THE BRONTËS OF HAWORTH :

YORKSHIRE'S LITERARY GIANTS -

Their lives, works, influences and inspirations

DAVID W. HARRISON

Cover photo: 'Top Withens' near Haworth, taken by author.
Part two photo section by author.

National Library of Canada Cataloguing in Publication

Harrison, David W. (David William)
    The Brontës of Haworth : Yorkshire's literary giants : their lives, works, influences and inspirations / David W. Harrison.
ISBN 1-55369-809-6
    1. Brontë family. 2. Authors, English--19th century--Biography.
I. Title.
PR4168.H275 2002   823'.809   C2002-903687-9

This book was published *on-demand* in cooperation with Trafford Publishing.
On-demand publishing is a unique process and service of making a book available for retail sale to the public taking advantage of on-demand manufacturing and Internet marketing. **On-demand publishing** includes promotions, retail sales, manufacturing, order fulfilment, accounting and collecting royalties on behalf of the author.

Suite 6E, 2333 Government St., Victoria, B.C. V8T 4P4, CANADA

Phone	250-383-6864	Toll-free	1-888-232-4444 (Canada & US)
Fax	250-383-6804	E-mail	sales@trafford.com
Web site	www.trafford.com	TRAFFORD PUBLISHING IS A DIVISION OF TRAFFORD HOLDINGS LTD.	
Trafford Catalogue #02-0622		www.trafford.com/robots/02-0622.html	

10   9   8

For my daughters Tara and Kyla,
and may all your hopes, dreams, and
aspirations for the future be fulfilled.

CONTENTS

AUTHOR'S NOTE

In the summer of 1993, while working on a graduate degree at my alma mater, the University of Manitoba, I signed up to do some summer, travel courses in the United Kingdom. In addition to our small group of eight students, we were joined by six, American graduate students from Indiana University. Together we were to study English Literature, drama, 'select' authors, make a brief study of the newly-implemented National School Curriculum in the U.K., and since the majority of us were teachers, we were also to visit several schools in both England and Scotland.

The two university groups met at Toronto International Airport, made some hasty introductions, and then flew on to Manchester, England where we arrived bright and early the next morning and boarded a bus to the historic city of Chester, built by the Romans in 79 A.D. The bus became our 'home on wheels' for a good part of our journey as we travelled from town to town, and from university to university. We spent the next five weeks in close quarters, and over that short period of time, we became a relatively close-knit group. And in addition to our studies, we managed to put together several, enjoyable social evenings of fun and entertainment.

At selected sites, we spent three, four, or five days at various universities, continued our studies, and worked on our major projects. Our travels and studies took us to Chester University, University of York, University of Durham, the Moray Institute in Edinburgh, and King's College in London. Of course, there were numerous other stops and studies along the way including the homes of authors like William Wordsworth (Grasmere and Ambleside), Robert Louis Stevenson (Edinburgh), Sir Walter Scott (Abbotsford), William Shakespeare (Stratford-upon-Avon), Charles Dickens (London), and John Keats and D. H. Lawrence (Hampstead Heath).

Early on in the trip, as we passed through the beautiful, hilly country of West Yorkshire, our group leaders, Prof. Peter Spencer (University of Manitoba) and Dr. Sharon Hamilton (Indiana University), decided to make a short, unscheduled stop for lunch at the village of Haworth, the home of the Brontës. The stop had a profound and lasting effect on me, for up to that time, my knowledge of the Brontës was scant indeed, but after a tour of the Brontë Parsonage Museum, and a short walk onto the moors behind their home, I was so intrigued and fascinated at what I saw, that I became 'hooked'. Then and there, I resolved to someday come back, revisit the area at my leisure, and delve more deeply into the lives of the Brontës.

Several years prior to my retirement in June, 1999, I decided to continue my research the Brontës, re-read the material which I had studied at high school and university, and launch into research of my own for both interest and pleasure. Some of their work I had never read, but the more of it I read, the more intrigued I became. Also, I must admit that my interest and investigation has delved more into the works of Anne Brontë who did not receive the same recognition, attention, and acclaim as that of her two, famous sisters. The following material, therefore, has a marked emphasis, and more detailed analysis, of *Agnes Grey* and *The Tenant of Wildfell Hall* since my curiosity and research led me in that direction.

In May 2000, I returned to West Yorkshire, stayed in the town of Shipley, and commuted almost daily to the village of Haworth. Each time I entered the village and walked up that long, steep main street, I could not help but feel a strong sense of history and be overcome with awe. These were the very streets they walked; these were the very shops in which they browsed, and at the top of the hill is the Black Bull Inn which their brother Branwell frequented much too often. My emotions always got the better of me, and I could not help but feel that I was treading on 'sacred' and 'hallowed' ground. My interest never waned; it simply increased.

In addition to two, lengthy tours through the Brontë Parsonage and Gift Shop, I spent time in the village and many hours on the Haworth Moors directly behind their home. This is where the Brontë children, from a young age, experienced the total freedom they became used to. It was there that they bonded with earth, sky, air, and moors to become 'one' with Nature, perhaps Emily most of all. Once 'connected', the bond could not be 'torn asunder'. Whether tourist, traveller, or literary researcher, it is easy to see why the timeless mystique of the area becomes so thoroughly captivating to anyone who unwarily ventures forth into its grasp.

On several occasions, I followed the paths across the moors, the same paths the Brontës used, past Penistone Hill and two miles beyond to Brontë Falls, a small, green 'oasis' amidst the blackened heath which they often visited by themselves or with friends. Sitting in the Brontë Chair, one can easily imagine Charlotte, Emily, or Anne pensively reclining there, and writing some of their youthful poems. And for brief respite, there are many fine spots for a picnic near Brontë Bridge or beside Sladen Beck which today trickles into Lower Laithe Reservoir at Stanbury.

Several times the Brontës took their friends Ellen Nussey and Mary Taylor to their 'secret' get-away for a relaxing morning or afternoon. Whether they enjoyed the peace, solitude, and 'communion' with Nature to the same degree that the Brontë sisters did is doubtful, but one cannot fail to be 'stirred' by its solemnity or enjoy its rugged beauty. For the more adventurous, another upward two-mile hike takes one to Top Withens, thought to be Emily's inspiration for *Wuthering Heights*. And from there, the hiker has a breath-taking vista and panorama of the seemingly endless moors, and the hills and dales below, from the top of Pennine Way. The grandeur of it all can easily transport you back in time, and one suddenly realizes that you are seeing what they saw, hearing what they heard, enjoying what they enjoyed, just as the Brontës did so very long ago.

Also within twenty or thirty miles of Haworth, one can easily visit Keighley, Bradford, Thornton, Halifax, Mirfield, Gomersal, Birstall, Hartshead, Bradford, and Leeds, all of which had some significance to the Brontës. All of these places are within easy reach by means of bus or train systems from either Keighley or Bradford. Today Bradford and Leeds are both large cities, but many of the older, historic buildings are still in tact, and in a similar condition, as the Brontës would have seen them.

To complete my pilgrimage, I made two separate side-trips well beyond the thirty-mile limits mentioned above. I wanted to see for myself Cowan Bridge School in Lancashire, near Kirkby Lonsdale, where four of the Brontë girls went to school, and two ultimately fell fatally ill. I also made the two-and-a-half mile walk they made each Sunday to Tunstall Church which still stands today, and I can only imagine the sheer misery those children must have suffered in the dead of winter exposed to blasts of cold, northerly winds. Secondly, I made a trip to Scarborough on the east Yorkshire Coast to visit the grave of Anne Brontë, the only Brontë not to be buried in the family vault of Haworth Old Church. Her grave lies just below Scarborough Castle in St. Mary's Churchyard Cemetery with a delightful, sunny, southern exposure overlooking a beautiful bay. These are the same beaches and bay she recounted in the closing chapters of *Agnes Grey*, and the rugged coastline alluded to in *The Tenant of Wildfell Hall*. One can easily see why Anne had such a close affinity with this alluring place of such great beauty, and which so greatly contrasted with her beloved, native Yorkshire hills, heather, and moors.

This book, *The Brontës of Haworth : Yorkshire's Literary Giants - Their Lives, Works, Influences and Inspirations* is the result of many years of pleasant research and a product of the interest and intrigue which has captivated me since my first visit to Haworth, West Yorkshire in 1993. Their timeless works, coupled with the sadness and tragedies of their lives, makes one marvel at the capacity of extraordinary human beings under extraordinary circumstances. Their works are a lasting legacy of English Literature to mankind and their lives are a lasting legacy of courage to human-kind, but one cannot help but wonder 'what might have been' had their lives been granted a 'full-measure' on this earth.

I know that I will return to all these places again, and for 'literary pilgrims' who plan to visit Haworth and the hills of West Yorkshire some day, they have a pleasant treat in store for them. And for those who do make the effort, their interest and understanding of the work of the Brontës will increase ten-fold, and their lives will be enriched and blessed by the natural beauty of West Yorkshire which so endeared the Brontë family.

March, 2002

INTRODUCTION

The lives of the Brontës is an interesting but tragic story. From the very outset, their lives took on a series of tragedies which plagued them almost from the moment they first set foot in Haworth, Yorkshire in April, 1820. Months before, in February of that year, Rev. Brontë was appointed the curacy and 'living' at Haworth while the family still lived happily at Thornton, near Bradford, some twenty miles away.

While in Thornton, the family was at its height of happiness. Their family of six children (Anne had just been born in January) was in full bloom, and everyone was prosperous and healthy. The preceding five years there had undoubtedly been the happiest of their lives, and four of their children, Charlotte, Branwell, Emily and Anne had all been born there. Maria and Elizabeth, their two, eldest daughters had been born earlier in 1814, and 1815, respectively, in their first home, Clough House, at Hartshead-cum-Clifton. But with the birth of Anne in January of 1820, and the appointment of Rev. Brontë to Haworth, their happy times were soon to come to an end.

The Brontë family arrived in Haworth in April, 1820, with seven ox-cart loads of furniture and household belongings which in itself must have been a spectacle and topic of conversation for the local villagers. Soon after their arrival and instalment into the Parsonage, Mrs. Brontë's health declined, and it had not improved since the birth of Anne in January. Throughout the summer and fall, the situation became even more critical and by January, 1821, Rev. Brontë expressed in a letter to a friend that his wife was critically ill, and he did not hold out much hope for her survival. In fact, it is believed that she had stomach cancer, and eight months later in September, 1821, she died. Their six small children were left without a mother, but this was simply the first of many tragedies to befall them.

Mrs. Brontë's sister Elizabeth, whom the Brontës called, Aunt Branwell, came to Haworth to provide interim assistance to Rev. Brontë and his six children. Both Maria and Elizabeth Branwell had come from a fine family which lived in the warm, southern coastal town of Penzance, Cornwall, and Aunt Branwell had no special liking for Haworth or North England, nor did she intend to stay. When the Reverend was unable to find a new wife, Aunt Branwell, out of Christian charity and duty, decided to stay and help raise her sister's children. She was a spinster of forty-four years when she arrived, and although she always dreamed of returning to Cornwall, there she would remain until her death, at age sixty-six, in October, 1842.

After Mrs. Brontë's death, life became 'settled' once again until 1824, when again a new, double-tragedy was set into motion. Rev. Brontë was determined to see that his children were properly educated, and when the Clergy Daughters' School, a 'benefit' school with subsidized fees, opened at Cowan Bridge, Mr. Brontë saw this as a God-send, and immediately enrolled four of his daughters as money became available and the children overcame childhood diseases. Maria and Elizabeth were enrolled in July, 1824, Charlotte in August, and Emily in November. The school practised an austere lifestyle, and living conditions there were extremely poor and far too harsh for young children. By early spring of 1825, both Maria and Elizabeth were withdrawn because of serious illness, and both later died of consumption in May and June, respectively; Charlotte and Emily were immediately withdrawn for their own safety by their father, and this probably saved their lives.

In his emerging years, young Branwell had become a highly indulged child; he was the only boy in a large family of girls, he was the idol of his father, and a favourite of Aunt Branwell. With the death of his two, eldest sisters, Maria and Elizabeth, he appeared to have some emotional problems in childhood which later manifested themselves into adult problems of a much more serious nature. As a result, his life was filled with a series of bitter failures; he regressed into drinking and drugs, and his life came to an abrupt end, at age thirty-one, in September of 1848.

The Brontë sisters, Charlotte, Emily and Anne, on the other hand, developed into one of England's most legendary, literary families which has gone down in the history of English Literature. But each of their life's journey was not without its 'bumps' in the road, and their literary efforts, fame, and fortune were perhaps the results of some of their failed efforts. Anne Brontë was the youngest but the first of the family to seek employment as a governess. Her first attempt was brief and unsuccessful and the second much longer and more successful, but still it was neither satisfying nor gratifying. Charlotte followed quickly with two different jobs as a governess with very similar results. In the interim, Emily held a teaching position at Law Hill, Halifax, and remained there for approximately six months, but one day she left abruptly.

The conclusion they arrived at from their failed and sometimes successful, but miserable, positions as teachers was to begin a school of their own. They followed this dream for several years, and after much planning, consideration, and Charlotte's and Emily's efforts on the Continent to better themselves and obtain their diplomas in areas of music, languages, and fine arts, they were ready. Their final plans were made, their curriculum was set, and advertisements were placed, but no one came. As disappointing as it must have been for them, it could not have been more fortunate for the world of literature, for it now left them with time for contemplation and writing. Today we reap the benefits of those early failures, since no finer family of writers has perhaps ever existed in the English-speaking world.

While Charlotte and Emily were on the Continent, and Anne was a governess at Thorp Green Hall, the Brontës were hit by another set of tragedies with three, sudden and unexpected deaths in the fall of 1842. In early September of that year, William Weightman, their father's curate, and favourite of the entire family, died suddenly of cholera. Early in October, Martha Taylor, a family friend and younger sister of Mary Taylor, Charlotte's close friend, also died of cholera while studying in Brussels, a short distance away from where Charlotte and Emily were boarding. Later in the same month, their beloved Aunt Branwell, who had been their 'mother' and mentor, died unexpectedly after a brief illness following twenty-one years of devoted service to Rev. Brontë and his six children.

After their first disappointing attempt at publishing their works, *Poems*, 1846, their literary fortunes took a dramatic turn for the better with Charlotte's, *Jane Eyre*, immediately followed by Emily's, *Wuthering Heights*, and Anne's, *Agnes Grey*. The London literari were taken aback, and by 'storm', by three, unknown, and mysterious writers by the names of Currer, Ellis, and Acton Bell from the North of England. Their books were instant successes, but in addition to these 'blockbuster' hits, was the added mystery which surrounded their identities which became the talk of fashionable London. Speculation ran rampant until July, 1848, when Charlotte and Anne went to London to clear up the mystery of the 'three Bells' to Charlotte's publisher, Smith, Elder & Company.

Emily never wrote again, for the general public that is, but Anne came out with her second novel, *The Tenant of Wildfell Hall*, one year later in June, 1848. These were the last of Emily's and Anne's writings since the fourth set of tragedies was about to befall them in rapid succession. Branwell's condition seriously eroded in the fall of 1848, and he died suddenly on September 24, 1848. At his funeral, a cold and wet day, Emily caught a cold and never left the house again only to die there three months later on December 19, 1848. And by this time, Anne was ill with consumption as well, and declining quickly. In only five months time, at the end of May, 1849, Anne, too, was dead; the tragic deaths of the three Brontës took only eight, short months. Now, Charlotte was alone in the world with her father, the aging and partially blind Rev. Brontë.

In October, 1849, five months after Anne's death, Charlotte's publisher released her second novel, *Shirley*, which received far less acclaim, and more critical reviews, than *Jane Eyre*. And from that point on, Charlotte, without any siblings with whom to confer, suffered from loneliness, despair, and deep depression from these traumatic losses. Her desire to write was thereafter considerably blunted, and she found difficulty completing any new efforts. Her next and final novel, *Villette*, was not finished and published until four years later in 1853. In the years from 1852 to 1854, Charlotte was seriously courted by her father's curate, Arthur Bell Nicholls, whom she later married in 1854. Her happy, married life was brief, and on March 31, 1855, Charlotte died, at the age of thirty- eight years, in the early stages of pregnancy after only nine months of wedded bliss. She was just three weeks short of her thirty-ninth birthday.

In the last years of her life, Charlotte began another novel, *Emma*, which was never completed, and two years after her death, in 1857, her first, failed novel, *The*

Professor, was published posthumously by Smith, Elder & Co., but more as a 'courtesy' to this renowned author taken in her prime than anything else. And so ended the brief and tragic lives of the Brontë sisters, three literary giants of Yorkshire, who have left such a lasting legacy not only for English Literature and the English-speaking world but also to the world at large. In 1861, Rev. Brontë died in early June without any heirs or grandchildren, and so the direct line of Reverend Patrick Brontë, and Maria Branwell of Cornwall, came to an end.

ACKNOWLEDGEMENTS

I would hereby like to thank the Brontë Society in Yorkshire and the National Portrait Gallery in London for allowing shots and photographs from their collections to be used in the production of this text, and the valuable information they provided along with the photographs. I would also like to thank the Parsonage Museum staff for providing detailed tours of the Brontë home during my two visits to Yorkshire.

I am deeply grateful to Barbara Whitehead for the tour provided of 'The Brontë Birthplace' at 72-74 Market Street in Thornton, Bradford. The delightful tour, and the discussion afterward with both Ms. Whitehead and Bernard Mayston, provided me with valuable insights into the origins, influences, and inspirations of the Brontës' early writings, and their literary careers which followed.

I found Ms. Whitehead's book, *Charlotte Brontë and her 'dearest Nell' - The story of a friendship,* to be highly interesting, well-researched, and a most valuable source of information on the special friendship of Charlotte Brontë and Ellen Nussey. After reading her book, one is thoroughly impressed with the importance of Ellen Nussey to the Brontë legacy and her great personal contribution to the preservation of invaluable, historical documents through her collection of Brontë letters from the time of their first meeting in January, 1831, until the time of Charlotte's death in March, 1855. Her unrelenting determination to preserve the letters, and the Brontë legacy, right up to the time of her own death in November, 1897, is to be strongly applauded.

My thanks are also extended to several close friends who provided me with much-needed encouragement through years of research and writing along with its many trials and tribulations, and my personal 'crises' added into the mix. These acknowledgements would not be complete without my gratitude being extended to a number of libraries, a host of librarians and their assistants, all too numerous to mention, in the collection of research material that was used in this book. The primary contributors included the libraries at the University of Manitoba, the University of Northern British Columbia, the University of British Columbia, the Prince George Public Library, and each of their extensive inter-library loan networks and services which managed to obtain materials, from 'far and wide', on my behalf for my 'long distance' studies.

PART ONE

THE BRONTË FAMILY:

THEIR LIVES

1

REV. PATRICK BRONTË (1777 - 1861)

The story of the famous Brontë family of writers cannot be told without first telling the story of Rev. Patrick Brontë, the father. First we must remember that he was there 'first' and that he was there 'last'. Only he saw the entire story unfold from the beginning to the end, and it was he who suffered all the agonies of the Brontë saga. He suffered greatly and only his strength of character as a man, and as a 'man of God', provided him with the strength to endure all the family calamities which would have most certainly brought any lesser man to his knees. He did not indulge in self-pity and did not repine over his losses; this was entirely incompatible with his outlook on life. He bore his grief with dignity.

Patrick Brontë was, in fact, born Patrick 'Brunty', but it appears that the family name was changed several times after he entered St. John's College at Cambridge. First it was changed to 'Branty', then to Bronté in honour of one of the family's great hero, Lord Nelson, who was honoured with the title, the Earl of Bronté, by the King of Naples, after one of his great victories. The family name was so close in structure and spelling that the change was made. It was not until 1811, that the Brontë name with the dieresis (ë) over the letter 'e' was used, in place of the acute accent, by the publisher of his first book of poetry, *Cottage Poems*. The dieresis was used simply because the printer had plenty of them but not the acute accents. Thereafter, the name 'Brontë' with the dieresis was used.

Patrick was born on St. Patrick's Day in 1777, at Emdale, County Down, Ireland, the first of ten children to Hugh and Eleanor (Alice) Brunty. And if we are to believe the writings of William Wright, *The Brontës in Ireland*, 1893, his father, Hugh, had an extraodinary and interesting upbringing which could easily have been the basis for Emily Brontë's classic novel, *Wuthering Heights*. The actual basis of these stories is still unverified, and is likely to remain so, but it appears that Hugh Brunty himself was renowned for being a raconteur and writer of verse, and, therefore, it is difficult to separate the 'truth' from the 'fictional story'.

What is known is that Patrick's father, Hugh, moved to the north of Ireland in the vicinity of Drumballyroney near the foot of the Mourne Mountains in a pleasant, pastoral setting. There he met and fell in love with the prettiest girl in the area who also fell in love with him. The young girl's parents opposed the marriage since they were Catholic and he was Protestant, but this was not a barrier to her love for Hugh. She renounced her Catholicism and married Hugh, much to the ire of her parents. They lived in a small, two-room, thatch cottage with dirt floors. Young Patrick was their first child and with the family constantly growing larger, they moved to a larger house.

As a young boy, Patrick was described as exceptionally quick and intelligent. His concern and interest for the welfare of others was shown early when at an early age, he started a school of his own to teach others less fortunate than himself. He also took older boys on 'rambles' during the summer holidays, and at age sixteen he was offered a position teaching at Glascar Hill Presbyterian School. His scholarly and teaching ability, and his concern for his fellow man, did not go unnoticed by his mentors and benefactors. In 1798, at age twenty-one, Rev. Thomas Tighe persuaded him to teach at the larger church school at Drumballyroney and became tutor to the minister's sons. Convinced that Patrick Brunty was 'university material' and destined for the church, Rev. Tighe used his influence and connections at St. John's College, Cambridge to gain admission for Patrick as a 'sizar'. This position allowed admission to students with great potential and little means to enter the college at reduced fees; the position also required the student to do menial tasks for wealthier, senior students.

In 1802, at the age of twenty-five, he entered St. John's College, Cambridge, the same school which his mentor had attended between 1771 and 1775. He arrived at the university with only £7 in his pocket and received another £5 annually from a benefactor. This was later raised to £10. During his stay there, although he was not of the 'society' and 'class' of many others, he earned their admiration and respect through his scholarship, determination, geniality, sincerity and his tall, impressive figure. He earned his B.A. four years later, graduating in 1806, at age twenty-nine, whereupon he immediately presented himself to the Bishop of London for Holy Orders.

His first appointment was to Wethersfield, Essex in 1806, where he spent his year of internship to the church. At the end of the year, on December 21, 1807, he was ordained a priest of the Established Church at Chapel Royal of St. James, Westminster. He returned briefly to Ireland and gave his first sermon as an ordained minister in the church at Drumballyroney where he had begun his 'calling'. During his stay at Wethersfield, Essex, he fell madly in love with Mary Burder who accepted his proposal of marriage, which was then strongly opposed by her parents. They were apparently opposed to his inferior 'place' in society and his humble and somewhat 'unknown origins'. In view of this, Patrick slowly 'backed off' and 'backed out' of the proposal. When he received his second appointment in early 1809, at Wellington, a mining town in Shropshire, he kept up correspondence with her for a year and then stopped. Mary Burder neither forgave nor forgot what he had done, and when he tried to renew her acquaintance for the purpose of marriage after his wife's death in 1821, he was sharply rebuffed by a 'stinging' letter of response.

While at Wellington, two important things happened which had an effect on him for the rest of his life. First was the meeting of his fellow curate, Rev. William Morgan, who became a lifelong friend. He was, in fact, the person who married Patrick to his new bride, Maria Branwell, later buried her in Haworth, and presided over several more family funerals and interments in the years following. Secondly, he met the widow, Mrs. John Fletcher, who described Yorkshire as 'the Goshen of our land' which influenced him to move there, possibly because it was so similar to his native land of Ireland. Rev. Brontë did, in fact, spend the rest of his life in Yorkshire and never left it, or even hinted at the desire to leave it.

His next appointment was to Dewsbury, Yorkshire near the end of 1809. He was quite popular among his parishioners and was both admired and respected by them because of his care and concern, his good deeds, not simply his reference to them, and his extempore style of preaching without reference to notes and scriptures. There, he earned the name, 'Old Staff' because he carried a shillelagh whenever he walked or roamed. He visited distant cottages, held services in working-class areas, and showed sincerity and compassion for their plight during the hard times of the cloth industry during the disruptions caused to trade by the Napoleonic Wars. He also showed himself to be brave when he stood up against some hostile bell-ringers who staged an unauthorized practise during the vicar's absence, a drunk who held up a Whitsuntide parade of boys and girls, and secured the acquittal of a wrongfully accused private in the army charged with desertion, a hanging offence.

His fourth appointment was to Hartshead where he became curate of St. Peter's Church, in March, 1811. The church was old, neglected and in dilapitated condition when he arrived; he immediately set about on some repairs. The following year, 1812, was to be one of the most important years in his life. In that year, one of the great Luddite riots occurred right 'on his doorstep' at Rawfolds Mill, which was owned by William Cartright. These were desperate times for mill workers who earned a meagre living which was now threatened by new machinery. The Luddites set out to smash machines and stop delivery by whatever means possible. Eventually, things got out of control and there were beatings, vandalism and murders. Although, Rev. Brontë was on the side of 'law and order', his sympathies were with the people who were just trying to make a living.

On the night of the attack on Cartwright's mill, the Luddites met secretly, disguised themselves and marched on Rawfolds Mill where a 'battle' ensued, many were injured and two men died. On their march to the mill, they passed nearby Lousy Thorn Farm where Rev. Brontë was lodging, but he was fast asleep and did not hear them. On several occasions, he spoke out against violence and lawlessness in his sermons, but when one clergyman was murdered on the moors, he 'traded' his shillelagh for two pistols, one of which he carried with him at all times on his walks. The riots not only had a lasting effect on Rev. Brontë himself, but played an important part in the writings of Charlotte in her novel, *Shirley.*

The second thing of great importance which happened that year was his appointment as 'examiner' of Classics at the new Woodhouse Grove School, a Wesleyan school for boys. The principal was John Fennell who was married to Jane Branwell from Penzance.

On one of his visits to the school, he met Maria Branwell, the niece of the principal's wife, who had come to join them, and carry out assorted duties, after the death of her parents. It was not long before the two fell in love. Rev. Brontë lived approximately ten miles away, but he came to see her often and walked both ways in the same day. Although she was described as small and plain, his future bride came from a prominent family of 'good stock' in Penzance, Cornwall, and was poised, elegant, and simply but tastefully dressed. She was described as patient, cheerful, pious, talented, meek and amiable. These qualities obviously attracted Mr. Brontë's simple tastes which were also reflected in his conservative style of living.

It was a 'love match' from the very beginning and their relationship proceeded rapidly. For Victorian times, it was considered a 'whirlwind' courtship of only two months when the Reverend proposed to her on the grounds of Kirkstall Abbey. They were married in a double ceremony, along with her cousin Jane Fennell, at the parish church in Guisely on December 29, 1812. It is also interesting to note that Maria's sister Charlotte was married on the same day, and at the same time, in Penzance, Cornwall. At this time, the newly-married couple moved into 'Clough House' on Halifax Road in Hightown, about a mile from the parish church at Hartshead. A year later, in 1814, their first child, Maria, was born and baptized in Rev. Patrick Brontë's church. In 1815, their second child, Elizabeth, was born, but she was baptized at the Old Bell Chapel Church in Thornton, Rev. Brontë's next post. In May of that year, he was offered a trade of 'livings' with the curate of Thornton, Thomas Atkinson, who wanted to be closer to his betrothed, Frances Walker, and Rev. Brontë accepted.

At Thornton, just outside present-day Bradford, they moved into a house on Market Street not far from the church. These next five years would be the happiest years of Mr. Brontë's life as well as those of his new family. In the parlour of the house in Thornton, four more children were born - Charlotte in 1816, Patrick Branwell in 1817, Emily Jane in 1818, and Anne in 1820. Shortly after they came to this house, they hired a young girl, Nancy Garrs, to help with the children and domestic chores. As the new additions arrived, Nancy's younger sister, Sarah, came to live with them as their second, live-in servant. Mr. Brontë at this time earned an annual salary of £200, and Maria Branwell had an annuity of £50. Although they were not considered to be rich, they were not considered to be poor and managed reasonably well.

The years of intense happiness in Thornton came to an end when he accepted a pertual curateship in the village of Haworth about twenty miles away. In April of 1820, the family packed up their worldly goods into seven ox-carts. They made their way through Denholme and across the moors to Oxenhope, into the Worth Valley, and up the steep main street of Haworth to the Parsonage. There they would stay to the end of their days. Mrs. Brontë was already suffering the first stages of cancer when they arrived, and within fifteen months of their arrival, she was dead. This was the first of a series of successive tragedies which dogged the family.

In the book, *The Life of Charlotte Brontë* written by Elizabeth C. Gaskell, the author is not exactly kind in her assessment of Rev. Brontë. She characterizes him as an eccentric and despotic with little regard for his family and who raised his children with 'cool detachment'. In some ways his actions may be construed as 'different' but her assessment was harsh, unfair and inaccurate. He was, in fact, a devoted, caring father who had a great deal of regard for his family. He was not the warm, cuddly type who played games with his children, but their interests were always foremost in his mind. Mrs. Gaskell based her opinion on the short time that she knew him, the few times they had met, her own preconceived ideas, and on occasion took the word of disgruntled, dismissed servants and 'idle gossip' which served and supported her preconceptions and dislike for him. This warped view of Rev. Brontë haunts him, even to this day, and even in death.

Others who knew the Rev. Brontë indicate that her indictment of him was definitely tainted, undeserved and misguided, but in any case you may judge for yourself. Some of the things that he did would be considered by some as 'odd'. For instance, he went to bed each night with a loaded pistol at his bedside; he ate his meals alone in his study; he sawed the backs off the chairs and made them into stools; he burned his children's leather boots, and he cut up his wife's silk gown. These may all sound like eccentric acts, but they each have an explanation. For example, he went to bed each night with a loaded pistol because of the political position he had taken on the Luddite Riots of 1811-12. Two men had already been murdered for their political beliefs; the fact that he was a clergyman was of little consequence. (See Ch. 19 Influence of Local Lore and History) Rev. Brontë and many other church leaders were against the actions of the Luddites which included intimidation, threats, rioting, destruction of property and even murder. These were things which he could not condone either as a 'man of God', or as a principled, law-abiding citizen. The pistol was needed as protection for himself and his family, and he always carried it with him on his walks on the open moors.

He took his meals alone in his study because he suffered from extreme, violent gastric attacks from certain foods, a condition which he suffered from early childhood in Ireland, and he preferred to be away from others while he ate. He took his meals in his study where he did his parish work, just as Aunt Branwell preferred to take her meals on a tray to her bedroom upstairs each evening. The only relief he obtained from this ailment was by drinking red wine, but he refused to do so on a regular basis for fear of what his parishioners might think of him if he was constantly purchasing wine. There were over 3,000 people in the village of Haworth, and many more in the parish, for whom he was responsible and as a result, he was a very busy man and could not always afford the time with his family which he would like to have given to them.

It was impossible for him to leave his pistols loaded for any length of time, so they had to be discharged. In the morning, he would often open his bedroom window, which overlooked the graveyard and faced the church, and fired it at the stone tower, or he would go out the back door and shoot onto the moors. The pock marks of his pistols can still be seen on the tower today. It is said that he often used the shooting of his pistols as a hobby and a form of therapy for the extreme stress and pressure which he often endured. At some point in time, believed to be in 1843 or 1844, after Emily returned from Brussels and all the other siblings were away from home, the Reverend taught Emily how to shoot a pistol and they practised in the front garden. For the Victorian period this would also be considered 'outside the norm' as an activty for a preacher, or a young lady, but while at St. John's College, Cambridge, military training for all young men was standard, and it was there that Rev. Brontë developed an interest in guns and the military. This was an interest which he carried with him for the remainder of his life.

As an Anglican minister, his religion and beliefs did not allow any degree of gaudiness or colour to show flamboyance. Therefore, when he thought that his daughters' boots were too 'showy', he burned them and had them replaced with plain, simple shoes. His wife, we must remember, came from a reasonably well-to-do family and these purchases of leather boots and silk gowns were, for her, considered 'standard' wear. For the Reverend, these were beyond his accepted 'norms.' His wife's silk gown was cut to ribbons for the same reason. He preached a life of simplicity and austerity and he felt that he and his family had to 'practise what he preached.' In an attempt to improve his daughter Maria's posture, however wise or misdirected it may have been, he cut the backs of the chairs and made them into stools. These may seem like strange acts, but his intentions were clear and purposeful. As a result, Mrs. Gaskell interpreted this subjectively and concluded that this was strange, 'eccentric' behaviour and that he was also indifferent to his children. Those who knew him well over the years solidly disagreed.

After his wife's death in 1821, Rev. Brontë approached not only Mary Burder with thoughts of remarriage but also two others. Another lady he approached before Miss Burder was Elizabeth Firth, who had become a close friend of the family while they lived at Thornton. She, too, turned him down, but they remained friends, and he wrote her a kind letter and said that he would deem it a privilege for his daughters to spend time with her since only good things could come from such a visit. Elizabeth Firth later married someone else.

Rev. Brontë had also made the same proposal to Aunt Elizabeth, who was one year his senior, but she, too, declined. She seemed happy in her spinsterhood, and no doubt 'had her hands full' looking after six, small, energetic children and managing the household as well. After this, the Reverend made no more amorous attempts and settled in at the Parsonage with the knowledge that he would now have to raise his children as a single parent. From then on he set about the task of rearing his children and carrying on the busy and time-consuming work of his parish.

The Reverend was always concerned about the education of his children since he had always seen the value of it and had himself gone through great efforts and made great strides to step out of poverty. For one of his circumstance from the farming community of Ireland to make it into higher education and graduate from Cambridge University was a slim chance indeed. While at home when the children were younger, he educated them himself as best he could, along with the teachings provided by Aunt Branwell. In 1823, Maria and Elizabeth were sent to Crofton Hall School in Wakefield, but the cost of tuition proved to be too much for their father's meagre income and they were withdrawn after only a few months. Another reason for withdrawal was that he learned of the new, much less expensive school at Cowan Bridge with fees subsidized (approx. £14 per annum) by the philanthropic Rev. William Carus Wilson, the founder and benefactor of the Clergy Daughters' School.

The new school opened in January, 1824, but due to setbacks caused by childhood diseases such as whooping cough and measles, Maria and Elizabeth's entry was delayed until July of that year. Charlotte was admitted in August and Emily was admitted in November. About mid-February of 1825, Rev. Brontë received a letter from the school indicating that Maria was very ill. He immediately removed her from the school and brought her home; she died of consumption on May 6, of that year. Shortly after Maria was buried, a second letter arrived announcing the illness of Elizabeth. He immediately went to Cowan Bridge on May 31, removed her from the school and brought her home. Seeing Elizabeth so ill and in such dreadful condition, he went back the very next day, June 1st, and removed Charlotte and Emily fully convinced that the school was a deadly threat to them as well. Elizabeth also died of consumption on June 15, 1825, but Charlotte and Emily survived.

From that point on, their father was even more conscious and concerned about their welfare, and evermore vigilant about all aspects of their life. After he removed them from Cowan Bridge School, which he referred to as 'that hateful place', he kept his children at home for the next six years, and only then was Charlotte allowed to go to Roe Head School in 1831, a school with a much better record and reputation for teaching and children's welfare than Rev. Wilson's Clergy Daughters' School. Rev. Brontë was more than adequately educated to provide basic education to his own children, since before he became a member of the clergy, he was a teacher in Ireland. But now parish requirements took up most of his time.

After morning prayers and a family breakfast, the Reverend would spend time teaching his children in his study. Then following an early lunch, he would again attend to parish duties in his study. For the remainder of the afternoon while the children were spending time with Aunt Branwell in various learning activites, or walking on the moors with Tabby, Rev. Brontë would be busy visiting parishioners in their homes, preparing sermons, or performing various church functions and ceremonies. In the early evening, the children would practise sewing or needlework followed by the Reverend reading various newspapers or magazine articles to them and then carrying on a discussion of what they had just heard, or listened to one of many stories told to them by their father from his worldly experiences. Such was their early education at home.

As most other parents of Victorian times, Rev. Brontë put a little more effort into his son's education than that of his daughters'. The reason for this was simple; sons of the family were 'heirs' and 'successors' to name and wealth and were expected to be educated, to learn a profession, and carry on the family name through their sons. Daughters, on the other hand, were expected to be 'married off' and introduced into their husband's line and family. Failing that, the sons were expected to support them if they weren't married and didn't have a profession or means of supporting themselves.

The rest of the family, and particularly Rev. Brontë, looked upon Branwell as the 'family hope' for the future. It would be Branwell that required the concentrated effort, the 'best education', supervision, guidance and professional training to prepare him for his future life. As a result, when young Branwell showed talent in several areas, particularly music, fine art and drawing, a 'master' was hired, at great expense to his father, to give him private lessons in these areas. Naturally, Charlotte, Emily and Anne also benefited in a 'secondary way' from these lessons given to Branwell. Later in their lives, their paintings and sketches were also noteworthy, and today we can still marvel at the variety of their talents. For Branwell, these lessons were to be the precursor to his entry to the Royal Academy of Art in London where he would earn a diploma and become a professional portrait painter, and perhaps more if his talents allowed. Plans for his life were well laid out, but none of them ever reached fruition.

The failures of his son, Branwell, were probably among the greatest disappointments and setbacks that the Reverend experienced in a vicarious manner; Rev. Brontë always succeeded at what he endeavoured through great effort, sacrifice and hard work. Branwell was extremely talented and should have done very well in the world, but it was not to be. Today, we can only 'analyze' and surmise at 'what went wrong' but one conjecture of seeming validity was Rev. Brontë's overindulgence of his only son, who was also the 'favourite' of Aunt Branwell, and some 'soft spoiling' by his sisters who always deferred to his preferences and demands. In her will of 1833, nine years before her death, young Branwell was not named, believed simply that he would do well in the world and would not need a dowry to become established as a professional and a gentleman, whereas Charlotte, Emily, Anne and another niece would. Upon her death in 1842, he received nothing, whereas his three sisters received just over £300 each.

Opportunity after opportunity, and failure after failure, Rev. Brontë finally lost hope for the great expectations of his son. He saw his great talents wasted and each and every opportunity squandered before his very eyes. As each new opportunity arose, the family's hopes rose once again only to be let down again, and each time they were more harshly dashed. The fact that Branwell had taken to drink at an early age (about fifteen years), and later to laudanum (liquid opium) to 'overcome' his rising sadness and depression, did not help the situation, and as one might expect, simply led to further, and worsening problems. By this time, the pattern for the remainder of his life was set, and his 'fate was sealed'.

The year 1842, was devastating for the entire family including Rev. Brontë. Once again, after seventeen years of 'relative calm' and stability in their lives, Aunt Branwell, who had been a 'surrogate mother' for the children for twenty-one years, suddenly became ill and died in October of that year at the age of sixty-six. Branwell was particularly hit hard, since she was the closest thing he had had to a 'mother' for his entire life after the deaths of his real mother whom he did not remember, and his two older sisters, Maria and Elizabeth, whom he did remember.

Only a month before this event, in early September, Rev. Brontë's curate, Rev. William Weightman, died suddenly of cholera. This was equally devastating and tragic to the Reverend since Rev. Weightman had been his curate for three years, arriving in 1839, and being a 'family favourite' with every one. He was young, handsome, popular, very promising, fun-loving, caring, and was loved and well-respected by all those who knew him or came into contact with him. His sudden illness and death was a shock and a 'blow' to Rev. Brontë who treated him like a son, the son he would liked to have had. In his funeral elegy for William Weightman, Rev. Brontë gave him high praise for his life and work during his short time on this earth; he was only twenty-six years old. A tablet to his memory is mounted on the side wall of the new church in Haworth and can still be seen there today.

For those like biographer and author Elizabeth C. Gaskell, who thoroughly castigated Rev. Brontë and later perpetuated this myth, they would have been wise to pay heed to all the good deeds he conducted not only for his parishioners and family, but also for the people of Haworth in general. He managed to obtain the first organ and bells for St. Michael's All-Saints Church in Haworth. His son Branwell who was taking music lessons learned to play it and became the organist for his father's church. Secondly he built a Sunday School in Parsonage Lane for the village children at which Charlotte taught near to the end of her days. Thirdly, he had small churches erected in some nearby villages, as well as purchased and repaired an old cottage which later served as housing for the destitute. Also, seeing the high, and disproportionate number of deaths in Haworth, and recognizing the source of the problem as impure, contaminated, community water supply system, he continually petitioned the government at Whitehall in London to seek help in improving and upgrading the water and sanitation system of their village. These are not the actions of a disinterested despot as 'painted' by E.C. Gaskell.

For his entire life, Rev. Brontë, like everyone else, used candles or 'rush lamps' by which to read. In time, this was very damaging to his eyes and by the summer of 1846, Rev. Brontë's eyes were in such poor condition that surgery was necessary for the removal of thick cataracts. For this he needed to go to Manchester, and in August of that year, Charlotte accompanied him there for the procedure. The operation, and his recovery in a dark room for one month, went well, and by late September he was back in Haworth, and by late October he was back to giving the occasional sermon in his church. It was also in this same month, one year later in 1847, that Charlotte presented him with her first, published work, *Jane Eyre*, a novel she had started while he was recovering in Manchester the year before.

Rev. Brontë was surprised, but not altogether shocked, at his daughter's new book, since they had always been interested in writing, constantly scribbled notes, had already published a book of poems, and he himself had published several small works. Surely the desire and interest in writing had been 'planted' early and 'rubbed off' on them, and he was proud of her accomplishment. Naturally, two months later when Emily and Anne came out with their novels, *Wuthering Heights* and *Agnes Grey*, he was equally proud of them. Since his eyes were still very delicate, he could not read their novels himself, but instead they each read theirs to him in turn.

It hardly seems possible, according to Charlotte's assertion that Branwell knew nothing of their publications right up to his death, whereas others claim that he did. It would hardly seem possible that he did not know, or at least he did not let on. If he was aware of their success in writing, this may only have deepened his own sense of failure. In any case, his condition got only worse, and his drinking and use of opium increased much to the dismay of his sisters, and especially his father. 'Village tradition' has it that his concerned father often went to the pub at late hours to collect him and literally carried him home from the Black Bull. Once again it shows that his father, although perhaps giving up hope for his future, did not abandon his son completely. He was still Branwell's father and the 'spiritual guide' of the family hoping for a miraculous change and recovery.

Another example of his caring for his wayward son, occurred after an incident in which Branwell came home highly inebriated and set his bed on fire. Emily beat out the flames and saved his life, but from then on, Rev. Brontë had Branwell's bed moved into his own front bedroom where he could keep a watchful eye over his son. It was a matter of safety and concern not only for Branwell but also for the entire family. It was there in his father's bedroom where Branwell finally took a 'turn for the worst' and died suddenly on September 24, 1848, early Sunday morning. Charlotte reported that her father was 'beside himself' with grief over his lost son. She wrote that, "he cried out for his loss like David for that of Absalom.... and he refused to be comforted". He took the loss of his son extremely hard and perhaps held out hope for his recovery and return to his senses even to the very last, but it was not to be. His son had long before given up hope for himself, but his father had not. Now it was all gone, and all he had left were his three daughters, but this, too, was to be short-lived.

Rev. Brontë's grief and suffering had hardly subsided when he suffered it again, twice more, in the following eight months. At Branwell's funeral, Emily became ill due to the cold and wet on the day of the funeral, October 1st, and quickly declined into serious illness. By December 19th of that same year, the Reverend and his family suffered another blow with the death and loss of their beloved Emily. And within weeks of her death and funeral, Anne was diagnosed with consumption in its advanced stages. Her life on this earth was now measured in months; another tragedy for the family was ready to unfold.

The grief from this tragic anticipation must have been great for Rev. Brontë as he watched his family, and friends, die off one by one as he grew older, but remained in rather good health himself. This time the tragedy would be apart from him and his home, but no less the loss, as Anne died on May 28, 1849, at Scarborough on the North Yorkshire Coast. To spare her father yet another funeral and more grief than he could possibly bear, Charlotte, along with Ellen Nussey, had Anne buried at Scarborough, where she died, in St. Mary's Churchyard Cemetery overlooking the sea, one of Anne's favourite spots. This seems to have helped somewhat, and after receiving the news of Anne's death and burial, Rev. Brontë urged Charlotte to remain where she was to take a well-deserved rest before coming home. Charlotte obliged and did not return until late June.

Now the Reverend had only one daughter, Charlotte, left and he became highly protective of her. Charlotte lamented on this sad situation to her publisher's reader and friend, Wm. S. Williams, after Anne's death in May, in a letter dated 04/06/1849, with this self-deprecating remark:

> They [Emily and Anne] are both gone now, and so is poor Branwell, and Papa now has me only - the weakest - puniest - least promising of his six children. Consumption has taken the whole five.... Why is life so blank, brief, and bitter I do not know -...

When Rev. Arthur Bell Nicholls proposed to Charlotte in December, 1852, Rev. Brontë 'exploded' in anger against him for several reasons, but perhaps, deep within, her acceptance would represent a 'final loss' to him, one which he cherished dearly, his only remaining daughter. Also, it would possibly mean that Charlotte and her new husband would take up a new 'living' and a new curacy elsewhere, and that he would then be left truly alone. This was possibly more than he could handle, and hence his very angry reaction and outburst.

Nicholls, seeing that he had so highly offended and angered Rev. Brontë, tendered his resignation early in 1853, and accepted another curacy nearby. Nicholls did not give up hope of marrying Charlotte, and he kept up a secret correspondence with her. In the interim, the new curate proved to be highly unsatisfactory, and Rev. Brontë was now able to see the strengths and positive attributes which he had overlooked in Nicholls before. With time, and Charlotte's gentle persuasion, her father soon 'mellowed' and acquiesced to her wishes. In the spring of 1854, Rev. Brontë finally gave up any opposition to the union of his daughter and A.B. Nicholls, and he returned as curate of Haworth. With little fanfare, equally little ceremony, and some secrecy, the wedding took place on June 29, 1854, at the Haworth Church. Rev. Brontë did not attend the ceremony, and the bride was 'given away' by her old friend and former headmistress, Margaret Wooler. Her best friend Ellen Nussey acted as bridesmaid.

After their honeymoon in Ireland, the new couple returned to Haworth and took up residence in the Parsonage. Charlotte, now with her added income from her book royalties, began to have changes made to the home. The old, 'peat room' was changed into a study for her new husband. Aunt Branwell's bedroom now became theirs and was enlarged at the expense of the children's playroom, decorations and paint were added, and for the first time, curtains were installed in the house. For the decades before, they were forbidden by her father because of his fear of fire caused by candles coming into contact with cotton or linen curtains or drapery. The graveyard held many victims of just such accidents, and Rev. Brontë had presided over many funerals, many of them children. Once again, he gave in to Charlotte's wishes to, at least, provide her with some small degrees of happiness, in an otherwise world of sadness and bleakness.

The following year, 1855, proved to be as devastating as 1821, 1825, 1842, 1848, and 1849. Her father had another 'hidden' concern about Charlotte's marriage, to any man, which he kept to himself. Charlotte was an extremely diminutive woman, and he secretly feared that if she became pregnant, it would be a cause for concern during child birth. Rev. Brontë had presided over hundreds of funerals 'in his day' from many causes, some of which were funerals of women who had died in childbirth. This, in his mind, must have been a major concern, for her safety and welfare, which caused his vehement opposition to her marriage.

In February of that year, their faithful servant of thirty years, Tabby Akroyd, died at the age of eighty-four years. The year was not starting out well. Also at this time, Charlotte was ill and not getting any better. First Charlotte caught a cold when she and her husband were drenched in a rainstorm on their way back from 'the falls' (now Brontë Falls) in November of 1854. Then again, a few months later in early January of 1855, she simply worsened her condition by walking through wet grass in thin shoes while on a trip to the Shuttleworths in the Lake District. From then on, her illness progressed into something far more serious.

Near the end of March, Charlotte slipped into delirium, wasted away with consumption, and also suffered complications from an early pregnancy. A short time before her death, she returned to consciousness briefly, demanded food and drink, but all was lost, and her situation was hopeless. When the doctor announced that the situation was 'terminal', Rev. Brontë spoke to Martha Brown and re-iterated his previous concern about her getting pregnant. In any case, it was a moot point, since it appears that Charlotte died of consumption, like the rest of her family, but her condition was complicated by problems early in her pregnancy. On the morning of Saturday, March 31st, 1855, she died in the presence of her loving husband and devoted father.

Rev. Brontë's family was now all gone. He had only his faithful servant, Martha Brown, his sexton's daughter, and Rev. Nicholls to console him, and attend to him in his old age. Five month's later, Martha's father, and Rev. Brontë's sexton and old friend, John Brown, also died. Rev. Nicholls and Martha Brown both remained with the Reverend until his death. In June of 1855, Rev. Brontë invited Elizabeth Gaskell to do a biography of Charlotte to 'set the record straight', since so many unauthorized articles were being written, with distortions and inaccuracies, about her and the family. Gaskell then began her now-famous biography and concluded it in 1857, as *The Life of Charlotte Brontë*.

Although Charlotte's father hailed it as a masterpiece, he easily and clearly saw how he was being portrayed in a highly negative light. Right to the very end, he was kind, forgiving, and magnanimous, happy about the positive portrayal of his daughter, Charlotte, to the public; he was not concerned about himself. In a letter to Elizabeth Gaskell after the release of the book, he wrote to her and thanked her for her work, but he also gently, but subtly, chastised her when he admitted to his many faults and added:

> ...being a Daughter of Eve, I doubt not that you also have some. Let us both try to be wiser and better as Time recedes and Eternity advances.

He lived for another six years, but throughout the winter of 1860 - 61, Rev. Brontë suffered from bronchitis and was tended to by Martha Brown and Rev. Nicholls. He died on Friday, June 7th, 1861, at the age of eighty-four. Large crowds attended the funeral, and he was buried in the family vault of the church, next to his beloved daughter, Charlotte. This was the end of the Brontë legacy, but only the beginning of its legend.

2

CHARLOTTE BRONTË (1816 - 1855)

Charlotte Brontë was born April 21, 1816, at Thornton, near Bradford, a sister to Maria and Elizabeth, her two older siblings. Although she may have been too young to know it, these were perhaps the happiest days of her life as well as those of her family. For five years from 1815 to 1820, the family lived on Market Street in the village where Rev. Brontë had been appointed perpetual curate at Thornton Church, just a few blocks away, and where the young family was being raised.

On June 26, 1817, the first and only son, Patrick Branwell, was born into the family, followed by Emily Jane on July 30, 1818, and Anne, born on January 17, 1820. Now the family was 'complete' and the Reverend and Maria, their mother, were overjoyed at the prospects of a beautiful family and a 'full life' before them. It was also at this time that Rev. and Mrs. Brontë took on a young girl, Nancy Garrs, from a local Bradford institution to help them raise their large, young family. Several years later, Nancy's sister, Sarah, joined her in her efforts. Both of them stayed with the Brontës until 1825 when both were betrothed, married and moved on. Charlotte, in later years, recalled her earliest thoughts of childhood, but none specifically made reference to their years at Thornton, Bradford.

In February, 1820, Rev. Brontë was offered a more prestigious, perpetual curacy and 'living' (church owned residence) in the more prosperous village of Haworth, high up in the Pennines on the edge of the moors, some twenty miles from Bradford near Keighley. For reasons of stability and especially a home for his large family, he decided to accept. In April of that year, seven wagons loaded with family belongings, six children, his wife and two servant girls made their way through Denholme and Oxenhope into the Worth Valley to the foot of the mile-long, upward climb to the village. At the top, they made a left-hand turn at the Black Bull Inn and followed the lane to the parsonage which was to be their home for the rest of their lives. It must have been both a 'spectacle' and an 'event' for the villagers, and his new parishioners alike, to watch this noisy, ox-cart procession.

Once inside the parsonage the children quickly explored their new home and new surroundings. From the window on the stair landing and the back bedrooms, they got their first glance of the seemingly endless purple moor which would later become not only their 'playground' and their 'refuge' from the 'world without' but also a 'backdrop' and essential element in some of the most revered writing in English Literature today.

From the front windows of the main bedroom, the children's study and playroom and the second bedroom, later to become the Reverend's and Branwell's bedroom, they could look out over the graveyard, the church with its tower, the village proper and onto distant Keighley four miles away. Today, the trees have grown to full height and the view that they could see so clearly is gone forever. The Parsonage is located on the highest point of the village and on the edge of the expansive moors behind them. The children quickly began to adapt to, and become firmly engaged and 'enmeshed' with, the environment and ecosystems of which they were to become a part in every sense of the word for their time, and forevermore.

Also, tragically, we must recognize that it was here that their world began to 'fall apart' and Charlotte, at its central core, gave witness to its gradual decline and eventual collapse. This move was the beginning of a series of family misfortunes that few people could endure and few families can compare to in its severity, intensity, and depth of destruction. One by one, the family succumbed to illness, despondence, and death in a series of tragedies which spanned almost forty years from 1821 to 1855.

When the family first arrived in Haworth in the fickle month of April, 1820, Mrs. Brontë was already unwell and falling into bad health. In fact, she had not been well since Anne's birth on January 17 of that year and did not recover even after their trek across the moorland to Rev. Brontë's new, Haworth posting. In a letter to Rev. John Buckworth dated November 27, 1821, Rev. Brontë stated that his wife was "taken dangerously ill on January 29 last..." He went on to explain that her illness was severe and protracted and that "almost every day of this long, tedious interval I expected her final removal".

Finally, on September 15, 1821, after a lengthy illness, thought to be cancer of the stomach, she died leaving her large family behind. She was the first of the family to be buried in the family vault beneath the church, and it was the first of the series of tragedies to befall them. Their mother's last words showed her concern for her children, "Oh God my poor children,..." And during the last few weeks of her life she refused to see them because of the trauma it would cause them to see her in such condition, and to her, knowing that they would soon be motherless.

After Mrs. Brontë's death, their Aunt Branwell from Penzance, Cornwall, their mother's older sister, came to 'fill the void' and offer solace to the children and assistance to the Reverend. She had no intention of staying and looked forward to returning home after things were stabilized and a measure of 'normality' was brought back to the shattered household. Also, it was assumed, and generally considered, that Rev. Brontë would soon re-marry and Aunt Branwell's services would no longer be needed. Such was not to be the case.

The Rev. made three attempts at re-marriage, first to Elizabeth Firth, a family friend as well as Charlotte's godmother and later benefactress, next, to a former lady-friend, Mary Burder, to whom he had proposed before Maria Branwell, and thirdly to Aunt Branwell herself. In all three cases he was rebuffed and refused, and from that point on, he made no more amorous attempts. Also, after reconsidering the situation, Aunt Branwell, out of a sense of duty and devotion to her deceased sister, Rev. Brontë, and the children, decided to stay, hoping perhaps to one day return to her beloved, coastal Cornwall.

Charlotte's recollections of this first tragedy were rather vague since she was only five years old and 'firm imprints' of the world about her were not yet made. The only living recollection she had of her mother was of Mrs. Brontë bouncing the young infant, Patrick, on her knee and playing with him in the parlour. From then on, her recollections were much more vivid and much more precise, and the successive tragedies became more real and traumatic and the results more highly devastating.

For the next four years, from 1821-1825, life for the Brontës once again settled into a routine that was for a short period free of personal tragedies. But, in the year 1824, an event occurred which set the family up for two more quick and successive tragedies, both linked to Rev. Brontë's desire to see his daughters properly educated. On his meagre, annual income of £200, it would be difficult for him to provide a quality education at expensive, private schools for all his children, but by what might have seemed a 'miracle', he was informed of a new school with affordable fees only a day's journey from Haworth.

The school was located in the Lune Valley, near Kirkby Lonsdale, Lancashire some fifty miles away. Cowan Bridge School had been set up by a wealthy clergyman, William Carus Wilson, of Tunstall as a clergy daughters' benefit school with subsidized fees. For clergymen of the day, and most certainly Rev. Brontë, such a school appeared to be a 'god-send' and an 'answer to his prayers' for a quality-education at modest, manageable fees of £14 per annum. Rev. Brontë was immediately interested and saw an opportunity to have his children educated in a 'systematic way' rather than the somewhat haphazard manner in which they were being taught at home.

The prospectus indicated instruction in : history, geography, use of globes, grammar, writing, arithmetic, and needlework as well as religious instruction. Extra fees were charged for instruction in French, music and drawing which were set at £3 per annum. The lure of the school was not only its low, subsidized fees but also an education founded on religious principles which Rev. Brontë himself believed in, adhered to, and practised in his daily life. Unfortunately, Rev. Brontë was completely unaware of the severity and almost fanatical way in which its founder, Wm. Carus Wilson, intended to carry out his training and instruction to reach his goals.

Maria and Elizabeth, the two oldest girls, were enrolled first on July 1, 1824, with high hopes and expectations for their future education. Charlotte was enrolled in August and Emily in November. It did not take long for these intelligent, young girls to 'size up' the situation at Cowan Bridge School, and when their father arrived at the school with Emily, Charlotte begged him not to enroll her and asked him to take her away as well. Children as they were, they realized that the harsh, cold, spartan conditions, severe discipline and strict regimen at the school were a threat not only to Emily but also to themselves.

Rev. Brontë, assuming that they were simply 'unaccustomed' to authority and used to their complete freedom at home were exaggerating their claims so that they could return to the comfort of their home, disregarded their pleas.

Cowan Bridge School was located in a 'bottom-land' where the 'Leck-fells swoop into the plain'. The flat, wet bottom-land was thought to be an ideal breeding ground for flying insects and mosquitoes carrying infectious diseases and made the location an unhealthy place to live. In addition to its poor location, the school had other major drawbacks such inadequate and improperly prepared food, lack of proper heating and generally unsanitary conditions, all of which contributed to conditions not conducive with the proper maintenance of growing children. William Carus Wilson, the school's founder and benefactor, also believed that two of the chief values that the school should foster were 'humility' and 'Christian resignation' which would best be taught by hardship, deprivation, spartan conditions, and stern and harsh discipline.

The poor location made the school open to the cold, northern winds in winter and often they awoke to wash basins skimmed with a layer of ice which they had to break through before they could wash their faces. The building itself itself was made of large, stone blocks which give rise to cold and dampness and was heated by fireplaces which themselves have a very low efficiency of heat production. On winter mornings they were often desperately cold, and when heat was needed, the smallest children were either shunted to the side or back while the older, bigger and more forceful girls took up the best positions directly in front of the fire.

The food also left much to be desired and was completely inadequate for growing children. Much of it consisted of burnt porridge which was, more often than not, quite inedible and other foods were not much better. On weekends, the children often went without eating altogether because the meals prepared for them were leftovers from the week before which were inedible in the first place. Therefore, it is evident that the food required for healthy, growing bodies of young children was simply not available to them. The lack of nutritious food was further compounded during the winter months when fresh fruit and vegetables were either very scarce or non-existent. It was later found that the food served the young girls was improperly prepared in highly unsanitary conditions by a less-than-cautious cook. She was promptly dismissed.

Sanitary conditions for washrooms in and around the school were also less than satisfactory with only one stone, outdoor privy for seventy students and staff. With the ground frozen in winter, and in spring a run-off, the contaminants from body waste and fluids may easily have entered the groundwater and contaminated sources for their pumps and wells. Such waste escaping into the groundwater may also have collected in stagnant pools where mosquito infestation was high and was in dangerous proximity to the school and its occupants.

To add to their misery was the general climate in which they lived. The winters in the north of England are harsh and cold with plenty of snow, ice and stormy weather, and the children were without proper hats, gloves and boots to meet the elements. As part of the harsh regime, the students were required to spend a minimum of one hour per day out in the fresh air in all kinds of weather; frost-bitten hands and feet were often the result, with little or no medical treatment for the young sufferers.

Sundays were perhaps the worst day of the week for Charlotte and the others since they were forced to go to Tunstall Church, almost three miles away, for services given by the Rev. Carus Wilson, the school's benefactor. To get there they had to travel on open roads and trails exposed to cold, northern blasts of winter winds. When they arrived at the unheated church, they were extremely cold and remained so all day. There they remained for most of the day, ate cold, box lunches, remained for 'even matins' and then marched home again in even colder weather. Sundays were certainly not days the children looked forward to.

In the early part of 1825, low fever and typhus broke out at the school. One of the first students to contract the disease was Maria, the eldest of the Brontë children, who was only ten years old. Her condition worsened, a letter was sent home to her father, and on February 14th, Rev. Brontë went to Cowan Bridge to bring her home. Elizabeth, Charlotte and Emily also asked to go home but their father had not yet realized the severity of the situation. Maria's condition did not improve, and on May 6, 1825, she died in the Haworth Parsonage. When a letter arrived that Elizabeth was now ill, Rev. Brontë wasted no time in removing her to Morecambe Bay nearby on May 31st. Seeing Elizabeth's poor condition, and now fearing for the worst for his other two daughters, he returned the very next day, June 1, and withdrew Charlotte and Emily before they, too, became ill. Elizabeth died only two weeks later on June 15, and Charlotte and Emily would never again return to that "hateful place", as Rev. Brontë later referred to it.

Many other children became ill with low fever and typhus; some were sent home, and others died at the school itself and were promptly buried at the Tunstall Churchyard Cemetery due to the highly infectious nature of the disease. In spring, when many children were ill, the school became an infirmary rather than a school and all classes were suspended. To facilitate the care-giving to the sick, the children who were well were given box lunches and allowed to roam in 'complete freedom' from morning till night. This suited Charlotte and Emily perfectly, and the freedom they had previously enjoyed at home was now restored. These proved to be the only 'happy days' they had at Cowan Bridge considering the grievous circumstances of their brief tenure there.

Years later, after considering the staggering loss of her two sisters, Charlotte developed a hatred for the school, its founder and benefactor Rev. Wilson, and particularly the teacher, 'Miss Scatcherd', who so terribly abused her older sister, Maria. She was the one who flung Maria to the cold, stone floor when Maria was desperately ill and begged to be left in bed one cold, winter morning in early 1825. Charlotte never forgave them, and in writing the novel, *Jane Eyre,* the infamous Lowood School was quickly and easily recognized as the one at Cowan Bridge, the sanctimonious Mr. Brocklehurst as Rev. Wilson, and the fictitious, genteel 'Helen Burns' as Maria Brontë. Thereafter, it did not take readers long, especially those who attended Cowan Bridge School as contemporaries to these events, to narrow down the list of persons who could possibly have written the novel and who identified 'himself' as 'Currer Bell'.

Once at home in early June, Charlotte and Emily witnessed the sad and rapid decline of their one remaining older sister, Elizabeth, and suffered the trauma of her death and funeral. This, of course, was heaped on top of the 'still-fresh' trauma of the death of their oldest and most beloved sister, Maria, who was their 'surrogate mother' since the passing of their real mother four years earlier. Now it was Charlotte's turn, at age nine, to 'pick up the reins' where they had left off and become 'mother', playmate, guardian and 'teacher' to her three, younger siblings. This 'post' she took seriously and kept loyally for the rest of her life.

For the next, five and one-half years, the Brontë children remained at home under the tutelage of their Aunt Branwell and their father. Rev. Brontë was already teaching and tutoring young Branwell Latin, Greek and literature, and now it was extended to include arithmetic and geography for his daughters. Later, a painting instructor was hired for Branwell, at great expense to his father, and a music instructor for all of his children. Aunt Branwell used her bedroom, next to the playroom, as a classroom for the children in which she taught them sewing and needlework as well as regular homemaking duties which was considered 'necessary' and 'standard' since their futures were seen as that of governesses, ladies-in-waiting, or wives. Charlotte's novels reflect her strong opposition to these firmly-held Victorian beliefs and her own bleak outlook.

In 1826, an event took place that had a profound effect on the Brontë children for the rest of their lives, particularly their writing careers, and that was no less the arrival of 'The Twelves', or toy soldiers. In May of that year, Rev. Brontë made a trip to Leeds, and as was his custom, he brought back some gifts for his children. He arrived late at night, and in the morning Branwell burst into his sisters' rooms and onto their beds with a box of painted, toy soldiers. The children were ecstatic and they each chose one beginning with Charlotte. Hers was the 'tallest' and handsomest and was immediately named, 'Wellington', after her hero, the Duke of Wellington. Emily's choice was dour and serious with a 'grave' expression, so they dubbed him 'Gravey' while Anne's had an odd, quizzical looking expression and was named, 'Waiting Boy'. Branwell chose a majestic, military man and named him 'Buonaparte'.

These simple toys later gave rise to their ever-growing imaginations which began to 'feed off' one another. By December, 1827, a year later, their first plays, which they 'acted out' in the children's study, began to take form. From then on, their active imaginations ran wild and the earliest beginnings of their writing careers took their first, formative steps. With their toy soldiers now vivid characters to them, each developed their own kingdoms and leaders which later led to the 'Great Glass Town Confederacy'. Four years later, while Charlotte was at Roe Head School, Emily and Anne in their ever-closer relationship as sisters, and in a spirit of individuality, formed their own 'break-away' colony of 'Gondal'. These writings of juvenilia were the forerunners of 'apprenticeship' to all their future, literary works. Some of this material has been preserved and can now be found in the Parsonage Museum Library.

In January of 1831, Charlotte set off on her second great 'adventure' to Roe Head School at Mirfield, some twenty miles away, which was run by the Misses Wooler. She stayed there for the next eighteen months and while there met two persons who would become her lifelong friends, Mary Taylor and Ellen Nussey. Mary Taylor and her family, especially Joshua Taylor the father, were highly influential in her thoughts, ideas and approaches to the social ills of the times. Both friends eventually outlived Charlotte and became 'first-hand sources' of information for Elizabeth C. Gaskell in the writing of *The Life of Charlotte Brontë*, published in 1857.

In the year and a half that Charlotte spent at Roe Head, she made great strides, particularly in her studies and in friendships outside her own family. In addition to Mary Taylor and Ellen Nussey, she also made friends with Martha Taylor, Mary's sister, and Miss Margaret Wooler, the headmistress of the school. The friendships she made there were to last her a lifetime. Miss Wooler was so impressed with the dramatic improvement in her 'star pupil', Charlotte, that she later offered her a teaching position which Charlotte accepted from 1835 to 1838. Years later in 1841, Miss Elizabeth Wooler wanted Charlotte to take over the entire school as she relinquished her position, and although Charlotte was inclined to accept, the situation changed at the last moment. Mary Taylor intervened with a suggestion that was even more tempting and alluring.

Of all the people she met, Mary Taylor, and the Taylor family, were certainly the most influential with their independent thought, strong personalities and 'maverick' ideas. Over the years, Charlotte visited them several times at 'Red House', a large, red brick house in Gomersal several miles from Roe Head. Mary Taylor was a radical free-thinker and fiercely independent in her thoughts, actions, and deeds, a personality trait which she picked up from her father. Joshua Taylor, a religious Dissenter, was a 'rebel' who could work only for himself, and as a cloth-dying merchant who did extremely well during the Napoleonic Wars, his fortunes declined somewhat after 1815, when the demand for military uniforms dropped off.

On one of her first trips to the Taylors, it did not take long for the topics of religion and politics to come into the discussion. Again it did not take long for Charlotte to realize that she was alone in her arguments against the novel and dissenting political and religious ideas of the Taylor family. Also, for the first time in her life, she came across views, opinions and arguments quite different from her own which had been fostered and ingrained in her since childhood; such diametrically opposed and divergent views must have come as somewhat of a shock to Charlotte at first. If it did nothing else, it forced her to review her own beliefs, recognize others, and search for arguments to back-up her own principles.

In Martha Taylor, Mary's younger sister whom they called 'Little Miss Boisterous', Charlotte saw an openness, happiness, cheerfulness and extrovertness, the likes of which she had never seen in anyone else before. The closeness of such a diverse family must have been an 'eye-opener' for one from a close, but sad, family which remained highly introverted for their entire lives. This openness of opinions and free exchange of ideas and beliefs could only have added to her ever-growing 'world view' of which she had been previously unaware. Added to this was, of course, the Taylor boys who were of Charlotte's and Branwell's ages. For the first time in her life, outside of her early years at Cowan Bridge, Charlotte was meeting both boys and girls of her own age whose ideas and interests were far different from her own. In fact, Mary Taylor was quite intrigued by

Branwell because for the first time in her life, she met someone of her own age of the opposite sex who had an intellect and rebellious attitude to match hers. But, for whatever reasons, the relationship did not develop, and failed to grow.

On the other hand, Charlotte met Ellen Nussey whose character could not have been more different than that of Mary Taylor's, and was also quite different than her own. Perhaps that is what drew these three together into three different friendships, each relating to each on different terms. Although these two friends of Charlotte's were so different, she managed to keep them both as lifelong friends and obviously interacted with each of them on different 'planes', and in different ways.

Ellen Nussey's family was also from a higher socio-economic class than Charlotte's and was more along the lines of the Taylors'. Both the homes of the Nusseys and Taylors could only be described as 'palatial' in comparison to the small, rectangular Parsonage of the Brontës. On Branwell's first trip to 'Rydings' in Birstall, the Nussey's new home after the death of Ellen's father, he described their home with its lawns, gardens and rookery as 'paradise'. Ellen's home was also used as Charlotte's model for 'Thornfield Hall' in *Jane Eyre*. On Mary Taylor's first visit to the Parsonage, Charlotte's home, she described it as 'claustrophobic'.

Ellen was a completely different kind of friend from anyone she had known before. She was not of the same lofty, engaging intellect as Charlotte or Mary Taylor, but she became a friend whom Charlotte could confide in, trust, and count on. Ellen remained in England for her entire life and was always there for Charlotte, and others in Charlotte's family, namely Anne, when they needed her. Mary Taylor on the other hand, spent time studying in Brussels, teaching at a boys' school on the Continent in Germany and then later left England for New Zealand in 1845. There she set up her own successful business and did not return until 1860, five years after Charlotte's death, but during this time they kept up a correspondence.

Ellen's greatest contributions to Charlotte was that she was a constant and steadfast friend from 1831, when they first met at Roe Head School as students, to the time of her death in 1855. Ellen also kept hundreds of letters sent to her by Charlotte over the years which later became a major source of information for research into biographies of Charlotte Brontë. Charlotte always accepted Ellen for what she was, did not expect more, and did not ask for more. One of Charlotte's last letter's before her death was to Ellen, a hastily scribbled note, in pencil, which was their last contact with one another.

After Charlotte's death, Mary Taylor and Ellen Nussey, who were both friends of Charlotte, and with one another, had a permanent split and 'parting of the ways' in their friendship because Mary no longer condoned the continued, public delving into the lives of the Brontës whereas Ellen acquiesced to its many demands. In fact, they were both excellent sources of information on Charlotte, but undoubtedly each was able to highlight different aspects and qualities in her character which they had brought out in her in their own unique way. Mary Taylor, herself an author in her later years, died in 1893; Ellen Nussey, who also wrote about the Brontës in *Reminiscences* (1871), died four years later.

In June, 1832, Charlotte returned home after eighteen months at Roe Head School and was now able to pass on and teach what she had learned to her three younger siblings. Once again the Brontë family was a cohesive unit and 'production' on their stories and poems for Angria and Gondal re-commenced with greater verve than ever, making up for 'lost time'. This situation continued for three years until mid-1835, when Miss Wooler offered Charlotte a teaching position at the Roe Head School which later moved to Dewsbury Moor a short distance away. Charlotte accepted.

In July, 1835, Charlotte assumed her new role as teacher, and along with her she brought Emily as a student whose fees she would pay from her own small salary. As well, Charlotte was also planning to contribute toward Branwell's education as an artist in London scheduled for the same year. By the time these fees and expenses were paid for by Charlotte, there was almost nothing left for herself. In a letter from her friend, Mary Taylor chided her for "giving so much for so little in return", but for Charlotte and others girls like Charlotte in Victorian times, this was one of the few, respectable occupations that women could engage in.

Emily, overcome by homesickness, did not last the first term and her place was immediately taken by Anne, Charlotte's youngest sister, who had not been to any previous school of any kind. Anne remained there as a student until December, 1837, and Charlotte remained there as a teacher for one additional year leaving in December,1838. By this time she had had enough of teaching which was 'draining her' mentally, physically, and emotionally, and usurping her time for creative thought and writing. Teaching, with added duties from early morning to late at night with no time for herself, just did not appeal to her; she felt 'trapped' and immobilized by the relentless demands. Finally she could take no more of it and resigned.

In the following year, 1839, after several months respite, Charlotte went out into the world again and took on the job as governess to the Sidgwicks at Stonegappe, Lothersdale where she remained from May through July. Once again the low pay, long hours, strenuous demands and lack of cooperation from both parents and 'charges' made her desire to return home even stronger. It was almost a year and a half later that Charlotte 'ventured out' again as a governess, this time to a Mrs. White and family at Upperwood House in Rawdon. Here, with a situation slightly improved over the last one, she lasted a full nine months, beginning in March,1841, and returning home in December.

The bleak future of a life as governess led Charlotte and her sisters to think of other directions their lives might take, although they were all still thinking in their restrictive, Victorian bounds of 'teaching' as being their only option and their only future. But, instead of being at the 'whim and fancy' of a master or lady of the house and their charges, they began thinking about the prospects of running their own school in their own village where they would be fully and completely in control. Such were their first thoughts toward being financially independent and not being a burden on their father, a thought which worried them considerably.

It was also about this time that Miss Elizabeth Wooler, about to give up her school at Dewsbury Moor where Charlotte had already been a teacher, offered her most-prized student the opportunity of taking over the school and becoming headmistress. Miss Wooler was convinced that of all the people she knew, Charlotte was the best-educated, the best-equipped, and the most highly motivated to take over the job as headmistress and revitalize the school. To Charlotte, the thought was more than appealing and could not have come at a more opportune time since both she and her sisters were looking into 'just such an opportunity'.

At first, Charlotte indicated to Miss Wooler that she was 'tempted' and may very well accept, but several things intervened which halted her initial, positive reaction and sent her off into another direction altogether. First of all, there were literally hundreds of private schools throughout England with which they would have to compete and to get an 'edge' on other schools, they would have to offer something other than the 'normal fare' of basic education. It would be necessary for them to offer additional 'extras' like French, German, and/or Italian languages, as well as music in the fine arts. These, Charlotte concluded, were an 'absolute must' if they were going to set up a quality school and attract students from near and far. At the time, neither Charlotte nor her sisters had any such qualifications or credentials in any of these areas mainly because private schools in England which offered such education was well beyond their father's means.

Secondly, Charlotte's influential friend, Mary Taylor, was urging Charlotte to come to the Continent with her for these attainments and credentials which could be had for half the cost found in English institutions. The level of teaching they would receive there, and the diplomas they would bear, would be equal to any they would receive in England. Added to Mary Taylor's encouragement was the urging of her last employer, the Whites, who heard of her plans and concurred with Mary's suggestions of studying in Europe. As well, Mary and Martha Taylor were both studying in Brussels and would like to have their friends close by. The Taylors were enrolled as students at the Chateau de Koekelberg, a pricy, Continental school beyond the means of the Brontës, but there were many other more modest 'pensionnats' which were well within their grasp.

Finally, in late 1841, it was finally agreed that both Charlotte and Emily would go to Brussels to further their education in preparation for starting up their own school. Aunt Branwell agreed to put up the loan, and in early 1842, they were on their way. On February 8th of that year, Charlotte and Emily, who needed each other for moral support, set out for Brussels with their father as chaperone along with Mary Taylor and her brother, Joe. After an overnight stay in London, they caught a 'packet' bound for Ostend and then proceeded to Brussels for their first European adventure.

Once in Brussels, they settled on the 'Pensionnat Heger' on Rue d'Isabelle near the centre of the city. Due to the fact that they were foreigners and compounded by the facts that they were highly intelligent, Protestants, and different in many ways from their regular students, M Heger soon realized that instruction for them must take on a different 'bent'. Some of their instruction was separate and private, and it was not long before M Heger recognized Emily's intellect as one of 'genius', even higher than Charlotte's in his estimation. He held Emily in great esteem, but the feeling was not mutual.

Charlotte and Emily were immediately set apart from the others because they were 'outsiders', English, Protestants and older than the other students at the school. They spoke mainly to each other and rarely engaged in any conversation with others unless it was absolutely necessary or unavoidable. Monsieur Heger, many years later in conversation with Elizabeth Cleghorn Gaskell, Charlotte's biographer, described them as 'scared-looking' with clothing that was not only considered 'odd' but completely 'out-of-fashion' with those of the day and fashion-conscious Continental tastes. As a result, Charlotte and Emily made very few friends during their stay there and Emily took an immediate dislike to the Hegers, especially Mme Heger whom she distrusted and warned Charlotte about. Later, when Charlotte became a teacher there in 1843, Emily's first impression proved highly accurate, and it was eventually Mme Heger's actions which led Charlotte to resign her post and return to England.

Their first eight months of studies in Brussels came to an abrupt halt when on November 2nd, 1842, they received a letter from home informing them that Aunt Branwell was desperately ill and suggested that they come home immediately. The very next day, they received a second letter informing them that Aunt Branwell had died on October 29th. They continued their packing and made haste to leave for home and arrived in Haworth on Tuesday, November 8th, but the funeral had already taken place and they would never see her again. Branwell took it especially hard since she was the closest thing that he had had as a 'mother' for the twenty-one years previous, and for many years, he was her 'favoured child'.

Emily was sad about her loss but extremely happy to be back at home and amidst her beloved moors; she would never leave them again. Immediately she took on many of the household duties and settled into a 'routine' of the 'domestic freedom' to which she was accustomed. By Christmas they were all home again, and it was an end to a sad and tumultuous year with not only the death of Aunt Branwell but also the deaths of their close and dear friends, William Weightman, their father's curate, on September 6th at Haworth, and Martha Taylor in Brussels on October 12th. Both had apparently died of cholera. In the space of just three, short months, they lost three of the dearest friends they had in the world.

When the New Year of 1843 began, with their lives re-aligned and re-assessed, decisions had to be made about their futures and Charlotte made the firm committment to return to her studies in Brussels, whereas Emily firmly decided to stay home and look after their father. Upon her return to Brussels, Charlotte not only continued her studies of French and German but was also hired on as a teacher of English. At first she considered herself fortunate, but as time went on, a letter to Branwell indicated her growing dissatisfaction and unhappiness. Much of this unhappiness had to do with her 'unrequited love' for M Heger, her instructor in French literature and headmaster of the school, with whom she had fallen in love.

When Charlotte first met M Heger, she was not immediately attracted to him and described him in very negative terms. This is reflected in both of her novels dealing with her time in Brussels and particularly 'Paul Emanuel' in *Villette*, who is, in fact, Monsieur Heger. To add to this, he was a Roman Catholic and she despised not only his religion but also his popish ways. The matter was even further complicated by the fact that he was a happily married man, with a delightful family of five children, who did not reciprocate her warm feelings and gestures. Years later, in 1847, the plot of Charlotte's first novel,

The Professor, was based on her strong feelings for him, although she reversed the genders and used a male protaganist, William Crimsworth, and the object of his desires was Frances Henri, a single-minded woman who was determined to make her own way in the world. The novel was rejected eleven times and was not published until 1857, two years after Charlotte's death.

Throughout 1843, Charlotte was a very solitary and isolated figure at the pensionnat who yearned to go home and be back among her own countrymen, family and friends. This was made clear in an entry she made in an exercise book in which she wrote, "I am tired of being among foreigners". By the end of that year, Charlotte once again had reached her limit and decided to leave since the situation with Mme Heger was becoming intolerable. Since Charlotte's growing attachment toward M Heger was becoming more 'visible', and her frustrations increased with his growing aloofness, Mme Heger's resentment toward Charlotte increased. The cordial atmosphere which had existed between them before slowly eroded, the 'friction' increased, and Charlotte even suspected that she was being spied on by Mme Heger through the treachery of another teacher.

Over the Christmas holidays of 1843, Charlotte turned in her resignation and made immediate preparations to leave. Just prior to this, she had completed her 'determinations' (exams) and would now receive a certificate to show her competence in the requisite areas which they had previously deemed necessary for setting up a school of their own. With the packing done, Charlotte said her 'good-byes' and left for Haworth arriving there on the morning of Wednesday, January 3, 1844. They could now set about the business of of setting up their own private school since they now had the background, the school, and the necessary 'capital' left to them by their Aunt Branwell. Each of the girls had received £300, but Branwell, because of his sinful and 'erroneous' ways was left nothing. These sums would not make them independent but would at least stabilize their incomes and financial situations for the next few years while they got themselves established. By mid-1844, a prospectus was drawn up, advertisements were placed in newspapers, and 'invitations' were sent to prospective students, in preparation for 'fall arrivals' at their school, but no one showed up. The reasons for their failure are pure speculation but we can venture to say that the remoteness of Haworth in North England was certainly one. They were well away from the main body of population in the south and the fact that it was a new, 'untested' and 'un-established' school were reasonably other considerations for 'non-attendance'. Although extremely disappointed at this new and unexpected setback, it gave more time for their literary genius to 'ripen' and flourish. The year, 1845, would mark a gentle turning point in their lives.

In May of that year, the first of a series of seemingly insignificant events began to unfold with the arrival of the new curate, Arthur Bell Nicholls, an Irish clergyman hired to assist Rev. Brontë with his parish duties. Little did Charlotte suspect that one day, nine years hence, that this man would play such an important part in both her life, and her death. In June, Anne returned home from her job as governess to the Robinsons at Little Ouseburn after almost five years of steady employment having resigned because of Branwell's unacceptable, immoral behaviour. He had been carrying on an affair with Mrs. Robinson, and after refusing to heed Anne's insistent demand to end the affair, she resigned. One month later, Branwell returned to Haworth having been shamefully dismissed from his job as tutor to young Edmund after Mr. Robinson learned of the affair. In a later letter to Branwell, Mr. Robinson threatened to shoot him on sight if he returned and set foot on his property. Finally, in mid-1845, they were all home again as one happy family, with the exception of Branwell.

With the hopes of opening a school of their own quickly fading, more continuous effort was being put into their writing, and in the fall of 1845, Charlotte 'accidentally' came across some pieces of verse written by Emily. (It is reputed that, in fact, Charlotte went into Emily's room unbeknownst to her, found some poems she had written lying on her desk, and read them. This was the 'accidental' discovery which Charlotte mentions, and this is why Emily was so furious.) When Charlotte broached the subject with Emily, she became furious with the knowledge that her most highly prized possession, her privacy, had been invaded and violated. Her writings were, in fact, meant to be solely for herself, and possibly for her sisters when the right moment presented itself, but not for the general public, since it would provide insights into her very private character and nature. It took Charlotte hours to calm her down and days to slowly re-introduce the topic of their poetry and possible publication. This was the beginning of their 'public writing career' and the beginning of a literary legacy which would go down in English, literary history.

After Emily 'settled down' from her fury, Charlotte began discussing the prospects, with her and Anne, of putting together a book of poetry with perhaps twenty poems from each of them. Again Emily firmly held to her intention that the poetry she wrote was for herself and no one else, but Charlotte was able to convince her that they were suitable for publication and Anne convinced her that they could keep their anonymity by using 'nom de plumes'. Finally, Emily was agreeable to this as long as there was complete anonymity. Charlotte and Anne concurred with this request and the book, *Poems*, began to take shape.

Their first attempts at finding a publisher for their book of poems did not go well, and they received many rejections by large, London publishers. Then, after an inquiry to an Edinburgh publisher, they were referred to the small firm of Aylott & Jones of Paternoster Row in London. Finally, in 1846, preparations were being made for publication, but although the publishers agreed to publish their book of poems, it would be done at their own expense of approximately £40. The publication went ahead in the spring, and *Poems* by 'Currer', 'Ellis' and 'Acton', the sisters Bell, was released in May, 1846. In early July, a review in the magazine, *Athenaeum*, praised the poetry of Ellis Bell but made little mention of the others. Two weeks later, in a letter to their publisher, Charlotte requested the number of copies sold and was disappointed by the response that they had sold only two.

In the latter part of 1845, and throughout 1846, Charlotte, Emily, and Anne had all embarked on a more ambitious project, their first novels, *The Professor*, *Wuthering Heights*, and *Agnes Grey*, respectively, and a new search was begun for a publisher of these three novels. Charlotte's work was ready first, in June, 1846, and was sent out to prospective publishers, but in each and every case, it was rejected and returned. Emily's and Anne's novels were ready in July and sent off together in search of a publisher willing to take their work. In contrast to Charlotte's "idiot child", as she later dubbed *The Professor*, *Wutherings Heights* and *Agnes Grey* were both thought worthy of publication and immediately accepted by Thomas Cautley Newby of London.

In August of 1846, Rev. Brontë's vision became so poor with thick cataracts that he was now almost blind and had to be escorted to Manchester for surgery. There, Dr. William J. Wilson, an eye-surgeon reported that his eyes were ready for an operation and fixed the date for the following Monday. Charlotte and her father took lodgings there since the he would require at least one month of recuperation and medical attention from a nurse. The operation went well, and her father, then sixty-nine years of age, seemed to recover as well as could be expected.

While Charlotte was there tending to her father, she began a new novel, *Jane Eyre*, which some have said is loosely based on a story of a mad woman locked in an attic in a house near Ripon. Charlotte visited there in 1839, while she was a governess for the Sidgwicks. Contrary to the widely held belief that Thornfield Hall with its battlements is based on Ellen Nussey's Rydings home in Birstall, others claim that it is modelled after Norton Conyers, the home where the 'mad woman' was said to have been kept, or North Lees, a home near Hathersage. Whatever the truth, the 'seeds were sown' for Jane Eyre, small and plain like herself, whom she said could just as easily be a heroine as someone tall and beautiful. She was 'bound and determined' to prove to her sisters that it could be done and upon this premise, the character, Jane Eyre, was created.

Upon their return, the Reverend's recuperation was hindered by Branwell who was in poor mental, physical and emotional condition, and who extended his misery on every member of the family. Charlotte continued her work on *Jane Eyre*, and at the same time continued to submit her first manuscript to various publishers, but without success. In all cases but one, the rejections were completely discouraging, but upon submission to Smith, Elder & Co. at 65 Cornhill, London, the publisher, although rejecting it, asked to see any of her future work first. By this time, *Jane Eyre* was almost complete and she hurriedly sent it off to them on August 24, 1847; their reaction and acceptance was immediate. The publishers were both delighted and excited with their newest novel and their new-found author, 'Currer Bell'. The manuscript was immediately put into production and six weeks later in October, 1847, *Jane Eyre* was published, and from there, Charlotte's career as a fiction writer began its meteoric rise.

To 'cash in' on the popularity of 'Currer Bell' and *Jane Eyre*, Thomas Cautley Newby Publishers immediately rushed into production the two manuscripts of Ellis and Acton Bell which they were holding since July of that year. *Wuthering Heights* and *Agnes Grey* were then published together in a single volume which was put on sale in December, 1847, complete with all the errors which Emily and Anne had already corrected and sent in. Naturally they were highly disappointed with their publisher who was seeking only to take advantage of the 'whirlwind' created by 'Currer Bell' and 'his' first novel, to maximize their own personal profits.

Although not all of the reviews of *Jane Eyre* were favourable, some were, and the most important things were that the book, considered the 'best of the season', was highly popular with the reading public and created a 'stir' in the literary community of London. Furthermore, not only did the book cause a sensation but it also raised the question as to the identity of this new, mysterious writer, completely unheard of before. The mystery was 'worth its weight in gold' in terms of advertisement, promotion and public relations for the companies involved. When *Wuthering Heights* and *Agnes Grey* were published with two additional new authors by the name of Bell, the mystery deepened and literary circles were 'abuzz' with speculation as to their identities. Not even the two publishers, Smith, Elder & Co. and Thomas Cautley Newby, had ever met, seen, or spoken with the authors, or knew anything about them; they were equally mystified.

In the months that followed, and as speculation grew about the mysterious authors, Charlotte kept their secret 'close to her vest' and even denied her authorship of *Jane Eyre* in two separate letter dated April 28, and May 3, 1848, to her dearest and closest friend, Ellen Nussey. Charlotte was determined to keep the secret, or at least as long as possible, because of the promise she had made to Emily regarding 'anonymity'. But as one might expect, such a secret could not be kept forever, and there were too many 'telling facts', and 'fictions too close to the truth' to escape notice by some. Many of the 'disguises' she used in *Jane Eyre* were simply too flimsy to mask the real identities of persons, places and events, and it did not take long for former students, teachers and others involved with Cowan Bridge School to recognize that 'it' was, in fact, the infamous 'Lowood School' and that 'Rev. Brocklehurst' was the school's benefactor, the Rev. William Carus Wilson. The discovery of the true identity of the 'Currer Bell' was not too far behind.

In the meantime, Anne was well on her way to the completion of a second novel entitled, *The Tenant of Wildfell Hall*, which she sent off to her publisher and was put into print in June, 1848. The book itself was loosely based on the life of their brother Branwell and his wasted years and misused talents. With speculation still rampant about the identity of the 'brothers Bell', and human nature being what it is, Thomas Cautley Newby hoped to capitalize on the new novel by 'Acton Bell'. It had been proposed by many varied sources that, in fact, the brothers Bell were really only one person, not three, and if this was so, Thomas Cautley Newby would stand to profit by it since they were now holding a manuscript by one of the Bells. Newby then construed and manipulated this thin possibility and loose conjecture to their favour.

With the popularity of *Jane Eyre* by Currer Bell still fresh in everyone's mind, T.C. Newby tried to 'palm off' Acton Bell's new book, *Tenant of Wildfell Hall*, as a novel by the popular and highly successful Currer Bell to Harper Bros., an American publisher. Smith, Elder & Co., Charlotte's faithful publisher in London, was understandably upset when they 'caught wind' of a second novel by one of 'their' writers through a foreign publisher and sent a letter of inquiry. When Charlotte received their letter asking for an explanation to the proposed new novel through an American publisher, both Charlotte and Anne were equally shocked. They then decided that the only way they could expose the treachery was by identifying themselves to Smith, Elder & Co. who could then 'challenge' T.C. Newby in their attempted fraud. Anne would accompany Charlotte, but Emily refused to go since she solemnly believed in maintaining her anonymity and personal privacy; she had only agreed to the publication of *Poems* and *Wuthering Heights* if complete anonymity could be maintained. Emily also warned that if ever her name became public, she would never 'pen' another line. Charlotte and Anne set out alone that very afternoon.

The trip did not begin well when they were caught in an afternoon thunderstorm as they walked to Keighley Station and were thoroughly drenched. From there they made their way to Leeds where they made their connection, and on the night train to London, they got little sleep and arrived tired, hungry and dishevelled. They stopped at Chapter's Coffee House, freshened up, had breakfast and set off for 65 Cornhill to meet Messrs Smith and Williams with whom Charlotte had been corresponding for over two years. It was a memorable meeting for all of them, and it was difficult to tell whose surprise and excitement was greater, Charlotte's and Anne's or the publishers. Undoubtedly, both W.S. Williams and George Smith were both shocked, surprised and amazed to find that the authors, Currer and Acton Bell, were, in fact, women and not men as they had assumed and considered them to be. For the next few days they were 'wined and dined' by Smith and Williams in various parts of London and were simply introduced as the 'Misses Brown'. At the Royal Opera House, they were somewhat 'ill at ease' in their odd, plain, and out-of-fashion clothing and 'awestruck' by the grandeur of the spectacle. On Tuesday, July 11, 1848, they returned to Haworth with many, exciting stories to tell and were 'weighted down' with numerous books which Messrs Smith and Williams had given them.

While in London, an unfortunate incident occurred which would remain to haunt Charlotte for the rest of her days. In the excitement of the introductions at Smith, Elder & Co. and revealing their identities, Charlotte blurted out and used the phrase, '...we are three sisters', which gave the final 'link' and clue to Ellis Bell's real identity. This was the second time that Charlotte had betrayed the privacy of Emily contrary to her wishes, and contrary to Charlotte's promise. Emily was furious, and as she had previously warned, she never again penned another line for the public-at- large. Several days later, a chagrined Charlotte wrote to Messers Smith and Williams expressing her regrets at her 'slip of the tongue' and cautioned and implored them not to expose the true identity of 'Ellis Bell'. Unfortunately, the damage had already been done, and Emily was not able to fully trust Charlotte again. If anything, she moved further and further 'away' from Charlotte, and closer and closer to her sister Anne.

The months to follow were some of the most difficult that Charlotte would ever have to endure. In a letter to Ellen Nussey in August of 1848, Charlotte indicated that Branwell was in poor condition and in a bad mental state. His continued use of laudanum and heavy use of alcohol drove him into steady decline, and having lost his 'will to live' after Mrs. Robinson's rejection of him, his ultimate fate was sealed. Shortly before his death, a close friend, Francis Grundy visited with Branwell at the Black Bull Inn and expressed shock at his wretched appearance. Several days later, early on Sunday morning September 24, 1848, Branwell took a turn for the worst and died. He was only thirty-one years old. It was another tragic loss for the Brontës and now the 'brilliant hope' of the family was now gone. Rev. Brontë had now only three remaining daughters to keep him company, but the tragedies for that year were not yet over.

Emily took charge of the arrangements and the funeral was held in the family church the following Sunday, October 1st, a cold, wet and chilly day. During the ceremonies, Emily caught a cold and from then on, she did not recover and went into rapid decline. She never left the house again and died after a lengthy illness on December 19, 1848, at the age of thirty. She, too, was buried in the family vault on December 22nd, only three days before Christmas. Of all the deaths and funerals, outside of Maria's and Elizabeth's so long ago, Emily's death hit Charlotte the hardest. And no sooner than Emily was buried, Anne's health ran into serious decline. Because of the two previous deaths of Branwell and Emily, both of consumption, a specialist, Dr. Teale, was called in immediately to examine and provide a diagnosis, and prognosis, for Anne.

The doctor's findings were the worst that could be imagined for she, too, was diagnosed with consumption in its advanced stages in the lungs. The prospects were not good, and Charlotte and Rev. Brontë knew the prognosis only too well. The possibility of alleviating and/or arresting the spread of the disease was discussed, and the clean, healthy air of the sea coast, which was known to favourably affect consumptive patients, was recommended. In a letter to Ellen Nussey on March 24th, 1849, Charlotte informed her of Anne's precarious health, its worsening condition, the prognosis, and the painful, unavoidable end. On the same day, a letter was received from Ellen inviting Anne to stay with her family in the hope that the change of air and diet might improve her situation. On April 5th, Anne made a new and different proposal that perhaps Ellen would like to accompany her to Scarborough, a seaside resort on the East Yorkshire Coast which Anne loved dearly. In the letter, she stressed to Ellen that she would be going along as a 'companion', not a nurse, and that hopefully Charlotte would go along as well. May was the month suggested for the journey, and although Charlotte and Ellen were against travel in such a 'capricious month', Anne prevailed by arguing that June and July are often worse.

On the first of May, Charlotte sent Ellen another letter outlining Anne's declining health and proposing times and dates for their trip to Scarborough to commence. It was convenient for them to meet at Leeds Station, and the departure was set from there for Wednesday, May 23rd, with a proposed stop at York. When Charlotte and Anne did not arrive at Leeds at the proposed time, Ellen went home and came back again the next day. When they failed to arrive a second time, Ellen hired a gig and set off for Haworth. Upon her arrival at the Parsonage, she discovered that Anne had been too sick to travel the previous day and, of course, there was no way that Charlotte could get a message through to Ellen. The next day, Thursday, May 24, 1849, Anne was somewhat better, and after Ellen's arrival, they all set out together and reached York later that day.

On the morning of May 25th, the trio took one last tour of York Minster Cathedral which never failed to put Anne in awe of its splendour. Later in the day, they arrived in Scarborough and took their pre-arranged lodgings in a beach-side hotel. The next day, the 26th, they walked and drove along the wide expanse of beach in a donkey cart, and Anne even took the reins awhile, according to Ellen's account. On the 27th, a Sunday, they talked Anne out of going to church, but in the evening they walked near the beach. The evening ended with a spectacular sunset resplendent in its beauty as if a portent marking the end to a short, but glorious, life; it was to be Anne's last sunset. For the first time,

Anne suddenly expressed a worried thought that perhaps she would die there, and not at home.

On Monday, May 28th, the last day of her life, she awoke at 7:00 A.M., had a light breakfast, and at 11:00 A.M. said that she 'felt a change' come over her body. Charlotte immediately sent for a doctor who informed them that she had but a short time to live, and although Anne wished to leave for home immediately, it was not possible. She was just too sick to travel. In the early afternoon, at 2:00 P.M., just like her sister Emily, she passed away quietly and calmly. Anne's final words to her were, "Take courage, Charlotte. Take courage."

To spare her father the grief and agony of yet another funeral, Charlotte made the decision to bury Anne in her beloved Scarborough in St. Mary's Churchyard Cemetery on a spot overlooking the sea. Only three people attended the funeral. A letter was immediately dispatched to Rev. Brontë reporting the bad news and the action she had taken. He responded by suggesting that Charlotte and Ellen 'stay on' and rest awhile after the ordeal they had just gone through. Charlotte decided to heed her father's advice and stayed almost a month at Filey and on Easton Farm in Bridlington, not returning to Haworth until the end of June.

Now with the exception of two servants, Tabby Akroyd and Martha Brown, and two dogs, Flossy and Keeper, Charlotte was alone in the world with her father. All her loved ones had been taken away from her, one by one. She had nothing left in the world except her father and her writing, the only two things which had any meaning to her now. Throughout her ordeal with the deaths of three siblings, her new novel, *Shirley*, which she had already begun, had been quietly set aside. After Anne's death, she slowly resumed writing, almost as therapy, and completed the manuscript. It was then picked up at the Parsonage by James Taylor, from Smith, Elder & Co., in early September. The next month, on October 26th, 1849, *Shirley* was released for sale in London, still under the pseudonym of 'Currer Bell'.

Charlotte's final novel was three years in the making, 1849-1852, and was a complete re-make of the ill-begotten and never-published, first novel, *The Professor*. The work on *Villette* was done in 'fits and starts', as her moods inclined her, due to bouts of recurrent depression after the deaths of Branwell, Emily, and Anne in close succession; the shock had not yet worn off. Inspite the presence of her father, the servants, and the dogs, she truly and deeply missed the companionship of her sisters, especially Emily's, who had both been such an important part of her life. Her loneliness was now deep and extreme, and her anxiety was profound.

Charlotte was not above holding a grudge, as she had against Wm. Carus Wilson as the indirect cause of her sisters' deaths, or 'lashing out' at individuals she thought deserving of her wrath. She lashed out against her good friend and headmistress, Miss Wooler, in December, 1837, when Anne had fallen into sickness, as being negligent and indifferent toward her health. The depths of Charlotte's depression, anxiety and stress were revealed in a letter of response to Mr. Williams at Smith, Elder, & Co. requesting the announcement of a firm publication date for her next book. Her irritation is reflected in the following passage:

If my health is spared I shall get on with it as fast as is consistent with its being done, if not well, yet as well as I can do it, *not one whit faster.* (Italics mine.)

Charlotte then continued on the manuscript at her own speed and *Villette* was sent off on November 20, 1852, three years after the completion of *Shirley.* This was to be her last novel.

In the years after Anne's death in 1849, Charlotte's social life took on new heights and a wider scope with trips to London, Manchester, the Lake District, and Edinburgh. Also she met with other notables such as William Makepeace Thackeray, George H. Lewes, Harriet Martineau, Elizabeth Gaskell, and Sir James and Lady Kay-Shuttleworth on trips to London. In some ways her trips to visit friends away from home may have been nothing more than an 'escape' from the lonely, dreary Parsonage whose silent walls 'resounded' with the echoes of her lost siblings.

Also, Charlotte's life was taking on an entirely new direction in another aspect of her life, since the new curate, Rev. Arthur Bell Nicholls's arrival in May, 1845. For all these years, almost on a daily basis, the Rev. Nicholls and Charlotte interacted by association and he had developed an interest in her; the longer he stayed, the greater his love and attachment to her became. At the moments of grief, anguish and despair, the Rev. Nicholls was always there as a spiritual guide and friend to console her. In December, 1852, as Charlotte described to Ellen in a letter, the Rev. Nicholls finally made a proposal of marriage to her and she told him that she would give him her answer in the morning. When she relayed this to her father, he became so highly incensed that he "worked himself into a state not to be trifled with". Charlotte therefore promised her father that he would receive a rejection the very next day not because she herself found the match objectionable, but simply to assuage her father's fury.

Rev. Brontë's reasons for rejection of A.B. Nicholls as a husband for his daughter are not exactly clear but have been merely alluded to. But for the better part, we can make reasonable assumptions and educated guesses about his highly emotional outburst against the prospect of his daughter's marriage. The first being that Charlotte was now his last and only child and his last and only daughter whom he wanted to protect to the best of his ability. Secondly, he was an old and lonely man, Charlotte had been with him for most of the last thirty-seven years, and he was now seventy-five. The prospect of Charlotte being married and leaving him was just something he found difficult to handle, especially after everything that had happened, and particularly at that stage of his life. Finally, since Rev. Nicholls had kept his feelings and emotions hidden [to wit: the prosposal came as a shock even to Charlotte], the shock of the proposal, the prospects by her 'acceptance', and that this man so close to him, had held secret and romantic feelings toward his daughter, may have seemed like something of a 'betrayal', hence his strong reaction and outburst.

Rev. Nicholls could only be described as a severe, grave, dutiful, religious and conscientious man, and when his proposal was refused, he handed in his resignation in May, 1853, and obtained a transfer to Kirk Smeaton, Pontefract, moving there in August. Inspite of his grave and serious manner, Rev. Nicholls was loved and highly regarded by his parishioners and a large send-off party and testimonial dinner was given for him by the people of Haworth before he left. But although he had been 'rejected', he did not feel 'rebuffed' and may have sensed that Charlotte would have preferred to say 'yes' rather than 'no' because the matter did not end there. From that point on, correspondence between Charlotte and A.B. Nicholls was carried on in secret over many months. Eventually, Charlotte had to admit to her feelings for Rev. Nicholls and slowly, gently, and patiently, she again broached the subject of marriage with her father. Also, with 'time' and 'distance' between them, Rev. Brontë may possibly have re-assessed the situation. Rev. Nicholls had provided a valuable service to the church, the parishioners, the village, Rev. Brontë himself and his family, and now he was gone. His absence was felt by everyone. Rev. Brontë may also have re-assessed the situation from his daughter's perspective of happiness, something of which she had had little in her own lifetime. Charlotte was now thirty-seven years old and her propects for future proposals and personal happiness were considerably reduced; the Rev. eventually gave in by 'attrition', and perhaps a small measure of guilt.

Finally on April 11, 1854, Charlotte wrote a letter to Ellen announcing her engagement to A.B. Nicholls, and the next day, April 12, she wrote a similar letter to her friend, Margaret Wooler, with the same news. Rev. Nicholls then renewed his post as curate of Haworth Church and resumed his duties there in June. Later that month on Thursday, June 29th, 1854, 'Charlotte Brontë' became 'Mrs. Charlotte Nicholls' in a brief, private ceremony at Haworth Church in which only two additional persons attended, Ellen Nussey and Margaret Wooler. Miss Wooler, in place of her father, who did not attend the ceremony, 'gave her away', and Charlotte's lifelong friend, Ellen Nussey, acted as bridesmaid and 'witness'.

The wedding was somewhat secretive, but when the ceremony began, word quickly spread and a band of villagers was waiting for them outside the church when the wedding bells tolled and they emerged. The happy couple then proceeded to Ireland, the birthplace of both her father and new husband, for their honeymoon. It was the first, last and only time that she would set foot on her ancestors' native soil. While in Ireland, they visited Killarney, Glengariff, Tarbut, Trolle and Cork, as well as many relatives along the way. While there, Charlotte made an interesting observation about her husband; he seemed to act like a completely 'different person' in his homeland. Although her married life was short, she found it highly enjoyable and was extremely happy, which friends later agreed they could see in her outward appearance. Rev. Nicholl's admirable qualities of being a faithful, affectionate, honourable and truthful person, and husband, came to the forefront during their short time together.

Charlotte became so devoted to her new husband, his efforts, his causes, and the demands of married life that she had little time for herself, and particularly for the "literary and contemplative". It is also interesting to note that the brief happiness awarded to her by marriage was to Charlotte, "better than to earn either wealth, or fame, or power". In brief, she had finally found ' true happiness', but 'continued happiness' on this earth was not to be hers.

At the end of November, 1854, Charlotte and her husband went to the falls (now Brontë Falls) to see a spectacular cascade after a brief snowfall which had quickly melted.

The walk is approximately two and one half miles from the Parsonage, and on their way home, they were caught in a sudden downpour. They were cold and wet when they got back. From this exposure, Charlotte caught the first vestiges of a cold which became much worse on a trip to the Shuttleworths at Gawthorpe Hall, Padiham. While visiting there early in the New Year of 1855, Charlotte went for a walk through damp grass in thin shoes. From then on, her health declined and she never recovered. On February 15, 1855, she wrote a letter to a Belgian friend telling her that she was ill and weak and expressed some kind words about her new husband. Only two days later, their faithful old servant of thirty years, Tabitha Akroyd, died at age eighty-four. A short time later, Charlotte scrawled a hasty, pencil note to Ellen telling her of Tabby's death, her own illness and weakness, and again, the kindness of her husband. This was to be her last letter to her, 'Dearest Nell'.

After weeks of illness, nausea and faintness, Charlotte began to descend into a state of delirium constantly requesting food and drink, but it was 'too late' and 'all was lost'. Early on Saturday morning, March 31, 1855, she briefly returned to consciousness, looked at her husband and said, "Oh, I am not going to die, am I ? He will not separate us, we have been so happy." A short time later the church bells told of her death to people miles away; she had died as the result of complications from the early stages of preganancy, as well as possible pneumonia and tuberculosis. Charlotte Brontë Nicholls had passed away at age thirty-eight, the same age as her mother who had passed away thirty-four years before. Her funeral was so well attended that only one member of each parishioner family was allowed into the small church; the remainder gathered outside and watched the coffin being carried from the house, through the graveyard and into the church. She was buried in the family vault with the rest of her family, except Anne, near the front, centre of the old church.

In the aftermath of Charlotte's death, many tributes were paid to her throughout England as the famed and mysterious 'Currer Bell', the writer Charlotte Brontë, and as a wife, Mrs. Charlotte Nicholls. She was a true literary giant of Yorkshire. Rev. Nicholls was as good as his word and stayed on in Haworth as the curate until the passing of Rev. Brontë in 1861, six years after Charlotte's death. Then he resigned, returned to his native Ireland, took up farming, and married his cousin, Mary Bell. He died on December 2, 1906, in Banagher, Ireland at the age of eighty-eight.

3

EMILY JANE BRONTË (1818 - 1848)

Of all the Brontës, Emily Jane was perhaps the most talented, the most enigmatic, the most analyzed, but the least 'documented' and the least understood; she remains inscrutable to this day. This view has largely been forged because of the limited amount of materials left behind, her reclusiveness, her shyness and her aloofness. She made few forays into the outside world, had no personal friends, except for those acquired in a 'second-hand nature' through Charlotte, and kept her thoughts and opinions to herself. Only after her death did Charlotte find a few press clippings, reviews on *Wuthering Heights*, and a few scribbled notes from years past. Beyond that, there is nothing extant, the original manuscript is gone, she wrote and received few letters, and left us only copies of her first and only novel and a few dozen poems. From these materials, brief notes about her life by Charlotte, and scraps of information provided by Ellen Nussey and Mary Taylor as our only sources, we must piece together her biography.

Emily was born, Emily Jane (after her mother's cousin Jane Fennell) Brontë on July 30, 1818, in Thornton (Bradford) where her father was curate. When Emily was born, she was the fifth child in the eventual family of six with her elder sisters Maria, Elizabeth, Charlotte, and brother Branwell all preceding her. These were happy times for the entire family with the children's bedroom and playroom above the parlour overlooking Market Street and the family's servant girls, Nancy and Sarah Garrs, across the back access stairway. It was in this room where they happily played together, learned their alphabet, and looked after one another. In this playroom today, one can still see an original wooden cupboard, and with only a little imagination, the children's laughter 'comes to life'.

In February of 1820, only a month after Anne was born, and after five years in Thornton, Rev. Brontë accepted the perpetual curacy of Haworth, a more prestigious curacy with a 'living', no doubt a major incentive to a Reverend on a small annual income and raising a large family. Emily, who was only two years old when they moved to

Haworth, and only three years old when her mother died in the fall of 1821, made no mention at any time of any recollections or made any reference to memories of her mother.

Like the rest of her siblings, when their mother died, she quickly gravitated to her older sisters, Maria and Elizabeth, as 'surrogate mothers', but this did not last either, since both of them perished in May and June, 1825, respectively, of consumption contracted while at Cowan Bridge School. Emily, too, was enrolled as a student there in November, 1824, and joined Maria, Elizabeth and Charlotte who were already there. When first Maria, and then later Elizabeth, became seriously ill, Rev. Brontë immediately withdrew Charlotte and Emily for fear that they, too, would contract the disease and die. For her entire life, Emily appeared healthy and managed to avoid dangerous and infectious illnesses.

In later years, Charlotte made reference to an incident at Cowan Bridge School which pointed out an important and interesting personal quality of Emily. Charlotte noted that at Cowan Bridge there was, in fact, a 'pecking order' of sorts within the student body which was generally based and graduated on the ages and sizes of the older girls who bullied the others into submission. This was usually done shortly after admission to the school, but when Emily arrived in November, although she was younger, smaller and weaker, physically, than many others, she soon became a school 'favourite' and was admired and respected by everyone. Charlotte explains and attributes this to Emily's 'strength of character', even at the age of six, which could not be bullied or intimidated. It was this 'strength' which immediately showed through and managed to earn her esteem and respect from her peers, the older students, and elders.

Physically, as a youngster and later as an adult, Emily was taller than her siblings, except for her father. At the age of three, Emily was already taller than Branwell at age four, and as tall as Charlotte at age five. In her teenage years, and as she grew into adulthood, she was tall, thin, graceful and lithe. At five feet, seven inches, she was considered 'tall' for a woman in Victorian times. The description of her features are conflicting whereas some say she was 'pretty', others have described her as not even being 'handsome'. But we can easily judge for ourselves, and although there are no photographs, we do have two 'likenesses' of Emily painted by her brother Branwell when she was about seventeen years of age.

After the Cowan Bridge School experience, Rev. Brontë decided that his and their interests would best be served if they stayed at home and remained under the tutelage of Aunt Branwell and himself. For the next ten years, 1825 to 1835, from the ages of six to sixteen, Emily remained at Haworth and during these formative years, she became firmly and closely attached to her home, freedom, 'domestic life', and the open moors behind the parsonage. Such an existence in a remote location brought Emily closer to nature in its every form and aspect, its beauty, and its solitude. These were the 'springs' which 'nurtured her soul', and to which she became so firmly engulfed that she would later find it impossible to be 'torn away'.

It was only a year after Cowan Bridge, in 1826, that Emily, like Charlotte, Branwell, and Anne chose a toy soldier from the box of twelve, which in many ways changed their lives, and in a 'round-about' way drew them into the field of literature. The toy soldiers were a gift brought home to them by their father, after a trip to Leeds, which was his custom. Emily's was a grave and serious looking fellow whom they dubbed, 'Gravey', and along with 'Buonaparte', the 'Duke of Wellington', and 'Waiting Boy' gave rise to, and fostered, their imaginative 'training' and learning which eventually led them to be productive writers.

With their toy soldiers in hand, their imaginations 'ran wild' and in December of 1827, during a seemingly dull evening that Charlotte suggested aloud, "Oh! suppose we each had an island of our own." They each began choosing an island and Emily chose the 'Isle of Arran'; next they chose leaders for their islands. Their choices were interrupted by the clock striking seven, and they were sent off to bed. The next day they resumed building their imaginary kingdoms and for the following six months their ideas 'flagged', but in June, 1828, they rekindled their spirits and began producing a small magazine, about two and a half inches by one and a quarter inches, made of blue paper from sugar bags.

The *Young Men's Magazine,* as they called it, was fashioned after Blackwood's magazine, a periodical of their father's which could always be found about the house. The small magazine served several purposes. First of all, the print in their magazines was so tiny that it was generally beyond the 'prying eyes' of adults who might try to invade their privacy and read them. Secondly, they could now develop their writing skills and wild imaginations free of any direct adult guidance, interference, or scrutiny. And it was here that their separate kingdoms were mapped and plotted, primarily by Branwell, into the Great Glass Town Confederacy. From these early stories, they began to write plays with their invented characters as primary forces, and later these plays were 'acted out' in the children's study and playroom next door to Aunt Branwell's upstairs bedroom. With these stories, poems and plays, they were already exploring form, 'voice', diction, and plot, a skill which would eventually help them write their adult novels.

At age fourteen, in 1831, Charlotte was sent off to Roe Head School for a second try at formal education leaving Branwell, Emily, and Anne behind. With Charlotte gone, their stories, plays, and poems for their magazines and the Great Glass Town Confederacy continued, but things were different now. Being the eldest, Charlotte was always the 'leader' with Branwell the 'second-in-command'. This went along well with Branwell's genius in devising, developing, and directing events in the Confederacy and Verdopolis, the capital, but now that Charlotte, the leader and 'enforcer', was gone, Branwell tried, but failed, to maintain 'control' over his two, younger sisters. They decided to 'branch out' on their own.

In Charlotte's absence, Emily and Anne began to grow closer together than ever before not only as siblings, with Branwell being the 'odd-man-out', but also in their imaginary kingdoms of confederacy. They now decided to secede from the Great Glass Town Confederacy, a bold and innovative step, and form their own new kingdom of 'Gondal', totally separate and apart from Charlotte and Branwell. It was only in response to their secession that Charlotte and Branwell created 'Angria', in 1834, after Charlotte's return from eighteen months at school in Mirfield. This perhaps gives us the first insight into Emily's independent, free-thinking, free-spirited, self-reliant, and determined nature.

The stories and poems written by Emily for 'Gondal' became a main pre-occupation with her for many years, even to the last years of her life. In a diary paper written on July 30, 1845, three years before her death, Emily recorded:

> My birthday - showery, breezy, cool. I am twenty-seven years old today..... The Gondals still flourish bright as ever. I am at present writing a book on the First Wars. Anne has been writing some articles on this, and a book by Henry Sophona. We intend sticking by the rascals as long as they delight us, which I am glad to say, they do at present.

Charlotte quit writing 'Angrian tales' about six years earlier in 1839, and there is some suggestive evidence that Anne also quit doing so shortly after the '1845 birthday, diary paper' was written. She had simply 'grown out of it' as an adult whereas Emily did not.

When Charlotte returned from Roe Head in June, 1832, the three younger siblings were the benefactors since she was now able to teach them what she had learned there and supplement the teachings of Rev. Brontë and Aunt Branwell. Once again their lives at the Parsonage stabilized for the next three years with the entire family under one roof again, but this changed in 1835.

In July of that year, Charlotte was invited back to the Roe Head School, by Miss Margaret Wooler, this time as a teacher. Charlotte accepted the offer, and now that Emily was seventeen years old, it was time for her to acquire more schooling, so she went along as a student, with her fees to be paid out of Charlotte's meagre teaching salary. Within a few, short months, Charlotte could see Emily 'slipping away', slowly at first, and then much more rapidly. No one but Charlotte knew her malady or the cause; it was not typhus, cholera, or consumption, the most prevalent illnesses of the day, but simply 'homesickness' in its severest form.

Emily went along to Roe Head School with the realization that some day she, too, would have to go out into the world and perhaps 'fend for herself' or at least earn an income to alleviate the burden on her father whose annual stipend was quickly becoming insufficient to support the lot of them. Emily was a responsible person and wanted to do what she could to help, but she became ill. Charlotte watched her slow decline and recognized what was happening; Emily could not live without her beloved moors and her close kinship with her sister Anne. Her homesickness became so severe that she could no longer function. Charlotte remarked about the incident years later,

> Liberty was the breath of Emily's nostrils; without it, she perished.

and:

> I felt in my heart she would die if she did not go home,...

Whenever Emily returned to the Parsonage at Haworth, her health improved imme-diately; she had lasted only three months at Roe Head, even with Charlotte's presence. When Charlotte went back to teach, she took Anne in her place, and Emily remained at home to help with domestic chores.

Emily was always happiest at home and did not yearn for travel or wider horizons like her sisters, and she was merely content to let others 'do it for her' and benefit from their reports and experiences. Emily is often described as quiet, reserved and withdrawn, but within her was a person of great loyalty, bravery and courage. One story told is how she bravely intervened in a fierce dog-fight and broke up the two, large combatants. Anyone who has ever witnessed such a horrific spectacle knows full-well, that it is an extremely dangerous practice which few persons, however brave, would attempt.

On another occasion, Emily, a staunch animal lover, saw a bedraggled looking dog come panting down the lane past the Parsonage kitchen door and went toward it to offer it comfort. Instead of accepting the comforting words and hand of Emily, the dog turned and snapped, tearing a gash in her forearm. Bleeding badly from the wound, she went into the kitchen, heated an iron to 'red-hot' in the stove and then used it to cauterize her own wound. Once again, this is an example of her own exceeding courage.

In later years, she showed her loyalty and bravery in an incident with Branwell. After Branwell had misused his talents and wasted his several opportunities to do well in the world, all of the family gave up hope for him, but Emily did not. In the evenings precisely at nine o'clock, Rev. Brontë would lock the front door, wind the clock on the stairway, and go to bed. Charlotte, Emily and Anne would often stay up later, discuss and some-times read each other their work, and then they, too, would go up to bed. Branwell often came in much later in a very inebriated state. Emily, out of loyalty to her brother, whom everyone else had forsaken, waited up for him, unlocked the front door, and often carried him upstairs to his bedroom. On one of these occasions, Branwell set his bed on fire, and Emily, smelling the smoke, came to the rescue, beat out the flames and saved his life, and probably that of the entire family's.

On another occasion, Tabby Akroyd, their faithful, old servant, who broke her leg in a fall on an icy street, was cared for by Emily. Also, after a two year absence from the Parsonage after this incident, Emily was instrumental in bringing her back into service inspite of her age. She also expected loyalty in return, and when, on two occasions, Char-lotte unintenionally 'betrayed her, Emily moved 'away' from her and 'toward' Anne who held her complete trust and confidence, that is, as far as she was prepared to give it. She never completely trusted Charlotte again, and even Charlotte sensed this ever-widening rift.

Emily had a deep love for animals and always kept a menagerie of pets close at hand. There were 'Grasper' and 'Keeper' the dogs, 'Hero' the hawk, 'Adelaide' and 'Victoria' the geese, 'Tiger' the cat, and a canary. This close relationship with animals and her continuous stream of pets indicated not only her deep love and respect for animals but also her close connection with Nature. As well, some psychologists may have some posi-tive things to say regarding her 'close connection' with animals and her reticence to deal with humans. And, it was this love of animals which caused her to resign her first and only job at Law Hill, Halifax.

In September, 1838, with a little more maturity, and determined to redeem herself after her short stay at Roe Head, Emily took a position as a teacher at Miss Patchett's School in Law Hill, overlooking the town of Halifax. For the time spent there, approximately six months, things appeared to go reasonably well, and Emily had a high regard for Miss Patchett, who also liked animals, and was an equestrian. Unfortunately, the regard Emily had for Miss Patchett was not fully reciprocated. She stayed there for half a year out sheer determination and personal resolve.

Emily, it appears, was not a good teacher for several reasons. First of all, she had neither a strong love for, nor rapport with, small children, particularly someone else's children who were misbehaved and ill-mannered, and they were afraid of her. On one occasion, it is said, she told her class that she much preferred the school mascot, a dog, to any of them. Also, in a letter to one of her sisters, she referred to teaching as 'slavery', since the total and complete freedom she had at home was now gone with extremely long hours, often 6:00 A.M. to 11:00 P.M., tedious duties, insubordinate and selfish children, and no time to herself.

The 'last straw' in Emily's brief, teaching career occurred on a 'ramble' which she often took with her students to 'commune with' and study Nature, not only for their benefit but also for her own, since she missed the tranquility of the Haworth moors. On this occasion, her attention was called to a commotion nearby, and when she went to investigate, she found a boy kicking a helpless, sick, or injured, hedgehog. For Emily who held such a high regard for animals and practiced a 'reverence for life', this was vicious, cruel, incomprehensible, inexcusable and unacceptable. In her instant rage and fury at such a despicable act, she lashed out and 'cuffed' the boy much to the surprise of everyone.

Naturally, upon returning to the school, the children went immediately to Miss Patchett, the headmistress, and reported Emily's 'cruelty' to one of her students. When Miss Patchett approached Emily and asked for an explanation with the intent of an investigation, disciplinary action, and possible dismissal, Emily did not deny the incident, make apologies, or seek forgiveness; she was much too honest for that. Instead, she simply responded that she was leaving, packed up her belongings and left that very day. So ended Emily's first and only attempt at full-time employment and foray into the 'working world'. The year following this event caused much speculation about Emily's enigmatic life.

The next twelve months of Emily's life have created a hint of mystery, perhaps by people simply 'looking for a mystery'. For the period following her tenure at Law Hill, from which she spent only six months and left in late February or early March, 1839, there are no records of her whereabouts. Most likely, they were quietly spent at home at the Parsonage until her next foray into the 'world without' in 1842, but there are no records, or mention made of her in letters during this time; therefore, much pure speculation has been made, much of which is too outlandish even to entertain or mention here. And without records or evidence, these wild speculations can neither be verified nor refuted.

Emily's next foray into the outside world was made in February, 1842. During the previous years, after all three sisters had gone into the world at large and tried their hands at being teachers and governesses, they each found the experience 'wanting', and being at the mercy of everyone else's whims and fancies, not much to their liking. It, therefore, crossed their minds that the only job for which they thought themselves suited, teaching, would take on a much more pleasurable aspect if they had their own school and they were, 'in charge' and 'in control'. Therefore, they were soon thinking along the lines of a school right at the Parsonage, a situation which would please them all extremely well since they would all be together, and at home. Various plans and ideas were considered, but the major stumbling block was 'capital' and the only source of such a basic necessity was their Aunt Branwell. Surprisingly enough, their aunt was amenable both to the plan and a loan; preparations then began.

When Charlotte was offered the job of headmistress, and the opportunity of taking over the new Roe Head School at Dewsbury Moor to succeed the retiring Miss Elizabeth Wooler, she was at first amenable to the idea, entered into some initial enquiries and negotiations, but later declined. Her thoughts and inclinations now took a new direction since she thought it best to first go to the Continent and improve her education. This, she thought, was both necessary and advisable, as well the most certain way of attracting students to their own school amidst the heavy competition in England for 'public school' students. Thus, when Mary Taylor suggested and invited Charlotte to go to Brussels and study there, at half the price of English schools, she was 'sold' on the idea. Charlotte, with Emily in tow, agreed to go, and Aunt Branwell put up the loan for their learning adventure. It was a year that they would not, and could not, soon forget.

Emily was never one for travel, leaving her home and family, her pets, and particularly her beloved moors, but she was honourable enough to realize that she could not be a burden to her father forever, and that their possible, future dependence on their brother Branwell, as was the custom in Victorian times, was looking rather shaky and doubtful. Also, if their own school was to be viable, Emily would be an integral part and must do her share. Therefore, it was with this in mind, and on these terms, that Emily agreed to accompany Charlotte to Brussels, and upgrade her knowledge in languages and literature, and her skill in music.

When they arrived in Brussels and settled into Pensionnat Heger, both Emily and Charlotte were not all that comfortable, being away from their own familiar surroundings, but they did have each other. They were set apart from the other students by their odd and old-fashioned clothing, the fact that they were both English foreigners and Protestants, the rest of the school being staunchly Roman Catholic, and the fact that they were much older than everyone else. From the very beginning, Emily made it known to Charlotte that she neither liked, nor trusted, the Hegers, especially Mme Heger.

Emily made a deep and lasting impression on Messr Heger who at once recognized her superior intellect and, "rated Emily's genius as something even higher than Charlotte's". Messr Heger, who provided this information in an interview many years later with Elizabeth Gaskell, commented that, "Emily had a head for logic, and a capability for argument, unusual in a man, and rare indeed for a woman". He went on with more praise saying, "She should have been a man - a great navigator," and how she could have made a difference to the world with new discoveries. Unfortunately, the respect and regard was not reciprocal, and Emily saw her teacher, Messr Heger as ill-tempered and 'waspish'. Emily in her extreme shyness spoke to no one except Charlotte, and only if the occasion forced or demanded it.

Their efforts and promise as knowledgeable teachers did not go unnoticed and well before their scheduled return to England, Mme Heger offered both Charlotte and Emily positions as teachers of English and music, respectively. In a letter to Ellen Nussey, Charlotte mentioned the offer and suggested that it would be unlikely that they would return in September since she was inclined to accept the offer, but she did ask for Ellen's opinion. Once again, the 'hand of fate' would intervene to alter any plans they may have had and the course of their lives which seemed to be dangling them on a yoyo-like tether.

The first news of impending tragedy came in mid-September, 1842, when they learned of the sudden, unexpected passing, from cholera, of William Weightman, curate of Haworth since 1839, on September 6th. He was a household favourite and like a member of their own family. He was extremely affable, well-liked and loved by everyone who knew him, especially Anne, and he brought many, much-needed, 'rays of sunshine' into their otherwise bleak and lonely lives. He was highly respected by all members of the family, his parishioners, and household staff, and it was generally regarded that both he and Anne were in love with one another. A short time later in mid-October, another 'ray of sunshine' in their lives, 'little Miss Boisterous', Martha Taylor, was suddenly torn away from them. She also contracted cholera while studying at the Koekelberg Pensionnat in Brussels and died very quickly. She was buried in the Prostestant Cemetery on the outskirts of the city.

Emily has sometimes been characterized as a 'mystic', and it was there in Brussels, and connected with the death of Martha Taylor, that such stories are based, born and nurtured. With the two families, Charlotte and Emily, and Mary and Martha Taylor, so close at hand and studying across town from one another, they were constantly in touch. One day a note arrived for Charlotte and Emily from Mary informing them that Martha had suddenly been taken very ill and that perhaps they should come and offer comfort. Charlotte and Emily immediately responded, but while on their way to the Pensionnat Koekelberg to see Martha, Emily suddenly commented that it was 'too late' and that she was dead. Upon their arrival, they were informed by Mary that Martha had indeed passed away in the night.

Years later, after Emily's death, a similar but far less credible, story began to circulate which fostered this same notion of Emily's mysticism. John Greenwood, a Haworth villager and local stationer who kept a diary, had several rare occasions to see the reclusive Emily Brontë. He claimed that on one occasion when Emily returned from a walk on the moors, her face was alight with almost a 'Divine glow'. Such stories may, and most likely have come 'to life' after her death and the fame and fortune of the Brontës had spread far and wide. The only other unverified story of Emily's 'mysticism' is that shortly after her own death, it is said that Charlotte briefly saw her ghostly apparition. Such stories simply exaggerate, possibly beyond reasonable proportion, that her mystic powers allowed her to reach out beyond the grave. We must gauge this report along side the story that Charlotte told when she was only five years old, and after the death of her mother, that she had seen an angel hovering above Anne's bed. Although adults were sceptical of her story, she could not be shaken from it.

On November 2nd, 1842, they received another urgent letter, this time from home, informing them that Aunt Branwell had suddenly taken ill and that perhaps they should come home. The very next day as they were preparing to leave, a second letter arrived informing them that she had died; they continued their packing and set off for home arriving there on Tuesday, November 8th. But their Aunt Branwell had already been buried in the family vault of the church. It was a sad homecoming for Charlotte, but even a sadder one for Emily because most of her pets were gone. It is generally thought that Aunt Branwell had, one by one, given them away or turned them loose. Emily was particularly incensed at the disappearance of Hero, the hawk, and demanded an explanation. As the story unfolded, Branwell wanted to be a 'hawker', like his sister Emily, but when he tried it, the bird flew away and never came back.

After her return from Brussels, Emily was determined not to go back, whereas Charlotte did. By remaining at home, Emily was back where she 'belonged' in her 'domestic bliss' and freedom, among the only 'friends' she ever had, and amidst the wild and lonely moors. She took charge of the domestic chores and looked after her aging father. Emily, as the Parsonage housekeeper, could now, in complete freedom, regulate her own life as she saw fit. Even when she was in Brussels with her sister, Charlotte noticed that she was again 'sinking' and slowly slipping away. The only thing that kept her going was her own resolution and determination not to fail again. The death of Aunt Branwell gave her a 'perfect opportunity' to return home, and remain home, once and for all. She never left home again.

The rest of the family at this time was apart from home with Charlotte back in Brussels, both teaching and studying for another year, and Anne taking Branwell with her to Thorp Green Hall in January, 1843, as tutor to young Edmund Robinson. Emily now concentrated her efforts on Gondal stories and poems and used the time to organize previous verse into two books, *Gondal Poems* and *'E. J. B.'* which today form part of her early writing grouped into their 'juvenilia'.

When Charlotte finally returned from Brussels in early January, 1844, their thoughts turned to final preparations for the school they hoped to open. With eagerness and anticipation, they went through all the necessary steps with plans and advertisements, but in the end, no one showed up. Although they were extremely disappointed when no one arrived, it turned out to be a 'blessing in disguise' for two reasons. Firstly, they now concentrated on their writings as never before, and this, of course, was very fortunate for them and the English literary world. Secondly, Branwell had become even more dependent on alcohol and drugs, and students living in the same house with him in his wretched condition would not have been compatible with offering a proper and suitable environment for young students of any age or sex.

Once again the Brontë household settled into a routine and for the next year and one half, everything was quite peaceful and uneventful. It was not until the 'discovery' of

Emily's poetry by Charlotte in the fall of 1845, that events took a fateful turn and led them into literary careers. Emily was highly incensed at her sister's intrusion into her privacy, as we read in Charlotte's 'Biographical Notice' to the second edition of Emily's novel:

> My sister Emily was not a demonstrative character, nor one, on the recesses of whose mind and feelings, even those nearest and dearest to her could, with impunity, intrude unlicensed; it took hours to reconcile her to the discovery I had made, and days to persuade her that such poems merited publication.

Eventually Charlotte was able to persuade Emily to take part in her suggested publication of their own poetry. Emily agreed only upon the condition that they remain anonymous, and upon Anne's suggestion that they use pseudonyms. They then set about their joint venture.

When they finally found a publisher, Aylott & Jones of London, it was on the condition that they pay the direct publication costs of approximately £40. Since they now each had a small inheritance of £300 from Aunt Branwell, they considered it a worthwhile investment and took up the offer of the publisher. Although, in the end, they sold only two copies from the entire run, thought to be 1000, it served two main purposes. They were now published poets, and it 'whetted their appetite' to publish again. Their second venture would be in prose, not verse, so they each agreed to try their hand at writing a novel.

One of the daily routines that occurred each evening was their father locking the front door at the stroke of nine, stopping in at the parlour door and gently admonishing his daughters not to stay up too late, winding the clock on the stairway landing and then proceeding to bed. Charlotte, Emily and Anne would then drop what they were doing and then proceed with a strange ritual. They would walk around and around the dining room table and openly discuss each novel, its progress, its plot, its characters, and perhaps make comments and suggestions on each other's work. And then once or twice during the week, they would read their works aloud to one another.

While working on their manuscripts, Charlotte learned, or at least confirmed, several of Emily's personal qualities which were growing ever stronger. Emily was a very strong-willed person, solemn, serious, reserved, shy to the point of timidity, meek, humble, and modest among others, but she was 'not amenable' to outside influences, and that included Charlotte's. She could be stubborn, uncooperative and intractable, which was annoying to Charlotte, and as for her spirit, it was indomitable, completely independent and 'altogether unbending'. And although with little formal education and without 'worldly knowledge', which may have been misjudged as naivety, there lay a pensive, tranquil mind with deep intelligence. Emily was also a person of deep loyalties, but in return, she expected the same from others, and once they transgressed these bounds, they were not easily redeemed or restored.

With the completion of their three novels, *The Professor* by Charlotte, *Wuthering Heights* by Emily, and *Agnes Grey* by Anne, they began anew to send out their manuscripts in search of a new publisher. Charlotte's manuscript was already 'making the rounds', since it was finished first, and Emily's and Anne's followed about a month later. On each and every occasion, Charlotte's was turned down, but by mid-1847, *Wuthering Heights* and *Agnes Grey* found a common publisher in Thomas Cautley Newby of London. Charlotte, having given up on *The Professor*, began a new novel, *Jane Eyre*, in August,1846, while she was in Manchester with her father who was having a cataract operation. *Jane Eyre* received immediate acceptance and publication by Smith, Elder & Co. of London, which immediately set Thomas Cautley Newby into motion to quickly publish *Wuthering Heights* and *Agnes Grey*, by the 'Bell brothers', to 'cash in' on Currer Bell's sudden fame and wave of popularity.

Emily's *Wuthering Heights*, and Anne's *Agnes Grey* were quickly put into publication in December, 1847, only two months after *Jane Eyre*. Regretably the rush to get these novels by Ellis and Acton Bell into print led to the original copies being published with many errors which had already been corrected and sent in by Emily and Anne. They now eagerly awaited reviews of their work, but when they did appear, the 'lion's share' of critics' attention went to *Wuthering Heights*, and they were not kind. The novel was so radically different from anything they had ever read that many of them expressed shock, outrage, astonishment, disgust and outright perplexity.

Graham's Magazine called *Wuthering Heights* a "compound of vulgar depravity and unnatural horrors". *Douglas Jerrold's Weekly* reacted that, "in *Wuthering Heights* the reader is shocked, disgusted, almost sickened by details of cruelty, inhumanity, and the most diabolical hate and vengeance". A reviewer in *The Examiner* commented:

> This is a strange book. It is not without evidence of considerable power; but, as a whole, it is wild, confused, disjointed and improbable.

These reviews and several others were clipped out, put away, and saved by Emily and later found by Charlotte, in a small container, in her writing desk after her death.

It is evident from these reviews that literary reviewers of the day were themselves in shock, knowing neither how to read or gauge material that was unlike anything they had previously encountered, nor how to react to it. They had read and reviewed many romantic novels and Gothic tales set in Moravia and distant places, but never a contemporary, Romantic-Gothic novel set in their own 'backyard' on the moors of the north of England. But the power and genius of the novel did not escape everyone, and although it may have been fashionable to join the 'chorus of voices' denouncing, berating and condemning *Wuthering Heights*, some were open and honest enough to 'sing its praises'. Such was the case in *The Palladium* in September, 1850. Later, Emily was referred to as a 'timeless genius', and her romance was compared to the tragedies of Shakespeare, but, of course, Emily did not live long enough to hear these words of praise for her work. She went to her death knowing only that her one and only novel was roundly condemned by literary critics throughout England. Not even her own sister, Charlotte, recognized it for the masterpiece that it was.

After the publication of their novels, the problem created by Thomas Cautley Newby, Emily and Anne's publishers, demanded an immediate resolution; Charlotte saw the only solution as being a trip to London to identify themselves. The trip solved the problem with Newby, but the relationship between the three sisters took a different direction from that point onward, particularly between Charlotte and Emily. Emily refused to go to London and had previously warned Charlotte that if ever their names became public, "Ellis Bell will never pen another line", and it now appears that she held to her threat. It was at this meeting that Charlotte excitedly blurted out, "...we are three sisters". Emily was always known as an honest, honourable, loyal and trustworthy person, and after making the statement that she would never write again, she fully intended to keep her word. Although, after her death, a brief correspondence was found between Emily and her publisher implying that a second novel had been considered, or at least solicited, no further work was ever found to indicate that this, in fact, was the case. If any such material did exist, it was probably destroyed by Emily herself, or by Charlotte after her death.

This was Charlotte's second 'betrayal' of Emily, and now that it was known that they were "three sisters", by Charlotte's own words, her true identity was now known, and the betrayal was complete. Their relationship was never the same again. Charlotte had first betrayed Emily by invading the privacy of her room and finding poetry on her writing desk in the fall of 1845. This first transgression was 'mildly' dealt with by Emily, but this second transgression was unforgiveable. Emily now withdrew from Charlotte and never fully trusted her again; their relationship 'cooled', and Emily gravitated more and more toward Anne with whom she felt much more at ease. Ellen Nussey commented in *Reminiscences* (1871) that after her first visit to the Parsonage in July, 1833, she noticed an early 'alliance', and close relationship, had already been formed between them :

> [Emily and Anne were]...like twins - inseparable companions, and in the very closest sympathy, which never had any interruption.

This, of course, described Emily and Anne's relationship in their early years, and it was further 'rooted' and 'bonded' when Charlotte was away at Roe Head School in 1831, and 1832. Often, the two of them would escape to the moors by themselves, asserting their growing independence, without Branwell as their guardian and protector. Their breakaway colony of Gondal, and their writings, again showed a closer kinship with one another, and a further distancing from Charlotte and Branwell. In a letter to Margaret Wooler, Charlotte once lamented about Emily:

> [she was] not quite so tractable and open as I could wish [but] I must remember perfection is not the lot of humanity...

It appears to indicate that Charlotte saw her 'intractability' as an 'imperfection' in her character, and not simply a viewpoint different from her own. The rift was there long before this and affected all of their relationships, one to another, which also affected Anne. In a poem entitled, 'Monday Night, May 11, 1846', and later re-titled, 'Domestic Peace' by Charlotte, Anne wrote:

> Why should such gloomy silence reign
> And why is all the house so drear
> When neither danger, sickness, pain
> Nor death, nor want have entered here?

It is evident that no outside elements have affected them, yet the atmosphere between them has been somewhat 'strained' and an air of tension existed. Charlotte's unintentional interference had upset the previous harmony and 'balance'.

Emily was not easily led, and Charlotte further lamented that she was not "amenable" to the "influence of other intellects" including her own which must have been frustrating for her. She again mentioned to Ellen Nussey that Emily will "not give an explanation of her feelings...", and again later, "I do wish I knew her feelings more clearly". Emily remained taciturn, withdrawn, unsociable, and 'unreachable' even to her own sister. Charlotte was now placed 'outside the envelope' of Emily's feelings, and there was no way that she could 'reach' inside. For Charlotte who saw herself as the 'head' and 'guardian' of the family, this must have been disconcerting.

When Branwell's downward spiral 'took a turn for the worst' and he died on September 24, 1848, Emily immediately took charge of the funeral arrangements, not Charlotte. The funeral was set for one week later on Sunday, October 1st, which turned out to be a wet, cold, miserable day, and during that time, Emily caught a cold. When she returned to the house after the funeral that day, she became ill and never left it again.

In the weeks that followed, it was soon noticed that Emily had more than just an ordinary cold, and her condition worsened. It was suggested that a doctor visit her and that her condition be properly diagnosed and assessed, but Emily refused, for whatever reason. Perhaps she did not wish to believe that her condition was consumptive, and therefore terminal, or perhaps as Charlotte saw it as just the opposite, and mentioned, "She sank rapidly. She made haste to leave us." This suggests that Emily perhaps lost the 'will to live' and simply wanted to hasten her own demise.

In those next few months, Emily demonstrated qualities and characteristics which were almost superhuman. These, they had always known about, but now they were tested to the extreme and she did not fail them. Emily was long-suffering, persevering, uncompromising, strong-willed, self-reliant, and determined. Throughout her ordeal, she refused to see a doctor, refused any help whatsoever, and continued on her regular household duties as though nothing was wrong. Charlotte commented about her physical determination ('Biographical Notice' to second edition):

> Never in all her life had she lingered over any task that lay before her, and she did not linger now.

As Emily's condition worsened and the physical erosion took place, she became slower at her tasks, but still she refused any and all help offered. When she awoke in the morning, she slowly and painfully dressed herself and went down to breakfast. As she became more emaciated and weaker yet, it took her an hour or more to perform these otherwise simple tasks which were now very laborious and 'taxing'. To Charlotte and

Anne, it was difficult to watch her steady and rapid decline. Charlotte could not comment without admiration ('Biographical Notice' to second editon):

> Day by day, when I saw with what a front she met suffering, I looked on her with an anguish of wonder and love. I have seen nothing like it; but, indeed, I have never seen her parallel in anything.

She continued her daily tasks in this manner for the next two months to the amazement of the entire household. But it could not last for long, and in it, Charlotte saw an irony ('Biographical Notice' to second edition):

> The awful point was, that, while full of ruth for others, on herself she had no pity; the spirit was inexorable to the flesh;...

And as a mortal being, Charlotte could only describe Emily's strength in these words ('Biographical Notice' to second edition):

> Yet, while physically she perished, mentally she grew stronger than we had yet known her.

and her perseverence as ('Biographical Notice' to second edition):

> Stronger than a man, simpler than a child, her nature stood alone.

Eventually, on December 19, 1848, a week before Christmas, the sad day of reckoning occurred, and after she awoke, dressed herself, and made her way downstairs, which took her an inordinate amount of time, she could not proceed with her household duties and laid down on the settee in the dining room. Still, she refused a doctor. Charlotte realized that these were probably her final hours, and determined to bring some little joy to her dying sister, went out onto the moors behind the parsonage looking for a sprig of heather. The moors were overlain with snow, but Charlotte persisted for over two hours digging through the snow here and there until she was finally successful. Charlotte rushed back with her 'prize' hoping to cheer her up, but Emily was beyond caring.

In the early afternoon, Emily finally whispered to Charlotte:

> If you will send for a doctor, I will see him now.

Charlotte quickly put on her coat and shawl and was about to leave when Tabby, the servant, asked where she was going. When Charlotte explained, Tabby quickly responded with words to the effect that, if Emily herself had asked for a doctor, then it was 'too late'. Moments later, they heard anguished cries coming from the front parlour; Emily's life was over. It was two o'clock in the afternoon. Emily Jane Brontë, age thirty years, was buried a few days later.

Such was the tragic end to one of English Literature's most well-read and deeply-analyzed writers in history. Her single work has been one of the most enduring pieces ever written, and we can now only wonder at, 'what might have been', if she had lived a longer, full life.

4

ANNE BRONTË (1820 - 1849)

The legacy of Anne Brontë is not quite equal to that of her two famous sisters, Charlotte and Emily, but it leaves much yet to be explored. In all the written work and background, least is said about her, and her works do not receive their proper acclaim, especially her second novel. Anne was in many ways different, and she was not exactly the quiet, subservient person that she was made out to be. She was intelligent, adventurous, congenial, and she had a mind of her own.

Anne Brontë has left behind two important novels, *Agnes Grey* and *Tenant of Wildfell Hall*. Neither of these two books have received the critical acclaim of those of her sisters, but they are not to be ignored. Each of these novels has much to offer. The novels of Charlotte and Emily were quite bold and different, and Anne's did not have the same dramatic appeal as *Wuthering Heights* and *Jane Eyre*. Her novels were merely overpowered and overshadowed by two masterpieces of English Literature.

Agnes Grey was a novel with a purpose other than simply profit; it was based on fact and was meant to send a message. The novel resulted from a culmination of years of experience as a governess in two different situations, neither of them much different from one another except in the ages of the chidren involved. The purpose of the novel was to expose and illustrate the hypocrisy of Victorian notions, and one's 'place' in society. It was not a 'grandstand' move to upstage her sisters or simply a wild attempt at fame and fortune; she had far too much integrity for that.

Anne was an especially warm, kind human being who loved and cared for her fellow-man and 'would not' and 'could not' find it in herself to verbally or physically abuse others. Mistreatment of others was just not in her character and her education and upbringing just would not allow it. Therefore, to go out into the world as a governess and to receive such cold, callous and cruel treatment as she did was, to put it mildly, a shocking entry into the 'real world' and society around her. It was reason enough for 'exposure'. Although the purpose and intent was not revenge, as some critics and analysts have accused her, its purpose was mainly to 'inform' with the ultimate hope of 'reform'. She strongly felt that it was a story which had to be told.

The novel, *Agnes Grey*, was an immediate 'hit' because it was one of the first of its kind, a hard-hitting tell-all, tell-tale book which exposed certain unspoken truths about high-society in Victorian England. Also, it was about this time, the second stage of the Industrial Revolution, that books began to proliferate and they were now within the financial reach of most readers. Naturally, human nature being what it is, readers of the day were exposed to inside gossip of the Victorian gentry, and they could now practise a new kind of 'voyeurism' into the 'dirty, little secrets' of the aristocracy. Even one of the families exposed in the novel, the Robinsons, recognized themselves. The eldest daughter, Lydia, wrote to Anne often after her fame had spread and continued to write to her to the time of her death. The Robinsons and the area they lived in, North Yorkshire, with holidays to the east coast, had a profound and lasting effect upon Anne.

The novel, *Tenant of Wildfell Hall*, was in some quarters condemned as 'vulgar'. Even Charlotte, in a letter to Wm. S. Williams after Anne's death, was highly critical of it saying, " 'Wildfell Hall' it hardly appears to me desirable to preserve." Charlotte again condemned it in the 'Biographical Notice of Ellis and Acton Bell' (Sept. 19, 1850) saying:

> The choice of subject in that work is a mistake; it was too little consonant with the character, tastes and ideas, of the gentle, retiring inexperienced writer.

These are harsh criticisms from her own older, protective sister who was shocked by Anne's subject matter and the explicit nature of its treatment.

One of the first things that a reader of *'Wildfell Hall'* will notice is the dramatic difference in style in the two novels. *Agnes Grey* is very direct, informative, and with limited conversation typical of non-fictions. On the other hand, *Tenant of Wildfell Hall* is, from the beginning, conversational with descriptive narrative much more so in the style of the novels by Charlotte and Emily. The plot, sub-plots, and characters are carefully attended to in the first several chapters, just as we find in *Jane Eyre* and *Shirley*, and are followed through to the end.

This lengthy novel is definitely a credit to Anne Brontë and is an indicator of what she might have done had she only lived longer. The improvement from her first novel, *Agnes Grey*, is remarkable. It also indicates her versatility and her ability to write two different novels in two completely different styles and formats. Her characterization and plot are both believable and interesting as well as the concept of the 'story within a story' which was definitely something new and different for the Victorian era. But it also retains some characteristics of the Romantic novel.

At the time of the publishing of *'Wildfell Hall'*, the novel *per se* was rising in importance and popularity. The general reading public was finding a new escape not only in and through the old classics as written by such writers as Sir Walter Scott but also from a new breed of writers such as Jane Austen, William Thackeray, George Eliot and, of course, the Brontës. Also, with improvements made by the Industrial Revolution, both paper and the production of books made them more universally available.

The public now had the freedom to enjoy a wide range of literature on a wide range of topics by an ever-widening body of writers and publishers. Through this literature, the reader was now able to fantasize and explore the inner lives and foibles of the upper classes. Before this genre of novel was established, they could simply enjoy stories told verbally, or passed on, by maids, servants, coachmen, footmen and governesses. Now, one of them, Anne Brontë, had not only the 'wherewithal' but also the ability to write it down in a palatable and interesting form for readers to enjoy in *Agnes Grey*. The reading public just loved it.

In addition to her two novels, Anne Brontë also left behind some poems which were first published under the pseudonym of 'Acton Bell', along with her two sisters who used the pseudonyms, 'Currer' and 'Ellis Bell'. These are thinly disguised pseudonyms for their real names, and the name 'Bell' was most likely taken from their father's curate, Arthur Bell Nicholls who first came into their parish in 1845.

The book called, *Poems*, by Currer, Ellis and Acton Bell was published at their own expense of £40 in 1846. It sold only two copies. Some of these poems give us further insight into the three, famous literary sisters of West Yorkshire. Anne's poems definitely give us insight into her thoughts, beliefs, loves and dreams. Although all three are known for their prose works, we must acknowledge and study their poetry as part of their literary legacies. Other than these, there are no manuscripts or materials extant, except for five letters and two diary papers left behind by Anne.

Anne was born in Thornton (near Bradford) on January 17, 1820, the last of the Brontë children. Shortly thereafter, Rev. Brontë accepted the curacy at Haworth about twenty miles away. The family packed up and moved in April of that year, and there they would stay to the end of their days. During her pregnancy with Anne, Mrs. Brontë was in poor health and after her birth, she never fully recovered her strength. After the move to Haworth, her health deteriorated further, and it was later discovered that she had stomach cancer which turned out to be terminal. Within eighteen months of Anne's birth, Mrs. Brontë was dead.

The Brontë children were now without a mother, and Mr. Brontë was now left with six, small children to care for. The eldest, Maria, was only seven. She quickly became the 'surrogate mother' to her younger siblings, and she was worshipped and adored by all of them. She provided them with the love, warmth, understanding and attention they badly needed.

Soon after Mrs. Brontë's death, her elder sister, Elizabeth Branwell, arrived from Penzance, Cornwall to help the Reverend in his transition period; Aunt Branwell had no intention of staying. It was generally thought that the Reverend would soon remarry and Aunt Branwell would then return to her beloved, native Cornwall. Unfortunately, Rev. Brontë was unable to find a new wife although he did make several proposals. We can only surmise that any prospective wife must have considered the daunting task, and enormous responsibility, of raising six, young, active, energetic children who belonged to someone else.

It soon became evident that Aunt Branwell's services would be required for a longer period, and her Christian sense of duty and charity would not allow her to leave. Elizabeth was a devout Methodist and this would eventually have a lasting effect on the Brontë children. Although she was kind and generous, she was not the warm, cuddly type and never developed a close, warm, physical, loving relationship that the children needed. She was greatly esteemed, highly regarded and respected, but her matronly form and strict, religious bearing could not replace the love and warmth which they had received from their mother, and sister Maria. She remained a spinster at Haworth until her death at age 66 on October 29, 1842.

Anne herself was a small, sickly child who suffered badly from asthma. After her mother's death, Aunt Branwell took the infant 'under her wing' and nursed her back to good health. After it was determined that she would be staying longer, Aunt Branwell took over Rev. and Mrs. Brontë's bedroom and used it as a nursery for Anne, and a classroom for the children during the day. She used this room as her own until her death, and Anne shared this room with her aunt well into her late teens or early twenties. As a result, Aunt Branwell had a greater influence over Anne in her early formative years than she did over Charlotte and Emily.

In her early years, Anne quickly adopted her older sister, Maria, as the most important person in her life. And likewise, Maria looked after Anne as she would her own child. Unfortunately this close, warm, motherly relationship ended all too soon when Maria, and then Elizabeth, died of consumption in May and June of 1825, respectively. Thereafter, Charlotte took over the role as 'protector' of the remaining Brontë children.

When Maria, Elizabeth, Charlotte and Emily first went to the Clergy Daughters' School at Cowan Bridge in 1824, Anne was at home with her only other sibling, Branwell, her older brother. As the youngest of the Brontë children, Anne was definitely adored, spoiled and protected by everyone; to some extent, it was over-protection. Also, being left home alone with Branwell was perhaps not the best thing that could have happened to her. He, too, as the only boy in the family, and a favourite of Aunt Branwell, became an overindulged child. This later had major repurcussions on his social and emotional growth and ultimately on the outcome of his life (see Branwell Brontë).

Anne, like the other children in the family, was taught at home by Aunt Branwell, her father, and later by Charlotte and Emily. She, too, was eager to learn, and in 1835, when Emily returned from Roe Head School, homesick after only a few months, Anne took her place. Anne remained there two years, but she, too, besides having a religious crisis, became homesick for the moors, her home, her family, and especially for Emily.

As older sister and brother, Charlotte and Branwell ruled over the younger Emily and Anne. But when Charlotte left for Roe Head in 1831, Branwell was unable to maintain 'control' over his two, younger sibling sisters. It was then that the two sisters began their new 'alliance' which lasted until their deaths. In fact, it was during this time that Emily and Anne made their 'break-away' colony of 'Gondal' which was so prominent in their early 'Juvenilia'. This undoubtedly was one of the more memorable and significant moments in their developmental period; they were now exhibiting the first signs of a new-found independence, and they no longer saw themselves as the 'young ones' to be dominated. Charlotte and Branwell continued on in their writings with the colony of 'Angria' after she returned from Roe Head.

Anne, like Emily, was tall and slender, and she was thought to be the prettiest of the three remaining girls. From the information we can gather, it appears that Anne was about five-foot five inches tall, and Emily perhaps an inch or two taller. For Victorian times, this was taller than average for girls of their day. Charlotte, on the other hand, was quite diminutive and smaller than average at four-foot ten inches, or perhaps eleven. No photographs of them (except for a contested one of Charlotte) are in existence although there are 'likenesses' in the form of artistic portraits and paintings. The most famous one is, of course, a painting of Anne, Emily, and Charlotte which was painted by their brother Branwell, and which now hangs in the National Portrait Gallery in London. A copy of that painting hangs in the main stairway at the Brontë Parsonage Museum.

If we believe Ellen Nussey in her book, *Reminiscences*, 1871, she described Anne as,

> ...her hair was a very pretty light brown and fell on her neck in curls. (she)...had lovely violet-blue eyes, fine pencilled eyebrows, and a clear, almost transparent complexion.

On the other hand, George Smith of Smith, Elder & Co. Publishers described her as follows:

> She was a gentle, quiet, rather subdued person, by no means pretty, yet of pleasing appearance.

These were observations made of her after Charlotte and Anne went to London (1848) to reveal their true identities and to quell rumours that Currer, Ellis, and Acton Bell were all 'one and the same'. The publishers were shocked to discover that their star novelist was, in fact, female.

Perhaps one of the most amazing things is that her own sister Charlotte never really had much confidence in Anne as a writer. When her mother, and later Maria and Elizabeth died, Charlotte assumed the protective, 'motherly' role over Anne. As a result, Charlotte was not completely able to 'let go' of Anne, nor was she able to recognize her adulthood in the form of freedom, freedom of thought, her developing personality, and her emerging individuality.

It was partly for this reason that Anne was 'bound and determined' to prove to Charlotte, Emily, and herself, that she was a capable individual who had never been given a chance to prove herself. As a result, in 1839, she answered an advertisement and became a governess at Blake Hall in Mirfield for the children of Mr. & Mrs. Ingham. She held on to this position even though she was verbally and physically abused by the children and emotionally abused by the parents. After only one term there, she was blamed for all the children's shortcomings and fired for 'incompetence'.

The children in her charge were completely uncontrollable, without any social norms of decency towards their fellow man and, therefore, unteachable. To further complicate matters, she received no help whatsoever from the parents; she was left entirely to her own devices. If anything, she learned valuable lessons about life, living, and 'place' in Victorian society, and it was this information which she presented in the novel, *Agnes Grey*, where the family was portrayed as the 'Bloomfields'.

Her second 'situation' was little better than the first (except in pay), and the children were older, but only a few years younger than Anne herself. She demanded £50 per year, twice what she earned with the Bloomfields, and managed to get it along with longer, seasonal family holidays. They, too, were greatly overindulged children who were not well-schooled and short on manners and civility. They were quite aware of their family's position and power and knew precisely where the governess 'fit in' near the bottom rung of the society's ladder. Also, they never let Anne forget her position on that ladder for any length of time. By words, deeds, and actions they constantly reminded Anne of her 'lower rank'.

It was only her strength of character and utter determination to prove her self-worth that she persisted in staying on. (The Robinsons of Thorp Green Hall in Little Ouseburn outside of York were portrayed as the 'Murrays' of Horton Lodge in *Agnes Grey*.) Here she stayed for more than four, long years from 1841-1845. Finally, in June of that year, she turned in her resignation, returned to Haworth, and remained there until her death four years later in 1849.

Her uninterrupted four-year tenure at Thorp Green Hall under difficult conditions proved, without equivocation, her strength of character, her determination, her skill as a teacher, and her will-power. She was a much 'stronger' person than most people gave her credit. Here she gained valuable experience and a new outlook on the upper classes, the Victorian gentry, and their faults and foibles which added tremendously to the valid content, interest, and credibility of her novel, *Agnes Grey*.

Many people had an influence on Anne from early childhood to her final days, and some, of course, had more influence than others. Perhaps the most noteworthy of these were her father, Emily, Charlotte and Aunt Branwell. Those of lesser importance would be her brother, her older sisters who died at an early age, the Taylors, and Ellen Nussey. In later years, and perhaps in a negative way, her influences included the Inghams of Mirfield and the Robinsons of Little Ouseburn whom she wrote about.

At an early age after the passing of her mother, perhaps the most influential persons were Maria and Elizabeth. Also, at about this same time, Aunt Branwell took over the care of Anne from her early infancy. The influence that her aunt provided was one of a 'mother figure', but which was somewhat devoid of a close, warm and affectionate relationship. That was filled by Charlotte and especially by Emily as time went on.

Although the primary caregiver, Aunt Branwell's influence was mostly of a religious nature. Her devout, Calvinist upbringing and her 'hell-fire'' brand of religious beliefs instilled in Anne the 'sinfulness of man' and a belief in a God who often responded with harsh, cruel and vindictive retribution. In later years, when she was able to think clearly for herself, she began to have some doubts about the God she was worshipping. She eventually had trouble reconciling herself with the God that Aunt Branwell worshipped to the kind, loving and benevolent God whom others, like her father, worshipped. This religious dilemma eventually took its toll on her.

During her stay at Roe Head School (1835-37), in addition to having a mild 'breakdown' of sorts, Anne also had a 'religious crisis'. The physical breakdown was one of nervous exhaustion coupled with a homesickness for her beloved moors and, her close friend and sister, Emily. Her religious and spiritual crisis coincided with her physical and emotional collapse. She oddly sought out the spiritual guidance of a Moravian minister from a neighbouring village. It appears that she experienced 'confusion' in her religious beliefs that each and every one of us experiences at one time or another in our lives. Aunt Branwell's beliefs as a Calvinist and a Methodist who lived by an austere, moral code presented a dark and brooding side to her religion which may have resulted in a 'religious melancholy', as Charlotte chose to describe it. Aunt Branwell's view of life may be summarized in one statement she made which said, "This world is a vale of tears. We are put here to suffer." This view conflicted with that of her father's which was much more hopeful and optimistic inspite of the family's recurrent tragedies.

Her father, her only surviving parent, was also a major influence in her life although he was accused of treating his children with 'detachment'. Once his wife died, he appeared to be somewhat lost in how to bring up his own children and seemed satisfied to leave the job to others. His 'cool detachment' from their learning and upbringing has often been described as benign neglect. But we must remember that he was always there as their spiritual guide, their father and provider. In this respect, he was steadfast and did not fail them.

Mr. Brontë was somewhat villified in the biography, *The Life of Charlotte Brontë*, 1857, by Elizabeth C. Gaskell who did not like Mr. Brontë and saw his 'detachment' as one of neglect. As a result of her personal dislike for him, she portrayed him in a very negative light. Her research was somewhat narrow and flawed and what she did not mention or take into account was that Rev. Brontë was well-liked and highly respected throughout the district. Besides his own family, he had literally hundreds of other families, many with severe problems, to minister to. Also, Gaskell's dislike of Mr. Brontë was based not only on her own prejudices from meetings with him but also that of two former, disgruntled employees discharged for incompetence. They had an 'axe to grind', gave biased reports, and this simply reinforced her own personal dislike of him.

Rev. Brontë was a very busy man, but when it was necessary for a firm, decisive hand, he was always there for them. Firstly, he sent his daughters to the Clergy Daughters' School in Cowan Bridge. When Maria and Elizabeth became ill, he removed them from the school, and the very next day he went back again and removed both Charlotte and Emily. Then, he saw to it that they were educated by Aunt Branwell, and himself.

Later he sent Charlotte and Emily to Roe Head School in Mirfield, and in 1842, when they decided to go to Brussels to further their schooling, he accompanied them first to London and then to Brussels. These are not the actions of one who was totally disinterested and 'detached' from the welfare and education of his children.

Also, while he was busy with the work of his parish, the children were well-taken care of by Aunt Branwell and the two older children. The children were well-behaved and were capable of amusing themselves and teaching one another. The few adults who looked after the Brontë children during their mother's illness, and afterward, always remarked on their extreme quietness and obedience, something quite different from most children of their age. Often they could hardly believe that there were actually children in the house.

The family, and especially the children, were quite self-disciplined and 'self-suffi-cient'. This we see from their early writings about 'Angria' and 'Gondal', their artwork, their poetry, and their rambles on the lonely moors behind their home which put them 'in touch' and 'in tune' with Nature. They seemed to have occupied their time well, although some may point out that they did not have much contact with the 'locals'.

In addition to a regular education by Aunt Branwell, they were also taught artwork, needlework, and other household skills such as cooking and cleaning. Most of this educa-tion came from either their aunt or their faithful, devoted servant, Tabby. In addition to supplying basic training of household management, which in Victorian times every woman 'must know', Tabby served another purpose even more important than the former. She was the family 'story-teller' and source of local folklore. From her, all the children learned about Yorkshire, its people, and notable events in times gone by; this later helped them immensely in their writing.

Since Tabby was a rough-hewn, West Yorkshire spinster[1] with a rough exterior and harsh accent, she provided a level of 'normality' and a connection to the outside world. The Brontë children had little or no contact with other children in the community, and the only other people they saw were the people at church, their father's curates, and the occasional visitor who came to the house to see Rev. Brontë, or on domestic business.

The only other person with whom they had constant contact, other than their father and Aunt Branwell, was Tabby. And while her older sisters were off to school, only Anne and Branwell were left at home to listen and learn from Tabby's wealth and storehouse of local history and folklore. Her stories undoubtedly spurred their imaginations and pro-vided a myriad of interesting characters which the children were able to engage and employ in their own stories and tales. The stories and characters offered an enriched background from which to choose their characters for their 'juvenilia', and later into their adult novels.

Perhaps the person who exerted the most influence over Anne was her sister Emily. Although Emily was not the type of person who sought to influence others (she was exactly the opposite), Anne eventually gravitated toward her. As time went on, she gradu-ally became more 'distanced' from Charlotte and Branwell, and Emily was closer at hand and more to her liking. In Emily, she saw qualities and characteristics which she admired and perhaps sought to acquire for herself. Emily was loyal, trustworthy, of strong charac-ter, and made an excellent confidante, which Charlotte was not.

In her formative years, Anne as a youngster was often left at home with young Branwell and Emily. Anne had more in common with her sister than her brother since Charlotte and Branwell had always had their own 'alliance', and Emily and Anne made up one of their own, perhaps equally out of need and desire. This resulted in the production of 'Gondal', a break-away colony, in their early writings. The stories and characters of

---

1   Some evidence indicates that she was, in fact, a widow from a farm near the village.

Gondal continued almost to the end of their lives. Emily never seemed to tire of it although near the end, Anne did.

Anne's brother, Branwell, was perhaps one family member who had varying influence at varying times upon her. At a young age and early childhood, Branwell definitely had a strong influence on all of them since he, too, had an extremely active imagination which he used for story-telling, story-writing and their plays. He was also an active member in their early plays which they produced and performed in the children's study. As time went on, Branwell became less and less of an influence on Anne as she moved her affiliation to her sisters and female adults of the family.

As Branwell got older and more raucous, and his problems became more serious, Anne still remained faithful and loyal to him. Although he had suffered failures in almost everything he had tried, Anne went out 'on a limb' and obtained a job for him at Thorp Green Hall where she herself was a governess. There, Branwell became a tutor to the young Edmund Robinson, but in this instance, she badly misplaced her trust in him.

When Branwell jeopardized everything and had an affair with Mrs. Robinson, it was then that Anne had had enough and resigned her position out of sheer embarrassment and humiliation. Branwell stayed on, but he was eventually fired when the affair was exposed and Mr. Robinson had had enough of him. Branwell returned home to Haworth and he was never to leave again. After that time, Anne lost faith in him, and he was not taken into their confidence regarding their writings and attempts at publication.

Other persons who were an influence in Anne's life included Charlotte's friends, the Taylors, and also Ellen Nussey who became a friend of Charlotte's at Roe Head in 1831. Ellen became a life-long friend to Charlotte as well as Anne. As the years went by, letters did pass back and forth between Ellen and Anne. In fact, Ellen Nussey went along with Charlotte and Anne on the final trip to Scarborough where Anne died. Mary Taylor, on her visits to the Parsonage, also had an effect on Anne with her free-thinking and open style of discussion. Their meetings were few in number, and brief, but they undoubtedly had a lasting effect.

No doubt the last people who had an influence on Anne, in the most negative ways possible, were the Inghams of Mirfield and the Robinsons of Little Ouseburn. From these two very negative experiences that she had with these two families, Anne received an 'education' of a different kind which inspired her to write *Agnes Grey*. The two families provided Anne with such a 'shock value' that the influence was permanent and unmistakable. For everything which she had been taught about love, caring, mutual respect and human dignity, these postings tested her to the limits of her endurance.

Anne has always been treated in a secondary way in relation to her two famous sisters, Charlotte and Emily. The 'lion's share' of criticisms and reviews have gone to *Wuthering Heights* and *Jane Eyre*, not *Agnes Grey*, and *Tenant of Wildfell Hall*. This is perhaps another of the great tragedies of the Brontë legacy, since both novels are of high quality and deserve much better acclaim, especially *'Wildfell Hall'*.

Readers and reviewers were so taken by *Wuthering Heights* and *Jane Eyre* that Anne's works were completely overshadowed. Reviewers, publishers and literary critics gave their time and effort to the two novels which provided the greatest 'shock value' and which were the most controversial. As a result, Anne's work, although not less interesting as a Victorian novel, was relegated to the 'back-burners' of criticism. This is unfortunate because it deserved closer attention, and in comparison to the novels of her sisters, hers was no less a masterpiece of social interaction focusing on spousal and alcohol abuse, separation and divorce, and the 'place' of women in society. She skillfully and masterfully handled all of these topics although somewhat too directly for some Victorian readers.

The tragedy of Anne Brontë was that she, too, died too young and well before her writing career had reached a 'peak', and before she had written a famous, acclaimed Victorian novel. She needed more time to 'blossom' and develop as a writer, but it was not to be.

When Emily died in December of 1848, Anne was already ill. She was in the initial stages of consumption, a disease for which there was no known cure at the time. Most people who were infected with it died from it. When Anne's health deteriorated still further, her father called in a specialist, a Dr. Teale from Leeds, who confirmed their worst fears. Anne was already in the advanced stages of consumption, but he still prescribed medicines and strict regimens of diet to follow for improved health. Unlike Emily who was a completely uncooperative patient, Anne was exactly the opposite and did exactly what was asked of her.

By late April, Anne's condition worsened to the point of being serious. The situation did not get better, and Charlotte was determined to do what was necessary to keep her alive. Anne suggested a trip to Scarborough on the North Yorkshire Coast and Charlotte made preliminary plans to travel there. Anne also wrote a letter to Ellen Nussey asking her to accompany them there. Over the years Ellen had become close friends to all of the young Brontës, and although she was more than willing, she was detained by visitors and could not leave until late April or May.

Anne loved the moors, but she also had a strong attraction to the beautiful Yorkshire Coast which she had come to know through her many trips there with the Robinsons during her tenure with them from 1840 - 1845. The precipitous cliffs, Scarborough Castle, the renowned sandy beaches, the glistening waters, the crashing waves, and mocking seagulls were a 'world apart' from her beloved, solitary moors, but she loved them equally. Anne was determined to see them one last time. Also, the fresh, clean, salt-sea air was thought to be highly therapeutic for consumptive patients and by going to Scarborough, Anne was not only fulfilling a 'last wish' but also 'clutching at straws' for improved health. Alas, it was too late.

On May 23rd, the day set for the departure, Ellen was to meet them at Leeds Station, a major train junction in the North of England. There they were to meet Ellen, change trains, and continue on to Scarborough with a stopover at York. Anne was determined to see the magnificent York Minster Cathedral one last time. Unfortunately, Anne was so ill that Charlotte dared not leave Haworth with her that day, and she had no way of getting a message to Ellen at Leeds to explain the delay.

Ellen waited patiently for them at Leeds Station[2] but they did not arrive. The next day, May 24th, when they failed to arrive again, she proceeded to Haworth by gig to find out what had happened. By then, Anne was better, and they all set off for York. At York, they stayed overnight, visited the vast and beautiful cathedral and then proceeded on to Scarborough where they stayed at a seaside hotel, arriving there on Saturday, the 25th.

On the 26th, the three of them managed several activites including a walk along the wide expanse of sandy beach, and later a ride on a donkey cart. Anne even took up the reins herself for a time, and at one point when the boy mistreated his animal, Anne scolded him. On Sunday, after breakfast, they dissuaded Anne from going to church, but later in the day Anne sat near the beach. The evening gave rise to a spectacular sunset which they enjoyed at the window. Thereafter, Anne's condition worsened, partly from the exertion of travel and partly because of the progression of the disease to its final stages. Charlotte then had an important decision to make; should she try to make it back to Haworth with Anne or simply 'stay put' in Scarborough. After difficult deliberation, she chose to stay.

On May 28, 1849, at about 11:00 A.M. after a light breakfast, Anne reported feeling a 'change' come over her body. Charlotte sent for a doctor immediately. His prognosis was that she was near death and had only a short time to live. He was quite accurate in his prediction and two hours later, at approximately 2:00 P.M., Anne passed away peacefully and quietly with Charlotte and Ellen at her side. Her final words were to her sister, "Take courage, Charlotte. Take courage." It was at 2:00 P.M. that her close friend and beloved sister Emily had also died only five months before. Anne was only twenty-nine years old.

The question of returning the body to Haworth for burial was not entertained very long for two reasons. Firstly, Charlotte wished to spare her father the grief and agony of yet another funeral, and secondly, Anne loved Scarborough and had often mentioned that she would like to remain there. Now, in death, it seemed that the proper thing to do was simply to have her buried there, and there she remains today.

The funeral ceremony was a simple one held at Christ Church[3], and she was buried on a gentle, sunny, southern slope of St. Mary's Churchyard Cemetery facing the sea, and just below Scarborough Castle. Even today, her grave is well-cared for and attended and covered with flowers. In literature, she may be referred to as the 'forgotten Brontë' or the 'other Brontë', but recently her works have re-surfaced and been re-reviewed and re-assessed more favourably than ever before. And today, she is certainly not part of a forgotten legacy; Anne Brontë's works are alive and well.

---

2   While waiting there, Ellen saw what she thought was an ominous signs; two coffin were being off-loaded from the train.

3   The funeral service was conducted at Christ Church since St. Mary's was under repair. Marg Wooler was the only mourner besides Charlotte and Ellen Nussey.

5

PATRICK BRANWELL BRONTË (1817-1848)

Perhaps the least known of all the surviving Brontë children is young Patrick (Branwell), the only son of the Rev. and Maria Brontë. He, too, died young at the age of 31, but he never published any material although he badly wanted to be a writer. It is also unknown as to whether he was aware of his sisters' fame and fortune even though they lived in the same house. It seems improbable that he could not have known about it, but there is no known acknowledgement or reaction to their works by him.

Being the only son in the family of six, with three sisters older than himself and two younger, there are indicators that he received preferential treatment in some quarters. Firstly, because it was Victorian times and it was the custom, and secondly because he was the only boy in a family of six children. He was always Aunt Branwell's favourite, and also being the only son, his father held out high hopes for him. Unfortunately, although perhaps the most intelligent, artistic, and gifted of all, he was clearly the least successful of the children. He eventually brought disgrace upon himself, his family, and particularly to his father.

Branwell was born on June 26, 1817, at Thornton (Bradford), the fourth child of the Brontë family. From an early age, he showed great promise; he was 'sharp' and highly intelligent. The entire family saw him as their 'great hope' for the future of the Brontë name. Also, in the Victorian era, all aspirations and future hopes were pinned on the sons of the family. Mainly they were seen as the heir to the family and the one who would carry on the family name. As well, they were expected to earn enough money to care for other female members of the family who were unmarried, or 'without station'.

All of Mr. Brontë's children were special to him, but young Branwell received special attention with thoughts to his future 'station' in life. Rev. Brontë hoped that one day he would become a scholar, an artist, or both. The Reverend remembered his own difficult path from poverty in Ireland to, and through, Cambridge University, and he wanted to make it easier for his only son. Although educated at home with the rest of his sisters, he received extra, personal tutorials from his father in classic languages.

Four of the girls were sent to the Clergy Daughters' School at Cowan Bridge in 1824, but young Branwell was kept at home with Anne to be educated by his father. The home education plan for Branwell did not go well for several reasons. The girls were usually very quiet, gentle, respectful, and tractable whereas Branwell was just the opposite. He showed signs of hyper-activity and of being a 'difficult' student from early on. These difficulties and negative qualities followed him for the remainder of his life; they did not get better, but only worse.

When Maria was seriously ill, a letter was sent from Cowan Bridge School to Mr. Brontë who promptly ordered a gig to go there and pick her up. Unfortunately she was too ill to recuperate and died on May 6, 1825, a few months after returning home. Elizabeth was now also ill and was withdrawn from the school on May 31st. Seeing how ill she was, and fearing for the welfare of Charlotte and Emily, he returned the very next day and withdrew them both. Elizabeth died on June 15th. From then on, the children were to be educated in their early years at home.

The effect of their deaths on the family was, of course, deep shock, sorrow, and grief, but for Branwell it was devastating. It left deep, permanent, emotional, and psychological scars. To him and the younger children, Maria had been like a 'mother' since their own had been lost years before. Now, she too was gone. Branwell flew into a blasphemous rage and hated God for what He had done.

He refused to believe that Maria, and now Elizabeth, were dead. He shut himself into the study and refused to come out. As was the custom to kiss a loved one as they lay in their coffin, Branwell refused to do so. He also refused to go to their funerals. Later, he wandered through the house hoping to see either Maria or Elizabeth. These are all obvious signs of severe mental distress for which he needed treatment but never received. In later years, he exhibited signs that he was 'godless' and his Bohemian lifestyle indicated that he was either 'godless' and lawless, or at least taunting and mocking God with his wild behaviour.

When he was a young boy, he had a violent temper and often threw temper tantrums. On one occasion at the Keighley Fair, he threw such a tantrum that he had an apoplectic fit and seizure and had to be taken home immediately. The fact that he was spoiled and catered to by his father, aunt, and sisters allowed him to develop without any self-control or self-discipline. The lack of these personal qualities and the inablility of self-denial ultimately led to his own self-destruction. Two other significant factors which had adverse effects upon Branwell were that he had no formal education outside of the home, and secondly, he had only minimal contact with other children and boys his own age outside of his own family which otherwise may have moderated his wild behaviour.

To provide some comfort to his young son (then seven) after the deaths of his two eldest sisters, Rev. Brontë moved him into his own bedroom where he could be close at hand to comfort him. There he remained until well into his teens, and again later in his life when he was deathly ill.

On one occasion, Rev. Brontë took his children to Oakwell Hall where the Roundheads had briefly fled during the Civil War. On one of the stain-glass windows is an inscription which can be seen even today. It reads:

"Kings are but slaves, when by their passions held,
But who commands himself, commands the world."

When his father read this to him, Branwell responded:

"When I'm grown up, I shall be my own king, master of myself."

How prophetic these words turned out to be as we see from the outcome of his own life; he was always 'his own master', but to his own detriment.

As a result of the deaths of his two eldest children, Rev. Brontë was paranoid about sending any of his children to any public or private school. As a result, Branwell was deprived of the opportunities to grow, develop, and socially interact with others his own age. Educators and psychologists are aware that a great deal of learning and social awareness comes just from co-mingling with other students and children their own age. This was completely denied to Branwell with the concomitant result of a raucous and 'wild abandon' approach to life and living.

This social interaction provides young children with learning the 'social norms' and 'limits of acceptability' of the society of the day. At any school, Branwell would soon have learned that there are certain 'norms', realities, and social graces which are acceptable and some which are not. Also, he would have learned about the 'authoritarian power structure' within a school, conformity to general rules and restrictions, as well as the penalties, punishments, and consequences of not adhering to those rules and conformities.

In addition to this, he would have learned about the 'pecking order' of society in which he lived and exactly where he stood in that order. He would have soon learned that there are 'good' and 'bad' people, those who will help you and those who will harm you, and of those who are meek, mild and submissive as well as those who are bullies, those who are abusive, and those who seek power and control. Without these confines, controls, rules, restrictions, penalties and consequences, he remained somewhat naïve to the 'ways of the world'. Also, he did not appear to have a strong sense of social and personal responsibility.

Without formal education and formal training in any specific area or trade, he lacked ambition, direction, and motivation. At one point Emily predicted his demise because she said that he was of "weak" character. Those who were near him and could help him toward these goals were afraid to be 'direct' or confrontational with him because of his very bad temper. By the time he reached his teens, he was 'explosive' as well as rebellious and sadly equipped to face the real world around him. All members of the family lived in fear of his rages.

At this time another external factor crept into the stream of elements which would eventually lead to his demise. This was his new and growing relationship with William Brown, the son of the church's sexton. He was older and more 'experienced' than Branwell and he led him into more serious 'temptations' and destructive follies. Naturally, as a young and naïve boy wanting to 'try his wings', exercise more personal freedom, and express his 'manhood', he gladly went along with his friend's adventures. About this time, he was even beyond the control of his own father, the last stop-gap on his road to self-destruction.

He also took up boxing, and on a trip to Roe Head in Mirfield to visit Charlotte (a 20-mile walk), he commented on his boxing ability and that he would soon be able to go drinking at the Black Bull with his new-found friend, William Brown. Charlotte could only shudder at the prospects and results of his newly-acquired freedom. When he finally did go drinking at the Black Bull, it was the 'beginning of the end' for young Branwell. In short order, Branwell ran up a large debt for which his father was liable. This was one time when a furious argument broke out between Branwell and his father. From that time forward, he only went into further decline.

As a young boy, Branwell often teased and taunted his sisters. Although he could be warm, witty and charming when he wanted to be, he often belittled them in front of their friends calling them 'small and ugly'. He became ever more abusive and developed a 'black heart' much like the characters he wrote about in his stories of Angria and Glasstown and in his plays. All this may have been a manisfestation of his inability to show love and affection toward others, much like his father.

When Branwell was in his mid-teens, he took an interest in art (oil, portrait painting) and showed that he had a considerable, natural talent. He painted a picture, now famous and in the National Gallery in London, of his three sisters and himself. The picture included Anne, Emily, himself, and then Charlotte, from left to right. After a comment by Emily that he appeared taller than the rest because he was 'standing on a box', Branwell took offence and painted himself out. A second theory is that A.B. Nicholls, Charlotte's husband, disgusted with his legacy, painted him out. Considering that A. B. Nicholls did some other odd things like folding the painting into squares so that only Charlotte would 'show' brings some possible credence to this odd speculation. A copy of this painting hangs in the main stairwell of the Brontë Parsonage Museum today.

Realizing that they may have finally stumbled onto Branwell's 'life work', his father hired a well-known art master, a Mr. Robinson from Leeds, to give Branwell painting lessons. Later, in 1835, with some training, more experience and 'letters of reference', Branwell was sent to the Royal Academy of Art in London. The money for the trip came from various sources including Aunt Branwell and Charlotte who earned it teaching at Roe Head School. She wasn't earning much, but she wanted to help and contribute to his education to get him started in life, just as she would do for Emily and Anne.

With great fanfare, Branwell was off to London to study art, learn a profession, later earn a living and even a name for himself. If he earned enough, he could not only support himself but assist his father and family at the Parsonage in Haworth. As a portrait painter, an art teacher and later as a creative, new artist, he could earn a comfortable living and perhaps make his fame and fortune. Everyone was satisfied that now, finally, Branwell was on his way to a successful life and career.

Several days later, Branwell showed up back at the Parsonage without any of his money. His tuition and living-expense money was all gone. The stories of what happened in London are varied. The most consistent story is that he spent it at a pub where sharp, 'city slicksters' soon duped the 'country boy' from the North out of his money. No doubt that with Branwell's penchant for drink, he was an 'easy target' and a willing accomplice. He was homesick and lonely in the big city, and one of the quickest ways to make new friends was to visit a pub and buy a 'few rounds'. It did not take long for his money to disappear.

Two other stories are also told. One is that he was 'mugged' and his money was stolen. A third, and more credible, story is that he went to the steps of the Royal Academy of Art, but after visiting the National Art Gallery and seeing the work of the masters, he became so intimidated and low in spirits and self-worth by comparison, that he just could not go in. Then, in despondency and loneliness, he spent his money on drink. In any case, he hastily returned in failure. Before Branwell even left, Emily had warned that he was both "weak" and "lacked resolution". Her insight into her brother's character was remarkably accurate.

Several years later in June of 1838, Branwell set himself up as a portrait painter at #3 Fountain Street in Bradford, lodging with the Kirby family. There he remained for a year and did paint some portraits, but it was not always enough to pay his rent. Often he would begin a portrait and then not finish it losing the commission for the work. Instead of concentrating on his work and finishing the portraits, Branwell would often go out drinking with his artist friend, J.B. Leyland, and associate, Francis Grundy, which simply reinforced his bad habits and put him deeper into debt. In time, he gained a bad reputation for unfinished work, and he was 'hounded' by creditors for his unpaid bills. In the face of mounting debt and persistent bill collectors, he left Bradford and returned to Haworth in May, 1839.

In January of 1840, Branwell went to Broughton-in-Furness as a tutor for a Mr. Postlethwaite and remained there until June of that year. It appears to be the only minor success which he had during his short lifetime. It was also during his stay here that he was able to meet and converse with Hartley Coleridge, the son of Samuel Coleridge, who was now by his own right, a succesful writer. During this visit, a 'germ' was planted in his brain for a wild scheme which would eventually lead to his downfall. It all resulted from his observation of other leisurely lifestyles and their method of success; he hoped to marry a rich lady and live in the same way.

In September of that year, Branwell finally landed a job as a clerk with the new Leeds-Manchester Railway at Sowerby Bridge near Halifax. At the beginning he did reasonably well, but for a person of his intellect and education, he thought it 'beneath his station' and became bored with it. In his off-hours, he fell into his old pattern of drinking at the pubs with his friends. Inspite of this, he continued to do well and was promoted in 1841, to clerk-in-charge at the slightly more distant post of Luddenden Foot.

Although his family was pleased with his promotion, Branwell himself was unhappy with it because of its more remote location. He was no longer able to go to the pub on lunch breaks, he had few people to talk to, and the nearest pub was miles away. When an assistant was finally placed under his charge, it gave him a perfect opportunity to delegate responsibility while he left to be with his friends at the pub for extended periods.

In the course of time, money from ticket sales went missing. One story is that Branwell absconded with the money for drink which, knowing his past history, seems a likely possibility. The second story appears to be that his underling was incompetent and avaricious, or both, and that *he* absconded with the ticket money. In any case, as the agent-in-charge, Branwell bore the responsibility and was fired for negligence in keeping the accounts. Once again he went home in disgrace in April, 1842.

Upon the death of Aunt Branwell on October 29, 1842, Charlotte and Emily were called home from their studies in Brussels where they were studying languages, and Anne was called home early for Christmas from Thorp Green Hall in Little Ouseburn outside of York. When she returned in January of 1843, after the holiday, she took Branwell along with her as a tutor for young Edmund Robinson, a boy of eight. Anne took a chance on Branwell and convinced the Robinsons that he would be a good tutor for the young Edmund who was to be educated apart from the Robinson girls.

The Robinson family took an immediate liking to Branwell and treated him more like a member of the family than a tutor and paid servant. Unfortunately for Branwell and the Brontë family, it proved to be the biggest mistake and greatest disgrace of his entire life. Branwell became infatuated with Mrs. Lydia Robinson, the mother, and she with him. They were flirtatious, very indiscreet, and they soon began an affair that everyone, except for the very young children and the husband, Mr. Robinson, knew about. Anne was shamed, humiliated, and highly embarrassed by Branwell's immoral behaviour. Anne blamed both of them because each of them should have known better. (Years later, in her first novel, *Agnes Grey*, the Robinsons are portrayed as the 'Murrays' of Horton Lodge.)

Although Branwell was infatuated by Mrs. Robinson and had an affair with her, it appears that this bright, young man had an ulterior motive for his actions. He was being crafty, scheming, and laying plans for future gains. Branwell had tried working for a living and found it disagreeable. He believed that it was 'beneath him' to labour in this world, and he believed that there was a much easier way of 'getting ahead'. Mr. Robinson was not well, and if he was to die, Branwell had thoughts of marrying the widow and simply stepping in as 'Lord of the Manor'. He would then be 'set for life', and all the necessary 'ingredients' for his greedy plot were there.

Branwell most likely got this mercenary idea from observing some of the poets he met in The Lake District while working at Broughton-in-Furness and members of the aristocracy and middle-class who were not in the habit of working. Others had married well, and as a result were not wanting for anything. When Branwell saw their 'life of leisure', he wanted the same. The only difference was that many of these marriages had been arranged through wealthy, upper-class connections, and particularly those who wanted their sons to be 'well-placed' in society. Branwell, on the other hand, had no such connections and would have to make his own. He saw a 'window of opportunity' with Mrs.

Robinson should the sickly Mr. Robinson pass on, and given his condition it seemed a possibility. If Mrs. Robinson would then marry him, his money problems would be solved.

When Branwell managed to infatuate and carry on an affair with Mrs. Robinson, she told him that she loved him more than her older husband who was ill and getting worse. Should he die, Branwell assumed that she would marry him, that his worries would be over, and that he would never have to work again. All seemed to be going 'according to plan' until the summer of 1845, when Anne, out of sheer disgust over her brother's actions, resigned her post and went home. She left in June but Branwell stayed on.

One month later, Branwell was dismissed for 'improper behaviour beyond description'. The elder Mr. Robinson was now aware of what was going on between the tutor and his wife. It is thought that the oldest girl Lydia, who had given Anne such a difficult time, was extremely sad to see her go and may have leaked the information to her ailing father soon after Anne's departure. Once again, Branwell returned home in disgrace. By this time all family members had given up hope on Branwell. Inspite of his dismissal, he still firmly believed that Mrs. Robinson would send for him and marry him after the death of Mr. Robinson. He anxiously awaited word from her and was firmly convinced that it was just a 'matter of time'.

As with the old saying about the 'best-laid plans' going awry, this case proved to be just that. No one could have foreseen the outcome, least of all Branwell, when his entire plan backfired into his face. At one point, Branwell's scheme appeared to be going exactly to plan when a short time later, the elderly Mr. Robinson did pass away. Upon receiving the news, Branwell waited in high anxiety for a message from his beloved Mrs. Robinson. He 'knew' that he would hear from her eventually.

Finally, as Branwell waited at home, a message arrived from the Black Bull Inn that a gentleman, a Mr. George Gooch (Mrs. Robinson's footman), was there to see him. Undoubtedly, this is what he had been waiting for, a message from Mrs. Robinson. In minutes, he was through the back entrance of the Black Bull in search of the messenger, and indeed he was from his beloved Lydia. But it was certainly not the message he was expecting.

The footman passed him a letter which informed him that he was never to return to Thorp Green Hall again under any circumstances and that he was not to have any future contact with Mrs. Robinson. Before his death, Mr. Robinson at least had the presence of mind to redraw his will in which he stated that if his wife was to re-marry to Branwell Brontë that all her wealth, assets, and property would be forfeited to successive heirs. When it came to wealth, position, and power, Branwell was the first to be sacrificed by his 'beloved'.

Branwell could not possibly have been more shocked, surprised, and devastated than he was. He was convinced that Mrs. Robinson was deeply in love with him and would marry him upon Mr. Robinson's demise. The new stipulation in his will had dashed all his remaining hopes. He was absolutely 'crushed', and from that moment on, his life went into a 'death spin'. His already heavy drinking increased, and in addition to this, he took more frequently to laudanum, which was readily available at the apothecary shop, to overcome his anguish and depression. Within months, his appearance altered drastically and he took on a 'frightening look'. Many of his close friends, including Francis Grundy, could hardly recognize him.

Branwell never worked again, and from all reports, it does not appear that he was ever again a productive person. His health continued to deteriorate, and in early 1848, he became infected with consumption. This, coupled with his heavy drinking, his opium use, and lack of proper food, put his health into a deadly, spiral descent. Often he was unable to get out of bed for days on end. At this point, he was placed in his father's bedroom which has a window overlooking the garden, the cemetery, the church, and beyond it, the Black Bull Inn.

Two weeks before his death, Branwell made a sketch of the 'Grim Reaper' at the foot of his father's bed coming to collect him. This sketch is now a part of the permanent collection at the Brontë Parsonage Museum. Only two days before his death on September 24, 1848, he was up and about and visiting at the Black Bull Inn. When he returned, he remained in bed and did not get up again. It was to be his very last venture outside the house.

Just minutes before his death, it is said that he asked those around him to help him to his feet because he wanted to 'die like a man'. (There is a good possibility that many of the actions of Arthur Huntingdon in the novel, *The Tenant of Wildfell Hall,* are in fact, descriptions of her own brother's drunkeness and opium altered state, witnessed by Anne herself.) Once again, the Brontës suffered through another family tragedy.

Martha and Hannah Brown, both friends and servants of the family, laid out his body for burial and his good friends, John and William Brown, placed it in the coffin. The funeral was held on Sunday, October 1, 1848, a cold, wet, and miserable day. And it was then that Emily caught cold and never left the house again after the funeral. (Three months later, she, too, died of consumption.) Branwell, like other members of the family, was interred in the family vault beneath the centre aisle of Haworth Old Church which is just outside their front door. And so ended the life of Patrick Branwell Brontë at the age of thirty-one.

The Brontë sisters. An oil painting by their brother Patrick Branwell Brontë (circa 1834) with Anne, Emily, and Charlotte (left to right). Branwell painted himself out of the picture.
(By courtesy of the National Portrait Gallery, London)

A pencil sketch of Charlotte Brontë by George Richmond in 1850, done at the request of her publisher in London.
(By courtesy of the National Portrait Gallery, London)

A pencil sketch of Anne Brontë (age 13) made by her sister Charlotte in April, 1833.
(Courtesy of the Brontë Society)

Plaster medallion of Patrick Branwell Brontë (1840s) made by his sculptor friend, Joseph B. Leyland, of Halifax. (Courtesy of the Brontë Society)

One of the few photos of Rev. Patrick Brontë (late 1850s). He believed that his high, silk cravat would protect him against bronchitis.
(Courtesy of the Brontë Society)

A photo of the Brontë Parsonage (early 1860s) before the gable wing was added in 1878, by the succeeding incumbent, Rev. John Wade.
(Courtesy of the Brontë Society)

Rev. Arthur Bell Nicholls, Mr. Brontë's curate, who arrived in May, 1845, and slowly won over Charlotte's heart. They were married on June 29, 1854, only nine months before Charlotte's death.
(Courtesy of the Brontë Society)

Mary Taylor, a close and respected friend of Charlotte's who left England, for New Zealand, in 1845, and did not return until 1860, five years after Charlotte's death. She was an inspiration to Charlotte in many ways. (Courtesy of the Brontë Society)

The Parsonage Dining Room in which the three sisters often met to discuss the progress of their novels. They walked around the table as they did so; this was a habit Charlotte picked up at Roe Head School in Mirfield in the 1830s.
(Courtesy of the Brontë Society)

Rev. Brontë's bedroom with a replica of his half-tester bed. The original was sold at auction after his death and never recovered. It was here that both Branwell and Rev. Brontë died in 1848, and 1861, respectively.
(Courtesy of the Brontë Society)

Haworth Old Church (circa 1860). It was torn down, except for its tower, and replaced in 1879, by Rev. John Wade who succeeded Rev. A. B. Nicholls in 1861. (Courtesy of the Brontë Society)

Some of the 'little books' written and bound by Charlotte between the years 1824 and 1830. Today they remain an important part of their 'juvenilia' historical records. (Courtesy of the Brontë Society)

PART TWO

THE BRONTË SISTERS:

THEIR WORKS

6

EARLY WRITINGS

When one looks at the works of the Brontës, one must first be conscious of the background of their lives, which I have already outlined, and their early writings as children, or their 'juvenilia' as it is called. For persons who wish to explore in more detail their first and early attempts, a student of their writings is advised to read Fannie Ratchford's, *The Bronte's Web of Childhood*, Columbia University Press, 1941. This early analysis is considered one of the better, if not the best, sources on the developmental stages of their childhood and writings. For the remainder of readers who seek a more general overview, I will briefly summarize this period in their lives.

The Brontë sisters, it appears, had an early interest in both reading and writing, which combined with the highly, active imagination of young children was a literary force 'in the making'. There were other extraneous factors which influenced and affected their writing, and these are addressed in Part Three. To what extent their older sisters, Maria and Elizabeth, were responsible for their early interest in reading and writing is not exactly known, but we do know that Maria was highly intelligent and an extremely precocious child. During their 'happy days' together as one cohesive family, the children spent many hours together in their playroom on the second floor of their Market Street home in Thornton. As precocious as Maria and Elizabeth were, and as intelligent as the other four children were, it is not inconceivable that they learned their alphabet there very early in life, and later at Haworth, under their tutelage and guidance.

Almost all their early writings, of which some has been preserved and others only in fragments, seem to have their earliest origins in 1826, and later. This, of course, is related to the toy soldiers which Rev. Brontë brought home for his children in late May or early June of 1826. Their already active imaginations seemed to be stirred and excited to even greater heights, and although their interest and ideas seemed to have languished for a short time, they were re-kindled on a cold, winter night in December, 1827. The incident was related earlier (p.38) of how, during a lull in the conversation just before bedtime,

Charlotte suggested they each 'own' an island of their own. The highly imaginative Branwell was the first to respond, and from there they each took their que, named various islands of interest to themselves, and later added their own 'heroic leaders' for each island and territory.

Although Charlotte later claimed credit for the initial idea, it appears that Branwell, with his 'stroke of genius' in the realm of imagination, was often the 'spark' who carried other ideas over, added a new element, or sent them off in a new direction. Branwell has often been portrayed as the 'pampered son' who never amounted to anything, but any researcher delving into his early writings of prose and poems cannot deny the great potential which he displayed. Unfortunately, because of many other factors, his path to greatness was 'waylaid', and we can only guess at the the great works his genius may have produced and unleashed.

After Maria's and Elizabeth's deaths, Charlotte and Branwell became the 'senior siblings' and, therefore, the 'leaders' whereas Emily and Anne were at first the 'followers', but this, of course, changed and took a different direction later. At first, some of their imaginations and oral stories began taking the direction of plays which they later 'acted out' in their playroom and bedrooms. Drama and acting definitely requires observation, interpretation, presentation, and a great deal of improvisation which developed their imaginations and creative skills still further. Their continued interaction with each other and each other's imaginary characters, plots, and ideas, was a stimulus and an 'early seed' to their later adult writings. All this was inadvertant and unwitting preparation for a much higher level of writing years away in their futures.

Their early plays included *The Young Men*, *Our Fellows*, and *The Islanders*, three plays which survive in written form today. In the last of these, each child selected three heroes, which they chose from their knowledge of history, the military, or politics that they had learned about from their father or their reading. Also, each child became a 'genii' with the special power of being able to bring the dead back to life; this is often interpreted as wishful thoughts on their part, for their two, dearly departed sisters and mother whom they longed to have back.

Each child had a territory which they named after their heroic leaders: Wellington (Charlotte's), Sneaky (Branwell's), Parry (Emily's) and Ross (Anne's), each with a capital city called, 'Glass Town', after the major centre and seat of government called, 'Great Glass Town', and later 'Verdopolis'. Together these four territories were part of a larger confederacy simply known as the ' Glass Town Confederacy'. To extend information to the territories and their inhabitants, Branwell designed, *'Blackwood's Young Men's Magazine'* which he modelled after *'Blackwood's Magazine'*, a periodical which his father subscribed to and Branwell hoped to write for some day. In addition to the 'Young Men's Magazine', Branwell was also responsible for the creation and design of maps and charts of where these new territories were 'discovered'. Later, when he tired of the magazine, he relinquished the editorship to Charlotte and began his own 'newspaper'. This gives us some indication that Branwell, although younger than Charlotte, had a very progressive, inventive imagination which was 'equal to', or better, than his sisters. While writing articles for this 'magazine', Charlotte used the pseudonyms, 'Charles', 'Arthur', 'Charles Wellesley' and 'Capt. Tree', all of whom were leaders of her territories.

One of the first divisions we see in the Brontë family takes place in 1831, when Charlotte went away to Roe Head School as a student. In Charlotte's absence, Branwell assumed 'control' of the Glass Town Confederacy, but Emily, now thirteen years old, and Anne, eleven, began to assert their independent thought and ways. Slowly they moved away from Branwell and the Glass Town Confederacy, but we can only speculate whether it was either a 'move away' from Branwell's aggressive domination or a natural desire, consistent with young girls their age, for 'independence' and 'separation' from boys. Whatever the reason, it was at this time that Emily and Anne 'broke away' from the Glass Town Confederacy and formed their own confederacy of 'Gondal'. Upon returning from Roe Head, Charlotte and Branwell continued their Glass Town Confederacy writings, but later, either in retaliation or response, they founded their own new confederacy of 'Angria', believed to have been started in 1834.

The writings produced by the Brontë children are, in fact, in greater volume and amount than anything they produced as adults which we now read as their literary classics. Their early 'juvenilia' was prolific and some of it is still extant, housed in the Bonnell Collection Library at the Brontë Parsonage Museum. Other material has been lost, and all of the Gondal prose produced by Emily and Anne is believed to have been destroyed either by Emily herself, or by Charlotte after Emily's death. What remains today is mostly Charlotte's writings which has provided researchers with sufficient material to analyze her development from 'young writer' to that of a great writer of 19th C. English Literature.

Another amazing aspect of their early writing is its size; it is truly 'microscopic' in some cases which make some researchers ponder how it was possible for *any* human hand to write in such small script. Even her friend Ellen Nussey made mention of her small handwriting which she noticed Charlotte using while at Roe Head; the print was also done in 'italics' which Charlotte explained was a habit she had picked up while writing for her 'magazine'. The reason for the minute size of their early writings is believed simply to be that it was meant to 'fit', or be proportionate with, 'The Twelves', or toy soldiers, each of which could fit in the palms of their hands. The paper used for the magazines was often that from blue-coloured, sugar bags cut into pieces one and one-half inches by two inches in size, and on each of these pages was printed 300 to 400 words, as many as one might find on a present-day, regularly typed 8 x 11 inch sheet with '12-point' type. The feat was truly amazing, and it is believed to have been the cause of Charlotte's extreme short-sightedness, which Ellen Nussey first noticed and remarked on, upon her arrival at Roe Head School.

At age thirteen, Charlotte gave more serious attention to the writing of poetry and did so for about the next ten years, but in a letter to Henry Nussey January 11, 1841, Charlotte makes it clear that she has given up on poetry and has moved on to the more serious writing of prose. She implies in her letter that she has matured and is advancing out of a youthful stage which seems to have originally spawned her interest in poetry. She wrote:

> At this age it is time that the imagination should be pruned and trimmed - that the judgment should be cultivated - and a few at least, of the countless illusions of early youth should be cleared away.

Much of Charlotte's early poetry was also written for the Angrian tales as well as articles and poems for *Blackwood's Young Men's Magazine*. By age twenty (1836), Charlotte had already written more than half of the poetry that she would ever produce, the bulk of the remainder being done in the next four years, and occasional poems thereafter. It was also at this time that Charlotte corresponded with England's Poet Laureate, Robert Southey, and although he did write back, he was anything but encouraging. This must have been extremely discouraging for Charlotte.

Other factors may also have influenced Charlotte to more or less abandon poetry and pursue prose and later novel writing. The first and most obvious was that Charlotte did not have a natural flare for writing poetry as did Emily. From her early childhood days, Charlotte's poetry improved somewhat and some are noteworthy, more as insights to the various events occurring at various times in her life, but she never matured and developed into a great poet. Secondly, Charlotte's talent was in the writing of prose, and this is what she is remembered for today. When their first book, *Poems*, was published in 1846, only two copies were ever sold, and although reviewers made comments on the work, the only praise for poetry was heralded to Emily, not to Charlotte or Anne. This, in itself, was probably a message clear enough for Charlotte to realize that her talent lay 'elsewhere', and she then pursued prose more vigorously.

Almost all of Charlotte's writing is based on her own experiences, extrapolations of her 'Angrian tales', or stories she had heard from her father and Tabby, their servant. Like most other writers, Charlotte felt more confident and secure by writing about topics and surroundings she was most familiar with. When she finally gave up writing poetry and Angrian tales in 1839, or 1840, her thoughts moved more toward topics which were 'grey and sober', and away from topics of youthful controversy and idealism. Charlotte had particularly been influenced by writers of her day like Southey, Wordsworth, Coleridge, Scott, and Keats, but perhaps even more so by Shelley, and Byron most of all; Byronic influences and characters can be seen in both Charlotte's and Emily's prose and poetry.

These youthful tales of 'Angria' and 'Gondal' fell by the wayside for Charlotte and Anne in their mid-twenties as they matured into adulthood, but it appears that Emily, still interested in them on her twenty-seventh birthday, may have been writing them to near the end of her life. It is also not known when Branwell may have given up on these tales and writing, but his later life was bound to alcohol and drugs, and not writing, at least as far as we know.

7

THE PROFESSOR

Charlotte's first attempt at writing a full-length, adult novel was *The Professor*, but researchers do not have any firm clues which indicate exactly when she began writing it. Since it is a novel about her experience in Brussels as both a pupil and a teacher, we do know that it was probably started after her return to Haworth in January, 1844. The only other indirect clue we have is that Charlotte, Emily, and Anne began their writing of adult novels after, or during, the summer of 1845, when the entire family was home again, this time for good. Their plans for a school of their own had fallen through, they intensely disliked being teachers and governesses, Branwell had miserably failed his fourth venture into the outside world, and the only activity which gave them pleasure was their continuous writing, but now it was branching out into something more serious than their juvenile writings of the past. It was then that they began their evening ritual of walking around the dining room table to discuss their plots and characters and sometimes read their work to one another after their father had gone to bed at nine o'clock. This was the beginning of their serious, adult writing.

If we refer to *Jane Eyre*, Charlotte's second novel, as an 'immediate success', we can then possibly refer to *The Professor* as an 'immediate and continued' failure. This novel had serious flaws and was criticized by publishers as being devoid of 'dramatic incident' to make it a 'saleable product' to the reading public. In all, the manuscript was rejected eleven times and was not finally published until 1857, two years after Charlotte's death, and even then only as a courtesy for its overall historic value to the memory of the author. Any critical reader of English Literature who has read *The Professor* would probably agree that this novel definitely fails to excite reader interest and make use of a suitably developed plot line. Also, the characters seem weak, ineffectual, and remain 'flat' in their development throughout the novel. Almost needless to say, the novel did not get 'off the ground', and Charlotte later often, self-mockingly, referred to it as her "idiot child". In 1850-51, Charlotte made extensive revisions and re-submitted it to Smith, Elder & Co., but again they refused it for more or less the same reasons as they did before. The entire novel appears to be unsalvageable and beyond redemption.

The Professor is a story based on Charlotte's experiences in Brussels, 1842 and 1843, where she went as a student to study French and elements of the fine arts which she could use as a teacher in her own school. Charlotte used 'William Crimsworth', instead of a female, as the protagonist who goes to the Continent to seek his fortune. There he takes on a job as a teacher and soon falls in love with a Swiss-Protestant pupil- teacher from the school who is in one of his English classes.

Like Messr Heger had been to Charlotte, a schoolmaster with an influence over her, Crimsworth has the same influence over Frances Henri, and he eventually became enamoured with her. Mlle Reuter's jealousy led to Mlle Henri's dismissal and Crimsworth's lengthy and determined search for her which finally ends successfully. The two pledge their love for one another and are married, set up a successful school, and work long, hard hours.

The story is romantic and moralistic in several ways. First, true love triumphs after Crimsworth's extensive search and unfailing love for Mlle Henri, and secondly, hard, dedicated work pays off in a successful school which draws students from far and wide. And finally, your dreams, like those of Crimsworth's to return to England and Mlle Henri's to go to England, are achieveable and attainable through perseverence. The last, of course, is not only moralistic but also patriotic since they wish to retire to England rather than stay on the Continent. In this they are successful after they earn their independence following ten years of work at their school and Crimsworth's teaching as a college professor.

In examining the real situation and background, *The Professor* is based on Charlotte's first and only great adventure outside of England, and her studies in Brussels where she was both a student of French,and a teacher of English. During her two years there, Charlotte fell in love with her instructor, Constantin Heger, who did not return her affections and love. M Heger was a happily married man and Charlotte was probably infatuated by one of the first males she had ever met outside of Haworth who was her equal in intellect, and her 'better' in cultural knowledge and human experience. He was definitely a person of much greater 'worldly' experience, and although Charlotte disliked M Heger upon their first meeting, she gradually changed her mind and developed a strong love and attachment to him. After her return to England, Charlotte wrote to M Heger on a number of occasions and he responded but a few times, and then finally stopped altogether, much to the dismay and angst of Charlotte.

To develop her experience in Brussels into a novel, it had to be disguised in such a way that the persons involved could not be directly identified although that was not always possible. Therefore, Charlotte kept Brussels as the 'background' and simply altered the characters; this is partly where her problems began. Instead of the female protagonist, herself, she changed it to a male, William Crimsworth, and the object of her affection, M Heger, became Frances Henri, a French-speaking, Swiss-Protestant whose ultimate desire is to live in England. As the narrator, Charlotte had to assume the thoughts, opinions, and 'voice' of a male, a situation for which she was not properly qualified and ultimately did badly. Here everything falls 'flat' since Charlotte was not only 'unworldly' but also did not have a good understanding of men. Charlotte's limited involvement with men, and her 'world of men', included her father, her father's curates, her brother Branwell, and Ellen Nussey's and Mary Taylor's brothers; all other encounters were only by way of brief introductions, conducting business in shops, and parishioners who came to the house to speak to her father. In this respect, her knowledge of men was incidental, superficial, 'narrow', and not widely founded or based. As a result, William Crimsworth comes across as stern and unsympathetic with blunt speech and behaviour which Charlotte associates with men, that is, the men of 'her world'.

Furthermore, Charlotte adds to her undeveloped plot and weak characters by numerous 'addresses' to the 'reader' in which she adds other, pertinent information which might not otherwise be known. It is something like the soliloquy of stage and drama, but in a novel it is much less dramatic, far less appealing, and in some cases annoying, insulting, and even demeaning to the reader. This habit of addressing the 'reader' is first found in their youthful tales and is a 'carry-over' from their early writing. A second device she frequently used which also became irksome was her use of French passages. She defended its use by saying that it would lose too much in the translation, but some readers saw it not only as bothersome but also as a 'showy display' of her language skills and quite unnecessary. For the readers who do not read French, they got neither the 'higher meaning' of the original French nor the 'base understanding' of a faulty translation into English. It was simply *all lost*.

To add further to the novel's problems, as alluded to above, the protagonist repeatedly becomes the soliloquist to provide the reader with 'his' inner feelings and outlooks. With this technique, one most effectively used in drama, she provides an 'inner dialogue' to project and reveal her innermost thoughts at given moments in the development of the plot. This is accomplished through encounters with the 'looking glass' in which she uses a 'mirror image' as a way to describe a character whose description might otherwise go unrevealed. These are all techniques and devices which we associate with imagery and with a writer who is highly 'image oriented'. If there is one saving grace about the problems which we can identify in this novel, and which contributed to its failure, it appears that Charlotte made all her major errors in this one novel, *The Professor*. By avoiding these same mistakes in her other novels, Charlotte made great leaps and strides toward success, and although critics found shortcomings in each of the successive works, they were still highly successful and today 'live on' as some of the greatest works in English Literature.

8

JANE EYRE

Charlotte Brontë is perhaps best known for her novel, *Jane Eyre*, although some will argue that her last novel,*Villette*,1853, is of superior writing quality, a product of her maturation as a writer and improvements on her three, previous novels. *Jane Eyre* was begun after it became obvious that *The Professor*, immediately turned down by seven publishers, and four more later, was never going to be published. Her only option was to start afresh and anew with an entirely new plot, new characters, and an approach substantially different from her ill-fated, *Professor*. In this instance, her instincts proved correct, since no amount of re-writing and revamping could 'revive' this manuscript which no publisher wanted.

The novel, *Jane Eyre,* was begun in Manchester in August, 1846, while Charlotte was attending her father after eye surgery. It is also interesting to note that prior to the writing of her second novel, she told her sisters with a degree of confidence that she would create a heroine who was small and plain, like herself, contrary to recommended 'formula' of the day. Heroes and heroines of the Romantic and Victorian era would be tall, handsome, rich and in the socially acceptable upper classes of aristocracy or nobility, whereas Charlotte was bound and determined to prove not only Emily and Anne wrong but also the writing establishment in general. In the end, Charlotte redeemed herself on every front but not without harsh criticism from some quarters as well as some reviewers and writers.

Another factor which played a part in Charlotte's writing at this time and stage of her life was the fact that she no longer had to work to earn an income since she and her sisters had each received a small inheritance from Aunt Branwell upon her death. Secondly, their plans for a school of their own never materialized and was now a 'dead issue', and the hope of Branwell every succeeding at anything and supporting them was rapidly fading. Finally, Charlotte had already had one book failure, knew that she could do better, and anxious to improve her writing and to redeem herself, set about with renewed resolve on her next novel.

Jane Eyre is a novel of an orphaned girl who lives with, and is cared for, by a Mrs. Reed, her aunt, who treats her badly and harshly. As a child of keen spirit, she does not always submit kindly or easily to her aunt's wishes and demands which eventually results in her being sent to Lowood Institution, a charity school for underprivileged children without 'means', for a proper education. After several years there under the austere and harsh discipline of its founder, Mr. Brocklehurst, she decided to leave and accept a job as governess for the daughter of a Mr. Rochester at a place called 'Thornfield Hall'. Neither she nor he was immediately attracted to one another, but as time wore on and they became more accustomed to one another, they soon fell in love, even though he was twice her age and they were from different social classes and backgrounds.

Jane Eyre finally consents to marry her employer, but she was not aware of the fact that he was already married, to a mad woman locked away in the attic. During the wedding ceremony, at the very last moment, Rochester's attempted bigamy is exposed and Jane flees Thornfield Hall in shock. With only limited funds, she makes her way by coach to Whitcross and then proceeds across the moors where she spends the night. The next day she arrives at Morton near complete exhaustion where she is taken in by Rev. St. John Rivers and two young ladies, whom we later find out to be her cousins. She stays with them and is brought back to health.

Although still in love with Rochester, Jane is almost persuaded to marry the Rev. St. John Rivers and accompany him to his mission in India, but at the last moment she hearkens to a 'telepathic call' to her from her beloved Rochester who is many miles distant. She leaves and returns to Thornfield Hall only to discover that it has been burned down, the mad woman has died, and that Rochester, badly burned and blinded in an attempt to save his mad wife, has retreated to Ferndean, one of his farms some thirty miles away. She quickly hires a coach to his manor retreat, the two lovers are re-united in peaceful bliss and harmony, and they are finally married and later produce a young son whose eyes are like those of Rochester.

In this her second novel, Charlotte wrote with much more confidence, freedom and openness, and showed a more daring and imaginative side of her writing which combined romance, intrigue, and suspense, in the proper proportions, to produce a first-rate, classic novel which was never again repeated to this level of excellence. The novel was an immediate hit and instant success in the reading salons of London. Such was the enormous success of Currer Bell's 'best-seller' that Thomas Cautley Newby immediately rushed the two manuscripts it was holding of Ellis and Acton Bells' into print. The book had caused a sensation in London and throughout the country; even William M. Thackeray set aside an entire day from his busy, writing schedule to read it.

The reviews on *Jane Eyre* were mixed and varied, but in most cases they were highly favourable since the general reader saw it as a delightful romance which illustrated, or at least allowed them to fantasize in their strict, Victorian times, that true love could traverse the bounds which separated the classes. This in itself was a 'novel' idea which appealed to the masses, but to those of the upper classes, it was seen as 'moral Jacobism' and an extension of Chartist thought. The mere suggestion of the social structure of English society being altered, challenged, or changed was an affront and a 'blasphemy' against a structure which they thought of as 'ordained by God'. On these moral grounds, Charlotte Brontë was seen by some as anti-Christian, coarse, contributing to 'ungodly discontent', and to some, reason enough to set her book aside.

On the other hand, reviewers who read the work with an 'eye to literature' and an objective mind which could pass beyond the restrictive views of politics, religion, and contemporary Victorian society saw the book as a powerful piece of writing. G. H. Lewes, in the *Westminster Review* of January, 1848, hailed it as 'decidedly the best novel of the season'. Others praised it for its vigorous style, its 'freshness', its 'power', in the literary sense, and its 'passion'. Other factors which accounted for its favourable reception were the elements of truth, sincerity and genuineness, which were sandwiched amidst the scenes of improbability and extreme coincidence. For the reader of romantic novels, the positive, artistic elements could easily override the few, obvious negative elements.

For those who are highly familiar with Charlotte's life and background, it is easy to see that many parts of the novel are 'autobiographical' and others are drawn from her background and experiences. Perhaps the first and most obvious one is that of her time spent at Cowan Bridge School which she identifies as an 'Orphan Asylum' and within it, the 'black pillar', Mr. William Carus Wilson, the founding benefactor of the school. Also, the harsh and brutal treatment of Helen Burns (Maria Brontë) by the abusive 'Miss Scatcherd', is not a scene which Charlotte ever forgot, or wanted to forget. Also, although a highly religious person, Charlotte found it very difficult, if not impossible, to forgive Rev. Wilson and 'Miss Scatcherd' for the hurt they had directly inflicted upon Maria, and indirectly upon the Brontë family at her death, and later Elizabeth's. These were touching, real-life situations with which most of the readers of the day could easily identify with, sympathize with, and react to in pure indignation.

Perhaps the most interesting element of the plot, a mad woman in the attic, is based on a factual incident known to Charlotte. After she resigned from Roe Head and returned home in December, 1838, she took a position as governess to the Sidgwicks at Stonegappe in May 1839. It was during her stay there that she became intrigued by 'Norton Conyers', a country house they visited near Ripon, where a madwoman had been kept locked in the attic. This gave rise to Bertha Mason, 'Mrs. Rochester' in *Jane Eyre*, and whose acts Rochester wished to conceal as actions of servant Grace Poole. Therefore, as preposterous as this element of the plot may seem, it is based on fact and became an integral part of the story.

Other parts of the novel are also based on fact as well. For example, both Charlotte and 'Jane Eyre' were governesses to wealthy families, and this is where she gained insight and background to put into this novel. Two years later in March, 1841, Charlotte took her second position as governess to a Mrs. White at Upperwood House, Rawdon, and remained there for nine months. While in these positions, she was directly exposed to English, high society and observed at close hand the faults and foibles of the two families. This was 'grist' for Charlotte's 'writer's mill'. Also, during her stay with Ellen Nussey at 'Hathersage', Derbyshire, in 1845, Charlotte adopted it as 'Morton', the home of Rev. St. John Rivers in *Jane Eyre*, as well as using the 'Eyre' family name which appeared on a memorial tablet in the local church she attended while visiting there.

Charlotte had two other sources of information, in addition to what she learned from Anne, which she could employ for her 'studies' of the upper classes, the Taylors of Gomersal and the Nusseys of Birstall. Mary Taylor and Ellen Nussey both became close friends of Charlotte's while they spent time together as students at Roe Head. During and after the years at their common school, Charlotte was invited to both their homes on numerous occasions, and likewise, Charlotte invited them to the Parsonage. The Taylors were perhaps the more 'interesting' of the two families because of their strong, individualistic attitudes, independent ideas, and free-thinking spirits coupled with a cavalier approach. Ellen Nussey, her mother, and her brothers were also of a higher, socio-economic class, but they were the complete opposites of the Taylors. The Nusseys were a demure and conservative family which followed conventional lines and would not go against the Establishment; the Taylors, among the 'nouveau riche', merchant-class, were independent mavericks bent on challenging established thought, belief, politics, social classes, and religion at every turn. Charlotte could not possibly have chosen two friends with such diametrically opposed views even if she had tried. This provided Charlotte with two sets of completely divergent thoughts and opinions on varied subjects. The time she spent with the Taylors gave Charlotte time to think and 're-think' many of her own thoughts and opinions which she considered 'true' and immutable. Later, in private, and in solitude, as she matured and had time to 'absorb' these new, and challenging, views on social issues, she applied some of them to *Jane Eyre*, but many more to *Shirley*.

Other dramatic incidents in the novel were taken 'from life'. For example, the fire in Rochester's bedroom which nearly cost him is life was drawn from an incident at home where Branwell, in a drunken stupor, set his own bed on fire. Charlotte used the same incident with Rochester where Jane Eyre beats out the flames and saves his life, and again later with Mrs. Rochester, the madwoman in the attic, setting Thornfield Hall ablaze, destroying it, killing herself, and severely injuring her husband. At the Parsonage, the fire set by Branwell was bravely beaten out by Emily, there was minimal damage, and there was no loss of life.

Besides Charlotte's moral and religious didacticism which we frequently find, one also notices her continued use of imagery, which is perhaps a hold-over from her youthful days of writing poetry, and also allegory. Charlotte's use of imagery is a well-developed talent in her writing, and she often digresses to 'paint' for her readers a vivid picture of her surroundings or a detailed sketch of a character. With it she is able to conjure up stark contrasts such as frost, ice, snow, and fire in winter scenes, and storms, sunshine, and rain for summer scenes. And each of these vivid scenes is closely related with 'human overtones' of mood, colour, and character. This is something which Charlotte, as an author, does well primarily because she and all her family members were so closely atuned with Nature's freedom and beauty to be found right out the 'back door' of the Parsonage on Haworth Moor.

Charlotte's use of allegory is somewhat more nebulous and elusive, since we are not certain precisely which is intentional, as opposed to that which the reader or reviewer 'reads into' it. Some of the allegory is just too obvious to be anything but intentional, and the less obvious have to do with the moral allegories which are perhaps more deeply hidden. Perhaps the most obvious allegoric symbolism is the use of the term 'black pillar' to describe how Rev. Brocklehurst of Lowood School appeared to Jane Eyre, a small child. Charlotte's image of Brocklehurst reflected through Jane's eyes is how she remembered Rev. William Carus Wilson, the founder of Cowan Bridge School, which brought back to her only very bad memories. For Charlotte, he represented a dark, evil force, a 'black pillar', which was responsible for the deaths of her two, beloved sisters through his drive for austerity, frugality, simplicity, abstemiousness, and his obsession with sin, punishment and damnation, inspite of his good intentions.

A similar comparison can be made if we take the imagery and allegory of Rev. St. John Rivers whom she portrays as icy, cold, reserved, and loveless without the warmth of human passion, much in the manner of Brocklehurst. Although Rivers represents the 'moral person' with good intentions, such as to take on a mission in India, Jane Eyre is tempted to marry him and go along with goodness and altruism in mind, but ultimately rejects it because it would be a 'cold' and loveless union. In Charlotte's real life, a similar situation arose when Henry Nussey, Ellen's brother, proposed marriage to her, and although tempted because Ellen would then be even closer as her sister-in-law, she felt that she and Henry did not have enough in common to make it a happy and successful relationship.

As a stark contrast to these two individuals, Rivers and Brocklehurst, whom she cast in an unfavourable light, we find Edward Fairfax Rochester, a man of unremarkable features, much like herself, who does not fit the heroic figure image so common to novels of the day. He was not handsome, dashing, or debonair as a reader of Victorian romance novels might have expected, but exactly the opposite. Victorian readers may also have found his moral values reprehensible, or at least highly questionable, since he was willing to commit bigamy to obtain the one he loved, but Rochester is also symbolic of other greater values, like love and determination.

Firstly, Rochester did not see his desire to marry the one he loved as an immoral act because he was tricked into the loveless marriage with Bertha Mason when he was very young and felt no obligation to her as a dedicated husband to wife. Secondly, he felt the same as Jane Eyre that true love transcends all bounds and boundaries although she was not willing to commit an illegal act. Finally, their love rose above social boundaries which would be considered highly objectionable to the social custom of the time, and especially to the English aristocracy and nobility. Both Jane Eyre and Edward Rochester were blind and oblivious to these social restrictions because of their regard, respect and love for one another. To some readers then, Rochester may have appeared as a 'black', Byronic hero, as opposed to a gallant hero of one of Scott's novels.

Even after Jane fled Thornfield Hall following the aborted wedding ceremony and arrived at the door of 'Morton', St. John River's home, and had time to reconsider the traumatic events which brought her there, she still loved Rochester enough to want to return to him. Although Charlotte objected to many of the social ills and prejudiced attitudes of high society and the times, she was still a moralist, and there were many behaviours she could not condone even in 'high fiction', namely bigamy. She may have found his act of attempted bigamy as deplorable, but this did not alter her 'true love' for the person himself. His willingness to marry one whom he loved, although from a lower social class, indicates his positive qualities of truth, honesty, dedication and the single-mindedness not to be controlled by external social rules, values, and 'truths'.

Only after the death of Rochester's mad wife and the 'telepathic call' which Jane 'heard' and responded to was the 'air of respectability' put back into their relationship. The dark, immoral, illegal aspect of their previous relationship and proposed marriage was now lifted and sanctioned in moral terms; they could now pursue their earlier relationship with honesty, integrity and dignity. Their true love and perseverence overcame the hurdles of age, social class, a traumatic break-up, the passage of time, and later Rochester's injuries, infirmities and physical handicaps to provide the reader with an endearing, and enduring, romance of hardship and torment to conclude with a happy-ever-after ending. And although events and actions throughout the novel may not have conformed to traditional romance novels of the time, which added to its intrigue and popularity, the ending was definitely 'classical romance'.

Other elements of the story which brought harsh criticism to the novel and its author were the type of relationship established between Jane Eyre and Edward Rochester, the manner in which they addressed one another, and particularly the liberties Jane Eyre, the governess, takes with her 'social superior', and 'elder', since he was twice her age, as well as her employer. It is not long before these two are portrayed as 'equals', in their relationship with one another, regardless of their class; the mere suggestion of equality between the two was highly contentious and considered disrespectful. For a governess to marry a man of wealth from the aristocracy and for the two to unite in marriage and carry on as 'equals' was received with horror and disgust by some in high society and treated as coarse, crude and contemptuous, almost to the point of 'social heresy'.

These were the views of the day, and today we can only read and objectively look at their comments with a century and a half of time between us, and a 'gulf' as wide from the Earth to the Moon in regard to differences and social change which have occurred since then. From our objective position of time, place, and change, one would have to agree with the brief analysis of G. K. Chesterton that *Jane Eyre* is 'one of the finest stories in the world', and, of course, today we view it as one of the masterpieces of English Literature.

9

SHIRLEY

This novel was originally entitled, *Hollow's Mill*, with another possibility of *Fieldhead*, and perhaps the original, former title may have been better suited since much of the main action is focused on the historic, Luddite Riots in Yorkshire which occurred around 1812. At this time wool export was almost closed down due to trade restrictions and stoppages brought about by the Napoleonic Wars. Many millworkers with families to feed were without jobs, and to complicate matters many mills were installing new machinery which would require even fewer workers.

The main action focuses on Robert Moore, a half-English, half-Belgian mill owner, who is caught amidst these riots which primarily opposed the introduction of second-generation, labour-saving devices of the Industrial Revolution. Mill owners wanted to reduce their labour costs, and workers saw it as a loss of much-needed jobs. As a result, new machinery deliveries were intercepted and smashed, people were injured, and the lives of mill owners were threatened; it was an 'ugly time' for both owners and workers.

To avoid financial ruin, Moore proposes marriage to Shirley Keeldar, an energetic, independent young lady of 'means', but she scornfully rejects his offer of 'economic union', being a person of ideals and principles. In the background remains Caroline Helstone, niece of Reverend Matthew Helstone, who loves him dearly and waits patiently for his love. In the end, things work out well when the Napoleonic Wars end, the wool trade is resumed, and Robert Moore brings prosperity back to his workers. The relationships for the two main protagonists, Robert Moore and Shirley Keeldar, also work out well since they are both re-united with love-interests they had before these events. Robert Moore is re-united with Caroline Helstone for whom he held affections before but which were derailed by thoughts of economic union with Shirley Keeldar, and Shirley is re-united with Louis Moore, Robert's brother, who was once her tutor.

According to Charlotte, *Shirley* was not meant to be a romantic tale with a 'happy-ever-after' ending, and some reviewers saw it as a varied collection of themes, as well as a romantic tale. On the first page of Chapter One, 'Levitical', Charlotte forewarns her readers that it would be "something unromantic as Monday morning".

If we disregard the continued, abortive failure of her first novel, *The Professor*, we would then refer to *Shirley* as her second major novel following on the heels of *Jane Eyre*. Naturally, Smith, Elder & Co. was anxious to see what their popular, new author, Currer Bell, would come up with as an 'encore' to her first, resounding success. The first draft of *Shirley* were begun in late 1847, or early 1848, but Charlotte's writing came to an abrupt halt with the quick, successive deaths of Branwell, Emily, and Anne, all in the space of eight months. With these three devastating and traumatic losses, Charlotte was not in the mood for writing, and she did not begin again until some time after Anne's death in May, 1849. Before the death of Branwell, she had almost completed the second volume, and it is possible that she resumed her writing not only to complete it and please her publishers but also as a form of therapy to take her mind away from the great sadness and anxiety which she was suffering at the time.

When Smith, Elder & Co. finally did receive the manuscript, there are indications that they were not totally pleased with it and wished to see some changes. Unfortunately, the publishers, knowing of Charlotte's losses and the agony she must be enduring, made 'suggestions' for improvement but did not 'push' nor 'demand' that these changes be made. Williams, one of the publisher's readers cited a lack of 'distinctiveness' and 'impressiveness' of the protagonists in the novel, as well as expressing 'alarm' over her portrayal of the three curates, Donne, Malone and Sweeting, which might have caused an unwanted, religious backlash for the publishers.

In the end, few changes were made for several reasons, the first being that once Charlotte finished a work, she was more than reluctant to go back and change anything, and she only wanted to move on to something else. Secondly, due to Charlotte's recent, personal tragedies and her 'delicate' frame of mind, the publishers were more willing to defer to their popular and profitable author's wishes rather than pressing forward their demands. In such a situation, they could still bring out a new novel by Currer Bell and perhaps, as time erased and healed some of the harsh wounds from her personal losses, her 'third' novel would be better; this was a gamble they were willing to take. As a result, *Shirley*, was released in October, 1849, two years after Charlotte's first successful novel, with her publisher's knowledge that the book had several flaws, was not a masterpiece on the level of *Jane Eyre*, but was a saleable and marketable product.

Unfortunately, the critics were not as kind and benevolent as Charlotte's publishers and some reviews were highly critical, not of the writing 'per se' since the writer was a skillful 'wordsmith', but of the structure, plot and unity of the work which they saw as 'badly wanting'. A thorough analysis of the plot and structure bears out this criticism, since it appears that the author was never clear as to the 'direction' the plot was taking, what the main action was to be, and precisely where it would all lead. As a result, the plot seems to 'wander' and is highly fragmented with no clear vision and direction, as though the plot was leading Charlotte wherever it happened to take her, rather than the reverse. In the opinion of F. B. Pinion, author of *A Brontë Companion*, he clearly sums up the fragmented plot with this observation:

> In *Shirley*, there are numerous irrelevances...... To some degree the novel became her 'Jew-basket', into which she tossed for good measure a miscellany of small articles to add to the principal contents.

If the reader or reviewer looks for a common, continuous thread of unity in the novel, it is elusive and difficult, if not impossible, to find. On the other hand, if we sit back, relax and read for pure enjoyment without a serious or critical eye, there are a number of highly interesting stories, each one of which might have been developed into a successful plot had the author taken the time and trouble to develop them separately. Had Charlotte focused on one theme or element and developed it fully with time, consideration and effort, *Shirley* could have been much closer to the quality and success of *Jane Eyre*.

Even today, one hundred fifty years after its release, one can still ponder the question, without arriving at a satisfactory conclusion, as to whether *Shirley* is a romance novel, a social commentary on selected topics, or a historical novel based on local, historical events in Yorkshire, the wool industry or the Luddite Riots of the early 1800s. From the change in the titles from 'Hollow's Mill' to 'Fieldhead' and then finally to *Shirley* itself, shows the lack of clarity and certainty, and the indecisiveness of the author which finally manifested itself in the disunity and disharmony of plot. Within each of these themes lies interesting stories, but they are not sufficiently tied together to provide the necessary 'cohesiveness'. In the end, Charlotte, a relatively inexperienced author, left herself 'wide open' to professional reviewers and critics who came down on her harshly and 'mauled' her badly.

As an example of the loosely assembled plot, we must only look at the relationship between Robert Moore and Shirley where the reader is firmly 'led on' to believe, almost to the last, that these two principal characters would eventually be united in matrimony to satisfy our instincts of a 'romance in the making'. The readers are then suddenly 'wrenched away' from this belief and hopeful romance and disturbingly sent off in another direction searching for new connections, and wondering how they could have so badly misread or misinterpreted the author's leads. Caroline Helstone who had been languishing on the 'sidelines' is then brought back into the picture as a love-match for Robert Moore, and his brother, Louis, appears to drop into the picture without a clear past and developed connection to the plot-at-hand, or the characters. This aspect of the novel is definitely 'unsettling', disconcerting, and baffling to the reader.

As the reader searches for that 'thread' of unity which may provide some coherence to the work, the main action, if one can identify it, appears to be the attack on 'Hollow's Mill'. This story, of course, is based on historical fact of the workers' attack on Rawfolds Mill, Liversedge in 1812, which was owned by William Cartwright. The owner, along with a handful of loyal workers and armed soldiers, successfully beat off the attack of rioting Luddites bent on entering the mill, smashing the new machinery inside, and intimidating the owner to reverting to the old ways with a higher dependency on manual labour. After twenty minutes of heavy fighting, the Luddites gave up their unsuccessful attempt, and upon withdrawing, left two badly injured, and dying, rioters behind. The two men were taken to the Star Inn, Roberttown where they died of their injuries. Other than this, one is hard-pressed to find other actions which are connected to the whole, and contribute to the general, overall plot.

G. H. Lewes, a seasoned critic and writer for *The Edinburgh Review* was candid and direct in his criticism of Charlotte's second novel. In one of his reviews, he stated:

> ... in *Shirley* all unity, in consequence of defective art, is wanting. There is no passionate link; nor is there any artistic fusion, or intergrowth, by which one part evolves itself from another. Hence, its falling off in interest, coherent movement, and life....

In the same article, he further criticizes her work identifying its fragmentary nature; he states:

> ... *Shirley* cannot be received as a work of art. It is not a picture; but a portfolio of random sketches for one or more pictures. The authoress never seems distinctly to have made up her mind as to what she was to do; whether to describe the habits and manners of Yorkshire and its social aspects in the days of King Lud, or to paint character, or to tell a love story. All are by turns attempted and abandoned; and the book consequently moves slowly,...

Charlotte was not amused. Prior to this review, Charlotte Brontë and G.H. Lewes had been on reasonably friendly terms with general, warm correspondences travelling back and forth between them, but after this harsh criticism of her work, however honest and candid it may have been, it seems to have put an end to their friendship. In fact, Charlotte was not one to take criticism lightly or easily, and her curt reply to Lewes was probably as shocking to him as his review was to her. The full text of her letter to him was:

> I can be on my guard against my enemies, but God deliver me from my friends.

Lewes, in particular, and other reviewers had more criticisms as well. Charlotte had been brought up in Yorkshire and was well-acquainted with Yorkshire speech, manners, and expressions which she often used in her writing. To Londoners of high society, and well-educated publishers and readers, some found the expressions 'coarse', the characters rough and disagreeable, their manners rude, their remarks flippant, and their colloquial expressions 'odd'. Also, the bounds of social class had again been traversed with the 'lowly' tutor, Louis Moore, pursuing Shirley, an aristocratic lady of wealth and refinement, and Robert Moore, a man of wealth and industry, being re-united with Caroline Helstone, the niece of a poor, country preacher. For many English readers, this did not 'sit well', but Charlotte did not exactly accept, nor was willing to submit to, the Victorian society belief in 'God's appointment', a belief that 'place' and differences in social class and structure were pre-ordained in Heaven.

This novel is noteworthy for two other reasons; the first being that this was the first novel completed after the deaths of all her siblings, and, of course, produced without their help, guidance, influence and suggestions. Now she was more highly dependent on her publishers for their help, but Charlotte did not always appreciate what they had to say in the way of comment. Secondly, it is the first and only one of her novels which does not have an 'autobiographical background' as a main thrust or theme; the others, *Jane Eyre* and *Villette* did, and they were much more unified and cohesive, and much more success-ful than *Shirley*.

Although Charlotte may have abandoned the thread of unity with an autobiographi-cal plot, or semblance thereof, the novel is 'chock full' of characters, places and incidents with which Charlotte was fully familiar. Perhaps the most notable figure of all is 'Shirley' herself who exhibits qualities and characteristics which are remarkably like those of Emily, a person of enormous 'inner strength', extreme courage, tremendous ability and great determination. She was a person for whom Charlotte held extremely high regard and respect above and beyond the fact that she was a beloved sibling. Chapter 28, entitled 'Phoebe', is simply a re-creation of the story how Emily was bitten in the arm by a dog in the lane beside their house, and with great courage, took a red-hot iron from the stove and cauterized her own wound without making a sound. Shirley Keeldar, with 'strength of character', independence, strong personal convictions, determination and 'sense of di-rection' is simply Emily in disguise. This is how Charlotte imagined her had she reached her full potential and developed and applied all her skills and positive characteristics in the 'world without', a world Emily rarely ventured into.

There are some other clear indicators that Shirley Keeldar was, in fact, her sister Emily. There are times when Shirley shows her keen love of Nature, poetry and particu-larly her love of animals, the most obvious being the dog, Tartar, whose description remarkably fits that of Emily's dog, Keeper. In the novel, Charlotte describes it: "Tartar was a rather large, strong, and fierce-looking dog, very ugly, being a breed between mastiff and bulldog,...". The descriptions of the two dogs are remarkably alike and the incident where Tartar forced curate Donne up the stairs recalls situations where Emily bravely handled and controlled her enormous dog, Keeper. A final clue is the use of the nickname, the 'Captain', for Shirley, since Emily had often been called the 'Major' at home. I would venture a guess that Charlotte also used her friend Mary Taylor, with her strong personality and business acumen, as the basis for her 'Shirley' character.

The Yorke family in the novel were clearly fashioned after the various members of the Taylor family and were readily recognizable much to the delight of everyone except Mrs. Taylor who was not amused with how she was portrayed. Charlotte had a high respect for Mr. Taylor (Hiram Yorke), but often wondered what drew him to his wife, since he was open-minded, hospitable, social, active and cheerful, and she was much the opposite. Rose Yorke was, in fact, Mary Taylor, Charlotte's lifelong friend who moved to New Zealand in 1845, and did not return until 1860, five years after Charlotte's death. Jessy, the passionate, happy, bubbly and loquacious one of the family was, indeed, Martha Taylor who died in Brussels of cholera in September, 1842, and was buried there in the Protestant Cemetery on the outskirts of town.

Many other characters in the novel were 'forged' after people Charlotte actually knew. Rev. Matthew Helstone was modelled after Rev. Hammond Roberson, a stern, 'military-looking' man whom Charlotte had once met at the church consecration when she was only ten years old. During the time of the Luddite Riots, he strongly opposed their unlawful and premeditated actions and for this stand, his life was threatened. Caroline Helstone, his niece, was a blend of the calm, quiet qualities she found in her friend Ellen Nussey and her meek and gentle, sister Anne, both of whom possessed quiet, reserved natures and personalities. The three curates, Donne, Malone and Sweeting, were all easily recognized by some readers as curates from the region of Yorkshire and village of Haworth, and through whom Charlotte saw an opportunity to mildly mock and 'poke fun' at changes and attitudes, in the 'modern Church', of which she did not entirely approve. Hortense Moore was later 'identified' as having an uncanny resemblance to a teacher and colleague Charlotte knew at Pensionnat Heger in Brussels, a Mlle Hausse. Joseph and Joshua Taylor are both likely candidates for the likes of Robert and Louis Moore, respectively, and the attraction of Robert Moore to Shirley Keeldar may have had a connection to a 'budding romance' between Charlotte's two friends, Joseph Taylor and Ellen Nussey, or perhaps even that of Mary Taylor and Branwell Brontë, although this is not certain.

Beyond the personal characterization of Robert Moore is the historical figure for whom he stands; this is none other than William Cartwright, the owner of Rawfolds Mill who bravely fought off the attack of the rioting Luddites at his mill on the night of April 11, 1812, with only the help of a few soldiers and a handful of loyal employees. Cartwright was not a popular person in the area, since he was a man of 'means', had lived abroad before coming to Yorkshire, spoke French, a reason for hatred in itself, and was progressive enough to bring modern changes to his mill, in spite of the workers' revolt and intimidations. A week after the attack on his mill, he narrowly escaped death at the hands of an assassin on his return home from Huddersfield, an incident which Charlotte used in the novel.

As well as individuals, there are a number of places which can be tied to places Charlotte was familiar with such as 'Hollow's Mill' which is in reality Rawfolds Mill at Liversedge, near Cleakheaton, owned by William Cartwright. 'Fieldhead', the house owned by Shirley is, in fact, Oakwell Hall, a beautiful, Elizabethan manor house, located near the tiny hamlet of Fieldhead, and which was once briefly used by the Roundheads during the English Civil War. Charlotte visited there with Ellen Nussey when she stayed at Rydings, Birstall, and they went together to visit the owners who were friends of the Nussey family. In the 1840s, the building was also used as a young ladies' boarding school. The oak panels and latticed windows are both mentioned in Chapter Eleven of the book; these were two things Charlotte clearly remembered from her visit there.

Finally, the novel is loosely connected by a number of social issues which are important and relevant to the author, and the fact that it was not meant to be a romantic novel was stated plainly on the first page as a 'disclaimer', of sorts, and a 'notice' to the reader should they be expecting something like the romanticism found in *Jane Eyre*. She states:

> If you think, from this prelude, that anything like a romance is preparing for you, reader, you never were more mistaken. Do you anticipate sentiment, and poetry, and reverie? Do you expect passion, and stimulus, and melodrama? Calm your expectations; reduce them to a lowly standard. Something real, cool and solid lies before

you; something unromantic as Monday morning, when all who have work wake
with the consciousness that they must rise and betake themselves thereto.

By focusing the 'main action' of the novel on the attack on 'Hollow's Mill', Charlotte was able to draw attention to the problems of the working poor in the mills of
Yorkshire, and elsewhere in England. This event has been mentioned several times, and
although Charlotte and her father, were against Luddism, and any unlawful riotous acts,
they sympahized with the plight of the workers and their families. Rev. Brontë had worked
with the poor through very hard times and saw their sufferings; these images and the
people's plight were definitely scenes common to Charlotte and her siblings. The Luddite
Riots occurred before Charlotte was even born, and occurred when her father was a young
curate at St. Peter's Church in Hartshead, but she knew the story well. In Charlotte's day,
another political movement called 'Chartism', and its followers 'Chartists', arose whose
aim it was to gain social and economic equality among the class of voteless British
labourers. This was a working-class political movement named after the 'Peoples' Charter' of 1838, drafted by William Lovett of the London Workingmen's Association to
demand suffrage, district representation, ballot votes, a repeal of the property qualifications for officeholders, parliamentary salaries and an annual Parliament.

These were social issues Charlotte was familiar with, and being sympathetic to the
workers' plight, she gave 'voice' to them through William Farren, a worker of Robert
Moore who lost his job because of newly-installed machinery. Although not a Luddite,
he sympathized with their cause but did not take part in any of their 'mob tactics'. In an
effort to show that not all mill owners were harsh, cruel and thoughtless toward their
workers, Charlotte's character, Robert Moore, made a magnanimous effort and jesture
by finding him a job as a gardener for Mr. Yorke once he became unemployed at the mill.
It is also possible that William Farren may have been modelled after the local mason, and
Rev. Brontë's sexton, John Brown of Haworth, who surprisingly was a very learned man.
In the novel, both Shirley and Caroline Helstone find William Farren learned, engaging
in conversation, and they loaned him books and gave him plants.

For the 'timeframe' of this book, 1811-12, the Industrial Revolution had already
been in full swing for almost fifty years, and its effects were beginning to 'show' on the
landscape, on society, and on the low-paid class of workers. The 'social cost' of the
Industrial Revolution could now be more fairly and objectively 'weighed' and 'measured' against the promises of prosperity which its progress was supposed to bring. It was
becoming evident that amidst the small margins of prosperity, there were a host of social
problems concomitant with this growth and 'progress'. There were problems of smoke,
smog, dirt and grime from the factories, poor housing conditions and sanitation, low
wages and poverty, widespread squalor, child-labour and crime. People left the rural
areas, and farming, and headed for large, industrial cities looking for work, all of which
simply compounded the problems at hand. Charlotte alludes to the wonderful days of
yore, when the valley was 'bonnie', full of nut and oak trees and inhabited by 'fairies', a
story told to her by Tabby, their household servant, who was a major source of country

lore for the Brontë children, and who was old enough to remember the 'days of old' before the coming of the mills and factories into the valleys of Yorkshire.

Charlotte also used *Shirley* to launch into two other issues which were a source of irritation for intelligent, ambitious, energetic persons, like herself, who were so highly restricted by the Victorian attitudes of the time, and which so clearly limited the occupations of women 'stuck between' high society and the lower, working class. The plight of women was clearly and boldly addressed in Chapter 22, 'Two Lives', on three, successive pages, where she both scornfully and plaintively seeks a change in attitude, primarily from the male bastions of power. Caroline Helstone gives 'voice' to the concerns of women in regard to opportunites for occupation:

> ...God surely did not create us and cause us to live with the sole end of wishing always to die. I believe in my heart we were intended to prize life and enjoy it so long as we retain it. Existence never was originally meant to be that useless, blank, pale, slow-trailing thing it often becomes to many,...

and in the next paragraph:

> I believe single women should have more to do - better chances of interesting and profitable occupation than they possess now. And when I speak thus I have no impression that I displease God by my words; that I am either impious or impatient, irreligious or sacrilegious.

This was an obvious retort to the criticism of *Jane Eyre* that the author was coarse, impatient, and unwilling to accept, 'God's appointment!', first as a woman and secondly the 'station in life' which that ordainment brings. Finally, Caroline made a lengthy plea to the 'men of Yorkshire' and the 'men of England' :

> Men of Yorkshire!.... Can you give them [women] a field in which their faculties may be exercised and grow? Men of England! look at your poor girls, many of them fading around you, dropping off in consumption or decline; or, what is worse, degenerating to sour old maids - envious, backbiting, wretched because life is a desert to them; or, what is worst of all, reduced to strive, by scarce modest coquetry and debasing artifice, to gain that position and consideration by marriage which to celibacy is denied. Fathers! cannot you alter things?

The other area of contention which Charlotte gives attention to is 'marriage', which at the time does not come across in a favourable manner in her eyes. Later, after she herself became married to Rev. A.B. Nicholls, she saw it in a completely different light and was much happier in her own marriage than she ever thought possible. We must also keep in mind that she was married for only a short time and was not able to give the 'institution of marriage' a long, objective look and may have, after years of marriage, changed her mind again. But in *Shirley*, before being married herself, she does not exactly cast a favourable view on marriage if we closely examine some of the marriages she alludes to in the novel.

The first issue regarding marriage is that of 'incompatibility', as we see from the separation of Caroline Helstone's parents shortly after she was born. She was sent as a child to live with her uncle Rev. Helstone, at Briarfield rectory, she never knew her real mother, and 'marriage' had failed this child; this was a single, given example, but it was also true for countless children in England. Only after her pining love for Robert Moore and serious depression forced her into illness did she discover that her nurse, Mrs. Pryor, was, in fact, her long, lost birth-mother. Mrs. Pryor had married James Helstone, the Reverend's brother, for several reasons, but the primary one was her 'unhappiness' and dissatisfaction with her life as a governess and she was seeking a way out, an 'escape', like many others in the same situation. 'Marriage', and 'marriage at any cost', provided that escape, but for many it proved to be only a temporary solution, and even a worse nightmare. Her husband, James, was handsome, but this was no substitute for love, and he soon proved to be cruel and lacking in morals. As a result of this disastrous, first attempt at marriage, Mrs. Pryor became disillusioned and did not pursue marriage a second time.

As a second example, we have only to look upon Robert Moore, a well-travelled and educated man, who took a liking to Caroline Helstone, his cousin, but was more than willing to sacrifice her for a 'economic union' with Shirley Keeldar to save his mill. Shirley was a highly principled person and rejected him sharply once she recognized his mercenary purpose. Although this may have been Charlotte's way of drawing attention to Victorian men and their attitudes, it is also an equal condemnation, not on marriages, but on 'loveless marriages' which are made purely for economic and social gain. In the end, Robert Moore 'comes to his senses', and once again pursues Caroline Helstone with true love in mind.

The same occurs between Shirley and Louis Moore, Robert's younger brother, who was her tutor years before. Shirley and Robert Moore had much to gain by their economic union to strengthen their position in society as well as their wealth in industry, but it was Shirley's strength of character, clear thinking, and principles which refused to go along with such a charade. This is Charlotte's commentary on so many marriages in England which were pre-arranged simply for the purpose of strengthening positions in Victorian society, a practise which Charlotte found most unacceptable, being a principled person herself. Once again, the recurrent themes of 'love conquers all' and 'love triumphs over all' obstacles, and traverses all boundaries of wealth and class, results in the final, happy relationships of the two, leading characters in the novel.

And finally, Charlotte points out, and makes an example of another marriage which eventually had a far more serious consequence, and that was the marriage of Mary Cave and Rev. Matthew Helstone. In his younger days, Hiram Yorke, was very much 'taken' by Mary, but she chose Rev. Helstone for his 'position' in society over Hiram. Rev. Helstone proved to be an uncaring and unobservant husband who was too busy and too involved to notice the 'decline' in his own wife who found herself living in a loveless marriage, slipped into despondency and severe depression, and eventually lost the 'will to live', and died.

With these examples in *Shirley*, Charlotte is pointing out, not the hopelessness of marriage, but the misguided reasons why people marry to begin with, and that marriage without love is senseless and futile. Charlotte is very idealistic on the topic of marriage, and, in fact, in her own lifetime turned down several marriage proposals simply because she did not feel love for the other person, and did not see the proposed marriage as having a 'future' based on the love, dignity and respect that she thought marriage deserved. Also, she did not feel that marriage should be based on an infatuation or sudden heated passion, and once referred to such a passion as 'une grande folie'. In the text of the novel she makes a more direct reference to this temporary type of passion:

> I don't think we should trust to what they call passion at all, Caroline. I believe it is
> a mere fire of dry sticks, blazing up and vanishing.

In a letter to Ellen Nussey, Charlotte said about marriage:

> [if] you can respect a person before marriage, moderate love at least will come after;
> and as to intense passion, I am convinced that it is no desirable feeling.

Charlotte herself does not have a clear view and understanding of men because of her limited experience with men, and these are echoed in the words Caroline speaks to Shirley as they discuss the topic of marriage:

> I wonder we don't all make up our mind to remain single,... We should if we listened
> to the wisdom of experience. My uncle always speaks of marriage as a burden; and
> I believe whenever he hears of a man being married he invariably regards him as a
> fool, or, at any rate, as doing a foolish thing.

and she also makes a statement, with some uncertainty, about the ability of men to hold a long-term committment and a sustained love for the same person:

> I often wonder, Shirley, whether most men resemble my uncle in their domestic
> relations, whether it is necessary to be new and unfamiliar to them in order to seem
> agreeable or estimable in their eyes; and whether it is impossible to their natures to
> retain a constant interest and affection for those they see every day.

In summary, author F. B. Pinion in *A Brontë Companion* : makes an excellent observation about the main protagonist, Shirley, and her overall importance to the elusive thread of 'theme', and more importantly 'unity' and 'cohesion' of the novel:

> Her [Shirley] most important role, from the literary point of view, is to express in
> words and action Charlotte's views on the Church, class divisions, party hatreds, and
> all forms of tyranny, injustice and corruption. She helps, in short, to give thematic
> cohesion to a novel which tends to sprawl.

In spite of the many shortcomings from a purely literary, but mostly technical, point of view, *Shirley*, with its many interwoven stories, makes an interesting study into Charlotte Brontë the author, the people of Yorkshire, the driving economic forces of the region, social dynamics and early pressures of Victorian society for change, several social issues of the day, her views on those issues, and particularly as they affected women in the middle classes and the limited opportunities afforded to them. Also, it was the favourite of many readers, mostly from North England and the three ridings of Yorkshire, including Charlotte's lifelong friend, Mary Taylor, who could easily identify with the Yorkshire surroundings and its people, many of the places and characters within the novel itself, and particularly 'Briarmains' her former home and her own family members, the 'Yorkes'.

10

VILLETTE

Villette, published in 1853, two years before Charlotte Brontë's death, was her last, complete novel. When it was released in January of that year, some writers and reviewers saw it as her best work, and for others at least, a vast improvement over *Shirley*, her second novel. And for the most part, the reviews on *Villette* were far more favourable than either of her previous works. The story is focused, has fewer central characters than *Shirley*, and it has excellent unity, theme, and 'cohesiveness', something which critics of her second novel said were severely lacking.

The novel, *Villette*, is once again loosely 'autobiographical' and follows the story of a young girl, Lucy Snowe, from childhood in England to adulthood in Belgium where she obtains a job as a teacher. Lucy has not exactly been blessed with wealth, beauty or 'connections' and must make her own way through life and support herself. Once established in the girls' school in Brussels (Villette), her abilities are recognized and she earns the respect of the headmistress, Mme Beck. There, by coincidence, she meets again John Bretton, her godmother's son, who is now a doctor to the school, but they are each unrecognizable to one another at first. She is attracted to him, but he is infatuated with the coquetish Ginerva Fanshawe whose main goal in life appears to be to marry into wealth and social standing. In time, 'Dr. John', as he is called, overcomes his infatuation for Ginerva and falls in love with with Paulina Home, Ginerva's cousin, who was a childhood companion of his, and who occasionally visited his home in Bretton in bygone days.

Lucy Snowe eventually passes over her fascination for 'Dr. John' and slowly and gradually is attracted to M Paul Emanuel, an irritable, excitable and oppressive professor at the school. She dislikes him upon their first meeting, but as time passes, she finds that he is really kind-hearted and has redeemable qualities. Slowly, he, too, changes and shows love, respect and esteem for the quiet, reserved Lucy, and she reciprocates. When he leaves for the West Indies on business, he sets her up with a school of her own, but upon his return there is a shipwreck, and readers are left to ponder his ambiguous fate, and the outcome.

Before Charlotte began this novel, she tried desperately to revise *The Professor*, but all efforts failed and Smith, Elder & Co. refused to accept it; the only alternative was to totally re-write the whole story. Fortunately, for Charlotte and the publisher, the re-writing of the story into a new novel, *Villette*, proved to be a 'wise move' and a complete success. Several factors accounted for this renewed success: first was the improvement in the plot; secondly, the characters had more 'depth' and showed growth and development throughout the story, and finally her adoption of the narrative technique which worked so successfully in *Jane Eyre* was re-employed. As a result, the entire novel presented a much 'tighter' and more 'cohesive unit' with greater continuity and sustained intensity than *Shirley* with its fragmented plot, and was more comparitive to her first success, *Jane Eyre*.

The plot of *Villette* is perhaps one of its major assets and can be praised in the fact that it is more fully integrated and 'tightly knit' than the far less effective plot of *Shirley* which is often described as 'loose', 'episodic', and poorly connected. The reviewers had far more praise for the former which they thought of as more consistent with the talents of Charlotte Brontë, which she had so clearly demonstrated in *Jane Eyre*, and much criticism for the latter because of a plot which had little unity. In *Villette*, the unification of plot, the linear development of the story-line with fewer digressions and addresses to the 'reader', and the long-term development of a few, key, central characters were combined in 'correct proportions' to make it a literary success, as well as a 'recovery' and a redemption from the severely criticized *Shirley*. So excellent is its plot that some critics say it is her 'crowning glory'.

The plot of the novel and its chief character, Lucy Snowe, are so closely integrated that it is difficult to separate them, and Lucy becomes an integral part of the story from the first paragraph to the very last. To compliment this central figure, Charlotte reverted to her first-person narrative which proved to be the 'binding thread' of continuity which was so effective in *Jane Eyre*. The story begins in Bretton, where Lucy Snowe lived with the Brettons and where we meet the central characters who later re-appear in the novel: Lucy Snowe, Mrs. Bretton, John Graham Bretton, Paulina Home and her father, Mr. Home, later the Count de Bassompièrre, who rises in wealth and social standing. From Bretton, Lucy proceeded to Miss Marchmont's estate, fifty miles from London, where she became her 'companion' and remained there until her death.

With only £15 in her pocket, Lucy Snowe went to London and then from England to the Continent to seek her fortune as her governess; it is there that the main action of the story begins. Upon landing in Boue-Marine, thought to be Ostend, Belgium, she was assisted by a handsome, young gentleman in retrieving her trunk. Later we learn that he is 'Dr. John' who makes calls at Mme Beck's Pensionnat, and Mrs. Bretton's son, Graham, whom she knew years ago in Bretton. Lucy also ends up at this same Pensionnat as a teacher-governess where she again meets Ginerva Fanshawe and learns to despise her for her foolish coquetry.

Lucy is soon drawn to the handsome, well-educated 'Dr. John', but gives up on him when she sees that he has become infatuated, first with Ginerva Fanshawe, and later Paulina Home, the now 'adult Polly' from their early days at Bretton when they were all children. They have all grown, gone their separate ways, matured as adults, and have again been 'thrown together' by circumstance and coincidence. Each has developed and matured in their own, unique way, and now a new set of relationships and interactions occur between them. The story re-integrates and re-combines the three, central characters who appear at the beginning of the tale; this intensifies and strengthens the central plot to a higher degree.

With the hope of a relationship between 'Dr. John' and Lucy Snowe fading quickly, Lucy is slowly, but surely, drawn toward an unlikely character, M Paul Emanuel, someone she found repelling by 'first impressions'. At the outset, Lucy found him highly irritable, demanding, hot-tempered, 'waspish', and something of a tyrant, but deep within he had admirable qualities which only time revealed as their friendship grew and their relationship developed. Lucy's meekness and gentleness was disarming and his fiery temper, aggressiveness, and dictatorial ways eventually gave way to kindness and consideration, and his anti-British, anti-Protestant feelings soon mellowed and gave way to love, respect, and admiration.

Mme Beck and Mme Walravens observed the growth of love and attraction between them and prepared schemes to keep them apart and prevent their 'union'. These interferences are, in fact, based on the spying which Charlotte was subjected to by Mme Heger when she suspected that there may be some form of relationship occurring between her husband and Charlotte. In the novel, Paul Emanuel takes his leave and Lucy feels that he has deserted her and searches for him everywhere only to discover that he has been setting up a school for her to direct in his absence. Paul Emanuel then sails for the West Indies where he will direct Mme Walravens' estate with the future of marriage to Lucy Snowe in mind. Once again, two of Charlotte's recurrent themes, 'love conquers all' and the 'dissipation of barriers and prejudices' overcome their intruders' malevolent actions.

The only part of the novel which is somewhat distressing and inconsistent with the preceding plot is its ending. In this novel, one is again led to believe that certain events are 'pre-scripted' and most likely to occur, and one of those events is a happy ending. Also, at one point the reader is led to believe that 'Dr. John' and Lucy will eventually find love and happiness, but that 'flame' is suddenly extinguished. And, once that is gone, the reader is propelled to a new 'conclusion' that Lucy Snowe and Paul Emanuel will overcome the obstacles of nationality, language, and religion and consummate their love in marriage, but this was not to be. The reader is then left to 'read' or 'write' one's own conclusion as to the demise of Paul Emanuel. Charlotte's intended ending was originally more tragic, and without 'doubt', but in an effort to please and appease her father, who preferred 'happy endings' rather than sad ones, she made it deliberately ambiguous. Unfortunately, I believe that this ending detracts in a serious way to the intended plot, and that *Villette* would have gained even more favourable reviews had the ending been one of 'classic romance', had he lived, or as a 'tragic romance' with the certain death of Paul Emanuel.

Recurrent elements which Charlotte Brontë uses in this novel, as well as *Jane Eyre*, is 'mystique' and the supernatural which may have their origins in her strong attachments, and those of Emily and Anne, to Gothic novels and Gothic romance. Her use of this element is reminiscent of the terror and suspense used by Horace Walpole, Ann Radcliffe, and M.G. 'Monk' Lewis in their Gothic novels, but Charlotte used it in a 'softer' sense. Charlotte used this element successfully in *Jane Eyre* and uses it again here with the sudden, mysterious appearances and disappearances of the 'nun', whose true story we do not learn until near the end of the novel.

The supernatural is also used effectively with great storms as preludes and forebodings of major events to follow. When Lucy is a companion to Marchmont, a great, spring wind-storm arose late one evening (Ch. IV.) :

> After a calm winter, storms were ushering in the spring. I had put Miss Marchmont to bed; I sat at the fireside sewing. The wind was wailing at the windows: it had wailed all day; but, as night deepened, it took a new tone - an accent keen, piercing, almost articulate to the ear; a plaint, piteous and disconsulate to the nerves, trilled in every gust.

And in the next paragraph she continues on about these forebodings:

> Three times in the course of my life, events had taught me that these strange accents in the storm - this restless, hopeless cry - denote a coming state of the atmosphere unpropitious to life. Epidemic diseases, I believed, were often heralded by a gasping, sobbing, tormented, long-lamenting east wind. Hence, I inferred, arose the legend of the Banshee.

In the morning, Miss Marchmont was found dead in her bed; she had died 'peacefully and painlessly' during the night.

In the second instance before Lucy dropped into 'agonizing depression' and delirium which led to physical illness and near collapse, she went to bed but not before the fall storms began (Ch. XV.) :

> About this time the Indian summer closed and the equinoctial storms began; and for nine dark and wet days, of which the hours rushed on all turbulent, deaf, dishevelled - bewildered with sounding hurricane - I lay in a strange fever of the nerves and blood. Sleep went quite away. I used to rise in the night, look round for her, beseech her earnestly to return. A rattle of the window, a cry of the blast only replied - Sleep never came.

When Lucy finally did fall asleep, she had a frightful dream in which she was challenged by 'Death' to leave this troubled Earth behind (Ch. XV.) :

> Amidst the horrors of that dream I think the worst lay here. Methought the well-loved dead, who had loved *me* well in life, met me elsewhere, alienated: galled was my inmost spirit with an unutterable sense of despair about the future. Motive there

was none why I should try to recover or wish to live; and yet quite unendurable was the pitiless and haughty voice in which Death challenged me to engage his unknown terrors.

And in the final chapters and paragraphs of *Villette*, M Paul Emanuel's return is presaged by yet another storm; its tenacity forewarns us and prepares us for a final disaster of great magnitude (Ch. XLII.) :

> The wind shifts to the west. Peace, peace, Banshee - 'keening' at every window!... That storm roared frenzied for seven days. It did not cease till the Atlantic was strewn with wrecks: it did not lull till the deep had gorged their full of sustenance. Not till the destroying angel of tempest had achieved his perfect work, would he fold the wings whose waft was thunder - the tremor of whose plumes was storm.

The reader is then left to imagine the outcome and whether Paul Emanuel returns, by the will of God, or perishes in the storm leaving Lucy Snowe with unrequited love, and yet another sad 'chapter' in her life. This ambiguous ending may also have another explanation which may have been somewhat 'symbolic' in that her association with Constantin Heger, with whom she was deeply infatuated, 'evaporated' from her life after she left Brussels and returned to Haworth. After only a few letters, he broke off communication with her, and she never heard from him again.

Metaphorically, the ending may have another interpretation related to the continued and successive tragedies which Charlotte had suffered throughout her life for which there were no clear and definitive answers. What is the meaning of life? Why do these tragedies happen? What purpose do they serve? Why do some people who are irreligious, ungodly, and 'non-contributory' members of society go through life 'unscathed' with no grief or tragedy? Why are some blessed and others, like the Brontës who adhere to God's laws, made to suffer so? These were the frustrating ironies which Charlotte had already witnessed and experienced in her own short, bitter-sweet life. The ending of *Villette* with its ambiguity may have simply reflected Charlotte's continued struggle with life's philosophical mysteries, which 'beg the questions', but provide no firm answers.

Charlotte Brontë also used another technique effectively in her writing, and that was parapsychology, and mystic events, first used in *Jane Eyre* when Rochester makes a 'telepathic call' which she 'hears' and 'answers'. After her return, the events prove positive, and the relationship, the novel, and the story is brought to a successful and happy conclusion with a romantic ending. In *Villette*, parapsychology and mysticism are used briefly in an 'out-of-body experience', once again presaged by a storm. As she made her way to the steps of a church, she felt herself failing, and "the giant-spire turned black and vanished from my eyes". She went on to describe the 'parting' of soul from body, and then its return (Ch. XVI):

> Where my soul went during that swoon I cannot tell. Whatever she saw, or wherever she travelled in her trance on that strange night, she kept her own secret; never whispering a word to Memory, and baffling imagination by an indissoluble silence. She

may have gone upward, and come in sight of her eternal home, hoping for leave to
rest now, and deeming that her painful union with matter was at last dissolved. While
she so deemed, an angel may have warned her away from heaven's threshold, and,
guiding her weeping down, have bounded her, once more, all shuddering and unwilling, to that poor frame, cold and wasted, of whose companionship she was grown
more than weary.

This 'out-of-body' description is remarkably similar to a number of modern-day reports published in books and journals about such paranormal experiences which leads us
to question whether she herself had such an experience, whether she 'designed' it from
pure imagination, or whether this was an experience related to her by her father, Rev.
Brontë, or someone else. Lucy then goes on in the next paragraph to explain how body
and soul were 're-united' (Ch. XVI) :

I know she re-entered her prison with pain, with reluctance, with a moan and a long
shiver. The divorced mates, Spirit and Substance, were hard to re-unite: they greeted
each other, not in an embrace, but a racking sort of struggle. The returning sense of
sight came upon me, red, as if it swam in blood; suspended hearing rushed back loud
like thunder; consciousness revived in fear: I sat up appalled, wondering into what
region, amongst what strange beings I was waking.

The desperate, reluctant feelings to have soul and body re-united may simply have
been a conscious or 'unconscious' reflection of her own feelings since Charlotte was
going through a severe, mental depression at that time. We must remember that she began to write this last novel two years after the deaths of Branwell, Emily, and Anne, and
now had only her father with whom to commiserate. No doubt he was a comfort to her, as
well as their stable and steady household servants, Tabby Akroyd and Martha Brown, but
it was just not the same without the camaraderie and counsel of her beloved sisters. Her
world was slowly 'collapsing' around her, and had been sporadically, since early childhood with the deaths of her mother and her two older sisters, Maria and Elizabeth.

The despair continued well into her adult life when in 1842, she was again 'rocked'
by three more tragedies all in the two months of September and October. In early September, William Weightman, someone who had brought a great deal of happiness into
their sad lives, died in Haworth of cholera, as well as Martha Taylor in Brussels who also
died of the disease in mid-October. Two weeks later, their devoted Aunt Branwell died
on October 29th; Charlotte was no 'stranger' to debilitating losses and anguish.

This tragic scene was repeated in September, 1848, December, 1848, and again in
May, 1849, when Charlotte's remaining siblings perished from consumption. Charlotte
then had difficulty completing *Shirley*, which had been well on its way to completion,
and even more difficulty with *Villette* once it was begun in 1851. There is little doubt that
Charlotte was in deep depression and suffering great mental anxiety from these unforgiving and devastating bouts of tragedy. Not only were they a severe test on her 'mortality'
but also a severe test of her religion, beliefs, and faith. With Mary Taylor now living in

New Zealand, Charlotte had only one good, close friend remaining in whom she could communicate and confide, and that was Ellen Nussey.

The entire novel, *Villette*, is based on Charlotte Brontë's experiences in Brussels, and although some events are 'from life', the majority are simply from the realm of her vast imagination. The scene early in the novel where she is in London and boards the packet, The Vivid, is based on fact. Upon Charlotte's return to Brussels in January, 1843, this time without Emily, after the death of Aunt Branwell, just such an incident occurred when she went to the Thames dockside late at night in search of her packet to Ostend. Fearing that she would miss its early morning departure, she decided to board it at night, something which was rather unwise and risky. Once at the dock, several rough boatmen argued over who would take her out to the ship, and when they did, they took advantage of her and grossly overcharged her.

A second incident of importance based on fact in *Villette* is her 'confession' in a Roman Catholic church. Charlotte was a very religious person and was 'born into' a Protestant house with her Reverend father, but she had little tolerance and sympathy for 'Romanism' and its Church. During her second year in Brussels, she did at one time go into St. Gudule Cathedral and partake in a confession to a priest, something which was foreign and alien to her as well as 'offensive' to her personal beliefs. It was done on a 'whim' to see what it would be like, but Charlotte may also have had a deeper 'crisis of faith' in which she searched for greater meaning to life, the answers which were not forthcoming in her own religion. Charlotte found the priest likeable, tempting, and persuasive, but once 'out of his grasp', she was determined not to go back (Ch. XV.) :

> Did I, do you suppose, reader, contemplate venturing again within that worthy priest's reach? As soon should I have thought of walking into a Babylonish furnace. That priest had arms which could influence me; he was naturally kind, with a sentimental French kindness, to whose softness I knew myself not wholly impervious.

When making the 'confession', Charlotte was extremely lonely and in a highly vulnerable state. In a letter to Emily after the incident, she told her about it, but asked that she not mention it to their father.

With Charlotte's deep commitment to the Established Church of England and her strong opposition to 'Romanists', 'Romanism', the Catholic Church, and the Pope, it was not long before she had a 'clash' on this subject with M Heger who was equally anti-Protestant, and was as much anti-British as Charlotte was anti-Belgian. Their differences of opinion resulted in lively, friendly debates over religion which ultimately served no purpose, since neither was willing to to bend to the other's arguments and commit apostasy; they were both equally strong adherents to their faiths. In the novel, Paul Emanuel falls in love with Lucy Snowe and is committed to marry her upon his return from Guadaloupe, contrary to the wishes of the Church, Père Silas, and his friends because she was a Protestant. Lucy saw his sudden departure to the West Indies so shortly after his affirmation of love and commitment to marriage as a 'banishment' and punishment for his love of someone 'outside' his own faith. Chapter XXXVI, 'The Apple of Discord', outlines at length their continued battle over religion, but in the end, these differences were subjugated to their love for one another.

From their first introduction, both Paul Emanuel and Lucy Snowe are at odds about their two, different religions, but Paul Emanuel is determined to change that. Being a lonely Protestant in a Catholic school in Belgium, Paul Emanuel and Père Silas make a series of unsuccessful efforts to convert Lucy to Catholicism, but she does not fall into their grasp and concede her beliefs. She is unshakeable from the tenets of her religion, and in spite of Père Silas's efforts and kindness, she still dislikes the Roman Catholic Church. She says of Père Silas (XV) :

> ... whatever I may think of his Church and creed (and I like neither), of himself I must ever retain a great recollection.

And in a letter to Ellen Nussey from Belgium in July, 1842, she echoed these same sentiments when she said, "...whatever Romanism may be, there are good Romanists", indicating that she was magnanimous enough to put aside her bias and recognize the 'goodness' of people regardless of their religion or beliefs.

Later Lucy mocks Catholicism after she found a lilac-coloured pamphlet which mysteriously found its way onto her desk for the purpose of persuasion and conversion to the Roman Catholic Church (Ch. XXXVI) :

> I remember one capital inducement to apostacy was held out in the fact that the Catholic who had lost dear friends by death could enjoy the unspeakable solace of praying them out of purgatory. The writer did not touch on the firmer peace of those whose belief dispenses with purgatory altogether:...

and then in the very next paragraph Lucy proceeds from its 'mockery' to the 'amusement' it provided her (Ch. XXXVI) :

> The little book amused, and did not painfully displease me. It was a canting, sentimental, shallow little book, yet something about it cheered my gloom and made me smile:...

Paul Emanuel is equally at odds with Protestantism and has been warned by Père Silas about the 'evils' of the religion and the danger of consorting with its followers. He tells Lucy (Ch. XXXVI) :

> It is your religion - your strange, self-reliant, invulnerable creed, whose influence seems to clothe you in, I know not what, unblessed panoply. You are good - Père Silas calls you good, and loves you - but your terrible, proud earnest Protestantism, there is the danger.

Lucy has very little good to say about priests in the Roman Catholic Church and refers to them as; "Oh, lovers of power! Oh! mitred aspirants for this world's kingdoms!"

(Ch. XXXVI) and ends this scathing pronouncement by reminding the reader that priests, too, would have a day of Judgement. She then went on to thoroughly castigate the 'pomp and ceremony' of Rome which she called - 'the glory of her kingdom'. She had been to numerous Roman Catholic services and ceremonies and was not impressed; she was highly critical of their rituals (Ch. XXXVI) :

> Neither full procession, nor high mass, nor swarming tapers, nor swinging censers, nor ecclesiastical millinery, nor celestial jewellery, touched my imaginaion a whit. What I saw struck me as tawdry, not grand; as grossly material, not poetically spiritual.

And finally to show Paul Emanuel that all their efforts, pamphlets, cajolings, encouragements, persuasions, and attempts at conversion had failed, Lucy spoke to him more candidly than ever before; she explained that (Ch XXXVI) :

> ... to show him that I had a mind to keep to my reformed creed; the more I saw of Popery, the closer I clung to Protestantism; doubtless there were errors in every Church, but I now perceived by contrast how severely pure was my own, compared with her whose painted and meretricious face had been unveiled for my admiration.

It is impossible to read any of Charlotte Brontë's books without seeing the influence of her religion on her own thoughts, beliefs, and morals, and the outcome of those beliefs is the occasional didacticism we see in her writings. Throughout *Villette* there are some references to her moralist view, but the entire chapter, mentioned above, is dedicated to the arguments from both Protestant and Catholic viewpoints, with the former given the more generous and gentle interpretation, and the latter seen in a negative light. Charlotte's strong Protestant views could not be mollified, and the basis for the arguments in Chapter XXXVI, may well have been loosely based on discussions she had with M Heger, but this is speculation. In both cases, neither could be enticed to embrace each other's religion; they each held firmly to their beliefs.

The final chapters of *Villette* have often been praised as some of Charlotte's best writing, and some of the best in English Literature. In *Aspects of the Novel* (1927), by E.M. Forster, the author points out that most novels fall flat at the end, but Charlotte Brontë's novel, *Villette*, is an exception with a very strong and powerful ending. Not only is the final chapter engaging to the very end, the preceding chapters are also noteworthy, since the author does an excellent job of re-introducing all the main characters that the reader met at the beginning, tied up 'loose-ends', and provided satisfactory explanations to the intervening years. As a result, many of the criticisms which were aimed at Charlotte Brontë after the release of *Shirley*, could not, and were not, levelled against this novel. She had redeemed herself and effectively silenced her critics. There were some criticisms, of course, but they were minor and of little consequence. To this day, some literary experts will fervently argue that *Villette* is truly Charlotte Brontë's finest work, and deserves much more praise and recognition than it then received, and is presently accorded.

11

WUTHERING HEIGHTS

Wuthering Heights by Emily Brontë is most certainly one of English Literature's most enduring and timeless classics and has perhaps been subjected to more intense scrutiny and analysis than any other piece of writing in history. Today, as it was then, the novel is occasionally re-scrutinized and re-analyzed by successive, new generations of readers and analysts still anxious to solve its many mysteries. Like Margaret Mitchell, the U.S. writer of the famed *Gone With the Wind*, (1936), it was Emily Brontë's first and only novel, and one which leaves a lasting, and sometimes permanent, impression on its many readers.

Wuthering Heights begins with Mr. Earnshaw's return from Liverpool with a dark-haired, dark-skinned, homeless boy, whom they name 'Heathcliff', under his coat, the initial act which sets the entire story into motion. Slowly Mr. Earnshaw grows closer to Heathcliff than his own son which results in Hindley, Mr. Earnshaw's son, learning to hate Heathcliff with a passion, whereas Catherine Earnshaw, Hindley's sister, learns to love him more than life itself. When Mr. Earnshaw dies, Hindley returns with his new bride and takes over Wuthering Heights, lowering Heathcliff, who is not a blood-member of the family, to the status of a servant. Hindley bullies, humiliates and degrades him to the point of self-neglect, and Heathcliff becomes hateful and spiteful and yearns for revenge.

After hearing Catherine say that she could never marry him because it would 'degrade' her, Heathcliff runs away and is not seen again for three years. He returns after that time with a changed appearance, that of an English gentleman and with wealth to match. Catherine in the meantime has married Edgar Linton, a wealthy, English neighbour of class and standing, and is carrying his child. Although Catherine is ecstatic at his return, the two soon resort to recriminations against one another and make each other miserable and resentful. Heathcliff, with his nature now being twisted with hate and revenge, is determined to destroy his perceived enemies, the Earnshaws and Lintons.

Hindley, his old enemy, invites Heathcliff to stay at Wuthering Heights since he now has money, and Hindley, addicted to drink and gambling, hopes to separate him from his new-found wealth. After a final visit with Catherine, and more accusations and recriminations, Catherine dies shortly after giving birth to a daughter, also named Catherine. Heathcliff's grief now gives added weight to his desire for revenge. He marries Isabella, Edgar Linton's sister, treats her horribly, and after she dies twelve years later, as his estranged wife, Heathcliff takes possession of their sickly son, Linton, and devises a plan to marry him off to his cousin, Catherine Linton, in an effort to secure their property and wealth.

After much gambling, Hindley has now mortgaged off all his property to Heathcliff and soon loses everything with nothing to give to his only son, Hareton, the last remaining Earnshaw. Hindley eventually dies as a result of his drinking, and Heathcliff becomes owner and master of Wuthering Heights. Later, when Catherine is forced to marry Linton, the heir to the Linton estate, Heathcliff is again the benefactor when his son dies. Now, through patience and timely manipulation, Heathcliff is the possessor of all the real property and wealth of the Earnshaws and Lintons. In addition to this, the two remaining offspring, Hareton and Catherine, are both under Heathcliff's power and control.

Having achieved his goals of revenge, Heathcliff finally turns to his ultimate goal of 're-unification' with his long-lost loved one, buried eighteen years before. Finally, in what appears to be a re-union with her spirit, he finds a 'new peace' and refuses to eat. After several days, he is found dead in his bed. Young Catherine and Hareton also forge themselves a new relationship and their marriage is set for New Year's Day.

No other novel in English Literature has ever met with so much controversy, interest and critical analysis; the interests, criticisms and analyses continue to this very day. After its publication in December, 1847, it was roundly condemned by a number of reviews and reviewers from every corner of England. Victorian readers were shocked, sickened, and disgusted at the vicious acts, events and characters found in its pages; it was a novel that readers of the day were not prepared for. It was both different from anything they had ever read and was completely unique; nothing like it had ever appeared before, or since. *Wuthering Heights* was condemned for its brutality, savagery, coarseness, wickedness, and disagreeable language and characters, as well as it 'improbability'. Readers of the day were neither prepared for its vivid brutality nor the 'monster' they came to know as 'Heathcliff'. One periodcal, *The Examiner*, had the following to say about *Wuthering Heights* :

> This is a strange book....It is not without evidence of considerable power; but, as a whole, it is wild, confused, disjointed, and improbable.

Amidst all the negative reviews, there were some which recognized its 'raw' and 'rugged power', its uniqueness, and its 'strange magic', as one North American review recorded it. No one came forward and hailed it as a masterpiece because it contravened so many of the conventions of the day, but they simply hinted at its 'power' as a piece of writing. This is as far as reviewers would go to praising it, but today with so much time having elapsed and great changes in modern society's mores and values, we are much more at liberty to praise its greatness of style and plot, the intensity of its characters, its vivid descriptions, and recognize it as masterful, artistic literature. In a review of the *Palladium,* 1850, two years after its first publication, Sydney Dobell was one of the first to give it the acclaim it deserved, praised its brave simplicity, and called it a 'triumph of description'. Dobell also found its use of the supernatural very effective. Today, we see *Wuthering Heights* as a work of pure genius.

One of the great mysteries which surrounds this book is just how a young woman from a remote part of northern England with such limited experience in human relationships, especially with men, could write a novel with such power and intensity. What was it in her emotional background and make-up which could have given rise to such powerful passion, revenge, hate, brutality and savagery? What was the source of these powerful passions so internalized by these fictionalized characters which sprang to life in her one and only novel. Had she written a second or a third novel, could she have re-created similar, powerful characters in an equally compelling plot? But that is a moot point, and will ever remain so, since she died a year after its publication, and no second work was ever published, or perhaps even attempted.

It has been suggested that Emily had several sources for the plot of her novel, the sources being Lord Byron, the poet, Hugh Brunty, her grandfather, and the story of Jack Sharp, which she learned while teaching at Law Hill, Halifax. Each of these may have contributed some parts to the story as a whole, and others may have been adopted, or adapted, from Byron's life to fit the plot.

The story of Hugh Brunty, Emily's grandfather, was, no doubt, a highly romanticized one passed down to the Brontë children by their father, Patrick. It appears that their great grandfather was a cattle dealer on the River Boyne in Ireland and often crossed the Irish Sea to do trade in Liverpool. On one of the return trips, a dark, dirty, almost naked boy was discovered in the hold of the ship, and when no one could be found to give him medical attention, or care for him, Mrs. Brunty adopted him and brought him home. Because his origins were thought to be in Wales, they simply called him 'Welsh', and Mr. Brunty decided to teach *him* the intricacies of trading instead of his own sons. In time, he became highly proficient in trade, and at the same time his character grew to be serious and morose, crafty and jealous. During a return trip after the largest trade and deal they ever made, Mr. Brunty died suddenly of a heart attack, but 'Welsh' denied knowing anything of the money, or paperwork, from the sale.

As a result, the Brunty's finances were thrown into disarray, and knowing nothing of the cattle business, the family was forced into poverty. Welsh later re-appeared, extremely well-dressed, and offered to carry on their business if Mary, the youngest daughter, would marry him, but he was rejected. Hurt and angry, he swore an oath that she would eventually marry him, that he would own their home, and scatter them like chaff.

As rent agent for their land, Welsh lured Mary into a compromising situation, and rather than have her family subjected to scandal, she agreed to marry him. They remained childless, and Welsh cunningly adopted one of Mary's nephews, Emily's grandfather

Hugh, with a promise to raise him and educate him properly. Instead, he received no education and was put to hard labour on a farm by Welsh who treated him harshly and cruelly. One of Welsh's workmen, his right-hand-man, was remarkably like 'Joseph' in *Wuthering Heights*, and Hugh's favourite dog was named 'Keeper', just like Emily's. His aunt Mary finally informed Hugh of his origins after witnessing his misery, and Hugh decided to escape, which he did.

In a daring escape, he swam the River Boyne to a neighbour's farm, and there he was helped to flee to North Ireland where he got work at a lime kiln. There he made friends with a young lad named McClory, who invited him home during a holiday, and there he met, and immediately fell in love with, his sister Alice, the most beautiful girl in the area. Their love was forbidden since he was a Protestant, and she Catholic, but on the day of her arranged wedding to a Catholic farmer, she eloped with Hugh Brunty, and they were married in a Protestant church nearby. The year was 1776, and their first child, Patrick, the Rev. P. Brontë, was born on March 17, 1777. This, in itself, is a remarkable story, and is an excellent basis for *Wuthering Heights* whether it was a pure fiction, or simply a romanticized version of their grandfather's origin.

The second story of interest which may have contributed to the novel is one which has many similarities to the first, and was learned by Emily while living and teaching at Miss Patchett's School at Law Hill. It appears that Jack Sharp, an orphan, was adopted by his uncle, a Mr. Walker, of Walter Clough Hall. The uncle raised his nephew to be a partner in his wool business instead of his own sons and eventually he became very proficient and took over the business. Jack then became very arrogant and domineering and was detested by the other members of the Walker family, just as Heathcliff was by Hindley.

When the uncle died, the eldest son and his bride reclaimed Clough Hall, but Jack Sharp removed all the furnishings and valuables to his new home at Law Hill. To further humiliate the family, Jack Sharp apprenticed Walker's young cousin into the business and corrupted him with drink and gambling. When the young cousin had driven himself into hopeless debt, the elder Walker was obliged to pay off his debts, to his own financial distress. Later, the cousin moved into Clough Hall and taught Walker's son to swear and misbehave, and he also revelled in bringing disharmony into the household. These events parallel many that we find in *Wuthering Heights* although it seems that Emily introduced other real-life incidents from the life of Lord Byron.

Emily and the other Brontës read a great deal of contemporary literature, and they were all intrigued and fascinated by the works of Lord Byron and Shelley, two renegade poets of their own era. In fact, Heathcliff appears to be a 'Byronic' character who acts with spite, hatred and malice to those who have caused him any injustice. One of the major incidents in Emily Brontë's novel, Heathcliff overhearing Catherine say that marrying him would be degrading, appears to be a 'page' from Byron's own life, according to Thomas Moore's recollections from Byron's memoirs.

Moore describes how Byron, as a young man, fell madly in love with his cousin, but he once overheard her say to a servant something to the effect, "Do you think that I could care anything for that lame boy?"[1] Byron, extremely sensitive about his lameness, and deeply hurt by this insensitive remark, ran off madly into the night and did not stop for miles until he reached a nearby village. This incident is parallel to Heathcliff's departure and disappearance for three years. There are also close parallels to Byron's poem, 'The Dream', (1816) in which he describes his love for his cousin and his failed first marriage; in the poem, the young boy goes abroad, returns a 'gentleman', the lady is stricken with madness, and they both live and die in a state of misery. Comparably, the incident in which Isabella throws her wedding ring into the fire after grinding it with a poker is similar to Byron's smashing of his pocket watch and throwing it into the fireplace in a fit of rage.

Emily appears to have absorbed and used ideas from her own experience and other sources as well. Heathcliff's extraction of a promise from the sexton to bury him beside Catherine with sides removed from each of their coffins so that they could be together for eternity is vaguely similar to a story in Blackwood's magazine (circa 1840s) in which a young couple, in love since childhood, were separated and later denied marriage, since she was betrothed to another. Her lover decides to murder her suitor in order to gain her hand, but immediately after their marriage, he is forced to flee when he is betrayed by a black-hearted villain, much like Heathcliff. After fleeing from the law, the lover returns to his wife at night and appears at her window; there is a joyous re-union, but several months later she dies and is buried in the local churchyard. The lover digs up the casket, and while embracing the body he is surprised by the police, having again been betrayed by the villain. Shots are fired and the lover dies and falls into the same grave as his beloved for a final, eternal union. Such writings may have provided Emily with some background and ideas for scenes in her own, creative novel.

The structure of *Wuthering Heights* is interesting and intriguing, but for some Victorian readers, its style and uniqueness of approach led to some confusion as well as criticism. On the other hand, a detailed analysis of the plot and its structure only leads one to observe and realize its absolute genius. From the outset to its final chapter, we can see all the elements fit together into a neat 'jig-saw' puzzle with no elements missing or left over; the plot is 'tightly bound'. All plot elements are eventually found to be essential to the main plot and its structure, and all the plot elements have a place in the continuum of the story. If it seems complex and confusing to the reader at the outset, the story become more apparent and understandable as the plot unfolds and progresses towards its conclusion.

The narration of the story with two principal narrators, Ellen Dean and Mr. Lockwood, the new tenant of Thrushcross Grange, gives the story credibility and authenticity to an otherwise incredible tale. Ellen Dean, the general narrator of the story, lends additional credence to the tale, since she was a childhood friend of the Earnshaws and Heathcliff and gives eye-witness accounts and direct testimony to its authenticity. Mr. Lockwood, the secondary narrator to the overall tale, provides dates which fix the actions and simply corroborates Ellen Dean's story. The overall effect of the two narrators and precise dates

---

1   Byron was born with club foot and went through life with a pre-occupation about his physical defect.

provides *Wuthering Heights* with a greater sense of reality, truth and 'genuineness' which keeps the reader from otherwise dismissing it as a wild tale of pure fantasy. It is probably one of the first works of English fiction to bridge the gap from terrifying and remote Gothic fiction to a more modern, contemporary novel placed in a physical setting with which readers were familiar.

The novel is a 'flashback' of events and 'begins' near the end with the arrival of Mr. Lockwood who encounters Heathcliff close to the end of his life and the second genera-tion of Earnshaws and Lintons strictly under Heathcliff's powerful grip. Lockwood's unscheduled stay at Wuthering Heights and his unusual, terrifying dreams set the story into motion and piques the reader's interest and curiosity as to the nature of its odd inhab-itants and what events led them to be thrown together. When Lockwood returns to Thrushcross Grange and must remain there to recuperate from illness, his curiosity leads him to question the housekeeper, Nelly Dean. Over the weeks of his recovery, he learns bits and pieces of the strange love-story of Heathcliff and Catherine, and the young Catherine and Hareton who reside there now. It is a compelling tale of the love, hate and revenge of a black-hearted villain overcome by a monomania which cannot easily be put to rest. Nelly Dean's recounting of the tale in segments and sections allows the reader to 'catch his breath' and piece together this vengeful tale and to recede into the past and investigate individual incidents which allow us to understand, clarify, and gain greater insight into the present situation.

Lockwood's two dreams set the story into motion and also set the tone for the twisted tale which is about to unfold before the reader. Dreams are often nothing more than our unconscious expressions of events and occurrences which impacted upon our conscious thoughts during the day. Lockwood's first dream may well have been activated by his anger towards Joseph and the attack of the dogs as he attempted to leave Wuthering Heights that day. In his dream, Joseph's wearisome and endless preaching were enough to arouse Lockwood to revolt, but when Joseph orders the congregation to rise up against him, a fight breaks out. The preacher's frantic rapping on the pulpit causes him to awake, only to find that the noise is caused by a fir branch tapping on the window pane.

He falls asleep again and the second dream follows immediately. This time he hears a tapping on the window, and when he tries to open it, he finds it sealed. In his determina-tion to stop the noise, he 'breaks' the glass and reaches into the night to break off the suspected branch. Instead of grasping the branch, he is seized by a small, icy hand from which he cannot free himself. He is overcome by terror and asks 'Who are you?', and the apparition answers that it is 'Catherine Linton'. In his frantic efforts to free himself from this horror, he pulls the hand inside the pane and rubs the hand on the broken glass until it is covered with blood. Lockwood then screams aloud in terror, Heathcliff rushes into the room, and the spell of dreams is broken. It is possible that Lockwood's second dream was triggered by his conscious observations of the names, 'Catherine Earnshaw', 'Catherine Heathcliff', and 'Catherine Linton' carved into the window casing.

In reality, Lockwood had not broken the pane, and he had not committed the savage act of rubbing a child's hand on broken glass to break its grip; it was only a dream, but to Heathcliff, it *was* a reality. When Lockwood returned to the room to get instructions from

Heathcliff for exit, he saw him open the window and heard him shout into the stormy night (Ch. 3) :

> Come in! come in!... Cathy, do come. Oh do - *once* more ! Oh! my heart's darling!
> hear me *this* time, Catherine, at last!

The stage is now set for a review of events of several decades past which brings the reader to this point. Both Lockwood and the reader are very curious to know just how these people of Wuthering Heights, so full of hate for one another, arrived there, and why they remain there.

Heathcliff is undoubtedly the central character of the novel, the black-hearted, hero-villain about which the story revolves, and the steady growth of his frustration, bitterness, and hatred for Hindley, and later others who stand in his way or gave him pain and suffering. One of the moral themes we may extract from this novel is the latent, animal instinct, and potential, within each of us for revenge and cruelty which if allowed to grow 'unchecked' may result in a fiendish type of character such as that of Heathcliff. Put in modern, clinical terms, Heathcliff has developed a psychosis as a result of his rough treatment from Hindley, his traumatic loss of Cathy, his overpowering desire for revenge on his enemies, and his monomaniacal search for a glance or conversation with the dearly departed soul of his beloved Catherine. These were the factors which twisted and warped his tormented soul into that of a living 'monster'. In the 'Editor's Preface to the New Edition of Wuthering Heights' [1850], Currer Bell (Charlotte Brontë), at the beginning of the second edition, had this to say about its principal character:

> Whether it is right or advisable to create beings like Heathcliff, I do not know: I scarcely think it is. But this I know: the writer who possesses the creative gift owns something of which he is not always master - something that, at times, strangely wills and works for itself.

The latter part of the above statement suggests that the writer is not always 'responsible' or 'in control' of a character he creates; in fact, the character may develop a 'power', 'personality' and 'life' of its own which then 'takes charge' and leads the writer rather than the reverse. Heathcliff is just such a powerful character.

Heathcliff indeed becomes a 'monster' out of control with his ever- spiralling hatred for the Earnshaws and Lintons who appear to have taken from him everything that is meaningful and dear to him. The first major blow to Heathcliff is the death of Mr. Earnshaw and the return of Hindley and his new wife, Frances, to take possession of Wuthering Heights. With Heathcliff being relegated to the position of a servant, suffering degradations, and being at the receiving end of Hindley's tyrannical rule and abuse, Heathcliff's 'inner fire' is ignited and begins to glow with hatred. And when Catherine rejects him and grows closer to the affections of Edgar and the Lintons, Heathcliff is further infuriated, aggravated and frustrated. The final blow comes when Heathcliff overhears Catherine tell Nelly Dean that marrying him would 'degrade' her; he runs off and does not return for three years.

Heathcliff heard only part of the conversation and had he not run out, he would have heard a fuller confession of Catherine's love for him (Ch. 9) :

> I've no more business to marry Edgar Linton than I have to be in heaven; and if the wicked man in there had not brought Heathcliff so low, I shouldn't have thought of it. It would degrade me to marry Heathcliff now; [2] so he shall never know how I love him; and that not because he's handsome, Nelly, but because he's more myself than I am.

This hurtful phrase caused Heathcliff to flee, and he not only missed hearing Cathy's declaration of love for him but also her explanation of why she was marrying Edgar Linton (Ch. 9) :

> Nelly, I see now, you think me a selfish wretch; but did it ever strike you that if Heathcliff and I were married, we should be beggars? Whereas, if I marry Linton, I can aid Heathcliff to rise, and place him out of my brother's power.

Her planned marriage to Edgar Linton was, in part, a plan to help Heathcliff and remove him from Hindley's tyranny, but whether this was an entirely altruistic act on Cathy's part is somewhat doubtful.

Catherine, like Hindley, at first disliked Heathcliff but later changed her mind. As they grew as children, they also grew closer to one another spiritually until the bond was indivisible. There's was not a physical attraction, and nowhere in the novel do we find any hint whatsoever of a lusty, physical relationship, close or otherwise, between them. Their love was beyond that and their union was both metaphysical and transcendental and remains so throughout the novel. In contrast, Catherine's relationship to Edgar Linton is purely physical, Earthly and secular, tangible and concrete. In her discussion with Nelly Dean, Catherine is aware of the differences in her two loves and explains them in this way (Ch. 9) :

> My love for Linton is like the foliage in the woods: time will change it, I'm well aware, as winter changes the trees. My love for Heathcliff resembles the eternal rocks beneath: a source of little visible delight, but necessary. Nelly, I *am* Heathcliff! He's always, always in my mind: not as a pleasure, any more than I am always a pleasure to myself, but as my own being.

In Heathcliff's absence, Catherine seems to be a different character altogether, and quite normal in every respect; it is only when Heathcliff returns that her personality alters so that she becomes moody, irritable, argumentative, demanding, excitable, bad-tempered, and generally unpleasant. Heathcliff's close proximity brings him again to mind, and obviously brings out the worst in her. In his long absence, Catherine had 'room' to forget him and concentrate on someone near at hand who loved her, cared for her, and showed her affection. These were reasons for Catherine's marriage to Edgar, in addition

---

2   This is where Heathcliff abruptly left.

to Hindley's encouragement, as well as the wealth and social standing such a marriage would bring.

Catherine and Edgar had been married only six months when Heathcliff returned, re-entered Catherine's life, and altered their prospective happiness together. When Heathcliff returned, he was a changed man, much to the surprise of Catherine, and especially to Edgar, who referred to him as a 'gipsy', the 'plough-boy', and the 'runaway servant' which emphasizes the 'social distance' he sees between them. He allows Heathcliff to visit his wife simply to indulge her and her seemingly bad health. Heathcliff's 'transformation' is nothing short of miraculous, and although there was speculation that he had been away in the army, we neither learn where he has been nor what has brought about the transformation, primarily because it is irrelevant to the story as a whole and would only be a useless digression. Heathcliff appears now as a well-dressed, 'tall, athletic, well-formed man' who stands 'upright', has a much older-looking countenance, looks of intelligence, and has 'no marks of former degradation'. Furthermore, for the time being, we discover, his disposition and demeanour have apparently also changed according to Nelly Dean's report (Ch. 10) :

> A half-civilised ferocity lurked yet in the depressed brows and eyes full of black fire, but it was subdued; and his manner was even dignified: quite divested of roughness, though too stern for grace.

but his 'coolness' and 'calmness' did not remain long, and Catherine's and Heathcliff's proximity to one another soon ignited a new round of 'storminess', anxiety and frustration in their relationship.

With Heathcliff's return and their renewed interaction, it required only a short time for Catherine to return their relationship to its previous level; soon everyone else is pushed to the outer fringes of their conscious thought, and 'their reality', and treated as 'nonentities', even Catherine's husband, Edgar. After several months of renewed visits, their relationship heats to a 'boiling point' and there are bitter accusations from Heathcliff and acrid recriminations from Catherine, each blaming the other for what has happened. Heathcliff is now, more than ever before, bent on revenge, and when he discloses his intention to marry Isabella Linton, who has shown a loving interest in him, simply for her portion of the estate, Catherine argues vehemently against it.

When Edgar tries to intervene, both Heathcliff and Catherine turn on him as an unwelcome interloper. With armed servants in the hallway prepared to bodily eject Heathcliff, Catherine locks the door, and with mockery and derision, challenges Edgar to throw Heathcliff out himself if he is man enough to do so. Such uncharacteristic behaviour of Catherine toward her own husband is indicative of a rapidly declining mental state brought about by Heathcliff's presence. After Heathcliff's departure, the scene between Catherine and Edgar gets even 'uglier', and she appears to be heading for a complete mental breakdown. These scenes simply confirm to the reader what we have known all along: that Catherine's real sympathies and love lie, not with her husband Edgar, but with Heathcliff, and there appears to be no possible escape from the dilemma. She is hopelessly trapped in marriage to one, and hopelessly separated from the other whom she cannot stand to be apart from. It is literally enough to drive her mad.

Catherine's inability to deal with, or escape from, the problems of adult life and reality cause her to regress to times and places long ago which were comforting and more to her liking and to her favour. She 'falls victim' to the past and delights in lingering and re-living a past of childhood joy and happiness, a lifestyle free of troubles and worries and pure, idyllic love for Heathcliff from whom she could not bear to be parted. As the troubles of reality increase and 'close in' on her, the more she regresses into the past and leans more heavily on the pure, unfettered love which she once knew between herself and Heathcliff.

In all of this, Edgar and Isabella Linton are simply hapless victims in the all-powerful, Catherine-Heathcliff love-relationship which dominates their lives and leads them onto the 'sidelines' as 'outsiders' wondering at their exclusion and what went wrong. Edgar and Catherine's future as a couple looked happy, hopeful and successful until the arrival of Heathcliff, and then suddenly everything 'came apart at the seams'. Edgar is simply an unwitting victim who attempts to intercede on behalf of his wife to stop Heathcliff's perceived interference, but instead she turns on him, along with Heathcliff, and Edgar finds himself a 'third party' to a lovers' quarrel. As a person, Nelly Dean had only good things to say about Edgar calling him kind, truthful, and honest which clarifies to the reader that the power of the Catherine-Heathcliff relationship is 'beyond' him, and that Edgar is neither at fault nor lacking in positive, personal qualities.

Isabella, likewise, is also a victim of Heathcliff's tyranny and simply a pawn in his scheme for complete revenge on all the Lintons. She is blinded by her own love and does not heed the advice of Edgar, Catherine, and Nelly Dean to remain clear of Heathcliff. Isabella dismisses them with indignation, and Catherine gives a stern warning of the dangers (Ch. 10) :

> Pray, don't imagine that he conceals depths of benevolence and affection beneath a stern exterior! He's not a rough diamond - a pearl-containing oyster of a rustic: he's a fierce, pitiless, wolfish man.... and he'd crush you like a sparrow's egg, Isabella, if he found you a troublesome charge.

She then goes on to outline the possible ulterior motives Heathcliff has for marriage to her (Ch. 10) :

> I know he couldn't love a Linton; and yet he'd be quite capable of marrying your fortune and expectations; avarice is growing with him a besetting sin. There's my picture: and I'm his friend - so much so, that had he thought seriously to catch you, I should, perhaps, have held my tongue, and let you fall into his trap.

Isabella then goes on to marry Heathcliff, contrary to good advice, and suffers the exact consequences which Catherine had laid out before her.

Following the quarrel with Heathcliff and Edgar, Catherine locks herself in her bedroom and Edgar shuts himself up in the library; each refuses to go to the other. After three days, Catherine emerges in a poor mental and physical state, much to the alarm of Edgar and Nelly Dean who find her wandering back and forth 'in and out' of delirium. Catherine predicts her own death, denounces her husband, and to make matters worse, the next day they learn that Isabella has eloped with Heathcliff.

After Heathcliff and Isabella's two-month honeymoon, they return to Wuthering Heights and take up residence there, much to Isabella's regret. In a letter to Nelly Dean, we learn that Catherine's warnings and predictions about Heathcliff have proven correct; Isabella has already been treated badly and Heathcliff has made her life miserable and unbearable. Catherine is about to have her baby, and the stage is then set for the main action of the novel, a final meeting of Catherine and Heathcliff. As Heathcliff has been forbidden to visit Catherine or set foot on Thushcross Grange, he inveigles Nelly to carry a secret letter to Catherine and set up a clandestine meeting for the two of them. To avoid a major scene between Heathcliff and Edgar, which may be the death of Catherine, and upon the earnest appeals of Heathcliff in which he compares his deep affection for Catherine to Edgar's pale version of his love for her, Nelly reluctantly agrees to make the arrangement. In his impassioned plea, Heathcliff states (Ch. 14) :

> ... for every thought she spends on Linton, she spends a thousand on me!...... If he loved with all the powers of his puny being, he couldn't love as much in eighty years as I could in a day. And Catherine has a heart as deep as I have: the sea could be as readily contained in that horse-trough, as her whole affection be monopolized by him. Tush! He is scarcely a degree dearer to her than her dog, or her horse. It is not in him to be loved like me: how can she love in him what he has not?

After four days, Nelly Dean has not yet delivered the letter, but when the Lintons and their servants leave for church, Heathcliff enters, and what ensues is one of the most powerful love scenes ever written in the English language which is a singular, classic demonstration of Emily Brontë's power in the portrayal of the extremes of human passion and emotion. The accusations and recriminations pass furiously from one lover to the other, and contrary to the tone and contents of their speeches, the reader is aware that beneath these sharp, verbal exchanges and rebukes is a deep-rooted, immortal passion which transcends a plane far above temporal love and earthly pleasures. Cathy accuses Heathcliff of 'killing her' and thriving on it as well, and Heathcliff responds sharply (Ch. 15) :

> Are you possessed with a devil,..., to talk in that manner to me when you are dying? Do you reflect that all those words will be branded in my memory, and eating deeper eternally after you have left me? You know you lie to say I have killed you: and, Catherine, you know that I could as soon forget you as my existence! It is not sufficient for your infernal selfishness, that while you are at peace I shall writhe in the torment of hell?

Overcome by momentary weakness, Catherine replies (Ch. 15) :

I shall not be at peace,... I'm not wishing you greater torment than I have, Heathcliff. I only wish us never to be parted: and should a word of mine distress you hereafter, think I feel the same distress underground, and for my own sake, forgive me!

And when Heathcliff walks away, Catherine speaks to Nelly Dean and reveals a tortured soul anxious to escape an earthly body (Ch. 15) :

Oh, you see, Nelly, he would not relent a moment to keep me out of the grave. *That* is how I'm loved!... That is not *my* Heathcliff. I shall love mine yet; and take him with me: he's in my soul. And,... the thing that irks me most is this shattered prison, after all. I'm tired, tired of being enclosed here. I'm wearying to escape into that glorious world, and to be there: not seeing it dimly through tears, and yearning for it through the walls of an aching heart; but really with it, and in it.

Heathcliff then scooped up Catherine in a powerful embrace, and while holding her, admonished her for betraying their love (Ch. 15) :

You have killed yourself.... You loved me - then what *right* had you to leave me? What right - answer me - for the poor fancy you felt for Linton? Because misery, and degradation, and death, and nothing that God or satan could inflict would have parted us, *you*, of your own will, did it. I have not broken your heart, you have broken mine....Do I want to live? What kind of living will it be when you - oh, God! would *you* like to live with your soul in the grave?

With Catherine near death, the thought of life without her is already tormenting Heathcliff and reveals that his life will be intolerable; with Catherine dead, it will be like living without a soul. This was the last time the two met. Shortly afterwards, Edgar returned from church, and when he entered the room, Heathcliff placed the unconscious Catherine in his arms, much to his astonishment, and quickly left. At midnight, Catherine gave birth to a daughter and then died two hours later.

After the death of Catherine, Heathcliff's character is warped and twisted still further with his pre-occupation for revenge on the remaining Lintons and Earnshaws and his relentless search for the spirit of Catherine. Although he feels her presence, he is never able to 'see' or 'speak' with her, and Mr. Lockwood gives witness to this at the beginning of the novel when he explains his dream to Heathcliff and later hears him calling out to Catherine and trying to entice her in. In spite of his many efforts, Heathcliff is yet unable to make contact and communicate with her, and she remains just out of 'reach', to his continued, grievous torment.

The reader can also recognize that the book has two distinct halves, the first of which includes Heathcliff, Catherine, Hindley, Mr. & Mrs Earnshaw, Mr. & Mrs. Linton, and Edgar and Isabella, or in other words, the first generation of characters and their interactions right up to the birth of the young Catherine Linton and the death of Catherine Linton, her mother. With the burial of Catherine, the reader enters the second half of the book, which takes on a slightly milder tone, with the second generation of characters, young Catherine, Linton Heathcliff and Hareton Earnshaw. Edgar and Isabella Linton and Hindley

Earnshaw act as 'transitional characters', and Heathcliff, of course, as the principal character is the 'constant'. To complete the continuum, and to add unity to the plot as a whole, we have Nelly Dean and Joseph. With his beloved Catherine gone, he then focuses on acquiring complete revenge, and his cruelty and brutality give him small portions of fiendish pleasure and satisfaction.

Even with the death of Catherine, and overcome by grief, Heathcliff still blames Catherine for everything that has happened, and looks forward to a new, spiritual relationship with her. Their love transcends this temporal life, and her death is not the 'end' but a 'new beginning' for them which will only reach an end with Heathcliff's death and their blissful re-union as spiritual beings united in 'their heaven'. When Nelly Dean explains that Catherine never regained consciousness, looked very peaceful, and added that she hoped - " may she wake as kindly in the other world!", Heathcliff scathingly retorts (Ch. 16) :

> May she wake in torment!... Why she's a liar to the end! Where is she? Not *there* - not in heaven - not perished - where? Oh! you said you cared nothing for my sufferings! And I pray one prayer - I repeat it till my tongue stiffens - Catherine Earnshaw,[3] may you not rest as long as I am living! You said I killed you - haunt me then! The murdered *do* haunt their murderers. I believe - I know that ghosts *have* wandered on earth. Be with me always - take any form - drive me mad! only *do* not leave me in the abyss, where I cannot find you! Oh, God! it is unutterable! I *cannot* live without my life! I *cannot* live without my soul!

This description of his grief and his tormented soul is nothing short of 'Shakesperian' writing at its finest. It also sets the stage for the second half of the novel and Heathcliff's perpetual, but unsuccessful, search for Catherine in an 'altered state' while he remains in his hell on Earth. With his soul already 'in the grave', he is here only in the tormented flesh until he can resume his place with Catherine which gives him time to prey on his 'enemies' and derive sadistic pleasure from his revenge.

Heathcliff is now able to exact his revenge on Hindley who at first invited him into Wuthering Heights to cater to his desire for gambling, but Hindley's scheme 'backfired' and he was forced to mortgage his property to Heathcliff to cover his gambling debts. Heathcliff's sadism knows no bounds and in addition to impoverishing Hindley through gambling, he abets his drinking which eventually leads to his death, and once Hindley is out of the way, Heathcliff can concentrate on Hareton, his son. At Hindley's funeral, we see Heathcliff's malicious plan for Hareton when he lifts him onto a table and says to the uncomprehending child (Ch. 17) :

> Now, my bonny lad, you are mine! And we'll see if one tree won't grow as crooked as another, with the same wind to twist it!

---

3   Note that in death, he no longer refers to her as Catherine Linton but 'Catherine Earnshaw' which removes her from her earthly obligation as wife to Edgar Linton. They are one step closer to their ideal union.

Here Heathcliff indicates metaphorically how he will twist and corrupt Hareton and produce the same result as Wuthering Heights has twisted and corrupted Hindley. Emily Brontë use this metaphorically since the trees on Wuthering Heights, exposed to the constant winds across the moors are all twisted and bent in the same manner and same direction. Now, with Hindley gone and Hareton under his control, he is free to twist and shape him in the same manner and complete his revenge on the Earnshaws and his father even though he is no longer there. His revenge on Hindley, even in death, on this young, innocent child is nothing short of diabolical.

When the young Catherine meets Hareton many years later, we see the full extent of Heathcliff's corruption on him, since he, too, has turned out more like Heathcliff, and just as cruel and brutal, than his own father, Hindley. Hareton has a wide vocabulary of foul language, has bad manners, is cruel and contemptuous, is unable to read and write, and has a host of bad habits which appear not to have been modified in any way. One of the first things young Catherine witnesses Hareton do is the hanging of puppies over the back of the chair, the same thing Heathcliff had done to Isabella's small dog when they returned to Wuthering Heights after their honeymoon.

In Nelly Dean's narration, the next twelve years of relative peace and quiet are simply 'glossed over' as 'the happiest of my life', but things were about to change once more. After Isabella left Heathcliff, she bore him a son, Linton Heathcliff, whom she raised herself near London, but when Linton was twelve, she wrote a letter to her brother Edgar on her death-bed asking him to take care of Linton. Without hesitation, he went to London, and after Isabella's funeral, he returned to Thrushcross Grange with Linton. Upon hearing of Linton's arrival, Heathcliff immediately sent Joseph to secure his son to Wuthering Heights as his legitimate, legal right. With the weight and jurisdiction of the law against them, they were forced to deliver Linton over to Heathcliff in spite of their fears and better judgement. Heathcliff relished his victory and now had another person to humiliate and degrade, and he later used him as an additional weapon in his arsenal of devious tricks for ultimate revenge.

Heathcliff now realizes that Linton is the 'key' and 'last link' to a complete and successful revenge plot over the Lintons. If Linton, the male beneficiary of all the Lintons' real wealth, should marry the young Cathy, he would than have supremacy after Edgar Linton's demise. Should Heathcliff himself pass away, his son would then be master of both houses, Wuthering Heights and Thrushcross Grange, something which he was not able to manage in his own lifetime. Not only would he be master of both houses but also young Catherine Linton, and Hareton, Hindley's son, would be under his control.

There was also a possibility of a second scenario, and that, of course, was that if young Linton should die and Heathcliff survive, which was a distinct possibility since Linton was not in good health, Heathcliff would inherit all, and be in control. Upon arrival at the Lintons', Nelly Dean described him as 'a pale, delicate, effeminate boy', and the next day when Linton arrived at Wuthering Heights, Joseph, after a 'grave inspection', suggested that the Lintons had swapped him for young Catherine. Heathcliff was anxious to meet Linton for the first time but referred to him as a chattel and an 'it', rather than a young child in need of fatherly affection. As Nelly arrived with the boy, he said (Ch. 20) :

> I feared I should have to come down and fetch my property myself. You've brought it, have you? Let us see what we can make of it.

After a quick perusal of his son Linton, Heathcliff exclaims half in admiration and half in derision (Ch. 20) :

> God! what a beauty! What a lovely, charming thing!... Haven't they reared it on snails and sour milk, Nelly? Oh, damn my soul! but that's worse than I expected - and the devil knows I was not sanguine!

Heathcliff does not see any of his own characteristics in his son, and after another close inspection of him in the house, he proclaims, "Thou art thy mother's child, entirely! Where is *my* share in thee, puling chicken?" showing his disappointment in the young boy. Upon leaving, Nelly cautions Heathcliff to treat the boy well, and Heathcliff assures him that he will be brought up as a gentleman to be superior to those around him. Heathcliff's plan of action was 'in place' well before Linton arrived.

Catherine and Linton do not see each other again for almost four years, and in that time the diabolical Heathcliff has hatched another devilish plot as only he could devise. Upon a walk on the moors, Nelly and Catherine have a 'chance meeting' with Heathcliff and Hareton, and Heathcliff invites them to Wuthering Heights. Heathcliff wishes to re-introduce Catherine and Linton with their marriage in mind. Nelly is reluctant, but Catherine is curious, and they finally return to Wuthering Heights where Cathy meets Linton who is now taller and has the bearing of a gentleman. In great contrast to Linton is Hareton who is gruff, crude, poorly educated, illiterate, in fact, and with many boorish habits. Catherine wishes to see Linton again, and when her father forbids it, a correspondence is set up surreptitiously only to be stopped later by Nelly. Heathcliff's plan of marriage between Cathy and Linton has now been interfered with and is in danger of failing, so Heathcliff decides to take more drastic action.

Another 'chance meeting' occurs near the fence of the Grange park. When Catherine falls off the wall onto the other side, Heathcliff tries to convince Catherine to come to Wuthering Heights to see Linton, whom he says is pining away for her and may possibly die. Once again, Nelly is insistent on declining the offer and manages to persuade Cathy not to go, but the next day, Catherine convinces Nelly to accompany her to Wuthering Heights to ascertain for themselves Linton's condition; they have unwittingly fallen into Heathcliff's perverse plan. Once there, they indeed find Linton in very poor health, and his symptoms appear to be those of consumption. Catherine and Linton express their love for one another and Linton wishes to make her his wife, but for the moment, Catherine wants only a lesser relationship more along the lines of a brother and sister. On their return to the Grange, Nelly acquires a severe cold, and neither she nor her ailing father is aware of her secret visits to see Linton in spite of Nelly's pleadings and insistence that she not go there again.

Heathcliff may appear to remain in the background, but his part as the central character and figure of the novel is not yet over; he is still the chief manipulator of events between Cathy and Linton, even in his absence. When Cathy's father learns of her secret visits to Wuthering Heights, he forbids her to go there and she obeys, but he also extends an invitation to Linton to visit the Grange. Linton, probably under Heathcliff's close supervision and direction, suggests a meeting on the moors, and Edgar Linton agrees only after his resistance is worn down by Catherine's and Linton's pleadings; their first meeting is anything but successful. Catherine, accompanied by Nelly, finds Linton in poor physical condition, and he expresses terror at having to return to Wuthering Heights, and Heathcliff, who wishes them to be married before Linton gets any worse.

At their second meeting on the moors, Heathcliff is determined to be more forceful in his actions to bring about his desired outcome when he perceives that 'time is of the essence'. As Catherine and Linton converse, Heathcliff arrives and is highly interested in Edgar Linton's condition, and once Heathcliff learns that he is dying, he is more determined than ever. Catherine and Linton must marry before he, too, expires, if his plan for total control of all the Earnshaw and Linton properties is to be fulfilled. Completely terrorized by Heathcliff, Linton piteously pleads with Catherine to accompany him back to Wuthering Heights which she and Nelly reluctantly agree to do. Catherine's father is dying and she is anxious to return to the Grange to tend to him in his final days, but Heathcliff has a more devious plan in mind.

Once at Wuthering Heights, the diabolical Heathcliff locks Catherine and Nelly in, and in an ensuing struggle to obtain the key, Heathcliff slaps Catherine senseless. They wish to escape their forceable detention but cannot find a way out, and Heathcliff is determined to hold them there until Catherine agrees to marry Linton. Finally, Catherine gives in and the two are married, but she is still held captive although Nelly is released and allowed to return to the Grange. Linton now shows his 'ugly' side, and he, too, keeps Catherine imprisoned. The four men sent to rescue Catherine return alone convinced by Heathcliff that she is too ill to travel, and the servant sent to bring back Mr. Green, the lawyer, also returns alone. The lawyer, Heathcliff realizes, must be kept from Edgar Linton at all costs to prevent him from changing his will now that Catherine is married to the dying Linton; Heathcliff has bribed Mr. Green as well to keep him away.

Catherine is finally released by Linton, and manages to escape through an upstairs window and returns to the Grange just in time to be with her father before he dies. After Edgar Linton's death, Mr. Green finally arrives and takes charge of the house on behalf of Heathcliff; his plan is now almost complete, and he is close to the possession of all the real property and wealth of both the Earnshaws and Lintons. With the burial of Edgar Linton, Heathcliff arrived the next day to 'collect' Catherine to Wuthering Heights to look after her new husband Linton, who is himself near death. While she is packing, Heathcliff reveals to Nelly Dean that after Edgar Linton was buried next to Catherine, he had the sexton remove the dirt from Cathy's coffin, and he opened it to look upon her face once more. The sexton had difficulty pulling him away. He was then convinced that she has returned to him, spiritually, after years of torture. (Ch. 29) :

> Now, since I've seen her, I'm pacified - a little. It was a strange way of killing, not by
> inches, but fractions of hairbreadths, to beguile me with the spectre of a hope, through
> eighteen years!

Heathcliff's revenge is almost complete but his evil, sadistic nature has not been fully satiated; he is determined to inflict more pain and misery on Linton, his own and only son, and his new daughter-in-law, Catherine. He refused the attentions of a doctor to Linton, and with only Catherine to care for him, Linton died several weeks later. By his contrivance, Heathcliff put the couple together, and now with his interference, he brings it to an end with the express purpose of collecting on Linton's holdings, which by 'reversion' go back to a male primogenitor. Catherine, now without money or friends to help her, and without anywhere else to go, is forced to stay on at Wuthering Heights, much to her frustration.

From this point on, the novel takes on a new direction for both Heathcliff and Catherine; the novel is in need of a conclusion, and the old, Catherine- Heathcliff relationship needs to be resolved. As well, the young widow, Catherine, the last remaining Linton, is again 'available', as is Hareton, the last remaining Earnshaw. These two love-relationships have to be satisfactorily resolved, one a temporal love, and the other, a pure, idyllic and spiritual one. The earthly love between Catherine and Hareton gets off to a shaky start, since they are from two 'different worlds' in regard to manner and culture, she being cultured and educated, and he being illiterate and 'backward', hidden away from the world at large at Wuthering Heights. But it is obvious that Hareton is infatuated with Catherine and willing to make changes to win her affection, and Heathcliff, it appears, is on his way to being re-united with his beloved Catherine. And for the remainder of the novel, although Heathcliff never relinquishes his hate, spite, malice, or chance for revenge on his 'enemies', his focus appears to shift toward his final re-union with the spirit of Catherine which he now 'sees' as real and within his 'grasp'.

Events are allowed to unfold and Lockwood returns to London after his recovery at Thrushcross Grange, with the intention of returning in the fall to settle up with Heathcliff. When Lockwood returns the following September, he discovers that things really have changed; at Thrushcross Grange he is not met by Nelly Dean but by an old woman smoking a pipe. He learns that Nelly has returned to Wuthering Heights, and he proceeds there to witness a happy, young couple, Catherine and Hareton, reading and then making ready to take a walk. He avoids them by slipping around to the kitchen entrance where he meets a joyful Nelly and the eternally, disgruntled Joseph. There Lockwood learns the rest of the story and what has transpired since he left. Heathcliff has just recently died, and under mysterious circumstances as well. Nelly gladly fills him in on the strange curiosity of his behaviour and his subsequent death.

Nelly describes how Catherine and Hareton, two unlikely lovers, slowly and cautiously grew attached to one another over the months. Hareton was at first shy and afraid, and Catherine treated him indifferently and contemptuously, but with the passage of time, they became accustomed to one another and their friendship grew to be one of a loving relationship. They now had an ally in one another to ward off the tyrannies of

Heathcliff and Joseph; together they have strength to face them and forge a hopeful future for themselves. Catherine had even dared to challenge Heathcliff after Hareton tore out Joseph's favourite bushes and Heathcliff admonished her for encouraging Hareton to do so.

It was this incident which led Heathcliff to carry out his last acts of violence as he grabbed Catherine by the hair and prepared to throw her into the kitchen. Suddenly, as he looked intently into her eyes, he relaxed his grip; it was something about her gaze which calmed and soothed him for the moment. Later that evening when Heathcliff entered the room and both Catherine and Hareton looked at him at the same moment, Heathcliff was taken aback as he noticed that both their eyes were like those of his beloved Cathy. This completely disarmed Heathcliff and from that moment on, he lost his will for revenge. He states (Ch. 33) :

> An absurd termination to my violent exertions? I get lever and mattocks to demolish the two houses, and train myself to be capable of working like Hercules, and when everything is ready, and in my power, I find the will to lift a slate of either roof has vanished!... I have lost the faculty of enjoying their destruction, and I am too idle to destroy for nothing.

Suddenly, to Heathcliff, Hareton seems, "a personification of my youth, not a human being:" and from that moment sinks deeper into his monomania for his beloved as he described how every aspect of his senses, and in all things around him, he sees Catherine. Heathcliff feels a 'change' come over him, but when Nelly questioned him on its meaning, he was not fully able to describe it. He is healthy, but he is losing the will to live (Ch.33) :

> ... I cannot continue in this condition! I have to remind myself to breathe - almost to remind my heart to beat! And it is like bending back a stiff spring: it is by compulsion that I do the slightest act not prompted by one thought, and by compulsion, that I notice anything alive or dead, which is not associated with one universal idea.

He then described to Nelly his wish for an end to this Earthly life (Ch. 33) :

> ... I have a single wish, and my whole being and faculties are yearning to attain it. They have yearned towards it so long, and so unwaveringly, that I'm convinced it *will* be reached - and *soon* because it has devoured my existence: I am swallowed in the anticipation of its fulfilment....O, God! It is a long fight, I wish it were over!

For the next few days, Heathcliff began to act very strangely: he ate rarely, he walked about and muttered to himself, he seemed joyful and pleased, and wished to be alone. One night he wandered out onto the moors and did not return until daylight, and when Nelly prodded him with her curiosity as to his whereabouts, he answered (Ch. 34) :

> Last night, I was on the threshold of hell. Today, I am within sight of my heaven. I have my eyes on it hardly three feet to sever me!

When Heathcliff uses the phrase, 'my heaven', he, of course, refers to his final, spiritual union with Catherine Earnshaw. He feels that it is close at hand, and he can 'see' her just a few feet away. In this Heathcliff can rejoice, and it brings about the notable change in his personality and demeanour. At night, Nelly hears him speaking to someone downstairs, and when she goes to investigate, finds him speaking to 'Catherine' who is not there in reality. Upon noticing Nelly, he suggests that he should send for Mr. Green in the morning to prepare his will. Nelly's Christian thoughts turn to his salvation and she suggests that he repent of his injustices, but Heathcliff claims that he has committed no injustices and has no reason to repent. For the villainous Heathcliff, exacting malicious revenge on the people who have degraded him, and caused him injury and suffering, such retaliation is fully justified and required no acts of contrition or repentence. Nelly then reminds him (Ch. 34) :

> ... from the time you were thirteen years old, you have lived a selfish, unchristian life; and probably hardly had a Bible in your hands during all that period. You must have forgotten the contents of the book, and you may not have space to search it now.

But Heathcliff is not concerned with a Christian burial or afterlife and its Heaven, he is only concerned with having *his* burial instructions carried out as *he* has requested, and particularly his special instructions to the sexton. He entreats Nelly (Ch. 34) :

> You and Hareton may, if you please, accompany me: and mind, particularly, to notice that the sexton obeys my directions concerning the two coffins! No minister need come; nor need anything be said over me - I tell you, I have nearly attained my heaven; and that of others is altogether unvalued and uncoveted by me!

The closest thing to an apology that Heathcliff utters are his words to Nelly, "I believe you think me a fiend! Something too horrible to live under a decent roof!", and then to Catherine (Ch. 34) :

> Will *you* come, chuck? I'll not hurt you. No, to you, I've made myself worse than the devil. Well, there is *one* who won't shrink from my company! By God! she's relentless. Oh, damn it! It's unutterably too much for flesh and blood to bear - even mine.

When Mr. Kenneth, the doctor, was called by Nelly to see Heathcliff in his last days of distress, he refused to see anyone, and bid everyone to leave him alone. The next day when Nelly noticed his window open, she used a spare key to enter his room and opened the panelled bed; there she found Heathcliff dead with a look of supreme happiness on his face (Ch. 34) :

> His eyes met mine so keen and fierce,...he seemed to smile....I tried to close his eyes: to extinguish, if possible, that frightful, life-like gaze of exultation, before anyone else beheld it. They would not shut: they seemed to sneer at my attempts; and his lips and sharp white teeth sneered too!

Old Joseph was quite pleased at Heathcliff's final demise, assumed that the devil had carried off his soul, and that Heathcliff 'grinned in mockery'. He fell to his knees and gave thanks that the rightful master, Hareton, was returned to Wuthering Heights, and ironically, the only person who appeared seriously grieved at Heathcliff's death was Hareton, the one who was 'most wronged' (Ch. 34) :

> He sat by the corpse all night, weeping in bitter earnest. He pressed its hand, and kissed the sarcastic, savage face that everyone else shrank from contemplating; and bemoaned him with that strong grief which springs naturally from a generous heart, though it be tough as tempered steel.

When the doctor was called, he was perplexed as to the cause of death, and Nelly did not mention that he had not eaten in four days nor his strange behaviour before that. Nelly, a friend of Heathcliff's since birth, saw to it that he was buried according to his instructions, much 'to the scandal of the whole neighbourhood'. But Heathcliff's spirit was said not to be at rest; stories arose that his apparition was seen 'near the church', 'on the moor', and even within Wuthering Heights. And Joseph claimed that he had 'seen two of 'em looking out his chamber window, on every rainy night since his death'. Also, Nelly had a strange story to tell of a shepherd boy, crying terribly', whom she had met with a sheep and two lambs and who refused to proceed along the path because he had seen Heathcliff and a woman and dared not pass.

Even in death, Heathcliff was a powerful and formidable figure, and Wuthering Heights remained a grim, dreary, windswept place which frightened Nelly who was happy to be returning to Thrushcross Grange with the young couple after their wedding vows on New Years' Day, 1803. Only Joseph and a young helper-companion would remain at Wuthering Heights to maintain it. As for Nelly, she believed the dead were 'at peace' and that talk of various sightings of the two, deceased lovers was simply a product of overly-active and creative imaginations, but these sightings also lend credence to the belief that Heathcliff and Catherine have finally been re-united in death., and raised their love to mythical proportions. And, as for Mr. Lockwood, he felt the same as Nelly after he inspected the three headstones on the moor and surveyed the quiet countryside (Ch. 34) :

> I lingered round them, under that benign sky: watched the moths fluttering among the heath and hare bells; listened to the soft wind breathing through the grass; and wondered how any one could ever imagine unquiet slumbers in that quiet earth.

With Heathcliff's death, the action has now moved 'full circle' from one generation to the next, although the action appears to continue at a different level from Heathcliff's 'unquiet soul' on Earth to an 'unquiet soul' in the spiritual world, if the stories are to be believed. For Cathy and Heathcliff, they were unable to obtain love, peace and harmony in their life on Earth, but they have achieved it in death if we believe the observations and beliefs of Nelly Dean and Mr. Lockwood.

One of the themes found in *Wuthering Heights* is that 'love conquers all' or 'love overcomes all', and even though Hareton was as wild, cruel, and vicious as Heathcliff, the love of young Catherine changed all that, and Hareton became a changed, loved, and respectable person. Nelly Dean witnessed the miraculous change and made this observation (Ch. 33) :

> His honest, warm, and intelligent nature shook off rapidly the clouds of ignorance and degradation in which it had been bred; and Catherine's sincere commendations acted as a spur to his industry. His brightening mind brightened his features, and added spirit and nobility to their aspect: I could hardly fancy it the individual I had beheld on the day I discovered my little lady at Wuthering Heights,...

For the second generation of Earnshaws and Lintons, Catherine and Hareton achieved the temporal, earthly love which eluded their predecessors, and the stage is now set for a peaceful and happy life of the young couple. The novel then ends on a peaceful note with the two couples finally at their own peace.

The two major themes which run concurrently through the novel are 'love', and 'hate and revenge', which in Heathcliff's case are inextricably tied. From the beginning we see the love of Mr. Earnshaw for a homeless orphan from Liverpool, Heathcliff, whom he brings home. This soon turns to the hatred of Heathcliff by Mr. Earnshaw's son, Hindley, but Catherine's suspicions of the new-comer soon turn to love which is returned in kind. This mutual love, which is not of this world, grows and becomes the dominant love-story throughout the novel. The other loves like those of Cathy-Edgar, Hindley-Frances, Heathcliff-Isabella, Catherine-Linton, and finally Catherine-Hareton, shrink by comparison, and are introduced by Emily Brontë simply to demonstrate to the readers the difference in depth, and kind, of these loves to that of Heathcliff-Cathy which dominates the novel. Firstly, none of these loves are as enduring as theirs, and secondly the love of Heathcliff-Cathy exists on an entirely different plane, one of a supra-natural, ideal love which cannot be attained on this Earth. Until then, they must both suffer the agonies of this temporal life and wait for the 'consummate' bonding of their souls in the afterlife in a 'heaven' of their own making. Until that time, they each seem only to add to each other's misery and grief, of which the primary cause is Cathy's marriage to Edgar Linton to better her social standing and obtain an earthly 'heaven'. The frustration of their love is pervasive throughout, and the 'love theme' is not finally resolved until Heathcliff's death near the end of the novel and his final re-union with Cathy in the spirit world.

The 'hate and revenge' theme also pervades the novel and can be found as a continuous thread through the entire novel which only clarifies and defines the character of Heathcliff as one filled with hatred, cruelty, brutality, violence, and sadism. As a basic premise, Emily Brontë seems to demonstrate that his disturbing, negative qualities are a result of Heathcliff's need for affection and his loss of love by Cathy in her marriage to Edgar, and that they only dissipate at the end of the novel when he feels the restoration of this love when her spirit returns to visit him. Thereafter, he immediately loses his desire for revenge and looks forward to his own death and a reunion with Cathy to the exclusion of everything else. And at the end we are left with a glimmer of hope for at least one happy ending, but this, of course, is done at the expense of several other potentially successful relationships within the plot.

Another interesting element of Emily Brontë's writing is the influence of the 'Gothic' which seems to have intrigued her and which she effectively employed. From the outset, the readers see this novel as an extraordinary and powerful tale with features of the super-natural, the fantastic, and ghostly spirits early in the story. Lockwood's night at Wuthering Heights is beset by fearful dreams and the ghost of Catherine Linton. Lockwood is gripped by the 'fingers of a little, ice-cold hand', and when it refused to let go, he said, "Terror made me cruel;..." and [I] "rubbed it to and fro till the blood ran down and soaked the bed clothes:..." (Ch.3) These ghostly, and ghastly, scenes are, of course, firmly intercon-nected with the wild, barren landscape of Wuthering Heights, Heathcliff's dwelling place in a remote and forbidding part of North England. She describes the windswept land-scape and wild scenery of Wuthering Heights as (Ch.1) :

> 'Wuthering' being a significant provincial adjective descriptive of the atmospheric tumult to which its station is exposed in stormy weather.[4] Pure, bracing ventilation they must have up there at all times, indeed: one may guess the power of the north wind blowing over the edge, by the excessive slant of a few stunted firs at the end of the house; and by a range of gaunt thorns all stretching their limbs one way, as if craving alms of the sun.

This wild, inhospitable landscape is only slightly mollified in the description of Thrushcross Grange which seems to be only a minor improvement. The scenery, land-scape, and terrain all seem to be 'magnified' and super-enhanced, almost to the level of being 'supra-natural', by its chief agent, Heathcliff, whose stern countenance and sallow complexion parallels his dark, dreary, and sombre personal qualities. The character and the landscape appear to go 'hand in hand' and complement one another, positively, as does the uniqueness of the servants, the sullen, sanctimonious Joseph, and the fearful Zillah.

Although these Gothic elements can be identified throughout the novel, perhaps the scene which has the most impact is found in the chapter where Heathcliff goes to the Grange to retrieve young Catherine after she had run away and attended her father's illness, death, and funeral. He encounters Nelly in the parlour and describes a scene which is nothing short of morbid and classically macabre. As the sexton was preparing Edgar Linton's grave alongside Catherine who had been buried eighteen years before, Heathcliff persuaded him to remove the earth from her coffin-lid. He describes to Nelly what he did next (Ch. 29) :

> ... I opened it. I thought, once, I would have stayed there, when I saw her face again - it is hers yet - he had hard work to stir me; but he said it would change, if the air blew on it, and so I struck one side of the coffin loose, and covered it up:...

---

4   'Top Withens' is about four miles outside of Haworth and is believed to be the model Emily used for Wuthering Heights. At the top of the Pennine Way, it is truly amidst a barren, wild, wind- swept and seemingly inhospitable landscape.

Heathcliff then goes on to bribe the sexton to remove one side of Catherine's coffin, not Linton's side, but the other so that the open side in his own coffin will match with hers, side by side, and the two of them can dwell together in eternity when it is his time to be buried. Nelly scolds him for being 'wicked' and disturbing the dead, but Heathcliff retorts (Ch.29) :

> I disturbed nobody, Nelly,... and I gave some ease to myself. I shall be a great deal more comfortable now; and you'll have a better chance of keeping me underground, when I get there.... No! she has disturbed me, night and day, through eighteen years - incessantly - remorselessly - till yesternight;...

Heathcliff's strange behaviour toward the end of the novel, and his unusual demise, as described by Ellen Dean, also adds to its Gothic 'flavour'. Nelly finds Heathcliff in the kitchen 'talking' to Cathy as if she was there, and he appears wildly and excitedly happy; he has now made 'contact' with Cathy in her spirit form. He follows the apparition's every move with his eyes although Nelly sees no one near him; he wishes to make his will and appears to be making preparations to leave this world for the next. Several days later when Nelly finds Heathcliff dead in his bed, she tries to recompose the hideous expression on his face, but fails; Heathcliff simply sneered back at her. And finally, the unnatural adds to the Gothic element when many stories are told of Heathcliff's and Catherine's ghostly meetings on the moors on 'rainy nights' and dark evenings 'threatening thunder', creating myths and legends which terrify the superstitious, local people. All of these elements appear to be combined in 'measured', but proper, portions which stimulated and titillated Victorian readers' interests, and no doubt frightened some, and terrifed others.

12

AGNES GREY

Agnes Grey is the 'fictional' story of a poor clergyman's daughter who decides to go out into the world to earn a living to help support her mother and father's income and also to 'test' herself in the world at large. She takes on the job of governess to Mrs. Bloomfield who is recommended to her by her aunt as, 'a very nice woman'. The situation is a disaster of the first order since the children are completely undisciplined and generally unteachable. Agnes is put in the awkward position of having to try to teach these overindulged children without having any recourse to restrain, punish or reward them. Without these necessary levers, the situation does not improve and eventually she is fired for 'incompetence'.

After returning home for a vacation, she again advertises her services and is soon offered another position of governess to the Murrays at Horton Lodge, seventy miles away from home. The salary of £50 per annum is twice that of her first situation, but she is treated only slightly better by the girls in her charge, Rosalie and Matilda Murray.

The only good to come from her attempts at 'occupation' in the world is her acquaintance with the new curate, Mr. Weston, who is the only one to show her any kindness. Eventually they both leave their situations at Horton but meet again when, by coincidence, they both re-locate to the town of A-. After resuming their friendship, and an introduction to her mother, Mr. Weston asks for her hand in marriage. She accepts and the two live happily ever after.

As a writer and a Brontë, Anne Brontë has always been compared to her two, older sisters and their works, and completely under-estimated in the bargain. Today that situation is being reviewed and revised, and closer scrutiny and reflection of her writings indicate that she possessed a 'depth of character' easily equal to that of Charlotte and Emily. And if her skill as a writer was not equal to that of her famous sisters, it certainly was not very far behind; George A. Moore (1852-1933) the Anglo-Irish novelist, in fact, called her 'the greatest of the Brontës', but unfortunately not too many critics would agree with that.

Anne Brontë's first novel, *Agnes Grey*, although classified as a fiction is, in fact, based upon Anne's life experiences as a governess between the years 1839 and 1845, at Blake Hall in Mirfield, and Thorp Green Hall at Little Ouseburn, near York. The book is actually an exposé of the contemptuous treatment of governesses and servants by families of nobility, aristocracy and upper classes in Victorian times. Although it was favourably received by the ordinary readers of the day for its behind-the-scenes insights, it was highly criticized by the aristocracy and nobility who did not like their beliefs, opinions, and lifestyles held up to review, close scrutiny, or ridicule. It was also highly critical of the education of the children of these families who hired governesses to teach their children and then 'hobbled them' in such a way as to make their efforts ineffectual, and any improvements impossible. And with conflicting sets of rules to follow, no progress with the children's education could be made. This was the situation which Anne Brontë found herself in, and which she describes through the eyes of 'Agnes Grey' at Wellwood Mansion.

From the very outset of the novel, Anne Brontë wishes to make it clear to the reader that *Agnes Grey* is a novel based on real events which she can 'candidly lay before the public' because she is "shielded by my own obscurity,[1] and by the lapse of years, and a few fictitious names," (Ch. 1) :

> ALL TRUE HISTORIES CONTAIN instruction; though, in some, the treasure may
> be hard to find, and when found, so trivial in quantity that the dry, shrivelled kernel
> scarcely compensates for the trouble of cracking the nut.

Among the criticisms of *Agnes Grey* by the upper classes were that the author, in fact, embellished and exaggerated some scenes of the children's bad behaviour, and they either 'could not' or 'would not' believe them to be true. One critic even accused her of promoting 'propaganda', but throughout her life, Anne Brontë was known for her scrupulous honesty and integrity. In her 'Preface to the Second Edition' to *The Tenant of Wildfell Hall*, Anne Brontë makes brief mention of these very criticisms of *Agnes Grey*, and says in her own defense:

> As the story of Agnes Grey was accused of extravagant overcolouring in those very
> parts that were carefully copied from the life, with a most scrupulous avoidance of
> all exaggeration,...

Charlotte Brontë also came to Anne's defense in the 'Preface to the Second Edition', to *The Tenant of Wildfell Hall*, attesting to her unwavering honesty, "... Anne Brontë would put her hand in the fire before she would compromise the truth:...".

---

1   Anne Brontë wrote under the pseudonym, Acton Bell.

Anne saw her writing as a social commentary, just as Charlotte did, which she thought important and worthy of address although she had no illusions regarding her total contribution (Preface to Second Edition, July 22,1848):

> Let it not be imagined, however, that I consider myself competent to reform the errors and abuses of society, but only that I would fain contribute my humble quota towards so good an aim; and if I can gain the public ear at all, I would rather whisper a few wholesome truths therein than much soft nonsense.

Anne Brontë always wrote with a purpose, or moral, in mind rather than just pure entertainment. After her first three chapters of *Agnes Grey*, in which she outlined many of the torments she had to endure from her charges, and admitting that these were but half of their 'vexatious propensities', she indicates her main purpose in writing the novel (Ch. IV) :

> ... but my design, in writing the last few pages, was not to amuse, but to benefit those whom it might concern:... if a parent has, therefrom, gathered any useful hint, or an unfortunate governess received thereby the slightest benefit, I amwell rewarded for my pains.

Although much of *Agnes Grey* is fiction, a good portion of it is based on the life experiences Anne herself endured at the hands of her employers and her charges. Of the three Brontë sisters, she was undoubtedly the most 'outgoing' and congenial, contrary to Charlotte who thought her even worse at making friends than she was, as well as the most adventurous and successful outside their homelife at the Parsonage. Anne was, in fact, the first of the Brontës to 'try her wings' and leave home for a full-time job as governess at Blake Hall in Mirfield in April, 1839, some twenty miles away. She also remained away from home for the longest period of any of her family, five years at Thorp Green Hall near Little Ouseburn. She was also the most successful in 'transplanting' herself to totally new environments without having to return home repeatedly to 're-group', 're-charge', and re-establish herself like her two older sisters. Anne Brontë is indeed much more worthy and deserving of praise and acclaim than she has been accredited with in the past; each of them was unique, and their writing styles differed.

At the beginning of the novel, we get what might be a true assessment of Anne's position within the Brontë family as the youngest of the children, one who had to 'prove her worth' to the rest of the family, and to herself. Although the situation is based on fiction, there may be an element of reflective truth in Agnes Grey's words of explanation (Ch. I) :

> I, being the younger by five or six years, was always regarded as the *child*, and the pet of the family - father, mother, and sister, all combined to spoil me - not by foolish indulgence to render me fractious and ungovernable, but by ceaseless kindness to make me too helpless and dependent, too unfit for buffeting with the cares and turmoils of life.

We also learn that Agnes also had a bit of 'wander lust', among her other qualities, when she expressed "a vague and secret wish to see a little more of the world." As well, she was disappointed that her offers of help around the house were mostly turned down, and "... although a woman in my own estimation, I was still a child in theirs." Both Agnes and Anne were eighteen years old when they went out on their first job as governesses, and both were determined to prove themselves: "You do not know half the wisdom and prudence I possess, because I have never been tried." (Ch. I) Agnes asserts herself and then points out to her sister Mary (Ch.I) :

> You think, because I always do as you bid me, I have no judgment of my own: but
> only try me - that is all I ask - and you shall see what I can do.

In her youthful exuberance and idealism, Agnes eagerly looks forward to her entry into the world and to make her way through it. She sees something exciting and, "... something exhilarating in the idea of being driven to straits, and thrown upon our own resources." She adds (Ch. I) :

> How delightful it would be to be a governess! To go out into the world; to enter upon
> a new life; to act for myself; to exercise my unused faculties; to try my unknown
> powers; to earn my own maintenance,...

Untrained as a teacher, she felt confident that her 'clear remembrance' of her own thoughts and feelings in early childhood 'would be a surer guide than the instructions of the most mature adviser'. This idealistic view and overconfident approach soon proved to be 'fatally flawed' once she was thrown into the maw of the real world, the standards of Victorian society, and the vicious cruelty of some people. Agnes's first encounter as a governess was with the Bloomfields at Wellwood House for £25 per year; in reality this was Anne Brontë's encounter with the Inghams at Blake Hall in Mirfield.[2] Hers was not a gentle introduction to the 'world at large', or to the position of governess. She expected to be greeted and treated with respect, civility and dignity, and like a member of the family, but soon discovered that this was not the case, and that the 'lot' and 'place' of a governess was little above that of a field-hand, servant, or maid. The entire experience was both humiliating and shocking to Anne who, up till then, had always been used to love, respect, civility, and tenderness.

Agnes Grey is not only the study of Victorian society and the trials and tribulations of a governess within that society but also a study of people and character. Throughout the novel we are introduced to a number of persons whose character and qualities are exposed. Anne Brontë, through Agnes Grey, is adept at exposing their short-comings and negative qualities, not by elaborating in detail as one might expect, but by describing the critical and noteworthy events and incidents in their simplest terms. She was convinced

---

2   Blake Hall was, in fact, not far from Roe Head where Charlotte, Emily, and Anne had gone to school.

that 'truth' would always rise to the top and prevail (Preface to the Second Edition, 'Tenant', July 22, 1848) :

> I wished to tell the truth, for truth always conveys its own moral to those who are able to receive it. But as the priceless treasure too frequently hides at the bottom of a well, it needs some courage to dive for it,...

Upon her arrival at the Bloomfields, she immediately received a chilly reception from Mrs. Bloomfield, and glowing reports about her children Tom, Mary Ann, Fanny, and Harriet. From the very outset she noticed that they were 'bold, lively children', and 'remarkably free from shyness'. These were all auspicious indicators, but Agnes soon hoped to be on friendly terms with them as their guide, mentor, teacher, and governess. Unfortunately, nothing like that was in store for her, and she found them all poorly behaved, poorly mannered, poorly educated, completely uncooperative, and sadly incorrigible.

The eldest, Tom, demanded most of her time and attention and the first indicator of things to come was when he commanded her to stand by and observe him ride his hobbyhorse for a full ten minutes 'watching how manfully he used his whip and spurs'. And when Agnes suggested that he not use them so on a real pony, he retorted, "Oh, yes, I will!... I'll cut into him like smoke! Eeh! my word! but he shall sweat for it." (Ch. II)

Young Tom Bloomfield's lust for savagery and cruelty never abated during Agnes's entire stay, and all of her efforts were in vain. While wandering about the garden, Agnes noticed some contraptions which Tom explained were bird-traps, and when she asked what he would do with them once he had captured them, she was informed that normally he gave them 'to the cat', or "cut them to pieces with my penknife". But his next captives he meant to 'roast alive', and when Agnes tried to point out the wickedness of such activities, he simply scoffed at her and reported that his father had done the same things, and that his Uncle Robson only laughed. It was obvious to Agnes that he was not learning worthy actions by 'precept and example' from his parents and elders, but just the opposite.

Although Agnes persevered and did not give up hope on her ideals, it did not take long for her to realize that she was fighting not only an 'uphill battle' but also a 'losing battle' with Master Tom and the others. In fact, Tom had another side to his nature which was equally bad as his cruelty; he was violent. In an effort to keep his sisters, and governess, 'in line', he used his hands and feet against them, and considering that he was a strong, growing, young boy, it was 'no trifling consequence'. And in his most violent moods her only recourse was "to throw him on his back, and hold his hands and feet till the frenzy was somewhat abated". (Ch. III)

In addition to stopping Tom doing what he shouldn't be, Agnes also had the added problem of trying to get him to do things which he should, such as learning and repeating his lessons, and reading. In many cases, he would staunchly refuse, and Agnes was increasingly frustrated at having no recourse to his firmly-fixed bad behaviour. For the mild-mannered Agnes, she had some clear solutions to Tom's problem (Ch. III) :

> A few sound boxes on the ear on such occasions, might have settled the matter easily enough:

and later in the same chapter (Ch.III) :

> Here again, a good birch rod might have been serviceable; but, as my powers were so limited, I must make the best use of what I had.... Patience, Firmness, and Perseverance were my only weapons; and these I resolved to use to the utmost.

As for the other children, Agnes was no more successful with them. Mary Ann's favourite pastime was 'rolling on the floor', or 'lying there like a log till dinner or tea time'; it was more of a test of wills than anything else, and each time Mary Ann was 'victorious', it simply served 'to encourage her for a future contest'; little by little Agnes Grey was losing ground to their persistent misbehaviour. No amount of threatening, scolding, entreating, or coaxing had any effect on Mary Ann, and when she tried to punish the child, she struck back with piercing screams which usually brought in her mother who then only found fault with Agnes.

When Fanny entered the schoolroom, Agnes had hopes of receiving a mild and pleasant child but that illusion quickly evaporated. Agnes soon found her to be mischievous, intractable, and 'given up to falsehood and deception'. Her favourite 'weapons' were spitting in peoples' faces and 'bellowing like a bull' when she did not get her way. Naturally, all of the problems with the children were charged to the 'incompetence' of the governess, and Mr. and Mrs. Bloomfield's less-than-obvious remarks about their children's deteriorating behaviour were made in Agnes's presence.

Agnes's problems originated mainly with the uncooperative parents who had overindulged their children, let their behaviour and manners badly deteriorate, and then brought in an unsuspecting governess to try to bring them back under control, as well as entertain and educate them. Without the proper parental backing and levers of rewards and punishments, Agnes soon recognized the futility of it all (Ch. III) :

> ..; but I had no rewards to offer, and as for punishments, I was given to understand, the parents reserved that privilege to themselves; and yet they expected me to keep my pupils in order.

Agnes's pupils were completely intractable and the only person they responded to was their father when he had completely lost his temper and patience with them. Agnes describes them as (Ch. III) :

> ... my pupils had no more notion of obedience than a wild, unbroken colt. The habitual fear of their father's peevish temper, and the dread of the punishments he was wont to inflict when irritated, kept them generally within bounds in his immediate presence.

Otherwise, they were completely unmanageable, and on numerous occasions when he happened to pass by as they were doing something forbidden, Mr. Bloomfield provided Agnes with stony glares of disapproval, or berated her in an uncivil tone.

The only flicker of hope and kindness which Agnes received and warmed up to was Mrs. Bloomfield Sr., who seemed to sympathize with her situation and recognized her need for more parental support, and more power to the governess's authority. In the grandmother, Agnes thought she had an ally, but later, after overhearing the senior Mrs. Bloomfield question whether she was a proper governess for the children, she recognized her "as hypocritical and insincere, a flatterer, and a spy upon my words and deeds" (Ch.IV). The only way that Agnes found to remain in the good graces of the grandmother was to constantly flatter her, but Agnes was too honest a person to do that and she soon fell 'out of favour' with her.

The only other character worthy of note in her adventures with the Bloomfields is 'Mr. Robson', the children's uncle and Mrs. Bloomfield's brother, a man Agnes describes as "a mixture of real stupidity and affected contempt of all surrounding objects" (Ch. V). As well, he was an ultra-chauvinist, 'the scorner of the female sex', a 'fop', and 'no gentleman'. In a very short time, he was able to undo all 'the good' that she had taken months to achieve, and he seemed to encourage, inflame, and bring out all their 'evil propensities'. Instead of correcting their faults, or even making an attempt, he simply laughed at their insubordination (Ch.V) :

> Damme, but the lad has some spunk in him too. Curse me, if ever I saw a nobler little scoundrel than that. He's beyond petticoat government already: - by G-, he defies mother, granny, governess, and all!

In Mary Ann, a child already highly susceptible to flattery, he encouraged her conceited notions regarding her appearance, and in young Tom, he encouraged brutality toward his hunting dogs, and animals in general. When Tom returned home from a day of hunting with a brood of nestlings in his hands, he was excited about beginning his tortures on them. After useless pleadings with him not to do so, and threats to Agnes if she intervened in his 'pleasures', she took a large, flat rock and killed them instantly out of sheer mercy. Young Tom was enraged and complained to his uncle. To add to the overall injury to Tom and the 'general good' which Agnes tried to do, Uncle Robson taught him to drink wine and spirits in an effort to make him 'bold and manly' and 'superior' to his sisters.

By the close of May, Agnes felt that she had finally made some progress with the children, but Mr. & Mrs. Bloomfield were of another opinion and terminated her employment at the midsummer vacation after only one term. They attributed their children's many shortcomings to the 'want of sufficient firmness, and diligent, persevering care' on her part, and, in effect, accused her of incompetency. Realizing the futility of answering back, she said nothing in her own defense, but in her heart she knew that she was not at fault (Ch. V) :

> Unshaken firmness, devoted diligence, unwearied perseverance, unceasing care, were the very qualifications on which I had secretly prided myself, and by which I had hoped in time to overcome all difficulties, and obtain success at last.

Agnes returned to the Parsonage for a brief respite after leaving Wellwood House, but she was tough and resilient, anything but defeated, and anxious to both try again and to redeem herself (Ch. V):

> I was not yet weary of adventure, nor willing to relax my efforts. I knew all parents were not like Mr. & Mrs. Bloomfield, and I was certain all children were not like theirs.... I had been seasoned by adversity, and tutored by experience, and I longed to redeem my lost honour...

Agnes was not to be deterred by her first, bad experience and decided to take a different approach for her second try. In her advertisement for a new position, she was bolder, more demanding, and more discriminating about her final choice. This time she demanded, and received, £50 per year, twice what she received from the Bloomfields, and two months holiday which she received without objection. Her new posting was with the 'Murrays' at 'Horton Lodge' near O - ; in reality, Anne Brontë's second appointment was with the Robinsons at Thorp Green Hall near Little Ouseburn outside of York. After several months at home, Agnes set out for her second posting, some seventy miles away.

When Agnes began her second employment on a wintry day at the end of January, 1840, she began a 'new education' of her own with a family quite different from the one she had left several months before. The 'Murrays' were an affluent family with two daughters, one only slightly younger than Agnes herself, and two sons. The children in this situation were all older and more under control, but their attitude towards their new governess was not much different than that of the Bloomfields. From the outset, Mrs. Murray outlined her expectations, Agnes's responsibilities, and stressed her children's comfort and happiness, but made no mention of hers.

In the second half of *Agnes Grey*, Anne Brontë focuses on a new set of characters and problems which shift dramatically to moral and ethical questions and principles related to her new charges, rather than the behavioural ones she had with the Bloomfields. For the most part, she concentrates on Rosalie, the oldest and perhaps most interesting of all the Murray children, but Matilda runs a 'close second'. From the outset, the problem of being a governess to the Murray children was best displayed by the mother who explained her expectations for their education (Ch. VII) :

> ... she seemed anxious only to render them as superficially attractive and showily accomplished as they could possibly be made, without present trouble [or] discomfort to themselves, and I was to act accordingly - to study and strive to amuse and oblige, instruct, refine, and polish, with the least possible exertion on their part, and no exercise of authority on mine.

Once again, in regard to discipline, her hands were tied, and if 'gentle remonstrance' did not work, she was supposed to report to Mrs. Murray. Also, it was clear to Agnes that no great exertions were to be made on their part which struck an ominous note. To compound matters, there were no set hours of instruction, and the children more or less decided when and where they wanted to hold classes without any consideration for their governess; as a result, their education was a rather haphazard affair.

Their mother's remarks regarding their education simply reflected Victorian views of the time. For daughters of the nobility, aristocracy, and middle classes, they were expected to marry into the same, or better, class to maintain their social standing and wealth. And both working for a living, or marrying into a 'lower station' in life, would most certainly result in a banishment of sorts from 'high society' with whom they previously consorted. Therefore, Mrs. Murray's instructions to Agnes were not surprising, since most families of standing wanted their daughters sufficiently, but not necessarily more, educated and established in the social ways and graces. Once married off, the daughter's parents were considered to have 'done their duty' and then they could perhaps concentrate on other young daughters; a solid, firm, and established education was thought necessary only for their sons who would eventually inherit the family property and wealth.

For young ladies such as Agnes Grey, who by birth were not born of either the nobility or aristocracy or into a lower labouring family, but somewhere in between, the job of teacher or governess was but one of the few options available to them. In such a position as governess, her young charges were therefore considered as much her 'superiors' as those of her employers, their parents, and this situation allowed the children to misdirect and abuse their powers over their governess, something which they often did. With the children of the Bloomfields, Agnes had not been so mindful of this formality, but now she was determined to be more punctilious, and she referred to her new charges by formal address hoping for an improved rapport with the young Murrays. In spite of this, Miss Murray was at first, 'cold and haughty', and then 'insolent and overbearing' and never lost sight for more than half an hour of who was the hireling, but as time wore on, Rosalie became very attached to Agnes. In Victorian times, it was important, and expected, for hirelings, servants, maids, and governesses to know, and acknowledge, their 'place' in life and society, and never to aspire beyond it.

Miss Murray, or Rosalie, the eldest of the Murray children, was sixteen years old, only three years younger than Agnes Grey herself, when they first met. Agnes described her as pretty, and later 'positively beautiful', tall, slender, perfectly formed, exquisitely fair, a 'healthy bloom', clear and bright blue eyes, very light brown hair, and small features. Her character was far less favourable although she was lively, light-hearted, and could be very agreeable. Rosalie's self-awareness of her own beauty, position, power, and social standing, coupled with her parents' constant indulgence, and her 'habitual scorn of reason' often made her 'testy and capricious'. Agnes soon made and assessment of Rosalie (Ch. VII) :

> ... she had never been properly taught the distinction between right and wrong; she
> had, like her brothers and sisters, been suffered from infancy to tyrannize over nurses,

governesses, and servants; she had not been taught to moderate her desires, to control her temper or bridle her will, or to sacrifice her own pleasures for the good of others;...

In spite of her failings and shortcomings, Agnes truly liked Rosalie, and with time 'won her over' because of her strong character, clarity of purpose, steadfastness, and adherence to principles, something which was perhaps new to Rosalie. Agnes eventually earned her deep, but hidden, respect because (Ch. VII) :

> I was the only person in the house who steadily professed good principles, habitually spoke the truth, and generally endeavoured to make inclination bow to duty;...

Agnes, the daughter of a poor clergyman, was an extremely moral person who strongly held to her belief and could not be tempted or swayed. Later, her natural attraction to Mr. Weston became a cause for anxiety and guilt, but Rosalie suffered no such qualms or anguish, and "soon was swallowed up in the all-absorbing ambition to attract and dazzle the other sex" (Ch.VII). Rosalie was also well aware of her own physical attributes and "knew all her charms, and thought them even greater than they were,..." (Ch.VII). For Agnes, vanity was a venial sin, but for her student, it was simply a game to be 'played out', and a normal, expected course of events, for a young lady in her position in the pursuit of a suitable husband.

To Rosalie and Matilda, Agnes Grey was an oddity, an enigma, and a perplexity from a 'different world' whom they had difficulty understanding and in reconciling their two different spheres of 'reality', that of Agnes's which was firm, immutable, and impregnable, and theirs which was firmly entrenched in materialistic values and beliefs which they had been exposed to, and had adopted, from early childhood. Agnes was kind and benevolent, and she displayed an unselfish side of humanity which they had never seen before, most certainly not from their parents. They saw in her a 'queer creature' who never flattered or praised them 'half enough', and one who was 'obliging, quiet, and peaceable' but who could also be 'agreeable and amusing', and who was beyond their reproach and beyond their persistent, wily manipulations. What confused and confounded them most about Agnes Grey was that (Ch. VII) :

> She had her own opinions on every subject, and kept steadily to them -..., as she was always thinking of what was right and what was wrong, and had a strange reverence for matters connected with religion, and an unaccountable liking to good people.

Their difference in attitudes, morals, and principles are vividly described in Chapter IX, 'The Ball', where Rosalie excitedly, proudly, and anxiously describes her debut and the 'conquests' she has made while Agnes had briefly returned home for a visit. Patiently, Agnes listened to the list of lords and gentlemen who were overwhelmed by her beauty, her scathing reports on each of them, and how she detested them all. It was obvious that her parents had already settled on Sir Thomas Ashby, whom she described as 'the wickedest', simply for his wealth and class, and Miss Murray was willing to acquiesce for those same reasons; love never entered the picture. Rosalie's statement, "... I must have Ashby Park, whoever shares it with me.", explains much with only a few simple words. Agnes, true to her form, and her beliefs, gently chastised Rosalie for her coquetish ways, and in so doing, Anne Brontë points out the faulty, snobbish perpetuation of the class system in Britain, something as a person she detested, and as a writer she was able to openly condemn.

Agnes did not fear 'temptation', nor was she one whose character could be easily corrupted, but she did fear slow and imperceptible changes which might be taking place in her own character simply by close and constant association with the Murrays. There were constant pressures upon her, and they produced constant concerns which she feared might weaken her own inner resolve in spite of herself (Ch. XI) :

> My only companions had been unamiable children, and ignorant, wrong-headed girls, from whose fatiguing folly, unbroken solitude was often a relief... But to be restricted to such associates was a serious evil, both in its immediate effects and the consequences that were likely to ensue.

and then (Ch. XI) :

> Habitual associations are known to exercise a great influence over each other's minds and manners. Those whose actions are ever before our eyes, whose words are ever in our ears, will naturally lead us, albeit against our will - slowly - gradually - imperceptibly, perhaps, to act and speak as they do.

Rosalie took delight in her charms, and also great pleasure in crushing Mr. Hatfield, the rector, who took a deep interest in her and pursued her with hopes and thoughts of marriage in mind. Although Agnes suspected that Miss Murray liked him more than all the others, and marriage was the ultimate goal, "but never for one like poor Mr. Hatfield, who has not seven hundred a year to bless him with" (Ch. XVII). It was not long before Lord Ashby proposed, and Rosalie accepted, that she encouraged Mr. Hatfield with flirtations simply for 'sport', and was determined to delay the wedding because she wished to pursue her coquetry a while longer. And even after humiliating and injuring Mr. Hatfield's ego, she was determined to win back his affections. When Hatfield did not respond to her re-newed attempts, Rosalie turned her sights on Mr. Weston, although he proved to be disinterested and impervious to her charms, which annoyed her. Agnes was disgusted with her actions, and it certainly raised questions in her mind about possessing 'beauty'; she said (Ch. XVII) :

> It is foolish to wish for beauty. Sensible people never either desire it for themselves or care about it in others. If the mind be well cultivated, and the heart well disposed, no one ever cares about the exterior.

and about 'vanity' (Ch. XVII) :

..., I could only conclude that excessive vanity, like drunkenness, hardens the heart,
enslaves the faculties, and perverts the feelings.

Anne Brontë's writing was not without moral and religious purpose, and through
Rosalie, and less so through Matilda, we learn the most important ones. After Miss Murray
was 'transmuted' into Lady Ashby, and her honeymoon on the Continent was complete,
the new Lady Ashby was anxious to display her new-found wealth and station to her
former friends and family. Upon her return to Ashby Park, Agnes was among the first to
receive an invitation to visit, this time as a friend and not as a governess, and although she
did accept, she did so with some hesitation. Knowing the intent and purpose of Rosalie's
marriage, it contravened Agnes's sensibilities and moral guidelines, and it disturbed her
to know that (Ch. XVII) :

... some people think rank and wealth the chief good; and, if they can secure that to
their children, they think they have done their duty.

Agnes's belief that Miss Murray's marriage to Sir Thomas Ashby was a grand mistake was completely vindicated after Rosalie returned as Lady Ashby with a very different
attitude and outlook on her new situation. In her letter to Agnes, she states (Ch. XXI) :

Alas! how far the promise of anticipation exceeds the pleasure of possession!... There's
a fine sentiment! I assure you I am become quite a grave old matron... pray come, if
it be only to witness the wonderful change.

And as Agnes and Lady Ashby walk through the park and spot Sir Thomas, Rosalie's
comment about her own husband and her marriage regrets came to the fore. The brief
comment is a revelation about her new-found wisdom and speaks 'volumes' about pre-
arranged, loveless marriages for the benefit and perpetuation of English high society (Ch.
XXIII) :

- filthy beast! Oh, I would give ten thousand worlds to be Miss Murray again! It is
too bad to feel life, health and beauty wasting away, unfelt and unenjoyed, for such
a brute as that!

Anne Brontë reinforces her belief in the wrongfulness of class marriages with the
example of Agnes Grey's mother who married a poor parson, much like her own mother
in real life, except in the novel she does it against her father's wishes. When Agnes's
father dies, her mother is contacted by her father asking her to renounce her 'unfortunate
marriage' and admit to the mistake of marrying into a lower class. Without hesitation,
she replies that her marriage was not a mistake, that the past thirty years had been extremely enjoyable, and to renounce her past would be tantamount to admitting that the
births of her two, lovely daughters were also 'mistakes'. This, Mrs. Grey was unable and
unprepared to do, knowing that with such a reply, she would forfeit her right to return to
the title of 'Lady Grey', as well as relinquish her inheritance. Both Agnes and Mary, her

sister, were in full agreement with their mother's response and were fully aware that the consequence was to do without a legacy. All this was done on a matter of principle, and in the end, all their grandfather's money and possessions were left to wealthy, unknown cousins.

Throughout the novel, we find there, interspersed between and within conversations, Anne Brontë's religious beliefs and views spoken through the words of Agnes Grey; some of these also reveal several religious crises which she herself had from time to time. When all Agnes's diligent efforts with the Bloomfield children failed, she appealed to God and tried to invoke his help (Ch. III) :

> ...; and night and morning I implored Divine assistance to this end. But either the children were so incorrigible, the parents so unreasonable, or myself so mistaken in my views, or so unable to carry them out, that my best intentions and most strenuous efforts seemed productive of no better result than sport to children, dissatisfaction to their parents, and torment to myself.

And when she had been in charge of the Murray children for some time, she sometimes questioned her own sincere, caring intentions (Ch. VII) :

> ... and sometimes, I thought myself a precious fool for caring so much about them, and feared I must be sadly wanting in Christian humility, or that charity which suffereth long and is kind, seeketh not her own, is not easily provoked, beareth all things, endureth all things.

The strong, religious passions of Anne Brontë are continued throughout Chapter XI in 'The Cottagers', in which she reveals that Miss Murray's visits to Nancy Brown, and others, are not exactly altruistic as we find Rosalie and Matilda making offensive and insensitive remarks directly in their presence. Often their visits there were for the sole purpose of amusement, or merely to fulfil their obligations as young ladies of the manor. They saw the cottagers as 'an order entirely distinct from themselves' and were condescending to them, sometimes gave them money or clothing, and believed that they had brightened their lives and their humble abodes by their visits, but, in fact, had only insulted or injured their pride. Anne Brontë also uses this chapter to air her views on the new generation of lack-lustre emissaries of the Church of England, like curates Hatfield and Bligh, to expose their shallowness and short-comings and, in contrast, to praise the many virtues of the new, young curate, Mr. Edward Weston, who truly cares about his parishioners.

Anne Brontë having been brought up by a clergyman father in a religious household has firm, fixed views as to worthy qualities of any human being, and particular views as to the requisite qualities of a curate which she offers up in defense of Mr. Weston. When the Misses Murrays derisively referred to Mr. Weston as, 'sullen' and 'morose', and 'an insensate, ugly, stupid block-head', Agnes saw him otherwise as having a mouth of 'character', a 'man of firm purpose', and 'a habitual thinker', and she was convinced that he was (Ch. XI) :

> a man of strong sense, firm faith, and ardent piety, but thoughtful and stern: and..., to
> his other good qualities, was added that of true benevolence and gentle, considerate
> kindness,...

These were the redeemable qualities of character she some day hoped to find in the man she loved, and in this hope, she was firm and unswerving.

Agnes, thereafter, often found herself upholding a defense of Mr. Weston against the 'abuses' of the Misses Murrays, and she soon discovered that she was falling in love with him. When she arrived at Horton Lodge one morning after walking with him, she quickly went to her room, closed her door, fell to her knees, and "offered up a fervent, but not impetuous prayer", in which she earnestly entreated the Lord that they be meant for one another. To assuage her seemingly 'selfish' prayer, she argues that her prayer is not entirely for herself, but for the happiness of two people. Later, her human, temporal, and physical attraction to Mr. Weston caused her to suffer pangs of guilt and conscience (Ch. XVI) :

> ..., which would too often whisper that I was deceiving my own self, and mocking
> God with the service of a heart more bent upon the creature than the Creator.

But then in an almost immediate reversal to her religious guilt, she considers another viewpoint which justifies, and perhaps rationalizes, her natural and human attraction to Weston (Ch. XVI) :

> We would do well to worship God in his works; and I know none of them in which
> so many of his attributes - so much of his own spirit shine [in] this his faithful ser-
> vant, whom to know and not to appreciate, were obtuse in sensibility in me, who
> have so little else to occupy my heart.

Anne Brontë, in her own life, suffered numerous family tragedies and had occasional religious doubts. These doubts are paralleled in the novel by Agnes who sometimes wondered whether she would ever have any 'pleasure' out of life after having suffered so much in her twenty-three years. She wondered if God heard her prayers and would grant her some 'sunshine' in an otherwise 'gloomy' life (Ch. XX) :

> Is it not possible that God may hear my prayers, disperse these gloomy shadows, and
> grant me some beams of heaven's sunshine yet? Will He entirely deny to me those
> blessings which are so freely given to others, who neither ask them or acknowledge
> them when received? May I not still hope and trust?

Agnes wondered what God's plan was for her regarding her life's work and whether her 'happiness' would come in this world, or the next (Ch. XX1) :

> Should I shrink from the work that God had set before me, because it is not fitted to
> my taste? Did not He know best what I should do, and where I ought to labour?... If

happiness in this world is not for me, I will endeavour to promote the welfare of those around me, and my reward shall be hereafter.

On Agnes's visit to Lady Ashby who is very anxious to converse with her and seek her counsel, Agnes again provides her with the same advice she had more or less given her before, and which Lady Ashby had rejected. Although Rosalie, now Lady Ashby, had gone to church on a regular basis, it was done so for social reasons of meeting potential husbands, and no other; she seems to have learned little and gained nothing from her regular, Sunday visits. Agnes is philosophical and advises her (Ch. XXIII) :

> The best way to enjoy yourself is to do what is right, and hate nobody. The end of Religion is not to teach us how to die, but how to live; and the earlier you become wise and good, the more happiness you secure.

Ultimately, Agnes Grey is favoured with happiness here on Earth with her marriage to Mr. Weston and blessed with three, wonderful children. The novel then ends on a religious note with Agnes spelling out a 'moral formula' for happiness and contentment on this Earth. Her goodness and simplicity shine through in her final summation (Ch. XXV) :

> Our modest income is amply sufficient for our requirements; and by practising the economy we learnt in harder times, and never attempting to imitate our richer neighbours, we manage not only to enjoy comfort and contentment ourselves, but to have every year something to lay by for our children, and something to give to those who need it.

The religious theme of the novel is also highly evident in the characters of Mr. Hatfield, the rector at Horton, and later in Mr. Weston, the new curate. Just as in *Shirley*, Charlotte's second novel, in which she gently chides the three curates Malone, Donne and Sweeting, Anne Brontë also criticizes and chides the Church of England and some of its 'ambassadors' for their less-than-sincere efforts in the form of Rector Hatfield. Agnes, through her recollections, exposes him for his many faults and shortcomings, and although he is handsome and a wonderful companion, Agnes sees him badly wanting as a rector. His character is highly symbolic of why many Church of England members turned to Methodism; it was a reaction to the Church's apathy for the needs and concerns of the poor, and its closer and stronger ties and connections to the upper classes. Hatfield's reactions throughout indicate that he is not a close friend of the poor and has little concern for their welfare whether physical, mental, social, or religious.

From her first few visits to the church at Horton, Agnes is not impressed by Hatfield and his sermons whose topics are far too serious and 'remote' to be of any great value or benefit to his wide array of parishioners. For Agnes, they were 'far too studied and too artificial to be pleasing' to her, but occasionally he would deliver (Ch. X) :

... a very good one, but sunless and severe, representing the Deity as a terrible task-
master, rather than a benevolent father. Yet,... I felt inclined to think that the man
was sincere in all he said; he must have changed his views and become decidedly
religious, gloomy and austere, yet still devout: but such illusions were usually dissipated, on coming out of church, by hearing his voice in a jocund colloquy.

Also Hatfield was a bit of a 'showman' and somewhat theatrical in the delivery of his
services, mostly for the benefit of his wealthy parisioners. Agnes saw him as vain and
ostentatious, and as he conducted his services, she described that he would often (Ch. X):

... mutter over a Collect, and gabble through the Lord's Prayer, rise, draw off one
bright lavender glove to give the congregation the benefit of his sparkling rings,
lightly pass his fingers through his well-curled hair, [and] flourish a cambric hand-
kerchief,...

Agnes also judged Hatfield by his actions towards her and other parishioners who
were not well-off, and usually ignored. After the church service was over, he often helped
the Murrays into their carriage as they left the church for home. Hatfield did this to
ingratiate himself with the lovely Miss Murray, and in so doing offended Agnes first by
not speaking to her, and secondly by shutting her out of the carriage. When it was brought
to his attention that Miss Grey, the governess, was not yet in the carriage, he made no
apologies and left the footman to 'finish the business'.

Hatfield's treatment of Nancy Brown, a poor, widowed cottager was even more deplorable. After several trips to see Nancy Brown, Agnes discovered that she did not care
for visits by either Mr. Hatfield or curate Bligh; Mr. Hatfield was particularly mean-
spirited. He would often find fault in the way she kept her cottage, her irregular church
attendance, and he was critical of her in other ways; besides that, his ministries to her
were anything but helpful or comforting. And when Nancy Brown suffered depression
brought on by religious melancholy and was having doubts as to how to interpret various
passages in the Bible, Hatfield was scornful and accused her of 'Methodism' and being
'among the Methodists'. He then insisted that the cure for all her problems was to attend
church regularly in spite of the fact that she was quite elderly, it was winter, she was in
poor health and suffered from rheumatism, and the church was over two miles walking
distance. He was anything but sympathetic to Nancy Brown and some of the other poor
cottagers like Mark Wood who suffered from consumption. When he visited them, he
insisted that the door be left open for fresh air without thought or regard for the sufferings
of Mark Wood and his wife to the cold.

After delivering a stern lecture to Nancy Brown on the merits of attending church
regularly, Hatfield made inquiries as to the Misses Murrays, and if she had seen them.
When she told him that she had just seen them go onto Moss Lane - "he kicked [her] poor
cat across the floor, an' went after 'em gay as a lark;". For both Agnes and Anne Brontë,
kind treatment of animals was always an important measure of a person's good character,
and in this regard, Hatfield failed the test badly. And to add to the insult, Nancy Brown
attended church one Sunday and decided to speak to Hatfield before the service, but he

ungraciously dismissed her, instructed her not to bother him again, and within earshot he referred to her as 'a canting old fool' when Mr. Weston, the new curate, asked him who she was.

Mr. Hatfield's actions and treatment of animals comes into play a second time when he hotly pursues Miss Murray. On a number of occasions, Mr. Hatfield would coincidentally 'happen by' Horton Lodge just when Miss Murray was beyond the park and near the road. Her purpose was obviously flirtation, and she misled him to believe that she was not only 'interested' but also that he had a chance at her hand in marriage. During one of these meetings by the roadside, Agnes was sent by Mrs. Murray to bring her home and she was accompanied by Matilda's dog, Snap, who was more fond of Agnes than her master. The dog was young and playful, and at the sight of Miss Murray ran ahead to greet her and play with her (Ch. XIV):

> But Snap, running before me, interrupted her in the midst of some half-pert, half-playful repartee, by catching hold of her dress and vehemently tugging thereat till Mr. Hatfield, with his cane, administered a resounding thwack upon the animal's skull, and sent it yelping back to me,... that afforded the reverend gentleman great amusement;...

To Agnes, this was proof that he was not a piteous, gracious, kind, and caring being that a rector of a church should be.

Mr. Weston, the new curate, was different from Mr. Hatfield in every way, and just as Anne Brontë characterized Hatfield as 'all the things a church rector should not be', she holds up Weston as 'everything that one should be'. There has also been much speculation as to whether or not 'Weston' was modelled after William Weightman, Mr. Brontë's curate from 1839 - 1842, whom all the Brontës simply adored and admired. It has also been a matter of speculation as to whether Anne Brontë and William Weightman were in love, and may have even been married had the course of events in their lives not been so tragic. Weightman died in September, 1842, after a very brief illness, and only a month and a half before Aunt Branwell died in late October of the same year.

In any case, he was a favourite of the family, and particularly Rev. Brontë, young Branwell, and Anne. In a letter which Charlotte wrote to Ellen Nussey, she mentions the flirtations between them in church as they sat for a service. With Weightman's death, Rev. Brontë lost an excellent curate, young Branwell lost a good friend, and Anne, perhaps, lost a future husband, but such a suppositon is a moot point. If William Weightman was the model for Mr. Weston, there were noticeable differences in their outward natures. Weightman was open, light-hearted, gregarious, and gay in spirit, whereas Mr. Weston is portrayed as quiet, serious, and sober. We might also more widely speculate that the ending of *Agnes Grey*, was a wishful scenario which Anne Brontë might have chosen for her own life with William Weightman, had he lived, or someone like him. Several of Anne Brontë's poems are also thought to be tributes to this man whom they so much admired.

Mr. Weston's stark contrast to Mr. Hatfield can be seen throughout the latter chapters in two ways: one is his caring attentions to his poor parishioners, and the other is his kind treatment of animals. On several occasions, Agnes meets Mr. Weston at either Nancy Brown's cottage or in her travels, and in each and every case, he treats Agnes with kindness, courtesy, and civility, something which Agnes had not seen since she had left home. And in time, just as Agnes finds herself slowly falling in love with Mr. Weston, he also finds himself falling in love with her. Their love is based on mutual courtesy, respect, and devotion rather than a type of flimsy cohesion based on vanity, flattery, lust, superficial glamour, or attraction to wealth and social standing, such as Miss Murray practised by flaunting her charms in her pursuit of a husband.

Mr. Weston's kind actions were immediately felt by the cottagers who distrusted and disliked both Hatfield and Bligh. The day after Mr. Hatfield called Nancy Brown 'a canting old fool', Mr. Weston showed up at her cottage to minister to her needs. He was more than willing to listen carefully and sympathetically to her doubts and fears which she had tried to express to Hatfield, but was rebuffed; Weston, on the other hand, was determined to try to ease her mind. Also, Nancy Brown related to Agnes that he was kind to her cat and only stroked it when it jumped onto his lap, unlike Hatfield who had given it a good smack in 'scorn or anger'. For Nancy and Agnes, this was a 'good sign' demonstrating that he was a person with a kind and caring nature. Mr. Weston gently contradicted some of the things Mr. Hatfield had said and then went on to stress the love of God and love of our fellow man (Ch. XI):

> ... and let us dwell in love, that He may dwell in us, and we in Him. The more happiness we bestow, the more we shall receive, even here, and the greater will be our reward in Heaven when we rest from our labours.

Once again, Anne Brontë's unshakeable and steadfast religious views are reflected through Agnes Grey's words, and demonstrates how she sought to direct her own life in pursuit of Earthly happiness.

Mr. Weston's kind nature was also demonstrated in two other incidents, both related to the poor cottagers near the Murrays. When Agnes was forced to remain in Nancy Brown's cottage until the rain let up, Mr. Weston appeared with Nancy's cat which had previously gone astray. Nancy had, in fact, been very worried about its disappearance, but Mr. Weston had rescued it from death at the hands of Mr. Murray's gamekeeper who was about to shoot it. In another instance, Mark Wood, who was suffering from consumption told how Mr. Weston, seeing that they had no fire in their humble cottage, generously paid for and sent over, a sack of coal to keep them warm and comfortable. Prior to that Mr. Hatfield had done nothing to help them and only rebuked Mrs. Wood for some minor 'omissions'.

Mr. Weston also treated Agnes kindly, and as an 'equal', whereas no one else did. As Agnes left church one Sunday, it was raining heavily but only Mr. Weston offered to share his umbrella as she walked to the Murrays' carriage, and once there, he offered his hand to assist her into it. This raised the ire of Miss Murray who, having lost Mr. Hatfield's attentions, was now determined to flirt with Mr. Weston in the short time she had remaining before her betrothal ball. On another Sunday after a church service as Agnes walked alone behind the Misses Murray, Mr. Weston came up behind Agnes who was admiring three primroses on a high bank just out of her reach. He reached up, gathered them, and gave them to Agnes which surprised her, since it was one of the few acts of civility and kindness she had received during her entire time at Horton Lodge. During that same meeting, the topic of 'Home', something almost sacred to both of them, was mentioned, and Mr. Weston enlightened her by explaining that there was something of even greater value which he had learned about, "... the power and will to be useful".

In the second half of the novel, we have a continuation of the social issue which the author began in the first half, the mistreatment of governesses at the hands of their employers, the nobility, aristocracy and upper classes of English society. Agnes's treatment by the Bloomfields was deplorable and improved only slightly at the hands of the Murrays. Her 'place' within the household was clearly indicated from the outset, and all members of the family, as well as the other servants, treated her with 'distance' and disdain. When they rode to church on Sunday, Agnes was crushed into a corner of the carriage, and Miss Matilda openly mocked her and asked how she could stand it. She ate her meals alone, or in the classroom with the children, and was constantly at their every beck and call; dignity, respect, privacy, and consideration were not too commonly found. 'Warmth' and love were completely out of the question.

On the Sundays when their capricious natures made them decide to walk back to Horton Lodge to enjoy the fine weather, Rosalie and Matilda talked as though Agnes was not there, and she was forced to walk behind them like an unwanted third party. To ward off the insult of their ignominious action, she pretended to be fully engrossed in the flowers, trees, or other aspects of nature which interested her, or as if she was "wholly absorbed in her own reflections". On one occasion at the church, Miss Murray took up Agnes's regular seat and forced her to take up a seat at the back with her back to the pulpit from which she could not see her beloved Mr. Weston. And when it was obvious that he was showing some interest in Agnes, Miss Murray gave her extra work to do to prevent her from going to church on Sundays. Miss Murray's malicious actions were a deliberate attempt to keep Agnes from Mr. Weston, and when he inquired of her whereabouts, they concocted lies and told him that she no longer wanted to come to church, and later, that she preferred her books to attending church.

The Misses Murray also misused Agnes's services as a governess by forcing her to do their tedious work such as sewing time-consuming, delicate fancy-work, stretching frames, stitching canvas, sorting wools and silks, counting stitches, and rectifying mistakes. Other demeaning tasks included finishing pieces they had become tired of, running errands, fetching and carrying, and doing their 'bidding' as commanded according to their whims. When Agnes finally did have some time to herself, it was often interrupted, as was the case when she tried to withdraw and read a letter from home. Miss Murray immediately commanded her attention regarding the upcoming ball with the comment (Ch. VIII) :

> Miss Grey, do put away that dull, stupid letter, and listen to me! I'm sure my talk must be far more interesting than that.

and to add further insult and injury, Miss Murray instructed (Ch. VIII) :

> You should tell the good people at home not to bore you with such long letters,... and above all, do bid them to write on proper note-paper, and not on those great vulgar sheets!

These are but some of the vexations they caused Agnes Grey and serve as examples to make her point and demonstrate their condescension, scorn, and outright contempt for governesses, and servants, whom they looked upon as 'beneath' them in the social strata.

The longer Agnes Grey stayed at Horton Lodge, the more she worried that she would become like them. Soon after arriving there, recognizing Rosalie's physical attributes, and learning of her coquetish ways, she expressed thoughts on the possession of 'beauty' (Ch. XVI) :

> I was sorry for her; I was amazed, disgusted at her heartless vanity; I wonder why so much beauty should be given to those who made so bad use of it, and denied to some who would make it a benefit to both themselves and others.

The vague and indirect implication that Agnes makes here is not too difficult to detect, and she soon found herself paying, "... more attention to dress than ever I had done before..." and in front of the looking-glass she would, "spend as much as two minutes in the contemplation of [her] own image...". But in such a 'study' she found no consolation (Ch. XVII) :

> I could discover no beauty in those marked features, that pale hollow cheek, and ordinary dark brown hair; there might be intellect in the forehead, there might be expression in the dark grey eyes, but what of that?

These were as close to confessions of vanity that Agnes would admit to, but as Miss Murray began accenting and promoting her charms to Mr. Weston just before her own wedding simply to lead another heart astray, Agnes rallied to her own defense with confidence and honesty in describing how she was more suited to Mr. Weston than Rosalie (Ch. XVII) :

> ..., I was more worthy of his love than Rosalie Murray, charming and engaging as she was; for I could appreciate his excellence, which she could not; I would devote my life to the promotion of his happiness; she would destroy his happiness for the momentary gratification of her own vanity.

For the first time, such a statement gives witness to Agnes Grey's small measure of jealousy toward Miss Murray, but at the same time she offers up a magnanimous gesture for Mr. Weston's well-being (Ch. XVII) :

> - but, if he could but know her hollowness, her worthless, heartless frivolity - he would then be safe, and I should be - almost happy, though I might never see him more!

Later we find that Agnes's fears for Mr. Weston were mislaid, and that he was both astute and well aware of Miss Murray's 'artful ways' and had early on recognized that she was both 'giddy and vain'. And when Mr. Weston did not respond to her in the carriage as they drove by, Miss Murray berated him by saying, "Stupid ass!... You don't know what you've lost by not looking this way!", and later, "... I intend him to feel my power -",and "acknowledge it too;" (Ch. XVI). Agnes's hopes for a friend, or perhaps even more, like Mr. Weston, are buoyed up by this disclosure, but again dashed when she reconsiders them as nothing more than, "Egregious folly - too absurd to require contradiction..."(Ch. XXI). Again she is self-deprecating respecting her own personal worth (Ch. XXI) :

> If you would but consider your own unattractive exterior, your unamiable reserve, your foolish diffidence, which must make you appear cold, dull, awkward, and perhaps ill-tempered too; -

But eventually, we see that both she and Mr. Weston are of one mind when it comes to kindness and respect for others; their mutual attraction is based on deeper emotional values and ultimately results in their 'union'.

As with Anne Brontë's deep commitment to moral purpose displayed throughout *Agnes Grey*, we also see her deep respect and love of Nature which she learned at an early age in the hills of Yorkshire surrounding her home. This love and respect for Nature shows itself in several places in the novel, one of the first being a spring-like day at Horton Lodge as she ventured out to visit a cottager (Ch. XI) :

> ... and the park with its glorious canopy of bright blue sky, the west wind sounding through its yet leafless branches, the snow-wreaths still lingering in its hollows,... and the graceful deer browsing on its moist herbage, already assuming the freshness and verdure of spring...

As Agnes trails the Misses Murray as they walk home from church one Sunday, she notices some primroses alongside the road. Her mind was immediately tele-transported back to her beloved hills of North England which she missed so much (Ch. XIII) :

> As my eyes wandered over the steep banks covered with young grass and green-leaved plants, and surmounted by budding hedges, I longed intensely for some familiar flower that might recall the woody dales or green hill-sides of home -

Mr. Weston overtakes Agnes in her walk, picks the flowers, and presents them to her; their conversation then turns to wild flowers, of which they are both especially fond. Agnes points out that her favourites are, "Primroses, blue-bells, and heath-blossoms.", three wild flowers commonly found on the moors of Yorkshire and the north of England.

When Agnes's father dies, and she and her mother must leave the place where the family has spent the last thirty years, and she her entire lifetime, she feels a great sorrow not only for leaving her home and village but also (Ch. XX) :

... the old bare hills, delightful in their very desolation, with the narrow vales between, smiling in green wood and sparkling water -

Agnes was always cognizant of the beauty of her physical surroundings, and perhaps unconsciously compared them to the beauty of her home. When she visited Rosalie in her new setting, she gave a comparative description of Ashby Park (Ch. XXII) :

... the park was spacious and beautiful - chiefly on account of its magnificent old trees, its stately herds of deer, its broad sheet of water, and the ancient woods that stretched beyond it,... but [it had] very little of that undulating swell which adds so greatly to the charm of park scenery.

Agnes was born among the hills, swells, dales, and valleys of the north and west of England, and therefore, flatter land without these physical elements and attributes was less appealing and caused her to miss her home country still further.

Although Anne Brontë had a strong attachment to the moorlands behind her West Yorkshire home in Haworth, she also developed a love for Scarborough and its coast and beaches in North Yorkshire. This resulted from the many trips taken there while she was governess to the Robinsons who often travelled there for vacations. The sights, sounds, and smells of the wind, water, beaches, and surrounding landscape proved very alluring to her; it was in stark contrast to the moors of Haworth which she loved so well. And I firmly believe that the contents of the final two chapters entitled, 'The Sands', and 'Conclusion', reveal far more about Anne Brontë than they ever do about the character Agnes Grey.

Therefore, when Agnes Grey and her mother had to leave the Parsonage after her father's death, it is not surprising that the town of A - (Scarborough in real life) was chosen as the sight of their new school which they were about to open. In spite of the fact that their home was 'a considerable distance from the sea', she still took great pleasure walking to the sea shore (Ch. XXIV) :

But the sea was my delight; and I would often gladly pierce the town to obtain the pleasure of a walk beside it,... It was delightful to me at all times and seasons, but especially in the wild commotion of a rough sea-breeze, and in the brilliant freshness of a summer morning.

and when she set foot on the sands and faced the 'broad, bright bay', she struggled further to express her strong feelings and emotions (Ch. XXIV) :

... no language can describe the effect of the deep, clear azure of the sky and ocean, the bright morning sunshine on the semi-circular barrier of craggy cliffs surmounted by green, swelling hills, and on the smooth, wide sands, and the low rocks out at sea...

It was perhaps these same recollections which brought Anne Brontë back to Scarborough only eighteen months after *Agnes Grey* was published when she was suffering through the final stages of consumption. In fact, she went there with the hope that the fresh, salt, sea air would improve her condition, and although this is true for the sufferers of the disease, Anne Brontë was far too advanced in the disease for there to be any hope of a miraculous cure. In any case, any student of the Brontës, and especially Anne Brontë, cannot help but notice the coincidental connection between her descriptions and the tragic, final days of her life in Scarborough. In the novel, it was on one of these walks that she accidentally met Mr. Weston again; the wide expanse of sandy beaches was a place of great beauty to her with 'brilliant, sparkling waves' (Ch. XXIV) :

> And then, the unspeakable purity and freshness of the air! there was just enough wind to keep the whole sea in motion, to make the waves come bounding to the shore, foaming and sparkling, as if wild with glee.

and not only did it provide her with vitality and a delight of the physical senses, but it also acted as a mental elixir as well (Ch. XXIV):

> Refreshed, delighted, invigorated, I walked along, forgetting all my cares, feeling as if I had wings to my feet, and could go at least forty miles without fatigue, and experiencing a sense of exhilaration to which I had been an entire stranger since the days of early youth.

After being re-united with her beloved Mr. Weston, and also her old dog, Snap, whom he had recovered from the rat-catcher in Horton, they slowly became re-acquainted and Mr. Weston was introduced to Agnes's mother, Mrs. Grey. In the final scenes of the novel, following a thunder shower which had 'a most beneficial effect upon the weather', Mr. Weston asked Agnes out for a walk, one which took them through the 'crowded streets' to the 'quiet outskirts of town'. During the course of their walk, Mr. Weston seemed 'grave and abstracted' which troubled Agnes, but (Ch. XXV) :

> ... as soon as we came in sight of the venerable old church[3], and the - hill[4], with the deep blue sea beyond it[5], I found my companion was cheerful enough.

They were just in time to see a 'brilliant sunset' at which time Mr. Weston professed his love for Agnes, and by telling her that she was the only suitable companion for him in

---

3 The venerable old church is most likely St. Mary's Church, in whose churchyard Anne was buried only eighteen months later.

4 The 'hill' is most likely the hill on which we find Scarborough Castle from which one has a magnificent view of the surrounding area.

5 Anne Brontë describes almost an identical scene in Ch.7 of 'Tenant' when Helen and a small group of friends go to the coast for a picnic day. There Helen is able to sketch rugged, coastal landscapes to use in later paintings.

the world, he proposed to her. Agnes Grey, who had dreamt of this day, accepted his offer and ended her diary with one, last addition (Ch. XXV) :

> ... I shall never forget that glorious summer evening, and always remember with delight that steep, rugged hill, and the edge of the precipice where we stood together watching the splendid sun-set mirrored on the restless world of waters at our feet - with hearts filled with gratitude to Heaven, and happiness, and love -

Anne Brontë then ends her fictional diary in a succinct way with one, final sentence, "And now I think I have said sufficient."

We can only marvel at the coincidence that just eighteen months later, Anne Brontë, dying of tuberculosis, went to Scarborough for her final days, and the night before her death after sitting quietly near the beach which she loved so much, they witnessed a spectacular sunset. Later, in retrospect, for Charlotte Brontë, this spectacle had been an omen which brought to a close the life of a wonderful human being, her beloved sister Anne, and the last of her siblings. Anne was buried there in St. Mary's Churchyard Cemetery overlooking the very scene she had described in the closing pages of *Agnes Grey*.

13

THE TENANT OF WILDFELL HALL

The Tenant of Wildfell Hall is the story of a young lady with a small son, Arthur, who moves into secluded Wildfell Hall. Little is known about her, her past, and what has brought her there. She is young, beautiful, and a talented painter, but the mystery of her past sets the local wags gossiping, and particularly about her seemingly close and mysterious relationship with her landlord, Frederick Lawrence.

Gilbert Markham, a young, neighbouring farmer, and narrator of the story, soon falls in love with Helen Graham, and her son becomes attached to him. Gilbert refuses to believe the gossip, but after overhearing Frederick Lawrence and Helen in what seems to be an intimate conversation, he assaults Mr. Lawrence savagely with a horse-whip, and when Helen realizes that a rift between herself and Gilbert Markham is imminent, she confidentially provides him with a diary to read which reveals her past.

In reading the diary, Gilbert discovers that Helen, at age eighteen, married the wealthy Arthur Huntingdon against the wishes of her family. After only a short period of domestic bliss, her husband's infidelity, drinking, and debauchery are simply too much for her to deal with. Fearing for little Arthur's welfare and uprbringing under such conditions, Helen flees to Wildfell Hall, and we discover that Frederick Lawrence is, in fact, her brother and owner of the property. He is simply providing her with a temporary refuge, and moral support, until the situation is rectified.

As a moral Christian devoted to duty, Helen returns to attend to her husband when she learns that he is dying; his wild lifestyle has finally brought him to an early end. Gilbert Markham eventually apologizes to Mr. Lawrence, and when he hears that Helen Graham is about to be married, he sets out in pursuit of her hoping to stop it. It turns out to be Mr. Lawrence's wedding and he is much relieved. The fact that Helen is now a wealthy heiress poses an imagined problem for Gilbert who fears his social inferiority, but for Helen this is not a barrier. In fact, she indirectly proposes to him, and the story ends with their happy union, and young Arthur will now have a proper, Christian up-bringing along with his new father, and new siblings.

Anne Brontë's second novel, *The Tenant of Wildfell Hall*, is clearly her more ambitious one of the two she completed in her short writing career. Clearly in this novel, as opposed to *Agnes Grey*, which was based on her own life experiences, she produces a major fiction novel equal in length to Charlotte's three successful novels, and perhaps equal in structure and complexity to *Wuthering Heights*, Emily's brilliant novel. It certainly indicates that as a young novelist, she was quite capable of imagination, creativity, and ingenuity. The complexity and organization of the novel also indicates a high level of intelligence and an extraordinary talent and ability to plan an intricate plot with a large number of characters.

Exactly where Anne Brontë got her material for this novel has been a subject of conjecture. There are some indicators that one of the major characters, Arthur Huntingdon, is loosely based on her brother Branwell, his wild escapades, and his apparent disregard for the quiet, pious life of the Brontë family. In fact, Charlotte Brontë was one of Anne's harshest critics after the novel was produced, and in her 'Biographical Notice of Ellis and Acton Bell' (Sept. 19, 1850), she said of her own sister's novel:

> The Tenant..., had likewise an unfavourable reception. At this I cannot wonder. The choice of subject was an entire mistake. Nothing less congruous with the writer's nature could be conceived. The motives which dictated this choice were pure, but, I think, slightly morbid. She had, in the course of her life, been called on to contemplate, near at hand and for a long time, the terrible effects of talents misused and faculties abused[1] ,...

and the effects of these observations 'near at hand and for a long time' were ('Biographical Notice') :

> ... hers was naturally a sensitive, reserved, and dejected nature; what she saw sank very deeply into her mind; it did her harm. She brooded over it till she believed it to be a duty to reproduce every detail (of course with fictitious characters, incidents, and situations) as a warning to others. She hated her work, but would pursue it.

The above explanation was given in defence of her sister's reason for writing this novel, and in another attempt to mitigate the strong criticisms, and some condemnations, of the work, she added her testimony to the author's honesty and integrity. "She must be honest; she must not varnish, soften, or conceal." And finally, in reference to her principles, she remarked ('Biographical Notice'):

> She was a very sincere and practical Christian, but the tinge of religious melancholy communicated a sad shade to her brief, blameless life.

---

1   This is a direct reference to their brother Branwell who misused and abused his talents.

These were words written in retrospect of her dearly, departed sisters whom she considered as less 'worldly' than herself; she described her sisters' knowledge and experience as ('Biographical Notice'):

> Neither Emily nor Anne was learned; they had no thought of filling their pitchers at the well-spring of other minds; they always wrote from the impulse of nature, the dictates of intuition, and from such stores of observation as their limited experience had enabled them to amass.

It is interesting to note the use of the phrase, 'stores of observation' since there is some evidence to support the suggestion that *The Tenant of Wildfell Hall* was borne not only of Branwell's dissolute ways but also from a tale of a vicar's wife who came to see Rev. Brontë about her husband whose lifestyle was highly irreverent, and anything but pious. He was a drunken profligate with many vices and was abusive to his wife and children, very much like Arthur Huntingdon. Rev. Brontë's advice to her was to leave him for good, once again much like Mrs. Huntingdon in Anne's novel.[2]

Seven years later, Charlotte Brontë makes reference to this same lady who, in fact, took Rev. Brontë's advice, left her husband, and with a great deal of perseverance overcame obstacles of agony, sickness, and suffering to successfully raise her child single-handedly and re-establish herself in society.[3] Being privy to the same information, Anne was certain to come into contact with this story, and others like it, which eventually provided an interesting 'mix' from which the basis of her second novel may well have sprung.

There is also a noticeable parallel to the lives of several other characters in the novel and real-life personages of the time. Lord Byron, a favourite of the Brontës, was also a source of evil and black-hearted villainous characters and heroes. In this novel, Arthur Huntingdon takes on certain Byronic features and characteristics such as his wild lifestyle filled with drink and debauchery, and Mrs. Huntingdon takes on the form of his first wife, Annabella Milbanke, Lady Byron, who married him, was said to be 'too good' for him, and was determined to reform him, but failed. One cannot help but notice the comparison between Byron's first wife and Helen Graham, who looks beyond all of Arthur Huntingdon's vices and shortcomings, sees only the good, dismisses all of her aunt's advice, and is convinced that she alone can change his ways and redeem his character.

The Tenant..., was first released in June, 1848, and due to its immediate success a second edition was called for and put into production in July of the same year. Some reviews had already been released which criticized the novel as coarse and brutal with too many scenes of debauchery, immoral conduct, and bad language which made it 'revolting' and 'disgusting' in the eyes of some. Others saw it as an 'eye-opener', but the positive critiques were few. In the second edition, Anne to put up a defence in which she acknowledged 'a few kind critics' and then lashed out at her detractors (Preface to the Second Edition, July 22, 1848) :

---

2   The story alluded to is seen in a letter (12/11/40) of Charlotte Brontë to Ellen Nussey.
3   The second letter to Ellen Nussey with this same reference was written on 4/4/47.

I must also admit that from some other quarters it has been censured with an asperity which I was as little prepared to expect, and which my judgement,... assures me is more bitter than just.

On several occasions, Anne Brontë almost pleads with her readers to recognize her honesty and sincerity in writing both *Agnes Grey* and *The Tenant*..., for she always writes with a purpose or moral in mind, and not simply to entertain. She explains ('Preface') :

My object in writing the following pages was not simply to amuse the Reader; neither was it to gratify my own taste, nor yet to ingratiate myself with the Press and the Public:..

and in reference to her characters ('Preface') :

..., but when we have to do with vice and vicious characters, I maintain it is better to depict them as they really are than as they would wish to appear.

Anne Brontë also uses this same 'Preface' to outline in more precise terms the true purpose of her writing, and the need for more openness :

Oh, reader! if there were less of this delicate concealment of facts - this whispering, 'Peace, peace,' when there is no peace, there would be less of sin and misery to the young of both sexes who are left to wring their bitter knowledge from experience.

and again in an effort to inform and make some minor contributions to 'change' in society's morals and attitudes ('Preface') :

... but I know that such characters do exist, and if I have warned one rash youth from following in their steps, or prevented one thoughtless girl from falling into the very natural error of my heroine, the book has not been written in vain.

The 'Preface' reveals the belief that she has a higher moral obligation than to just amuse or 'to give innocent pleasure' to her readers, albeit if that is a by-product, she makes no apologies for it. Her ambitions are not simply limited to ".... producing 'a perfect work of art': time and talents so spent, I should consider wasted and misapplied." And, as for 'such humble talents as God has given', she attests that she will put them to their 'greatest use'. For Anne, it was always 'purpose' before pleasure ('Preface') :

...; and when I feel it my duty to speak an unpalatable truth, with the help of God, I *will* speak it, though it be to the prejudice of my name and to the detriment of my reader's immediate pleasure as well as my own.

The plot and structure of *Tenant* is well-organized, but complex, and has come under scrutiny and criticism as 'awkward'. The plot begins with Gilbert Markham writing a lengthy letter to his friend Halford commenting on a new and mysterious neighbour,

Helen Graham, and her small son. The lady deflects all inquiries about her past which is intriguing to Gilbert and grist for the gossip mill of the neighbours. The mystery deepens and is only unravelled when Helen gives Gilbert her journal to read, minus the last few pages; the mystery is resolved detail by detail and page by page. After the completion of the events of the diary, Gilbert Markham again takes up the narration and completes the remainder of the story.

Many reviewers saw this as an unnecessarily complex plot presentation, although its times and sequences are evidence of a great deal of intricate planning, along the concentric, narrative lines of *Wuthering Heights*, and only a shade less than the genius of her sister Emily. Within the novel are two separate and distinct love stories, one with Arthur Huntingdon and its sad, inevitable ending, and the other with Gilbert Markham and a happy, but predictable, outcome. Anne Brontë's unwavering religious and moral principles and sense of propriety would not allow her to transgress these boundaries, even in fiction. Therefore, Helen's two loves, and two lives, were not allowed to overlap anywhere in the novel much to the increasing frustration of Gilbert Markham; the revelations in the journal were a great relief to him but provided no solution to his own problem.

Although indicators show Helen's feelings gradually leaning toward Gilbert, at no time did she completely give up on her dissolute husband nor did she allow her feelings for Gilbert to get out of control. As a dutiful, Christian wife, she was morally bound to take back her husband if he was penitent and gave up his degenerate ways. She explains to him (Ch. 33) :

> When you tire of your sinful ways, and show yourself truly repentant, I will forgive you, and, perhaps, try to love you again, though that will be hard indeed.

Religion and marriage are persistent themes throughout the novel, and prior to her marriage to Arthur Huntingdon, Aunt Maxwell gives Helen several pieces of advice on choosing a life-partner which she thinks advisable and worth noting (Ch. 16) :

> Receive, coldly and dispassionately, every attention, till you have ascertained and duly considered the worth of the aspirant; and let your affections be consequent upon approbation alone. First study; then approve; then love.

and then on personal qualities (Ch. 16) :

> Principle is the first thing, after all; and next to that, good sense, respectability, and moderate wealth. If you should marry the handsomest, and most accomplished and superficially agreeable man in the world, you know little the misery that would overwhelm you, if, after all, you should find him to be a worthless reprobate, or even an impracticable fool.

Aunt Maxwell has one more piece of advice for Helen since she recognizes her as a young woman of beauty which can sometimes bring its share of misery. Her aunt warns her of certain 'kinds' of men (Ch. 16) :

..., beauty is that quality which, next to money, is generally the most attractive to the worst kinds of men; and, therefore, it is likely to entail a great deal of trouble on the possessor.

Anne Brontë, and therefore Helen Graham, voices strong opinions against pre-arranged marriages which were so common in upper society in England to preserve their wealth and standing. She was of the determined mind that love and marriage was a matter of personal choice, and her choice alone. When her aunt indicates that Mr. Boarham has already sought permission from her aunt and uncle to seek her hand in marriage, Helen is outraged. She responds abruptly to her aunt (Ch. 16) :

I hope my uncle and you told him it was not in your power to give it. What right had he to ask any one before me?

and to the persistent Mr. Boarham, whom she detests, she applies her rigid principles and becomes obdurate and highly assertive (Ch. 16) :

I tell you plainly, that it cannot be. No consideration can induce me to marry against my inclinations.

After both Milicent Hargrave and Helen Graham were married and with families, they were much more 'wise to the world', and ready to provide their opinions. Milicent, having married Ralph Hattersly, who is not much better than Huntingdon, is afraid that her younger sister will not listen to her advice; she implores Helen to speak to Esther (Ch. 32) :

..., I wish you would seriously impress it upon her, never, on any account, or for anybody's persuasion, to marry for the sake of money, or rank, or establishment, or any earthly thing but true affection and well-grounded esteem.

And later, when Walter and Mrs. Hargrave are insistent that Esther marry Mr. Oldfield, an older gentleman whom she disliked intensely, Helen urges her not to give in to their demands (Ch. 41) :

You might as well sell yourself to slavery at once, as marry a man you dislike. If your mother and brother are unkind to you, you may leave them, but remember you are bound to your husband for life.

Helen gives Esther still more advice on keeping her emotions in check, and under control until the proper time (Ch. 41) :

When I tell you not to marry without love, I do not advise you to marry for love alone - there are many, many other things to be considered. Keep both heart and hand in your possession, till you see good reason to part with them;...

When Helen Graham is separated from her husband, Walter Hargrave relentlessly pursues her with protestations of love, but to no avail. Helen, a highly principled person, has no second thoughts about repeatedly rebuffing his advances, and she sets out her beliefs on the subject to make it clear to him that she will not enter into any unholy relationship with him or anyone else (Ch. 37) :

> - and if I were alone in the world, I have still my God and my religion, and I would sooner die than disgrace my calling and break my faith with Heaven to obtain a few brief years of false and fleeting happiness -

In spite of all the advice of Aunt Maxwell, and Helen's own good intentions and personal guidelines for a partner of choice, she is desperate to keep aloof from the likes of Mr. Boarham and Mr. Wilmot, and she eventually succumbs to Huntingdon's charm and good looks. On several occasions, Huntingdon 'rescued' her from these two, distasteful individuals which simply endeared him more to her each time. With buoyant, youthful confidence, her misplaced belief in physiognomy,[4] and her strong, Christian charity, Helen thoroughly believed that she could save Huntingdon from his vices and follies, and ultimately from his self-destruction. To 'leave the ninety-nine and save the one lost soul'[5] was, to Helen, thought to be the ultimate, Christian act of charity.

And if she 'hates the sin', she 'loves the sinner'. She explains to her aunt her hopes to re-direct the 'merry, thoughtless profligate' as her aunt described him (Ch. 17) :

> No; I should not wish to guide him; but I think I might have influence sufficient to save him from some errors, and I should think my life well spent in the effort to preserve so noble a nature from destruction.

Like Lady Byron, Helen believes that once married, her Christian beliefs will be a strong influence on Huntingdon, and if he had transgressed in the past, she will happily spend her life seeking his redemption (Ch. 17) :

> If he has done amiss, I shall consider my life well spent in saving him from consequences of his early errors, and striving to recall him to the path of virtue.

Helen is also of the belief that all of God's creatures, good or bad, are worth saving, and nothing could be more honorable than a Divine calling to redeem a lost soul. In spite of the warnings of her aunt about his ignominious past, Helen, blinded by love, looks only to the positive and the glory of God's work. She explains her joy (Ch. 18) :

> There is essential goodness in him; and what delight to unfold it! If he has wandered, what bliss to recall him! If he is now exposed to the baneful influence of corrupting

---

4 Charlotte and Anne were both believers in this pseudoscience of facial features revealing a person's character within.

5 This refers to the Christian parable of the shepherd leaving the flock to save one lost lamb.

and wicked companions, what glory to deliver him from them! Oh! if I could but
believe that Heaven has designed me for this!

and in reference to his faults, Helen proclaims that, "the worse they are, the more I long
to deliver him from them". (Ch. 20)

At one point prior to their marriage, Helen and Arthur have a disagreement, and she
fears that she has lost him to Annabella Wilmot, also a dissolute character. Helen ago-
nizes over the potential loss, and the fact that he has fallen for one who is so unworthy of
his affections. Helen believes that only she can do his affections justice and bring him
true happiness. She commends herself as more caring of Huntingdon (Ch. 18) :

> She cannot appreciate the good that is in him: she will neither see it, nor value it, nor
> cherish it. She will neither deplore his faults nor attempt their amendment, but rather
> aggravate them by her own.

Eventually, Huntingdon proposes and Helen accepts. After a Continental honeymoon,
and a year of wedded bliss, Helen begins to see things from a different perspective. Prior
to her marriage, she was more than willing to believe that all of her husband's faults were
due to outside influences, but 'repairable'. The causes ranged from an overindulgent
mother and an overly-strict, selfish, miserly father, and a host of degenerate friends, all of
whom contributed to his demise. And Helen firmly refused to believe her aunt's description of his 'jolly companions' (Ch. 17) :

> ... whose chief delight is to wallow in vice, and vie with each other who can run
> fastest and furthest down the headlong road to the place prepared for the devil and
> his angels.

Now, her aunt's warnings were coming back to haunt her as well as expose her own
youthful errors of judgment, and in particular, errors in judgment of character. It was not
long before Helen realized that her husband had little intention of mending his ways; in
fact, if anything, he was getting worse. After only a few months of marriage, Helen
makes an entry into her diary, 'Feb. 18, 1822', that if she had known more about her
husband, she probably would not have allowed herself to fall in love with Huntingdon
and marry him. She chastises him in the hope of a sincere change (Ch. 23) :

> You are not without the capacity of veneration, and faith and hope, and conscience
> and reason, and every other requisite to a Christian's character if you choose to
> employ them; but all our talents increase in the using, and every faculty, both good
> and bad, strengthens by exercise: therefore, if you choose to use the bad, or those
> which tend to evil, till they become your masters, and neglect the good till they
> dwindle away, you have only yourself to blame.

After two years of marriage, an entry in Helen's diary shows that 'wedded bliss' has
since faded and that their differences in views and opinions have widened from a rift to a

chasm. She now seems resigned to the fact that her husband is undoubtedly a confirmed hedonist; she states (Ch. 28) :

> ... he is a man without self-restraint or lofty aspirations - a lover of pleasure, given up to animal enjoyments: he is not a bad husband, but his notions of matrimonial duties and comforts are not my notions.

Anne and Charlotte Brontë also had their own clear views of women's 'place' in society which were radically different from the views of the Victorian England in which they lived. They saw no reason for the gendered division of labour, and particularly the vast fields of employment open to men, and the limited fields open to them. The existing view that women would become mothers and 'home managers' is sharply criticized by Helen when she condemns Huntingdon's view of a 'wife' (Ch. 28) :

> ... his idea of a wife is a thing to love one devotedly and to stay at home - to wait upon her husband, and amuse him and minister to his comfort in every possible way, while he chooses to stay with her; and, when he is absent, to attend to his interests, domestic or otherwise, and patiently wait his return; no matter how he may be occupied in the meantime.

After a trip to London in which Arthur spent four months there, he returned in a deplorable state, consistent with Helen's fears, and reports from Walter Hargrave, who found his derelictions and degradations even too much for himself, a former profligate cohort, to bear. When Helen remonstrates with Arthur and says, "You have shamefully wronged yourself, body and soul, and me, too;..." (Ch. 30) he simply retorts, and commends himself for his own 'fast-living'. He replies (Ch. 30) :

> I've lived more in these four months, Helen, than you have in the whole course of your existence, or will to the end of your days, if they number a hundred years;...

Finally, after years of effort, and Arthur's continued desire for wine and spirits which made him unnaturally 'peevish' and 'irritable', Helen finally recognized the futility of it all, and the dashed hopes of trying to redeem the man she loved. She simply gave up (Ch. 30) :

> ..., for I saw it all in vain: God might awaken that heart, supine and stupefied with self-indulgence, and remove the film of sensual darkness from his eyes, but I could not.

The bitterness of defeat and sense of hopelessness pervades her thoughts, and now she 'abhorred the sinner as well as the sin', a markedly changed opinion from her optimism of pre-marriage and early marriage. She now appeals to a higher source; for a Christian, there is always 'hope' (Ch. 30) :

> Yes, poor Arthur, I will still hope and pray for you; and though I write as if you were
> some abandoned wretch, past hope, and past reprieve, it is only my anxious fears -
> my strong desires that make me do so; one who loved you less would be less bitter -
> less dissatisfied.[6]

In the last days of his life, Huntingdon becomes closely attached to Helen, and would
not let her out of his sight even for a moment. He knew that death was near, recognized
his faults and transgressions, and struggled with the thought of a death-bed confession.
He was at least lucid enough in thought to discuss the matter with Helen and points out its
irony; it may also be an insight into Branwell's religious doubts (Ch. 49) :

> Are we not to be judged according to the deeds done in the body? Where's the use of
> a probationary existence, if a man may spend it as he pleases, just contrary to God's
> decrees, and then go to heaven with the best - if the vilest sinner may win the reward
> of the holiest saint, by merely saying, 'I repent.'?

For all of Huntingdon's misdeeds, one must at least recognize his honesty since asking for repentance would simply be a hollow and insincere jesture on his part. His reply to
Helen is straightforward, honest, and sincere, "I can't repent; I only fear." (Ch. 49)

A similar warning, and plea, was issued to Mr. Hattersly whose profligacy he himself
began to recognize, and wished to part company with them and their wicked ways. On
several occasions, his wife, Milicent, had pleaded with Helen to speak to her husband.
Helen advised him in a fashion consistent with her religious views and was similar to
advice she later gave to her own husband in his last hours. She told Hattersly (Ch. 42) :

> ... you cannot make amends for the past by doing your duty for the future, inasmuch
> as your duty is only what you owe to your Maker, and you cannot do more than fulfil
> it - another must make amends for your past delinquencies. If you intend to reform,
> invoke God's blessing, His mercy, and His aid; not His curse.

Anne Brontë also had firm views on raising children, and, of course, these views
were even more firmly developed and planted after her years as a governess to the Inghams
and Robinsons, and which were so clearly enunciated in *Agnes Grey*. Here again, in this
novel, both her husband and little Arthur, her son, are used to expound her beliefs on
raising a child 'properly' in Victorian times. She can see the final results of a poor upbringing in her own husband, and lays much of the blame for his shameless conduct,
absence of goals, and shiftless ways on his parents. She is determined not to make the
same mistake with her own children. She summarizes what she believes is the problem
(Ch. 25) :

> ... he has no more idea of exerting himself to overcome obstacles than he has of
> restraining his natural appetites; and these two things are the ruin of him. I lay them

---

6   These feelings are highly reminiscent of the Brontë sisters' feelings for their brother Branwell;
    he resisted their efforts, but they never lost hope for his salvation.

both to the charge of his harsh yet careless father, and his madly indulgent mother. If ever I am a mother I will jealously strive against this crime of over-indulgence. I can hardly give it a milder name when I think of the evils it brings.

In her diary entry of December 25th, 1822, after one year of marriage, she reports events, feelings, and changes in emotions, especially toward her newborn child whom she sees as a 'gift from God'. Her revelationary, and tempered, views are evident in the following passage (Ch. 28) :

> Now I am a wife: my bliss is sobered, but not destroyed; my hopes diminished, but not departed; my fears increased, but not yet thoroughly confirmed; and, thank Heaven, I am a mother too. God has sent me a soul to educate for heaven,...

One year later in her entry of December 25th, 1823, she expressed her first fears about Arthur's upbringing, particularly at the hands of his father, whose heart he has captured. She recognized fears of her own indulgent propensities toward her son as well (Ch. 28) :

> He has won his father's heart at last; and now my constant terror is, lest he should be ruined by that father's thoughtless indulgence. But I must be aware of my own weaknesses too, for I never knew till now how strong are a parent's temptations to spoil an only child.

In the above passage, Helen finally recognizes the reality, and difference, of raising a child of one's own, as opposed to educating someone else's child. This was an opportunity that Anne Brontë herself never had, but she was intelligent enough to be able to empathize with this situation, and may even provide a 'window' into her own inner thoughts on child-rearing, if she had been married and blessed with children.

The fiercest exchanges on child-rearing cover a number of pages in the novel, in Chapter Three, and involves Helen Graham, Mrs. Markham, and Gilbert Markham. And later Rev. Millward hears of it and lashes out at Helen's views with equally firm, but diametrically opposed, views. The entire debate begins when Helen makes a polite, social visit to her neighbours, the Markhams, and Mrs. Markham tries to force wine upon the mother and the boy. When Helen refuses and states that she has done everything she can to make him hate it, Mrs. Markham is appalled, feeling that she will not make a 'man' out of him. She lectures Helen (Ch. 3) :

> - 'well, you surprise me! I really gave you credit for having more sense. The poor child will be the veriest milksop that ever was sopped. Only think what a man you will make of him, if you persist [in] - '

And when Helen defends her decision, Gilbert Markham comes to his mother's aid and engages in a philosophical discussion on whether temptations should be removed altogether from a child's 'path', or whether he should be exposed to them, but learn to avoid them. Such is the argument which Gilbert Markham presents (Ch. 3) :

> If you would have your son to walk honourably through the world, you must not
> attempt to clear the stones from his path, but teach him to walk firmly over them - not
> insist upon leading him by the hand, but let him learn to go alone.

The debate as to whether or not temptations should be 'removed' continued between the three and then proceeded onto the topic of education of the young. Mrs. Graham was hesitant to send her boy to school, and Mrs. Markham argued against keeping him at home saying that she will make a 'Miss Nancy' of him and only indulge his 'follies and caprices' by doing so. And when Mrs. Markham sees that she is losing the argument, she explains that she will send the vicar to see Mrs. Graham, and that he will set her straight 'in a minute'.

From there the argument advanced onto the differences in the education of boys and girls. Whereas Gilbert Markham argued that boys should be 'strengthened' to resist temptation by leaving 'obstacles' in their paths, he was against exposing girls to these same obstacles and temptations. This Helen argued was unreasonable because it was a 'double-standard', or that he regarded women to be "so feeble-minded that [she] cannot withstand temptation". She prefers that both learn from others' experiences (Ch. 3) :

> You would have us encourage our sons to prove all things by their own experience,
> while our daughters must not even profit by the experience of others. Now I would
> have both so benefit by the experience of others,... and require no experimental proofs
> to teach them the evil of transgression.

When Rev. Millward is told about Mrs. Graham's 'unorthodox' views of childhood education, he is shocked and strongly disagrees with her approach. He believes that all wine and spirits are part of the stores of 'Providence', and that not to partake of them is unsound and misguided. The Reverend responds vehemently to the news of Mrs. Graham's approach, as described by Mrs. Markham (Ch. 4) :

> Wrong! - criminal, I should say - criminal! Not only is it making a fool of the boy,
> but it is despising the gifts of Providence, and teaching him to trample them under
> his feet.

In spite of the special efforts and precautions Helen took for her son, she eventually 'lost ground' with him in a 'battle' of good influences she was trying to set for him, and the evil encouragements which her husband was trying to instill in their son. She describes the battle of wills (Ch. 36) :

> If, I, for his good, deny him some trifling indulgence, he goes to his father, and the
> latter, in spite of his self indolence, will even give himself some trouble to meet the
> child's desires: if I attempt to curb his will,...he knows his other parent will smile and
> take his part against me.

The father then never troubled himself to think of the difficulties he had caused in the raising of his son, and the mother was left to cope with the problems he had wrought. Helen is doubtful of her husband's aims, and the only consolation which she can see in this difficult situation is that her husband often makes himself absent on trips to London which gives her time to repair the 'damage'. It appears that her advantage of influence is slowly being eroded, and that her husband's only motives are simply spite and torment (Ch. 37) :

> ... from motives of mere idle egotism, is pleased to win to himself; making no use of it but to torment me and ruin the child. My only consolation is that he spends comparatively little of his time at home, and,... I have a chance of recovering the ground I had lost.

The issue of parental guidance and influence was the one which finally brought matters 'to a head' and resulted in Mrs. Huntingdon's plan to make an escape to New England where she would start a new life, and be at a distance where Arthur's father would no longer be an influence. This plan was foiled, and she eventually 'stole away' to Wildfell Hall, but the issue was still the same, that is, getting her son out of the reach of her husband. Seeing her son being badly influenced by her dissolute husband, and his profligate companions, was more than she could endure (Ch. 39) :

> ...[he] learned to tipple wine like papa, to swear like Mr. Hattersly, and to have his own way like a man, and send mamma to the devil when she tried to prevent him.

Eventually, she makes good her escape to Wildfell Hall, and this is where the story begins when Gilbert Markham meets his attractive, new neighbour who lives in an isolated farmhouse under mysterious circumstances. Mrs. Huntingdon, now 'Helen Graham', has gone there to escape her husband's wrath and detection, since he is only interested in taking back his son, and raising him to be a 'man'. This is the point around which the main action of the novel revolves and also which triggered the chain of events which sets the novel into action.

Many reviews of *The Tenant...* criticized the novel for its coarseness, brutality, profanity, scenes of debauchery, and infidelity which some classes of Victorian society preferred to forget and overlook rather than scrutinize. It was these prejudicial reviews which reduced the novel's critical acclaim, and the level of recognition it so rightly deserves.

Early in the novel there is one scene which was, by Victorian standards, considered to be excessively brutal, and therefore offensive and distasteful. This was the scene in which Gilbert Markham, after garnering suspicions of Mr. Lawrence's attentions to Helen Graham caused him to cogitate and imagine an unholy union between them, spurred him into aggressive, and violent, physical action. Gilbert met Mr. Lawrence on the road, engaged him in an acrimonious conversation, and then out of sheer rage, and momentary jealous insanity, committed a grievous, unprovoked assault on Lawrence with his riding whip. The whip was tipped with a 'massive horse's head of plated metal' which he brought down on his head with 'savage satisfaction' and inflicted a serious head wound.

After the attack, Gilbert Markham saw a 'deadly pallor... overspread his face' and 'red drops' trickle down his forehead before he fell backward from his saddle to the ground. When he 'lay as still and silent as a corpse', he worried that he had killed him and returned to check. Seeing that he had simply been stunned by the fall, he rode away, but returned a second time from a 'voice of conscience' and perhaps a measure of guilt. This time he found him in 'a recumbant position on the bank' soaked in his own blood. It had been raining and he was covered in mud, and after some effort to help him, Mr. Lawrence mounted his pony in a stupor and rode off. Later that day, Gilbert heard a story that Mr. Lawrence had been 'thrown from his horse and brought home dying'. Gilbert made no admissions to his vicious attack, and Mr. Lawrence was magnanimous enough not to implicate Gilbert in the events of the morning. Such callous violence was not something Victorian readers were accustom to digesting in the course of their fiction; it was beyond the 'norms' of propriety and behaviour.

Hand in hand with this brutality was Huntingdon's mistreatment of his favourite cocker, Dash, which jumped on the settee to lick his face, and for this he was rewarded with a 'smart blow'. When the dog refused to answer his call a half-hour later, Huntingdon picked up 'a heavy book and hurled it at his head'. Helen immediately let the dog out to protect it from its master, picked up the book, and returned to her reading. Later, when she was going to bed, and he requested her to stay, he verbally abused her and called her a "confounded slut". To add to this profanity, Anne Brontë used the phrase, 'damn it' (ie d—n it) on several occasions, and in one case even used, 'G - d d — n me...' which for Victorian times was highly profane and quite offensive as well as a blasphemy. Several other invocations to the 'devil' (ie. d — l) throughout the novel would also have been viewed in the same way. In our present-day standards, this is very 'mild', but for Victorians it was 'shocking', coarse, vulgar, and unacceptable.

Anne Brontë, and Charlotte Brontë as well, often portrayed men as rough, boisterous, and often rude, perhaps out of lack of experience with well-mannered men, or just to focus on some of their worst tendencies. It was frequently scenes which involved men, and their companions, in drinking sessions which led to the criticism of 'coarseness' in her novel. Branwell, her brother, who is often thought to be the model for Arthur Huntingdon, may also have inadvertantly and unwittingly provided background information for all their novels. Branwell's use of alcohol and continued drunkeness, his rough and abusive language, and his eventual downward spiral through the use of laudanum are the most likely sources of the Brontë sisters' writing and references to men and their behaviours, which at times seemed odd and inexplicable to them. Their encounters with other men outside their immediate surroundings were very limited and could not have provided any extensive or direct experience for their novels.

Although her brother Branwell had faults and committed indiscretions, he was extremely intelligent, a brilliant conversationalist, and very well-liked; beneath these faults was a very likeable and popular person. In a conversation Helen has with Hattersly regarding personal reform, he is reluctant to give up his friend because of his dissolute ways (Ch. 42) :

> ...he's such devilish good company is Huntingdon, after all - you can't imagine what a jovial good fellow he is when he's not fairly drunk, only just primed or half seas over -we all have a bit of liking for him at the bottom of our hearts, though we can't respect him.

These were the same feelings that many people like Francis Grundy and J.B. Leyland had about her wayward, but fun-loving, brother Branwell.

Another reference which Helen makes which was applicable to both Huntingdon and her brother had to do with an 'occupation' which would have done much for both of them and kept them out of the reach of temptation. In an entry in her diary, Helen makes reference to her husband as 'lusty and reckless' and 'full of mischief', like a child. She has a solution for these 'idle hands' as she explains in the entry (Ch. 25) :

> I wish he had something to do, some useful trade, or profession, or employment - anything to occupy his head or his hands for a few hours a day, and give him something besides his own pleasure to think about.

Huntingdon had wealth and did not need to work. Branwell, on the other hand, needed both steady work and an income for a livelihood, and to offset his wild lifestyle which caused him to lose all of his jobs. He had the mental wherewithal to do extremely well, but the jobs he obtained he considered beneath his 'station' in life, and he was disdainful of them. Branwell's 'idle hands', which made for 'devil's work', frequently got him into trouble, and eventually led to his downfall, just as with Huntingdon.

Early in the novel, and shortly after Helen's marriage to Huntingdon, they have their first quarrel which begins when he insists on recounting to his wife an affair he had with an older, married woman.[7] Helen was not exactly interested in hearing of his prior escapades and intrigues, and he became angry when she asked him to stop. Later, as they sat across the room from one another in silence, she felt certain that he would have liked to exact revenge on her. She implies that had the weather been better, he probably would have set off on his horse, and (Ch. 24) :

> ... had there been a lady anywhere within reach, of any age between fifteen and forty-five, he would have sought revenge and found employment in getting up, or trying to get up, a desperate flirtation with her;...

Her husband's interpretation of the marriage vows also seems to differ widely from hers and are contentious. After he commits his first indiscretions with Lady Lowborough, she cautions him, but Huntingdon simply brushes them off as 'nothing'. Helen disagrees

---

7   This story is thought to be based on Branwell's affair with Mrs. Robinson at Thorp Green Hall. Anne attributed most of the blame to Mrs. Robinson who was older, and married.

and poses the question, "Can I love a man that does such things, and coolly maintains it is nothing?" Huntingdon angrily replies that she is breaking her marriage vows in which (Ch. 27) :

> You promised to honour and obey me, and now you attempt to hector over me,... I won't be dictated to by a woman, though she may be my wife.

and moments later, Huntingdon reveals his double-standard, when Helen points out that had she committed the indiscretion, he would no longer love her. His 'Victorian attitude' is clearly evident in his protest (Ch. 27) :

> The cases are different,... It is a woman's nature to be constant - to love one and one only, blindly, tenderly, and for ever - bless them, dear creatures! and you above them all - but you must have some commiseration for us, Helen; you must give us a little more licence,...

The scenes of degradation and drunkeness we read about when Huntingdon invites his friends to their manor for the hunting season sets the stage for debauchery, and later events directly connected to their separation. It was a custom of the times for men of wealth who could leave their estates in the hands of managers to sometimes stay away for weeks at a time. Land owners with large estates would invite their friends for 'fall shooting', and they would often remain there for perhaps a month or more. It, therefore, does not require too much imagination to realize the goings-on that accompanied such gatherings when men and alcohol were combined.

One of the first descriptions of Lord Lowborough show him to be a desperate fellow who, along with his friends, had given way to drunkeness, gambling, and debauchery and was now without a fortune and looking for 'an heiress to retrieve it'. To his credit, Lowborough later renounced this approach, married for love, and completely reformed himself, and although he still consorted with his same friends, he strongly resisted their efforts to bring him back to his old dissolute ways. Lowborough's wife, Annabella Wilmot, a true coquet, married him solely for the position and title, and became 'Lady Lowborough'. She had no love for him and continued to flirt, especially with the wild and handsome Arthur Huntingdon with whom she is enamoured. Their indiscretions are a precursor to the main action which unfolds later.

The scenes in the novel which were considered particularly scandalous and distasteful occur during the hunting season when Huntingdon's friends all descend on Grassdale Manor, much to the dismay of the new Mrs. Huntingdon. All of the guests like Grimsby, Hattersly, Hargrave, and Annabella, with the exception of Lord Lowborough, were up to 'no good'. Annabella was determined to carry on her flirtations with Mr. Huntingdon, right under the nose of his wife and her own husband, while the others launched into heavy drinking and outright tomfoolery. In her journal, Helen berates two of their male guests; she writes (Ch. 31) :

Those two detestable men, Grimsby and Hattersly, have destroyed all my labour against his love of wine. They encourage him daily to overstep the bounds of moderation, and, not unfrequently, to disgrace himself by positive excess.

Helen fully recognized the negative effects the others were having on her husband, but as a dutiful, Christian wife, she calmly resigned herself to the fact and seeks to make the best of it. She reports (Ch. 31) :

... I have found it my wisest plan to shut my eyes against the past and future, as far as he, at least, is concerned, and live only for the present; to love him when I can; to smile (if possible) when he smiles, be cheerful when he is cheerful, and pleased when he is agreeable; and when he is not, to try to make him so -

The next day, after the ladies had retired from the drawing room, the men began drinking and causing an uproar. When Lowborough could stand it no longer, he retired with the ladies in the adjoining room, only to be ridiculed by his wife, and then he retreated to the garden. When Hargarve later followed Lowborough's exit, Hattersly tried to prevent his departure, but he managed to escape his grasp, and when Lowborough returned, Hattersly seized him. Hattersly was bound and determined to drag Lowborough away and force him to drink until he was drunk, but he resisted. Lowborough clung to the door-post and could only be released from Hattersly's cluthces by applying a live candle to his hand. Once released, Lowborough was not seen again until morning.

The scene which immediately followed was equally unpalatable to Victorian readers since it showed mistreatment of women, particularly wives, at the hands of their inconsiderate husbands. When Lowborough escaped, Milicent Hattersly tried to sneak away after being completely humiliated and embarrassed by her husband's disgraceful behaviour. Hattersly observed her departure, called her back, and gripped her arm tightly to prevent her release. Her brother, Walter Hargrave, stepped in to protect her but was rebuffed by a violent blow to the chest and an epithet of curses for interfering between a man and his wife.

Finally, Helen stepped in and berated Hattersly for taunting his wife and explained that she had been disgraced in front of others by his actions. Hattersly then cursed his wife and threw her to the floor. Huntingdon, the host, was overcome by fits of laughter, which simply infuriated Hattersly even more. Hattersly further responded by hurling a footstool at the head of his host, followed by a fusillade of books, thrown one by one. When that did not put an end to Huntingdon's laughter, he physically attacked him. The evening ended when Grimsby, Hattersly, and Huntingdon, all inebriated, supported each other noisily up the stairs. Such scenes of disgraceful conduct would certainly not have endeared the author to the upper classes of Victorian readers for the negative exposure it provided. Other similar scenes appear throughout the better part of the novel, and all include the misbehaviour of the men while in each other's company.

To add to the disgraceful conduct of the men are the actions of infidelity between Lady Lowborough and Arthur Huntingdon. During the first stay of the visitors at the manor during the first year of their marriage, Helen caught her husband seriously flirting with Annabella and warned him; he promised never to repeat it. With their second visit, an elaborate scheme was set up by Hattersly, Hargrave, Grimsby, Annabella, and Huntingdon to enable the two, illicit lovers to secretly carry on in the garden behind the backs of Lord Lowborough and Mrs. Huntingdon.

When Helen went out to look for her husband, he was surprised to see her there, expecting Annabella of course, and insisted that she go back inside the manor for the benefit of her health. Once inside, Hargrave engaged Helen in a 'long game' of chess, as a diversion, while Grimsby and Hattersly acted as 'look outs' against Lord Lowborough on behalf of his friend, Huntingdon. After the game, Hargrave, seeking to make a personal gain from Huntingdon's downfall, implied that Arthur and Annabella could be found together in the shrubbery. Refusing to take Hargrave at his word, Helen made her way to the garden only to find that it was true and have her worst suspicions confirmed. She heard subdued voices, and then the conversation of her husband and Lady Lowborough in which he admitted to Annabella that he no longer loved his wife. When she asked Huntingdon if he still had any love for his wife, he replied, "Not one bit, by all that's sacred!" (Ch. 33) This infidelity, in effect, was the 'final straw' which brought their marriage to an end, and ultimately caused Helen to seek asylum at Wildfell Hall.

After her discovery, Helen confronted her husband on his infidelity. Since he could not deny the facts, Helen informed him that they were 'man and wife' in name only and that she would prefer to leave. Helen is forced to stay since he will not allow her to leave with their son; tensions between them run high. And when Lord Lowborough discovers what has transpired between the host and his wife, he was livid with anger and invoked a 'deadly execration' to Huntingdon. Huntingdon merely shrugged it off as 'unchristian' and flippantly offered up his own wife to him (Ch. 38) :

> ... I'd never give up an old friend for the sake of a wife. You may have mine if you
> like, and I call that handsome - I can do no more than offer restitution, can I?

and after Lowborough departs, he makes the same offer to his profligate friends when they chide him to seek her pardon. He replies (Ch. 39) :

> ...what wife?... look you, gentlemen, I value her so highly, that any one among you,
> that can fancy her, may have her and welcome - you may, by Jove, and my blessing
> into the bargain!

Adding insult to injury, Huntingdon continued to correspond with Lady Lowborough and had the audacity to show his wife the letters which he received from her. With their marriage rapidly deteriorating, and Huntingdon's negative influence on their son, Helen saw few options except to escape to a place where no one could find them. Even more important than her marriage was the negative effect of her husband's influence on their young son which Helen could no longer tolerate; her progress with young Arthur was always rapidly undone when her husband returned from one of his journeys. She complained that he would (Ch. 37) :

...[do] his utmost to subvert my labours and transform my innocent, affectionate, tractable darling into a selfish, disobedient, and mischievous boy; thereby preparing the soil for those vices he has so successfully cultivated in his own perverted nature.

The stage was now set for their move to Wildfell Hall.

Anne Brontë's writing could never be separated from her religious beliefs which are continuously portrayed, and continually surface, throughout the novel by way of her characters, their actions, and discourse which have already been quoted previously to display, and give voice to, her thoughts on marriage and child-rearing. Her beliefs, although perfectly evident throughout, are not overpowering, but firm, and do not develop into didactic fanaticism or lengthy, religious harangues. The references are constant, unswerving in controversy, direct, and moderate, but they leave no doubt as to where the author stands on many social issues, her moral grounds, and religious beliefs.

Before Helen's marriage to Huntingdon, during her idealistic period of 'pure love', she defends him to her aunt saying that "his worst and only vice is thoughtlessness". And when her aunt retorts that "thoughtlessness... may lead to every crime," Helen again comes to his defence and proclaims that even if she fails, she can always fall back on God who will (Ch. 20) :

> ... in the fulness of time, gather together in one all things in Christ Jesus, who tasted death for every man, and in whom God will reconcile all things to Himself, whether they be things in earth or things in heaven.

Later, Helen found her husband's attitude toward Lord Lowborough's sufferings both cavalier and deplorable. Huntingdon and his friends thought nothing of using his misfortunes as a source for their gaiety. Helen's basic instincts of common decency, courtesy, and empathy for the sufferings of others arouses her indignation towards her husband. He relents under pressure, and asks for her guidance; she sternly directs him (Ch. 22) :

> ... that, in future, you will never make a jest of the sufferings of others, and always use your influence with your friends for their own advantage against their evil propensities, instead of seconding their evil propensities against themselves.

Huntingdon's idea of religion is quite different from that of Helen's; he sees it as something aloof and abstract, and not concrete and near at hand. His world is secular and materialistic, and since he has always enjoyed the fruits of his inherited wealth, without any efforts, he appears to have no pressing need for religion. His wife's consistency, and constancy, in her morals, religion, beliefs, and values is something he finds difficult to deal with. In a discussion with Helen about his reform and his need for religion to guide him, he is critical of her and forthright about his beliefs. He tells her directly (Ch. 23) :

> - you are too religious. Now I like a woman to be religious, and I think your piety one of your greatest charms, but then, like all other good things, it may be carried too far.

> To my thinking, a woman's religion ought not to lessen her devotion to her earthly lord.

This is a very interesting and revealing response since he sees piety as a 'charm', and he seems to imply that it is fine for other people, but not himself. Also, his use of the phrase, a 'woman's religion' reveals that Helen's view, or understanding of religion, is perhaps somewhat different from his view and a 'man's religion', with different focuses. From this exchange, we see that the author recognizes two different views of life, man's and woman's, and that these differing views may 'spill over' into religion even though religion is 'universal' and gender has no bearing. His view appears to be that the husband, her 'lord', should be primary and at the centre of her attentions and devotions in this secular world, and religious piety should be 'secondary'. Helen's view could not have been more diametrically opposed, and she believes in the equality of husband and wife, not his superiority. She replied making it perfectly clear as to her own priorities when it comes to man and God. Nothing, including a husband, supercedes God; she replies (Ch. 23) :

> I will give my whole heart and soul to my Maker if I can,... and not one atom more of it to you than He allows. What are you, sir, that you should set yourself up as a god, and presume to dispute possession of my heart with Him to whom I owe all I have and all I am, every blessing I ever did or ever can enjoy - and yourself among the rest - if you are a blessing, which I am half inclined to doubt.

Helen's eventual love for Gilbert Markham has had no more deleterious effect on her religious beliefs and persuasions than her initial love for her husband, Arthur Huntingdon. When she and Gilbert enter into a discussion of 'love', Gilbert thinks only of his earthly love for Helen, but Helen cannot be separated or seduced from 'perfect love in heaven'. It is never really out of her sight, and secular love for both Arthur and Gilbert will always be fleeting, and temporal, as opposed to the timeless love of heaven. Helen resorts to the wonders of Nature and metaphorically compares the caterpillar to butterfly cycle to the true love that awaits them in heaven. She answers Gilbert's narrow, earthly view of love with these words (Ch. 45) :

> ... I do know that to regret the exchange of earthly pleasures for the joys of heaven, is as if the grovelling caterpillar should lament that it must one day quit the nibbled leaf to soar aloft and flutter through the air, roving at will from flower to flower, sipping sweet honey from their cups, or basking in their sunny petals. If these little creatures knew how great a change awaited them, no doubt they would regret it; but would not all such sorrow be misplaced?

Obviously, Gilbert's beliefs do not have Helen's degree of depth, or understanding, nor does it appear that he has given it much thought. Her first 'blind' marriage to Huntingdon has taught her many important lessons, and she is intent on not making the same mistake in a second marriage. Helen appeals to his sense of imagination and what awaits them in heaven, and at the same time issues him a terse warning if he cannot comprehend it. She outlines her thoughts of heaven (Ch. 45) :

> But, Gilbert, can you really derive no consolation from the thought that we may meet together where there is no more pain and sorrow, no more striving against sin, and struggling of the spirit against the flesh; where both will behold the same glorious truths, and drink exalted and supreme felicity from the same fountain of light and goodness - that Being whom both will worship with the same intensity of holy ardour, and where poor and happy creatures both will love with the same divine affection? If you cannot, never write to me!

It is both clear and evident that she intends to approach her second relationship, and possible marriage, with greater care than the first where the love of both will be subservient to the love of God. If this cannot be, and she cannot obtain a sincere commitment from him, she will forego her love for Gilbert and all its earthly pleasures.

The Brontë sisters were all closely attuned and attached to Nature and the wonders of its beauty, and it was always part of their writing. Whenever Anne made mention of Nature, her writing immediately altered and became elevated and cloaked in deep, narrative description which offered a refreshing change of pace from the rest of the story's elements and actions. One evening when Helen needed a slight respite from her guests, she retired to the library where she looked out the window onto a beautiful scene. Her description is almost poetical (Ch. 38) :

> ... out upon the west where the darkening hills rose sharply defined against the clear amber light of evening, that gradually blended and faded away into the pure, pale blue of the upper sky, where one bright star was shining through,...

Then, as Gilbert frantically sought out Helen after a reasonable period of mourning, and after an erroneous report that she was about to be re-married, he approached Grassdale Manor in a gig and described the grounds in its winter beauty (Ch. 52) :

> - the park as beautiful now, in its wintry garb, as it could be in its summer glory: the majestic sweep, the undulating swell and fall, displayed to full advantage in that robe of dazzling purity, stainless and printless - save, one long, winding track left by the trooping deer - the stately timber-trees with their heavy laden branches gleaming white against the dull, grey sky; the deep encircling woods; the broad expanse of water sleeping in frozen quiet; and the weeping ash and willow drooping their snow-clad boughs above it -

And finally, in a description more ascribed to the tenacity of Nature in all its hardships, she finds a winter rose[8] which she plucks from outside her window and offers to Gilbert (Ch. 53) :

---

8 The scene is vaguely reminiscent of Charlotte's search for a sprig of heather in the snows of winter as Emily lay dying in the parlour.

> This rose is not so fragrant as a summer flower, but it has stood through hardship
> none of them could bear: the cold rain of winter has sufficed to nourish it, and its
> faint sun to warm it; the bleak winds have not blanched it or broken its stem, and the
> keen frost has not blighted it.

The greatest suspense in the novel is found near the end where Gilbert hears of the
proposed wedding of one of the Lawrences. He believes it is Helen who is to be married,
but he is misinformed and the suspense created draws the reader into the plot and propels
him onward. It is sufficiently intriguing and suspenseful to hold the reader's attention
through the last few chapters. The suspense is sustained through all his travel tribulations; Gilbert is gripped with fear right to the moment where he sees the bride through a
shrouded veil and finally realizes that it is not his beloved Helen. In fact, it is Esther
Hargrave and Mr. Lawrence is the groom which brings a happy ending to another story.
Esther has defied her parents, and in the end, took Helen's earlier advice, and married
Frederick Lawrence, a gentleman, for 'true love' instead of wealth, social standing and
materialistic gain.

The main story also has a happy ending with Gilbert Markham set to marry Helen
Graham, but not without adversity, and Gilbert overcoming what he sees as a formidable
barrier. He is particularly concerned about the fact that Mrs. Huntingdon is now a lady of
wealth and standing, and that Mr. Lawrence, and not necessarily the recently widowed
Mrs. Huntingdon, will 'reject' him, or at least speak against him. The difference in their
social standing, he fears, will keep them apart. He bitterly ponders the objections Mr.
Lawrence might have against him (Ch. 50) :

> ... perhaps he would think me too poor - too lowly born, to match with his sister? yes,
> there is another barrier: doubtless there was a wide distinction between the rank and
> circumstances of Mrs. Huntingdon, the lady of Grassdale Manor, and those of Mrs.
> Graham the artist, the tenant of Wildfell Hall; and it might be deemed presumption
> in me to offer my hand to the former -

And just prior to this, as Gilbert made his way to Staningley Hall in search of Helen,
two of his fellow passengers speak of the Maxwell estate which has recently been willed
to a new, young heiress. Their conversation does not raise his dwindling hopes and fears.
One of them notes that, "... she'll be a fine catch for somebody", while the other replies
(Ch. 52) :

> There'll be lots to speak for her! - 'fraid there's no chance for uz - (facetiously
> jogging [him] with his elbow, as well as his companion) -...No offence, sir, I hope?...
> - I should think she'll marry none but a nobleman,...

This exchange does not allay his fears; it only makes them worse. When the coach
does finally stop at Staningley Hall gate and Gilbert exits, the passengers are extremely
surprised, and Gilbert is anxious about the reception he will receive. In the end, it proved
only to be an imagined barrier, for Helen's magnanimous view did not perceive any

barriers between them. They were married 'on a glorious August morning' in 1846, had children of their own, and thereafter lived a happy, rewarding life.

The novel itself shows Anne Brontë's great power and style as a writer, and had she lived longer, there is a good possibility that she could have equalled, or surpassed, Charlotte in supremacy. Anne died at the age of twenty-nine, and had written her first major, fiction novel at age twenty-eight, whereas Charlotte wrote her first, unsuccessful novel, *The Professor*, at age thirty and lived to be ten years older than Anne. Many analysts and reviewers hold the belief that great things were yet to come from Anne, but, of course, fate intervened and it was not to be. From Anne's first novel, *Agnes Grey*, to her second, *The Tenant of Wildfell Hall*, one can see tremendous changes, advances, and improvements, even though the character and nature of the two novels are quite different. George Moore (1852 - 1933), one of Anne Brontë's greatest fans, hailed her as the best of the Brontës, and likened her to Jane Austen. He strongly felt that she had a great future as a writer, with the possibility of surpassing many other notables of the day, but, of course, this is sheer speculation with too many variables and imponderable factors to have any merit other than a fruitless debate.

The one thing we do know about Anne Brontë is that she stands among the 'giants', and we realize that she is far more deserving of acclaim than she received in her own lifetime, and even today, in the shadow of her two, famous, older sisters, Charlotte and Emily.

'Clough House' on Halifax Road, Hightown, was the home of the new Mr.& Mrs. Brontë after their marriage on Dec. 29, 1812. Both their daughters Maria and Elizabeth were born here.
(Photo by author)

'St Peter's Church' in Hartshead-cum-Clifton. Rev.Brontë was curate here from 1811-1815. On today's structure, only the tower is original; the church itself was rebuilt in 1881.
(Photo by author)

'The Brontë Birthplace' is found at 72-74 Market Street in Thornton, near Bradford. Charlotte, Branwell, Emily, and Anne were all born here between 1816-1820. Their father was curate at Thornton Church nearby.
(Photo by author)

'Brontë Parsonage'. The Parsonage today serves as a museum to the Brontë family of writers. The Parsonage was purchased in 1928, by Sir James Roberts and turned over to the Brontë Society.
(Photo by author)

'Haworth New Church'. The Old Church was torn down and rebuilt in 1878-1879, by Rev. John Wade who succeeded Rev.Brontë and Rev. A.B. Nicholls as the new perpetual curate. Only the original tower remains.
(Photo by author)

'Main Street, Haworth'. The long hill with its cobbled street leading up to the church and Parsonage. The cobble stones were laid sideways to give horses' hooves more purchase up the steep slope.
(Photo by author)

'Cowan Bridge School'. Four of the Brontë girls attended here in 1824-1825, and it was here that both Maria and Elizabeth fell ill, and later died at home. It was disguised as 'Lowood' in *Jane Eyre* .
(Photo by author)

'Tunstal Church'. Each Sunday, Cowan Bridge students were marched three miles to attend services here. They remained the day in the unheated church and ate their box lunches in the small room above the porch.
(Photo by author)

'Parsonage and Graveyard'. Even in the 1840s, the church graveyard was 'overcrowded', and decomposing bodies were believed to have contaminated the village water supply causing many illnesses and deaths.
(Photo by author)

'Haworth Moor'. This is the path the Brontë children often took over the moor, past Penistone Hill, and on toward Brontë Falls, a green 'oasis' amid the blackened heath.
(Photo by author)

'Brontë Chair'. On this oddly-shaped stone, with the comfort of a chair, the Brontës were known to have often rested. It is also thought that they may have taken time to 'contemplate' and write poetry here.
(Photo by author)

'Top Withens'. This former house at the top of Pennine Way is four miles above the village of Haworth, and two miles beyond Brontë Falls. It is thought to have been the inspiration for 'Wuthering Heights', the home of the Earnshaws.
(Photo by author)

'Roe Head School'. Charlotte attended school here from January, 1831 to June, 1832. In the summer of 1837, it was moved to Healds House in Dewsbury Moor. Charlotte taught in both locations from 1835-1838.
(Photo by author)

'Red House, Gomersal'. This was the home of the Taylor family. Charlotte visited here several times and was exposed to political, economic, and religious views quite different from her own. It was the model for 'Briarmains' in *Shirley*.
(Photo by author)

'Oakwell Hall'. This Elizabethan Manor became 'Fieldhead' in Charlotte's novel, *Shirley*. Two references in Chapter 11 call attention to the 'oak panels', and the 'old latticed windows'. Charlotte visited here with her friend, Ellen Nussey.
(Photo by author)

'Bradford'. The town of Bradford was occasionally visited by Rev.Brontë to obtain items not available in Haworth or Keighley. Branwell spent one year here, 1838-1839, as a portrait painter.
(Photo by author)

'Parsonage and Church Lane'. This lane previously led to the side, kitchen door of the Parsonage. Today, the gable wing is the dominant feature. To the right (out of view) is the Sunday School and the sexton's house.
(Photo by author)

'Haworth Station', Keighley is a part of the Worth Valley Railway which went into operation in 1867. The station is found at the foot of the steep road to Haworth.
(Photo by author)

'Scarborough'. The wide, sandy beaches and rugged cliffs of this town were well-loved by Anne Brontë who spent time here with the Robinsons when she was their governess. The final chapters of *Agnes Grey* are 'played out' here.
(Photo by author)

'Anne Brontë's Grave'. When Anne Brontë died in Scarborough, Charlotte made a snap decision to bury her there. Her grave is in St. Mary's Church Cemetery overlooking the sea she loved so much. (Taller headstone in foreground with white splashes on back.)
(Photo by author)

PART THREE

INFLUENCES

AND

INSPIRATIONS

14

BY WAY OF INTRODUCTION

When we examine the writings of the Brontës, as we do with any other authors, we must thoroughly examine the influences which directed, molded and shaped their personal lives, their writings and their motives. In some exceptional cases, authors may be motivated by some past incident or experience which became a singular, solitary motivator, or driving force, a 'monomania' of sorts. With respect to the Brontës, this is definitely not the case; their influences and motivators were an intricate web of experiences, first hand and vicarious, and influences whose 'weights' and 'gravitations' produce a 'writer's mass' which is too imponderable, and incalculable, to dissect into parts or segments for analysis. But upon careful study, we are assured that the 'sum of the parts' definitely equal the 'whole' which makes the 'final product', their lives and their contributions to English Literature, so inviting and intriguing.

Any preliminary research into the Brontës indicates that the influences on their lives were many and varied; some were obvious and others not, some were significant and others moderate, some were from the present and others from the past, but they all contributed in some small measure. Also, each and every writer must be studied within their 'writing context' which reveals factors which are 'closer to home' and obvious as well as others which are beyond their control, abstract and intangible. To this list we may add such factors as the country (England), the area (Yorkshire), the village (Haworth), the times (Regency and Victorian) in which they lived, the moral and social values of the era, the science and technology which encompassed them (Industrial Revolution), the history and the politics of the world in which they lived (Imperialism), the past history and politics which brought them to their 'present day' (French Revolution and Napoleonic Wars), other writers, poets, activists, and people of influence in their day, immediate family members, their friends and servants, and specific incidents of note (personal tragedies) which had a particular impact on their lives. This is by no means a definitive list, nor have I intended it to be, but I do suggest that it is one which is reasonably comprehensive, and as for sorting out their individual values, weights, measures, and degree of import, I suggest that such an exercise would prove of little value beyond academic debate.

As the reader works his/her way through the final section on the 'influences' of the Brontës, one may occasionally lose track of the objective of Part Three and deem it to be tangential, or digressive. To a degree it may be, but in my own defence, and in advance, I would like to point out that none of us live in a 'vacuum', including the Brontës, and the influences of politics, religion, society, social values, transportation, communication, and innovations in science and technology, affect each and every one of us, but, of course, in different ways. By these independent summaries and 'digressions', I, therefore, hope to draw together the network of 'threads', and 'loose ends' which weaved the 'cloth' that played such an important part in the fabric of the lives of the Brontës of Haworth in the first half of the 19th Century.

Once again, in advance, I would like to point out to the reader the various influences which the Industrial Revolution had on the Brontës in a more direct and obvious fashion. During Rev. Brontë's youth and early days, as a curate and father to a young family, railways were not part of his 'tecnological world'. Most often he daily walked many miles from farmhouse to farmhouse, and village to village, or for longer trips hired a gig for transport. In his later years with the advent of the steam engine and people transport by railways, he did travel to and from Manchester for his eye surgery. But he was not fond of the new technology and used it only when it was a necessity. The railway was a giant leap in technology for a man who sometimes had walked up to forty miles in one day.

When the Leeds-Manchester Railway was first developed, Branwell was hired on as a booking-clerk at Sowerby Bridge, Halifax (Sept., 1840) and the following year was promoted to clerk-in-charge at Luddenden Foot, two miles distant. Had he remained with the railway, his chances of promotion would have been excellent, and the new technology could have provided him with a successful, lifelong trade, but he soon lost interest. And, in the years following Aunt Branwell's death, Charlotte, Emily, and Anne used part of their inheritance to invest in railway shares. It is said that they were wise, cautious, and frugal investors who followed the value of their shares with great interest. They saw the new railway as a solid investment for the future and were intelligent and astute enough to recognize the prospective value of these new shares in an exciting new technology.

In later years, the Brontës, particularly Charlotte, came to use the railway with much greater frequency. Charlotte, Emily, and Mr. Brontë used the railway to get to London in February, 1842, to catch a 'packet' to Ostend, Belgium, and again on their return. The 'packet' was a steam-powered, paddle-wheeler, another product of Industrial Revolution technology. Charlotte made four trips in total across the North Sea, but Emily only two. In later years, Charlotte, Emily, and Anne used the railway to travel to York, Scarborough, Manchester, and London. It later became a very important part of their life for travel about the country, and especially for Charlotte after the deaths of her siblings when she travelled frequently to keep her mind occupied.

The effects of mills and factories not only on the social condition of the people but also the detrimental effects on the landscape were noticeable to all. The pall of smoke from factories burning coal changed the once clear, green valleys to a veil of smoke and smog which often did not dissipate until late morning or early afternoon. In cities like Halifax, Bradford, Leeds, and London, the effects were highly noticeable, and for country folk from the fresh, clean air of the Haworth Moors and upper Pennines, such conditions may very well have left a negative impression of 'cities' and 'industry'. And, in particular, it may have helped to drive Emily from her job in Halifax back to the 'natural reserve' and pristine beauty of the moors behind the parsonage.

Both Rev. Brontë (b.1777) and Tabitha Akroyd (b.1771) were born at the very beginning of the Industrial Revolution, and much of their youth was spent in the pre-Industrial Revolution days, long before mills and factories arrived in the West Riding of Yorkshire. On several occasions Tabby made reference to the days of 'yore' before industry arrived when 'fairies' could still be seen in remote valleys. These are perhaps noticeable 'markers' of change which she saw, and disliked, even in her own lifetime. For Tabby who was not formally educated, the changes were probably much more significant, poignant, and difficult to cope with than for the much more sophisticated, 'worldly', open, and progressive-minded Rev. Brontë.

The Industrial Revolution also affected the Brontës in other ways of which I will comment in greater detail later, but suffice it is to say at this moment, that prior to the birth of the Brontë children, certain events related to changes and developments in science and technology led to important historical events in West Yorkshire which became part of the local lore. This body of facts, knowledge, and traditions from the past were part of their heritage which they could not escape. Much of this is reflected in their writings, but perhaps, none so dramatically and directly than the events in *Shirley* which deal with the history of Luddite Riots over a period of years from 1811 to 1816. The local lore was brought to their attention and instilled in them, for the most part by Tabby Akroyd, their servant, but the information on the Luddite Riots was provided to them mainly by their father, who was a young curate and lived at the centre of the most important riot and events of the Luddite uprising.

Also the Industrial Revolution and the sudden rise of the new, merchant class in British society played a far greater role in the lives of the Brontës than many care to acknowledge. Mary Taylor, the Taylor family, and their lively, extroverted nature, had a profound effect on Charlotte, and the rest of the Brontës in a secondary way as acquired friends. The Taylors were a quintessential example of this new class with their new-found wealth, and especially their Dissenting views and radical ideas which challenged the Establishment and shook the very foundations of Charlotte's religious and political beliefs.

Perhaps one of the most profound changes to come out of this era which affected the Brontës more directly than they imagined were the improvements and changes being made in the printing industry. For the first time, scientific changes, improvements, and inventions in the printing industry resulted in books being printed in larger volumes, with greater speed and accuracy, better distribution systems, and most importantly at a lower cost. This lower cost finally put written material within the means of the lower classes and widened the readership tremendously. Formerly, the high cost of books excluded a large number of potential readers, but now the readership was expanded to include the large base of the population pyramid who were previously excluded. These technical changes, along with the development of the novel, were coincident with the literary efforts of the Brontës and which eventually allowed them, along with their tremendous talents, to have their books published and gain the fame which it provided.

15

VICTORIAN TIMES

Each and every one of us is, to a large degree, a product of our times, and, of course, the Brontës and their writings are a reflection of those times. Our social and moral values are a precipitate of our general times 'filtered' through a vast network of ever-increasing 'inputs' from radio, television, newspapers, magazines, travel, telecommunications, and especially today, the world-wide web of the internet. Who can possibly, clearly predict what our new influences will be several decades hence, or even one decade from now when science and technology is advancing, not by leaps and bounds, but by the giant strides of a colossus. Can you imagine trying to explain our technology of the 21st Century to someone from the Victorian era? Perhaps someone like Branwell Brontë or his sisters with their keen intellect and wonderful imaginations could have more easily grasped our explanations, but others would most certainly have been lost in total incredulity and amazement, or simply wondered which asylum had released us.

Each generation usually recognizes a 'difference' or a 'gap' between themselves and their parents, and between themselves and their grandparents, a 'gulf'. These 'differences', 'gaps' and 'gulfs' are the result of changes in the society in which they live and work, the changes in social and moral values, and the advancements in science and technology. Each generation is born into a new era, their 'modern era', only to find it, several decades down the road, to have been supplanted by yet more changes, some significant and meaningful and others not, and another 'modern era'. This has now become a 'way of life', which we accept, and with the ever-increasing speed and rapidity of these changes assuring us that the dynamics of our present life will not remain the same, we expect even more. Even the Brontës could see the changes in their own time.

The Brontës were under the same types of influences with some dramatic changes occurring about them, and they, too, had one foot stuck in the past, and the other poised to step into the future. Their writings show evidence both of inertia holding them back in the past, and progressive, dynamic ideas propelling them into the future. Their inertia was a product of their conservative, religious up-bringing and their Conservative, high-Tory politics, while their dynamic and progressive thought showed through as 'early feminism' in several of their novels. Charlotte Brontë, particularly, makes the case most stridently in *Shirley*, and Anne Brontë does so to a lesser degree in *The Tenant of Wildfell Hall*, for an expansion to occupations for women in Victorian England. Both were critically chastised for expressing such 'unnatural' beliefs.

Their writings are of note, not only as enduring classics of English Literature, but also as notable thrusts of early feminism for uncovering and exposing, through 'concealed plots'[1], the shortcomings of a society which upheld the rank and 'station' of individuals, particularly of women, in Victorian times. The views of Victorian society which appears to have had a 'place' for everyone in every 'station' of life was highly objectionable to any free-thinking, intelligent person who recognized its sheer folly. Also, the entrenched view that women's intellect was less than their male counterparts is deplorable and ludicrous, but it was the prevailing view of the day. The fact that women were excluded from almost all professions, employments, and positions of power and authority in government is morally reprehensible, but, once again, those were Victorian times and those views and beliefs were rarely challenged. And, if challenges were made, direct or indirect, they were roundly and soundly criticized, denounced, and condemned, often on moral, political or religious grounds.

A closer examination of Victorian times gives us a better insight and understanding to the social class structure of the era. Naturally, one must go even further back, to times of feudal lords and barons, to trace the history of landed gentry in Britain, but almost needless to say, it was still firmly established in the 1700s and well into the first half of the 19th C., the times in which the Brontës lived. The Brontë children were all born during the time of the Regency (1811 to 1820), when the Prince of Wales, the Prince Regent, was acting on behalf of his father King George III who suffered from insanity thought to be caused by porphyria, a genetic disease, although this is sometimes disputed.

Although England is founded on a Constitutional monarchy, and has been for quite some time, its laws and social structure are firmly based and embedded on the tradition of land ownership. Such firmly founded traditions which span almost a thousand years is not easily dissipated or eroded, especially by a government whose members were primarily from the landed gentry and made up the ruling class. Major changes were not made, or seen, until the Reform Bill of 1832, which abolished 'rotten boroughs' and enfranchised large, industrial cities and propertied middle- class, the Reform Bill of 1867, which gave the vote to urban dwellers, and finally in 1884, the Reform Bill which extended it to agricultural workers. Changes for the proletariat came very slowly in England.

The nobility in England were fortunate to survive the spate of revolutions, and revolutionary forces of republicanism, which were sweeping Europe and North America in the late 18th C. Throughout, the English nobility were able to keep their large estates in manageable holdings within their families, acquire even more land by favourable mar-

---

1   S.M. Gilbert and S. Gubar make this hypothesis in <u>The Madwoman in the Attic: The Woman Writer in the 19th C. Literary Imagination</u>. Yale Univ. Press, 1979.

riages, and secure their holdings from the effects of partitions and partible inheritances by supportive laws. Also, they managed to keep out unwelcome outsiders and persons of lower rank from 'infiltrating' and 'diluting' their noble, blood lines. The Law of Entail enforced the passage of estates to the closest, and eldest, male heir, which did a great deal to strengthen and enhance their hold on land and power. Such inequities did not go unnoticed, and it once prompted Benjamin Disraeli to comment, "England is made up of two nations - one rich, one poor", in reference to the great disparity among its people. Disraeli was not only a politician and Prime Minister but also a writer and novelist who wrote to engage social conscience about the urban and rural poor of England. Some of his writings definitely forshadowed future social legislation such as slum clearance, public health reform, and improvements in working conditions, which he later introduced. Unlike Charles Dickens who simply wrote about poor social conditions, Benjamin Disraeli was in a position to both write, and then act politically.

The incomes between rich and poor showed a wide gap with most factory and agricultural workers at, or below, the poverty line. In Queen Victoria's day, the wealthiest, the Duke of Bedford, earned £300,000 per year, an equivalent of $20 million in today's currency, and $90 million at the old exchange rate of approximately five dollars to the £ British. The Duke of Marlborough, at Blenheim Palace, earned £37,000 per annum, or about nine million dollars at today's exchange rate. Workers at the very other end of the wage scale, working as a farm labourer and living in squalor, might earn 1s 6d per week, or approximately £3 per year. Their food consisted primarily of 'bread and drippings' with the occasional piece of bacon. Others earning more than this meagre sum might look forward to broth, soup, potatoes, and dumplings.

Labourers in London seemed to fare somewhat better, and although still at the poverty line, or below, earned up to 15s per week with almost two-thirds going to food and the remainder towards rent, heat and light. 'Getting ahead' was clearly not in their future; it was simply a life of labour, poverty, misery and death, usually at a very early age. Dock workers and tradesmen earned as much as 50 - 100% more, and tradesmen in demand or with special skills, could earn up to £2, or more, per week. Workers in factories in the mid-19th C. might earn anywhere from 12s - 24s per week; young girls were paid less at 5s - 10s per week, and young children were often paid only 2s 6d to 5s per week for a twelve to eighteen hour shift per day.

Maids and servants might expect to earn £10 - £12 per year; apprentice clerks £20 per year; junior clerks £80 per year, and Anglican clergymen between £200 - £400 per year. Rev. Brontë himself earned approximately £200 per year, but bishops often earned £2000, and the archbishop of Canterbury just under £20,000 per year. Doctors, lawyers, and headmasters of high-standing, public schools often earned up to £1000 per year. Teachers and governesses, depending on the family and the situation could earn anywhere from £20 - £50 per year. It should also be mentioned that in addition to their salaries, which may appear low, maids, servants, governesses and farm labourers often earned additional perquisites commensurate with their position. A maid, servant, or governess, for example, would receive, in addition to their meagre wage, free room and board, and in some cases additional clothing to fit their 'station'.[2]

'Class within class' was not uncommon, and the usual divider among nobility and aristocracy was not only annual income and size of mansion and property holdings, but more particularly the number of servants one had. Depending on wealth, the number of servants could vary widely from three or four, to dozens. The Duke of Bedford had forty-two male servants at his London home, Thomas Coke sixty, and at Wentworth House it was calculated that the staff was close to one hundred, seventy regular servants and thirty 'upper' servants. Horace Walpole was known to have a staff of about ten servants at his Strawberry Hill home.[3] The larger staffs, twenty or more, would include a variety of domestic servants such as housemaids, lady's-maids, kitchen-maids, chamber-maids, scullery-maids, nursery-maids, butlers, stewards, cooks, bakers, valets, porters, govern-esses, coachmen, footmen, grooms and gardeners. Those with extremely large incomes who wished to be even more pretentious would show their extravagance with such other servants as under-butlers, postilions, lampmen, candlemen, pages, ushers, boot-boys, messenger-boys, garden-boys, chaplains, librarians, tutors, bird-keepers, apiarists, wa-ter-men[4], and even a gong-man[5]. The latter few were extreme, of course.

Another distinction which separated the classes, and classes within classes, was the ability to own and operate a 'carriage', and hence the name, the 'carriage people'. When children were sent to 'smart schools' to upgrade themselves in hope of bettering them-selves, they were often 'grilled' upon entry by other students about their family's income, the number of servants they had, and whether or not they owned a carriage. Once this 'interrogation' was complete, the students could then determine where the new student 'fit' in on the social ladder relative to the others. Not having a carriage, and having per-haps only three or four servants would most certainly put one near the bottom of the social scale, since that would be an absolute minimum requirement.

The Brontës were by no means poor, but they were by no means wealthy. Their father's income was approximately £200 per year, plus the value of the 'living' which was provided free of charge. Aunt Branwell who lived with them for twenty-one years had an annuity of £50 per year, and, therefore, we can also reasonably assume that Mrs. Brontë had the same annuity benefit during their eight years of married life before her death. Rev. Brontë's income was sufficient to provide them a reasonable standard of living, but it was far from extravagant; this was not only a result of low income but also a reflection and expression of their religious beliefs, and habits of simplicity and frugal-ity which they all practised.

Upon Charlotte's arrival at Roe Head School in January, 1831, it did not take long for the other students to 'size her up' for their official 'placement' within the student body.

---

2   These statistics were garnered from <u>The English A Social History 1066 - 1945</u> by Christopher Hibbert. Harper Collins, 1987.

3   Ibid.

4   Carried water and filled jugs in each of the rooms.

5   This person went about the hallways striking a gong and announcing breakfast, lunches, din-ners, etc.

Although the number of students at Roe Head was quite small, individuals were still 'ranked' according to their wealth and social standing in the 'outside' world. Charlotte arrived in a hired gig wearing old-fashioned clothes of very basic simplicity. Her diminutive stature and very poor eyesight gave her the appearance of a little, old woman. A simple investigation revealed that Charlotte was the daughter of a poor parson, not among the well-to-do, and 'ranked' well below others at the school like Mary Taylor and Ellen Nussey. Charlotte made a very poor first impression, but it did not take long for them to develop a great deal of respect for their new friend due to her positive, personal qualities, extensive knowledge, story-telling abilities, her fine mind, and keen intellect. Her initial situation at Roe Head was vaguely similar to her father's when he entered St. John's College, Cambridge as a 'sizar' with subsidized fees. He, too, came from a very poor Irish background, but his positive outlook, commendable character, agreeable manner, fine bearing, and keen mind earned him respect and esteem from his fellow students who came from wealthy families and were well above his lowly class and 'station'. These factors in Patrick Brunty's favour soon 'melted away' the class differences and he was accepted into their 'fold'. Although social standing and wealth were the two most distinguishing factors which separated the classes, they were on rare occasions, as with the Brontës, overcome.

Education and admission to expensive public schools was well beyond the means of Rev. Brontë for his large family and meagre income. As a result, the Brontë children, although reasonably well-educated by their father and Aunt Branwell, lacked the benefits of a rigorous, well-defined, well-rounded, systematic education in their formative years which professional schooling could have provided. It was not until Roe Head School, well after their disastrous and abortive years at Cowan Bridge School, and at Pensionnat Heger that they learned subjects systematically taught by professional teachers. Once again it is a moot point to try to delineate the prospective benefits which any formal education may have had on their writings, but, of course, as with others, the Brontës and their works were a summary collection of their numerous experiences. And, for us to imagine how these changes might have altered their classic writings seems almost heretical, for why would anyone wish to see any changes to such greatness, and such timeless classics.

Another factor which shaped their backgrounds and limited their social expansion was their remote location in the north of England. Had their situation been different, and had they lived in Penzance, Cornwall, home of their maternal grandparents and their mother's home, the Brontë children would perhaps have been introduced to 'polite society' to which Aunt Branwell longed to return. There they would have been introduced to the 'social circle' of their mother, aunt, and grandparents, but this was not to be. Also, their distance from London, at least in the pre-railway era, reduced their access to the refinements of theatre, music, art, and cultural pursuits in general, to which they seemed so keenly adept and naturally talented. Only in later years, after July, 1848, when Charlotte and Anne made their sudden appearance in London to identify themselves to their publishers were they exposed to these social refinements which were completely foreign to them before, except through magazines and newspapers. Anne died within a year, but

Charlotte, on her occasional visits to London, took advantage of these cultural opportunities for the next few years. Her last visit to London was made in January, 1853, just at the time of the publication and release of her last novel, *Villette*.

16

YORKSHIRE - HEATHER, HILLS, AND MOORS

No matter how we may try to deny it, we are all part of our geography, and to varying degrees, it influences us, shapes us, and becomes a 'backdrop' and 'measuring tool' for all other environments we live in and encounter. These influences often stay with us for the rest of our lives, or become a nagging, unconscious reminder of our 'roots'. For some, like Emily Brontë, the local environment of geography, terrain, topography, flora and fauna becomes our own 'personal ecosystem' and 'terrarium' in which we live, breathe, and exist. For Emily it was the 'umbilical cord' of life which connected her with Nature and sustained her through her short stay on this earth. For others, the magnetism of our home environments might always be there, ready to draw us back, but is not powerful enough to keep us there or prevent us from exploring beyond its 'field of power'.

For the Brontës, West Yorkshire had an alluring magnetism which always brought them back, like a moth to a flame, and in the end only Anne Brontë was able to 'break free' of its powerful grasp and is buried in Scarborough where she died. Yorkshire, in the north of England is an area of great scenic beauty with dramatic moorlands, green valleys and picturesque villages dotting the landscape. This large area also has a variety of contrasting terrains and topographies from a rugged coastline in the east, to the flat expanse and lush meadows of the south near Spurn Head, and finally the rolling, verdant hills and the endless expanse of heath and moor in the uplands of the West Riding along the Pennines. Charlotte and Anne, and Emily to a lesser degree, experienced Yorkshire's geographical variety and incorporated them in some of their works. Rev. Brontë was first drawn to it when a friend's wife referred to Yorkshire as the 'Goshen of England'. In some respects, Yorkshire with its green hills and dales bears a striking resemblance to Ireland, and although this may have lured him into the region at the outset, many other circumstances kept him there for the rest of his life. In any case, from his first arrival in Yorkshire in

1809, there the Brontës remained and became firmly attached and rooted to Yorkshire, Haworth, and the wide expanse of moors just out their back door.

The general variety of terrain can find its direct origins in the Ice Age and its aftermath with large ice-sheets carving out valleys, and later glacial meltwater sculpting them into the gentler and rounder formations which we see today. With the arrival of the Angles, Saxons and Jutes, the terrain developed slowly into the topography of farms, hamlets, villages, roads and bridges that are there presently, which the Brontës observed in their lifetime, and that which can still be seen there today. For some, the real 'taste' and 'flavour' of Yorkshire can only be found in the remote villages, hamlets, countryside, and bleak moorlands with its network of intriguing and rugged walking paths of Pennine Way in West Yorkshire to the gentler walks of Cleveland Way of the North York Moors.

The Yorkshire Dales, now a National Park, north of Haworth and Skipton provide an excellent example of terrain, topography, people, and its industry and historical development. Made up of three principal dales, Swaledale, Wensleydale, and Wharfdale, they are a contrast to the high moorlands, and attest to the variety to be found in the area. Carved out by glaciation, the region has been slowly transformed by twelve centuries of habitation by people of Norse and Anglo-Saxon heritage. The diversity of farms, cottages, villages, castles, and abandoned abbeys spread over the area provide the region with sufficient appeal to draw tourists from the world over. The prosperity of Swaledale was founded mainly on wool and is particularly with famous for its sheep which graze and traverse the harshest slopes even in the harshest weather. The medieval market town of Richmond with its large, cobbled market place still draws visitors today. The town of Reeth, originally a lead-mining town which was later drawn into wool production, and the local 'Buttertubs', provide an interesting geographic phenomenon.

Perhaps the part of Yorkshire which most people today can associate with is Wensleydale, made famous by books of James Herriot and the television series 'All Creatures Great and Small'. This is the landscape that most people are familiar with and associate with Yorkshire, and expect to see. The area was originally famous for its cheese and butter-making which goes back to the founding of Jervaulx Abbey and its monks. Near the village of Hardraw is to be found England's tallest, single-drop waterfall made famous by Blondin, a Victorian daredevil, who crossed it on a tightrope. As well, Asygarth Falls on the River Ure was sufficient in its beauty to encourage England's greatest Victorian landscape painter, J. M. W. Turner, to paint it in 1817. All of the above illustrate the variety and beauty of Yorkshire, which is markedly different from other areas of England, and make it a continued, and major, attraction for visitors.

Although there is little evidence that any of the Brontës actually travelled to the areas just mentioned, they are part of the geographic area in which they lived. There are some individual sites, though, of which we do know that some of the Brontës, and particularly Charlotte, visited. On one occasion, Charlotte, Emily, Anne, and Branwell were all invited out to Bolton Abbey, established in 1154 but now in ruins, by Ellen Nussey with the intention of a 'surprise party' and introducing her to her family and some friends. Unfortunately the plan 'backfired' since the Brontës were extremely shy and reticent, except for Branwell, when it came to meeting new people. Charlotte was incensed and far from amused.

Charlotte was also somewhat familiar with Scarborough and to the south of it, Bridlington, where on several occasions she stayed at Easton Farm with Ellen Nussey, the first time being in September, 1839. After Anne's death in Scarborough in late May, 1849, both Charlotte and Ellen, who accompanied them, remained behind to recover from their ordeal at the behest of Rev. Brontë. They spent nearly a month in the area, at Filey and Easton Farm before returning home. Charlotte returned to the area, alone, in June, 1852, and visited Anne's grave. Again in September, 1853, Charlotte visited Marg Wooler, her former headmistress at Roe Head and now a friend, who had retired to Hornsea in the East Riding.

We also know that Charlotte used assorted geographic elements from the areas she visited in her novels. It is thought that she conceived the basic idea of Bertha Mason, Rochester's wife and the madwoman in the attic, when she visited Norton Conyers near Ripon with the Sidgwicks while she was a governess for their children. They stayed at Swarcliffe near the town of Harrogate and visited Norton Conyers while in the area. The old story of the madwoman locked away in the third-storey attic was just too intriguing for her to forget. Also, during her stays with Ellen Nussey at her home in Rydings, Birstall, Charlotte mentally 'stored up' its image and later used it as a basis for 'Thornfield Hall' in *Jane Eyre*. The house was surrounded by lawns, chestnut trees, fruit gardens, a rookery, and the house itself had 'battlements round the top'[1] which Charlotte mentions in the novel. During her first visit there in 1832, in which she was escorted by her highly excitable brother Branwell, he exclaimed as he was leaving her behind that he was leaving Charlotte, 'in paradise'.

This same area provided a number of other inspirations for Charlotte and her writing. Near Rydings is 'Red House' in Gomersal, the home of the Taylors which Charlotte used as the model for 'Briarmains' in *Shirley*, and the lively Taylors were presented as the 'Yorke' family. In the novel, Charlotte mentions the painting of 'a night eruption of Vesuvius' which Mr. Taylor obtained on a trip to Italy, and the stain glass windows, both of which are still visible in the sitting room there today. In the novel, the author says, "Those windows would be seen by daylight to be of a brilliantly-stained glass, purple and amber the predominant hues..."[2]

Again, only a short distance away is Oakwell Hall, also in Birstall, which provided the inspiration for 'Fieldhead', the home of Shirley Keeldar. The building is a large, imposing Elizabethan manor built in 1583, and once was briefly occupied by the 'Roundheads'[3] as they fled during the English Civil War. In the 1840s, it was a girl's boarding school and Charlotte and Ellen, whose family was friends of the owner, visited there. It must have left a striking impression on Charlotte since she used it as one of the

---

1 Jane Eyre, Chapter 11, p. 86.
2 Shirley, Chapter IX, 'Briarmains', p. 112.
3 Followers of Oliver Cromwell and the Parliamentary party in the English Civil War of 1640-1660 who opposed the royalist Cavaliers.

main residences in the novel, *Shirley*, and made mention of the oak panelling and windows in Chapter Eleven, 'Fieldhead':

> The old latticed windows, the stone porch, the walls, the roof, the chimney stacks, were rich in crayon touches and sepia lights and shades.

and later, in the same chapter:

> The brown-panelled parlour was furnished all in old style, and with real old furniture.

Today the home is open to visitors as a museum of a 17th C. home, and one can see the feature which Charlotte describes. Also, it was here that Branwell saw the inscription on a glass window which seemed to have a profound effect on him for the rest of his short life. It inspired him to live life 'on his own terms'. The inscription reads:

> Kings are but slaves when by their passions held, But who commands himself commands the world

and Branwell responded something to the effect that he was going to be 'master of himself' which he was, but to his own detriment.

The area was alive with inspiration for Charlotte. She also used St. Peter's Church in Birstall, which she attended while visiting the Taylors or Nusseys, as the model for 'Briarfield Church' in *Shirley*, as well as the vicar, Rev. W. M. Heald, as the model for 'Rev. Hall'. 'Hollows Mill', in the same novel, is the scene of the violent Luddite attacks and is based on Rawfolds Mill, Liversedge, the site of the real attack on April 11, 1812. William Cartwright, the owner of the original mill, is the model for the heroic character, Robert Moore. Another possible model for 'Hollows Mill', as described in *Shirley*, is perhaps fashioned after Hunsworth Mill, a woollen dyeing and finishing mill owned by the Taylors. 'Hollows Cottage' owned by Robert Moore in the novel may also have been inspired by 'Hunsworth House', the home of Mary Taylor and her brothers after they left 'Red House' in 1841. Charlotte was a visitor there as well.

Much of the story, inspiration, and background for *Shirley* came from stories told to her by her father, Charlotte's own knowledge of the area, and other pieces of history which she picked up from people like the Taylors, the Nusseys, and others she met while at Roe Head School, and later. St. Peter's Church in Hartshead where her father was curate during the time of the Luddite attacks in 1812, inspired 'Nunnely Church'. It was here that Charlotte's eldest sister, Maria, was baptised before they moved to Thornton. The church was set in a tranquil countryside much like it is today, and not far away is Kirklees Hall which appears as 'Nunnwood', or 'Nunnely Hall'. Kirklees Park includes the old site of a nunnery, and historically what is said to be the site of Robin Hood's grave. Also, just south of Whitby, a picturesque town on the coast of North Yorkshire and which dates back to a monastery founded there in the 7th C., is Robin Hood Bay, a place where Robin Hood is said to have kept a boat in case he needed to make a quick escape.

The local village is said to be thoroughly networked with ingenious hiding places beneath floors and behind walls for contraband of the many smugglers who lived in the area in days gone by. The area is truly rich with history and has no shortage of history or sites which can inspire any fledgling or accomplished writer.

For Anne Brontë, the cities of York and Scarborough were of major interest and curiosity. Anne's interest in Scarborough went back to the days when she was a governess for the well-to-do Robinsons at Thorp Green Hall near York. The family took their vacation at the 'Queen of Watering Places' as Scarborough was then called. On her visits there, Anne simply became enthralled by the scenery, the coast line, its sandy beaches, the wind, water, waves, and the salt-sea air. Nothing could have been more different than her home in Haworth, but over the years, it held a magnetic attraction for her, and in her final days, she yearned to go back there, just one more time.

In addition to making a last visit to Scarborough, Anne also insisted in stopping in the city of York to see the Minster one last time as well. The city of York is truly historic, and although much of it has the appearance of a medieval city with Elizabethan-style buildings, as in the 'Shambles', its history goes well beyond that to Roman times. The Minster is the largest, Gothic church north of the Alps and holds the largest collection of stain glass windows in Britain. It is truly a sight to behold, and one Latin inscription near the entrance to the vaulted Chapter House sums up its situation clearly. It says: "As the rose is the flower of flowers, so this is the house of houses." It was this church which left such a stirring impression on Anne Brontë that she just had to see it one last time.

The city of York can most easily describe itself as 'layered', since as in many towns and cities in Britain, one house or building is simply built 'on top of' the last one, using its foundation for the new one to be built. In the Roman Bath Pub near the centre of Old York, they discovered an ancient Roman bath while excavating to add more space beneath the building. To preserve and maintain its history, windows have been built into a portion of the pub overlooking the Roman bath, and visitors and patrons today can look at this well-preserved feature of its ancient past.

Leeds and Bradford were also cities that the Brontës were familiar with. Bradford is today a city of almost half a million people, and in the Middle Ages it was an important and thriving market town. Its trade was further boosted by the building of a new canal which allowed more raw resources to be brought into the city for manufacture. In the early 1800s, many German textile manufacturers settled into one area of Bradford which became known as 'Little Germany', and later became famous for its worsted wools. One of these, known as 'Berlin wool', was later in high demand throughout the area, and England. On occasions when supplies were needed which could not be obtained in either Haworth or Keighley, a trip would be made to Bradford where chances were much better for its procurement. It was also in Bradford, at #3 Fountain Street, where Branwell Brontë set up his portrait studio in June, 1838, in the home of the Kirbys and remained there for one year.

Leeds, even larger than Bradford, and today with a population greater than 700 000, is Britain's third, largest provincial city. The Brontës often made trips there since it is the northern hub of transportation, and major connections, especially for the railways, must be made there. The city was highly prosperous during Victorian times as an industrial city of woollen mills, and it was also well-known for its arcade of covered shops. Leeds is of particular interest to Brontë history and their legacy, since it was there that Rev. Brontë purchased a box of twelve, painted toy soldiers for Branwell on one of his trips in late May, 1826. Branwell shared them with his sisters, the soldiers were each named, and they eventually developed 'characters' and 'personalities' of their own. These toy soldiers are thought to have been the 'seed' which set their highly imaginative minds to work to their high levels of creativity, and the 'source' of their prolific, early 'juvenilia'. Today, Leeds is still an industrial city, but it is also a thriving, cultural centre for the north of England.

There can be little doubt that of all the influences that geography, terrain, and topography may have had on the Brontës, that of the village of Haworth, and the Haworth Moors behind their home, were the most influential, particularly for Emily Jane. Emily's *Wuthering Heights*, and Anne's *The Tenant of Wildfell Hall*, seem solidly situated in the local area, as do many of their references to Nature in their poetry. In fact, Emily was so firmly attached to her home and its surroundings that she could not 'break free', or live without them. Within three months of leaving home and enrolling at Roe Head School, at age seventeen, Emily became so homesick that her medical condition became serious; in fact, she was dying. Although her illness could not be diagnosed by 'outsiders', Charlotte instinctively knew what caused her problem and took her home to Haworth; within days, she was better. Her two, additional forays into the outside world, to Halifax (Sept., 1838 - March, 1839), and Brussels (Feb., 1842 - Nov.,1842), were both abortive and short-lived. And, when Charlotte returned to Brussels to teach, and study, in January, 1843,[4] Emily decided to stay at home, a place which she dearly loved and was firmly attached, to look after their ageing father and take charge of household duties. But, perhaps more than anything, Emily just wanted to be back amidst her beloved moors and close to Nature.

The village of Haworth had its first census taken in March, 1851, as part of a national census, and although this was several years after the deaths of Branwell, Emily, and Anne, it does provide us with insight into the community, the people, the economy and its structure, and the world in which they lived. At that time, there were just over 3500 people in the town and its immediate surroundings with about 660 houses and families. The rural economy was, of course, agricultural with sheep-raising being the primary occupation. Other animals were also raised, mostly for their own and local consumption, but the nature of the area made farming in the upper reaches somewhat more precarious, and closer to the subsistence level.

The major employer was textiles, the wool industry in particular, in several occupations which included wool combers, wool weavers, both power and hand[5], and 'spinners'. Most of the work was labour intensive and done by hand employing men, women and children, and although there was still a great deal of child labour exploitation, children worked only in the morning, and attended school in the afternoon. Other occupations in the village, not related to textiles, included tailors, dress-makers, shoe-makers, bonnet-

---

4   They had briefly returned home for Aunt Branwell's funeral in November, 1842.
5   There is said to have been more than 1200 hand looms in operation in Haworth in 1840.

makers, clog-makers, carpenters, joiners, one plumber, excavators, one glazier, butchers, shop-keepers, inn-keepers, servants, stone masons, labourers, several professional people including clergy, doctors, an architect, several school masters and mistresses, and an assortment of other people including the disabled, unemployables, annuitants, and pensioners.[6] Such a survey gives us an excellent insight into the make-up of the community, and although late into the lives of the Brontë family, it is still very indicative of the times in which they lived. Oddly enough, Charlotte Brontë and Ellen Nussey, who happened to be visiting the Parsonage at the time, had their 'occupations' listed in the 1851 census as 'none'.

From this census, and information we can glean from other sources, we find that the community, like its people, was self-sufficient in many ways. The local people with their self-reliant ways and 'hard-work' ethic were typical of their Norse and Saxon heritage. For items the community could not provide, they were required to walk or ride to Keighley some four miles away, or take a day-long trip to Bradford or Leeds. These larger centres, more often than not, could meet their needs for goods not available close to home. The main mode of transportation was still by foot for closer distances, then by horse, gig, or carrier's cart for longer trips where some comfort and protection from the elements were required. Rev. Brontë, in his younger days, sometimes walked forty miles in a single day, and even young Branwell accomplished this feat when he was about fourteen years old, walking from Haworth to Roe Head, Mirfield, a distance of twenty mile each way.

What the 1851 census did not reveal were some chilling facts and statistics about life, death, and life-expectancy in the decade prior to the census in the village. During the Victorian era, the phenomenal growth in many towns, villages, and larger cities, without the corresponding improvements in water and sewage systems, led to an equally phenomenal death rate. The village of Haworth had neither a proper water supply nor sewage system for its original, small population, and when the population grew suddenly, their sanitation problems were simply compounded. The threat of consumption (tuberculosis) and cholera were ever-present scourges which reared its 'ugly head' from time to time and took many lives. The winter of 1833-34, was particularly bad when there were approximately thirty deaths in the village, and between 1840 and 1850, there were a total of 1344 recorded burials in the churchyard which attests to the devastation caused by these diseases.

The average age at death was a young twenty-five, and close to forty percent of all children perished before the age of six, a very high mortality rate. When this information is matched against the early demise of the Brontë family members which poignantly brings our attention to the tragedy of life in Victorian times, we see that their life-spans did not fall too far outside the 'norms' for some, and exceeded it in others. In contrast to their short lives, one occasionally finds individuals who defied the odds and lived long, healthy lives, like Rev. Brontë, and their servant Tabby Akroyd, both of whom lived to the ripe, old age of eighty-four with only occasional mild illnesses in between.

---

6   This information was obtained from a pamphlet of a local, but unidentified, source which is entitled, 'Haworth 140 Years Ago'. The information was taken directly from the 1851 census.

The Parsonage itself is a two-storey, Georgian-style brick house, built by the Church trustees over the years 1778-79 with ten rooms, if we place the main entrance and children's study above it, as two, separate rooms. It remained relatively unchanged for almost seventy years until the 1850s, when Charlotte began to make some changes after income from her writing made it possible. Until that time, it remained plain, simple, and very basic in every respect. Although its furnishings were sparse, they were adequate and comfortable and manifested their religious beliefs and frugal means and ways. After her first visit there in the summer of 1833, Ellen Nussey commented positively on its spotless appearance throughout, but Mary Taylor only described it as 'small' and 'claustrophobic'. Mary's comments are understandable, since she lived in 'Red House' in Gomersal which was considerably larger, had many more rooms, and was far more spacious. Ellen also noticed its sandstone floors throughout the lower level and main stairway to the second floor, and in the 1830s, the house was also devoid of wallpaper and floor carpets, except for those in the dining room and Mr. Brontë's study.

With Charlotte's newly-acquired wealth, and growing desire for more comforts, her father finally acquiesced and allowed Charlotte to add such refinements as blinds and curtains, which had been previously been strictly forbidden, wallpaper to some rooms, and occasional, new carpets. Following Charlotte's engagement to Rev. A. B. Nicholls in 1854, renovations were made to the house which included an enlargement to her bedroom which had formerly been her aunt's, and before that her parents' bedroom. The bedroom was enlarged at the expense of the children's study, and prior to this, the dining room was enlarged at the expense of the main entry hall, and at the same time, an archway was added in the main hallway. The peat room, previously entered only from the outside, was quickly altered to provide a study for Mr. Nicholls, with a doorway added into the main hall, prior to his taking up residency there as Charlotte's new husband.

The kitchen with its large, cast iron stove was usually the warmest room in the house and acted as a congregating area for the Brontë children. Later, it became one of Emily's favourite rooms after the death of Aunt Branwell. When Charlotte decided to go back to Brussels in January, 1843, Emily decided to remain behind and take over the main housekeeping chores, and look after her ailing father. Emily soon became the chief, bread-maker, and it is village legend that as she worked and baked, she often propped up books to read, or studied German. Emily had a penchant for simple housekeeping duties and domestic chores like ironing, and with it perhaps found a soothing comfort and 'freedom'. She continued these duties well into the latter months of 1848, and even though she was very ill, she insisted and persisted in the daily, domestic chores of their home.

The greatest changes to the Parsonage occurred after the death of Rev. Brontë in 1861, when his replacement, Rev. John Wade completely demolished the back kitchen and made it into a passageway, removed the kitchen range, added several fireplaces, and in 1878-79, added a large, gable wing at one end of the house. This addition was not very popular with Brontë enthusiasts who saw it as an 'outrage' and an affront to the family that had made it famous. After the deaths of the Brontës, as early as the 1860s, people came from near and far on a 'pilgrimage' of sorts to see the Brontë home.

The Parsonage was 'home' to the Brontës, but the moors behind it were their natural playground. Most often the Brontë children went out the side door and directly onto the moors behind their home rather than through the streets of Haworth. The children were shy, reserved, and 'self-sufficient' in playing by themselves in their own, imaginative world. The moors lured and beckoned them into its grasp, and they were drawn to it by the qualities of its peace, serenity, solitude, its natural beauty, its natural reserve, and the freedom it provided. They could simply spend hours there, intrigued, delighted, enthralled, and entranced by the wonders of Nature at their doorstep.

The moors, a vast and windswept wasteland which extends for miles in the upper reaches of the Pennines in central and northern England, consist mainly of heathers, ferns, coarse grasses, a few, low shrubs, and the occasional tree leaning against the direction of the prevailing winds. These bleak tracts of land are agriculturally marginal at best and suitable only for grazing hardy, upland sheep. Only a handful of hardy and stubborn farmers were brave enough to live on the edge of subsistence, in isolation, and to confront on a never-ending basis, the unrelenting forces of wind and weather which make it so wild. The Haworth Moors provided them with tranquility, escape, a land of exploration, and a place to commune quietly and regularly with Nature in the form of bugs, insects, birds, animals, and a wide variety of plants and flowers to investigate and admire.

Not far away from the Parsonage and across the moors, they arrived at an 'oasis' in the moorland with green grass, a waterfall, and a slender beck, like an island amid a vast ocean. There they could stop and rest, have a picnic, enjoy the cool springs which seep out of the hills, splash in the crystal clear waters of the beck, or enjoy the waterfall as it sometimes thundered down and cascaded over the rocks. Near the base of the waterfall is a peculiar, chair-shaped rock which provided a relaxing respite as they read their books or created their poetry. Today these are named the 'Brontë Falls' and the 'Brontë Chair' (also Brontë Seat) with a small bridge over the beck now known as the 'Brontë Bridge'. From this point, visitors may, just like the Brontës did a century and a half ago, continue their trek to the top where it meets the Pennine Way, and 'Top Withens', a farm situated high above the village. The view from the top is breath-taking and is thought to have provided the inspiration for the Earnshaws' home and the opening description of *Wuthering Heights*.

From this vantage point one becomes carefree and 'immune' to the cares of the world with the vast expanse of seemingly endless, purple moor outstretched below, and the big, wide-open sky above. The air is fresh, clean, and breezy with larks and linnets winging and singing their way to their nests, and hawks soaring high above watching and waiting anxiously for an unsuspecting fieldmouse or leveret to break its cover. Here, one is 'next to God', and the pervading feeling of 'communion' and 'oneness' with the Universe, which overwhelms the observer, may well have been the inspiration for Emily's novel, and some of her poetry.

Beyond the immediate vicinity of the Parsonage, Haworth, and the Haworth Moors, Emily had little experience of the world at large except for brief visits to Keighley, Bradford, and in later life, near her 27th birthday, a trip to York with Anne. Emily's other experiences included her short stay at Roe Head School, a trip to Manchester with Charlotte, and her time in Brussels, also with Charlotte. Her only other experience included her six month teaching stay at Miss Patchett's School at Law Hill, Halifax near Bradford. Halifax was then an industrial, textile town whose history goes back to the Middle Ages, and with the arrival of the Industrial Revolution, the Pennines became the 'backbone of industry' in England, and the wool trade brought an economic boom to the region.

The town of Halifax was a 'sea' of mills, and from Law Hill, one could look down on the wide expanse of factories and mills below. It is also believed that the great, prophetic, epic poem 'Jerusalem' (1820), by William Blake, and its vision of 'dark, Satanic mills' were, in fact, inspired by the town of Halifax and this blemished sight which clearly displayed and represented the ugliness of man's, material world. Blake was a revolutionary in his thoughts and writing, and his work, like Emily's *Wuthering Heights,* was not fully grasped by his contemporaries. His work and insight show us that he was a 'Romantic', a visionary, and an original environmentalist. Emily, on the other hand, was spurred by her Pantheistic philosophy and approach to her immediate environment. These scenes of 'ugliness' of the industrial world, and her experiences at the school, where she saw, 'first hand', the ugliness of man toward one another and to poor, helpless animals, may well have provided Emily with the impetus to return home to the peaceful, quietude of the Haworth Moors. After her return from Brussels in November, 1842, Emily never left home again except for brief periods.

17

THE INDUSTRIAL REVOLUTION

Just as our morals and values are shaped by the society of the times in which we live, and which have such a profound effect upon us, so do the politics and economy of our times. Changes and upheavals are bound to have both direct and indirect effects on our 'material world', the one in which we live and cannot escape, and perhaps to a lesser degree our 'personal world', the one in which we interact with society and the technological changes that the era provides, depending upon our degree of involvement. Up to the time of the Industrial Revolution, changes were painfully slow in coming on both the social and technological level, but suddenly over a period of a hundred years, the 'floodgates' opened and science and technology brought many changes 'on stream'. With more and more technology available to us, the 'snowball effect' takes over, and today, in the 21st C., we can very well understand its effect. Unfortunately, at the time, people were perhaps less able to cope with the changes that the new technology which the Industrial Revolution brought, and this was the time that the Brontës lived.

The Industrial Revolution began in the textile industry in Great Britain and did so for many reasons. Before the coming of modern technology, the Industrial Revolution, and the 'factory', textiles were made by hand in an extensive 'cottage industry', or 'domestic industry', throughout Britain. From the Middle Ages, Britain was productive in textiles, both cottons and woollens, but its production was labour intensive. From the raising and shearing of sheep to the spinning of yarn, the weaving of cloth, and finally making finished goods, everything was done by hand, usually in homes, cottages and villages throughout the country. The 'domestic' industry was well-established and had been for hundreds of years. For the cottagers, it was ideal, since they remained at home, worked their own hours in the comfort of their own home, took their tea breaks and meals at their will, and woke up and went to bed at their leisure and according to their own schedule without a boss looking over their shoulder. The system worked very well, and we need not look very far today to see modern technology of the 21st C. trying to emulate the 'cottage industry' technique with stay-at-home office-work programs; the hands of time have gone 'full-circle'.

Although this situation was ideal for the cottagers, it was not always ideal for the merchant-vendors who financed the operation and was the general overseer for the welfare of his workers, and the collector of finished products. The merchant was a businessman and ultimately there to make a profit. In many cases, the merchant owned the cottages, the spinning wheels and the looms and rented them out to its occupants who in turn paid rents out of the proceeds of the sale of yarns and cloth. But human nature being what it is, several problems arose for the merchants which were of concern to them. The problems included maintaining the quality of the yarn and cloth, detecting portions held back and 'skimmed off' by the cottager for private sale, keeping their workers on a schedule to meet minimum quotas, and dealing with increased competition from other merchants enticing some workers to switch their allegiance as the demand for workers increased. Skilled, productive, and loyal workers with good attitudes were becoming scarce and increasingly hard to find; as a result, productivity and quality remained the same, or declined, but their costs continued to rise making them less and less competitive.

To establish the general causes of this situation, we must take a step back and take a general overview of the larger, economic picture affecting Britain at that time. British expansion and British Imperialism in the 1700s and 1800s gave rise to a large number of colonies throughout the world which provided Great Britain with raw materials. Added to this was the increase in demand for British goods and products within Britain and in the colonies themselves. Often the growth and demand outstripped the supply which increased the cost of goods and the competition for raw materials, and particularly the skilled labour to provide the finished product. The rise in production costs resulted in the loss of the 'competitive edge' they once enjoyed; the obvious solution was to keep down production costs with more efficient ways of manufacturing, but practical answers were not forthcoming until the 1740s, and later.

Since labour and raw materials were relatively 'fixed', the only way that output could increase was by better and more efficient production methods. New technology was needed to take them to the next level, but in the first few decades of the 1700s, the required technology was just not available. Until the mid-1700s, most spinning of yarn was done using the old-fashioned spinning wheel where yarn was produced one thread at a time. It was not until the arrival of the innovative, 'spinning jenny' (invented by James Hargreaves in the 1760s), the 'water frame' or 'throstle' (invented by Sir Richard Arkwright) and the new and improved 'spinning mule' (invented by Sam Crompton in the mid-1700s) that efficient production again increased, costs were lowered, and the competitive edge regained. 'Machinery' was the 'god-send' and the answer to the prayers of merchants who earlier had seen no way out of their dilemma.

The next stage of advancement in the textile industry had to do with improvements in the area of weaving, which up to the early 1800s had been carried out mostly by handlooms, not powerlooms. The earliest invention of importance was probably that of John Kay in 1733, called the 'flying shuttle', but it was primitive, unreliable, and sometimes dangerous. It was not until 50 years later that the first, steam-powered looms (invented by Edmund

Cartwright, 1780s) made their appearance, and the new, all-metal, powerlooms were designed in the early 1800s. By the 1830s, Great Britain had approximately 125,000 powerlooms and handlooms became relegated to specialty items still too complicated for available technology.

The Industrial Revolution, once started, fed off itself with increasing demands in every section requiring new solutions and new machinery to solve new problems. Originally, power for the earliest factories was provided either by the water wheel situated along streams and besides waterfalls or machinery moved by 'raw' horse power. It did not take long for forward-looking individuals with inventive minds to realize that this just would not do; steam-engines which generated tremendous horsepower to drive the new machinery was the answer. Early steam-engines had serious drawbacks, and it was not until the improvements to this new invention by James Watt (1760s) of Scotland that steam-engines could be effectively 'married' to new machinery to be useful, effective, and efficient. These inventions coupled with advances in machine-tool technology allowed for better and better machines to be manufactured with higher and higher productivity and efficiency.

The new technology of making machinery required to smelt and produce iron, and the two, basic raw materials, coal and iron ore, were widely available in Britain. Coal was also needed in abundance for the running of steam-engines to power the machinery in textile mills, and since most of Britain's coal was found in South Wales and the Pennines, much of the textile industry developed there. And due to the historical development of the textile industry, production of cotton was found mainly in Lancashire, and west of the Pennines, while woollen production was usually located in Yorkshire, and generally east of the Pennines.

Great Britain's ability to produce large quantities of iron quickly made it the leading industrial nation in the world, and the wealthiest. The beginning of the Industrial Revolution also coincided with improvements in iron production, the first being the switch from scarce, and expensive, charcoal which fuelled the smelting furnaces, to coking coal, inventions which improved the quality of iron itself by use of new 'puddling' techniques and the move away from 'pig iron' to integrated rolling mills. When improved high-grade ore from the colonies was used instead of Britain's low-grade iron ore, and the above inventions were employed along with steps in the iron making mills which combined them under one roof, England became the world's leading, top-quality iron producer.

With the growth in the Industrial Revolution, another revolution of sorts also began as a result of the first; it was the 'transportation' revolution. Until the early 1800s, Britain's system of roads was limited to 'say the least', and roads were generally in poor condition and not meant for mass transportation over long distances. The excellent present-day transportation system in Britain is a direct result of the requirements brought about by the Industrial Revolution with the great demands for iron ore, coal, heavy machinery etc., an extensive transportation system had to be developed to meet the growing needs. The movement of coal, as an example, from its source to mills where it was used to power mills required a much improved system, and not only must the system be improved, it had to be cheap and efficient.

It did not take long for mill owners, operators and designers to 'size up' and understand the new economic forces at work which made mills profitable. Mills had to be as close as possible to sources of heavy, bulky coal, and the cheapest method of transporting large quantities of coal was by water. Therefore, in addition to improvements in roads, new canals for barges and their heavy cargoes were being developed throughout England. Canal building in Britain continued for about four decades from the 1760s to the early 1800s, and at its height had 4800 kms of canals networked throughout Britain. The coming of the railways which had a more universal application with greater capacity and more flexibility soon began to compete with canals to a degree that perhaps few could have forseen. By the 1850s and 1860s, the canal system was becoming redundant, soon became obsolete, and today is nothing more than a 'curiosity' for tourists. The Manchester Ship Canal, inaugurated in 1894 by Queen Victoria, is perhaps one of the few exceptions and is still used today.

By the 1840s, railways were being built at an ever-increasing rate and criss-crossing much of Britain. Added to the advantages of railways for industry was its usefulness for 'people transport'. Roads in Britain were in poor condition, turnpikes were few, wheeled transport was very slow, and the cost of carriages, road tolls, and inns were often prohibitive for most of the working class. The advent of the railway changed all that, and its low cost, high speed, and ease of use, made it an 'immediate hit' with the public at large. The railway era brought on an entirely new aspect and dimension to the people of the Victorian era, and particularly for the people of the lower classes who could now quickly move from one city to another in search of work at mills and factories, at a rate that was affordable to them. For those living in the city, it now meant that a day or weekend trip to a 'watering-place' along the coast, or an 'outing' to the 'country' was now possible for a modest sum. And, to the new, young up-coming generation who would come to have railways as part of their technological heritage and culture, the railways were seen as a field of new opportunities, new adventures, and part of a new 'social revolution'.

18

THE FRENCH REVOLUTION

The French Revolution (1789), and the resultant French Revolutionary Wars (1792 - 1802), and Napoleonic Wars (1804 -1815), affected everyone in Britain to various degrees, and although these events occurred before the birth of the Brontë children, their effects were still being felt many years afterward. At the beginning, the French Revolution met with the approval of the British people, but later their opinions changed when news of the 'Reign of Terror' began in the 1790s. It was the first, major European revolution in modern times, and it followed on the heels of the American Revolutionary War which Britain had lost. The revolutionaries quickly overthrew their monarchy, executed the royal family, ended the privileged positions of the nobility and aristocracy, did away with traditional institutions, and replaced them with democratic rights and a republican-style political system run by the people.

The ideas which fomented the Revolution were new, exciting, and 'explosive' to the people of Britain who continually suffered under a rigid, class system of nobility and aristocracy which kept them in their 'place', suppressed rights and freedoms of the individual person which today we take for granted, and kept the lower classes in poverty. Such modern, aggressive thinking and bold actions of the French people were intriguing, interesting, and alluring to the under-privileged people of Britain. Long had they suffered in silence and accepted their lot, and now they witnessed people from the lower classes in other nations overthrow their 'betters', take charge of their government, start afresh and anew and begin a new society based on the equality of all people, at all levels, and from all walks of life. Such an avant-garde concept was certainly inviting enough to consider, and 'liberty, equality, and fraternity' which had been achieved in France were desirable outcomes which were more than appealing to the lower ranks and classes in Britain. English nobility and aristocracy shuddered at the threat such ideas posed to the structure and stability of their own society and country.

In France, as in England, a new, middle-class arose during the last half of the 18th C., and this new power soon began to challenge the status quo and the rigid establishment of the nobility and clergy. While Louis XVI, Marie Antoinette, and the French nobility basked in luxury and splendour, the new, middle-class and land-owning peasantry bore the brunt of the tax burden. This burden had been borne in relative silence for centuries, but the sudden awakening as the result of the Enlightenment brought challenges from every quarter. Now the idea of the individual man having 'power' and 'rights', and taking charge of his own destiny, was no longer just a dream but a distinct possibility within their grasp. On July 14, 1789, the people of France rose up, attacked the Bastille, and took their first step toward their own freedom. An equally important step was taken on August 26, 1789, with the adoption of the 'Declaration of the Rights of Man and the Citizen' by the newly formed National Assembly. This document basically rejected the absolute power of the monarchy, substituted it with the 'natural rights of man', sought fair taxation for its people, and self-determination and personal freedom of the citizen, based on the 'rule of law'. The excessive power and control of the French monarchy and nobility were now at an end; the people had taken control.

The implication of the French Revolution for the English monarchy, nobility, and aristocracy brought fear and apprehension to its upper classes. The threat of these revolutionary ideas were real and immediate, and whether or not the same series of events would occur in Britain was a question which was on everyone's mind. Fortunately for the English upper classes, these events did not repeat themselves for several reasons, the first being the new, French government's aggressive actions and pre-emptive strike against Austria. The new Revolutionary France was now seen as a threat not only to European nations but also to England as well. The people of England, from all classes, began to unite under the threat; the French Revolutionary Wars had begun, and they continued for a decade from 1792 to 1802.

The First Coalition of nations on the Continent, which included England among its numbers, was defeated in battles throughout 1793 to 1795, as well as the Second Coalition in 1799 - 1800, which fared no better. Only in Egypt did Britain manage to keep the great general, Napoleon, at bay. Britain was determined to maintain the balance of power in Europe so that no single nation would be supreme and in so doing would maintain its own 'supremacy'. But Britain now had a new fear, the rise of Napoleon Bonaparte who rose through the ranks of the French Army to become a general, and ultimately the Emporer from 1804 to 1814. Once he crowned himself 'Emporer', the Napoleonic Wars began; Napoleon seemed unstoppable and won battle after battle becoming the master of Europe. Britain feared, and prepared for, an invasion and had it not been for Admiral Nelson's victory over the French fleet at Trafalgar in 1805, England may have fallen.

It was during this perilous time that the young Patrick Brunty was studying at St. John's College in Cambridge that he, like others, were forced to take military training. It was something that Patrick truly enjoyed, and this is where he learned about guns, weapons, and artillery. He seriously considered entering the military as a profession, but his loyalty to his sponsors and benefactors, who assumed he would become a teacher or 'take his orders', overrode his desire to become an army officer. His love for the military, and guns, was something he carried throughout his life. After he became a curate in York-shire, he purchased two pistols for protection during the tumultuous times of the Luddite Riots. From that time on, he never went on walks onto the moors without a pistol, and for many years after that, he kept a loaded pistol at his bedside at night.

The Napoleonic Wars also had direct effects on trade and commerce with Continental countries as a result of actions taken by France against Britain. After France's naval defeat at Trafalgar, Napoleon ordered all European countries under his control to close their ports and markets to British goods which severely crippled England's textile industry. The riding of West Yorkshire with its many woollen mills was particularly hard hit, and the economic devastation it caused its many families who depended on it as a livelihood brought many people down to the level of abject poverty. As a young curate in Essex, Shropshire, and later in Yorkshire, Patrick Brontë had to deal with many crises of a personal and financial nature for his poor, parish flock. These problems, along with his own personal tragedies later, and the advent of modern, labour-saving machinery which put people out of work and sparked the Luddite Riots, made Rev. Brontë highly sympathetic to the plight of his parishioners, and earned him a good deal of respect wherever he served.

Although England was successful against France in the Peninsular War in Spain between 1808 - 1814, the closing off of European markets by the French hurt England economically. In response, England set up a naval blockade of French ports and that of its allies with the result that England became involved in yet another war, the War of 1812, with the Americans who saw the blockade as an act of aggression. The Treaty of Ghent was signed in late 1814, and everything simply returned to the status quo. The last battle, the Battle of New Orleans, was actually fought two weeks after the signing of the peace treaty which was unknown to the opposing sides of that famous battle.

The situation between England and France, and its allies which included the United States, did not stabilize until after Napoleon's defeat at the Battle of Waterloo in 1815, his final exile and incarceration on St. Helena Island in the South Atlantic, and finally his death in 1821. Without the heavy burden of taxes for war, and its recovery, Britain was now able to flourish unfettered and without the restrictions which a nation on a war-footing impose. Britain was on its road to recovery, and with the Empire covering one quarter of the world's land and people combined with the wealth of its raw resources, there was nothing to hold back its rapid growth and eventual success. Roads, canals, and the railway were built, people worked feverishly in its mills and factories, domestic and foreign markets and its colonies clamoured for its goods, and literature and science flourished. British production was growing rapidly, and there was no doubt in the minds of the British people that their country was in the midst of a national economic and social revolution. This was the political and economic world in which the Brontë children were born and found themselves in their teens and early adulthood.

The effect of the French Revolutionary Wars, and more particularly the Napoleonic Wars, on England was long-lasting and affected everyone for generations afterward in several ways. Firstly, it provided a shortage of manpower since over 500 000 men had been drawn away to fight in the British Armed Forces. Many of the vacancies in mills, factories, and industry in general, then had to be filled by women and children until the men returned. Many never returned and the shortage of manpower continued until the next generation. But on a different note, the shortage of men meant a shortage of 'husbands' which had a deleterious effect on the social fabric of the country. In these Georgian times, and for one or two successive generations, this effect was to be felt by the female population of Britain and more women became 'old maids' and spinsters.

One must keep in mind that during these times, genteel women were neither expected nor encouraged to enter into any profession, or engage in any form of trade. They were simply expected to be suitably married off, reduce the burden on their family finances, and produce the next generation of children who would also be expected to marry into 'good society' when their time came to make a marriage commitment. If they were not married by the age of thirty, and the likelihood of spinsterhood loomed large, they might be judged 'failures' by the harsh terms of Victorian society. This very issue, and the determinations and efforts genteel Victorian parents to marry off their daughters into other families of wealth and standing is a recurrent theme in Jane Austen's novels, that of Elizabeth Gaskell, and others.

For females in the lower ranks where the possibility of marrying into a higher, social rank was next to an impossibility, but successfully portrayed in the novel, *Jane Eyre*, by Charlotte Brontë, the reality and purpose of marriage was quite different than that of the nobility and aristocracy. The reasons may have ranged from one of true, mutual affection to an 'economic union' of necessity, and in many cases simply to avoid the stigma attached to being a spinster. Once married, a young woman's social standing increased immensely, and hence we understand the greater meaning of Lydia Bennet's words to her eldest, unmarried sister Jane in *Pride and Prejudice* after her own marriage to Mr. Wickham: "Ah, Jane, I take your place now, and you must go lower, because I am a married woman". Lydia then proceeded to her mother's right hand and accompanied her into the dining parlour which indicated that through her recent marriage, she was now 'one step up' on the social ladder, and 'above' that of her unmarried sister even though she was the eldest.

With the hopes and desires of many women to be married, their chances in the upper ranks were reduced, or enhanced, by the level of their own wealth; the greater their wealth, the greater their chances for an early marriage. In the lower ranks, the 'wealth factor' was far less important, and greater importance was attached to beauty, sex appeal, and positive attributes of character. A newly-married couple in the lower ranks would then face the reality of life's cruel hardships together, usually at a subsistence level. Unfortunately, in the early 1800s, and well into the 1830s and 1840s, the shortage and scarcity of available men of marriageable age was still being felt as a result of the Revolutionary and Napoleonic Wars. Those women whose chances of marriage were 'marginal' or 'slim at best' under ideal conditions, for whatever reason, now found their chances significantly reduced, and the number of spinsters in England rose sharply. 'Polite society' was not always kind to these women, and the contempt and 'social slight' shown them were roundly condemned in Charlotte's novel, *Shirley*.

19

LOCAL LORE AND HISTORY

With the arrival of Tabatha Akroyd in the fall of 1825, while the Brontë children were still quite young, came a rich source of local lore and history. The children, always anxious and eager to hear stories of the people and incidents which they could use in their own writing, could not possibly have chosen or found a better source than this fifty-four year old widow who had lived in the area her entire life. 'Tabby', as she was called, was neither educated nor sophisticated; in fact, she was an exact opposite of their erudite father. Such were the extremes of diversity in education and approach which stirred their interests and imaginations. They would often gather in the warm kitchen to help out with the daily, domestic chores, and at the same time be treated to stories passed down through the generations. As one can imagine, stories of the odd, curious, and weird occurences and happenings in the remotest parts of Yorkshire and North England were related to the children now and again from Tabby's extensive respository of local lore. These stories added to their knowledge of local history which they 'stored away', recalled later, and adapted and 'employed' into both their juvenilia and their adult writings.

Perhaps the story of greatest significance to their writing was told to them on many occasions, not by Tabby, but by their own father about the rise of Luddism, and as a 'living witness' to one of the greatest of all Luddite Riots, the attack on Rawfolds Mill, Liversedge in 1812. Charlotte later used this historical information in the novel *Shirley*, which was highly criticized for its loose and fragmented plot. Critics levelled the accusation that the authoress could not decide whether she was writing a 'romance' or simply telling a tale of Yorkshire history. Since there are smatterings of both, the 'yarn' was poorly 'spun', and the entire novel ends up to be a loosely, episodic tale based on the Luddite Riot which appears as the main action of the story.

For those interested in local, Yorkshire history, Luddism, and the Luddite Riots, one can easily identify various incidents within the fictitious plot and a host of characters who were real-life people, and only thinly disguised. For this reason, Charlotte's second novel had a definite, local appeal, particularly when individuals could be identified as seen through the eyes of the celebrated author, Currer Bell. But for critics, it provided a broad target which they easily hit with stinging rebukes over its plot and structure, and for the general reader elsewhere, *Shirley* was a let down after the immensely popular and successful *Jane Eyre*. Had Charlotte taken more time to plan the novel and isolate which theme and topic she wished to pursue and make all other actions secondary sub-plots, the book may have appeared more 'focused' and been more successful. Also, had she kept her original title, 'Hollow's Mill' and concentrated on the actions of the Luddites, issues behind Luddism, and the reasons for their dissatisfaction, it would have been far more successful. Unfortunately, the fragmented nature of the book may partly be related to the fact that Charlotte was highly distracted and emotionally distraught since it was written over the period of 1848, and 1849, a most grievous time when three of her siblings became ill and died in quick succession.

The causes of Luddism were many, but its roots of discontent went back many years. It had its origins in the growing discontent of the broadest base of the population pyramid, the working class and the common poor. The people of Britain had, for many centuries, been law-abiding citizens, and the differences of social classes was begrudgingly respected, but after centuries of serfdom and later poorly-paid farm labourers, this respect was wearing thin. With the coming of the Industrial Revolution, many new products were being created, but they were totally out of reach for the masses because they received so little remuneration for their work. And perhaps the thing which grated them most was the fact that it was their toil and effort which produced the new wealth for the nation, and their masters, yet they were not allowed to share in the new prosperity. This became the 'bone of contention' and the 'sticking point' between the ever-widening gap of rich and poor in England.

In France, this exploitation of the poor by a mocking monarchy which flippantly told them to 'eat cake' when they had no bread, and an uncaring and arrogant nobility finally reached its breaking point in 1789. The working poor of France would not endure it one day longer with the final result being the abolition of the monarchy, their execution, and a wholesale slaughter of its nobility. The possibility of a parallel uprising was now ever-present in the minds of the English monarchy, nobility, and aristocracy. Very little had been done to narrow the gap between the 'two nations' which existed in England, 'one rich, one poor'. England's saving grace probably had a lot to do with the rise of a new, middle-class which exerted economic, financial, and political pressure on the British government which slowly brought about much-needed changes, but at a very slow rate. Other factors included Britain's historic respect for 'law and order', and the fact that the bitter hatred which propelled the people of France to violent revolution was not present to the same extent in England. Also, the new middle-class, who were neither members of the nobility nor aristocracy, was proof enough that common people could make some headway if proper opportunites presented themselves.

The working poor of Britain had much with which to be discontented; with the prosperity brought about by the Industrial Revolution, only the upper and middle-classes benefited, and the poor remained poor. The price of corn (grains) was a food staple and along with their rents kept rising, yet their wages remained the same, or even declined. New taxes were being added to an already heavy tax burden; improvements in their working conditions were not forthcoming; trade unions were banned, and new machinery from the secondary stages of the Industrial Revolution were putting even more poor people out of work. Many people were on the verge of starvation and destitute; they had nothing to lose, and instant death from a soldier's bullet was far more preferable than a slow and painful death by starvation. The working poor had been 'squeezed' at every conceivable turn and had no one to speak for them or act on their behalf in the Parliament of Britain.

England was not immune from revolts, and a look at past British history brings to mind the Peasants' Revolt of of 1381, led by Wat Tyler and John Ball which resulted when the actions of the government attempted to increase taxes and roll back wages to a level prior to the Black Death when labour was plentiful and wages low. The march to London by Tyler and his mob led to property destruction and death. In the end, concessions were made to the demands, but they were quickly revoked once the mob dispersed and returned to their homes. In 1780, the Gordon Riots[1] in London continued for four days which left over 800 people dead and inestimable property damage. The mob was angry not only because of the repeal of anti-Catholic legislation but also against foreigners, mainly from Ireland, who took away their jobs by reducing wage expectations.

Thirteen years prior to the Gordon Riots, a number of disturbances, mainly food riots over higher prices, rocked England in the years 1756 and 1757. The fact that the Parliament of Britain was controlled by the landed gentry who refused to give any concessions to the poor, and, in fact, endeavoured to keep them even more underfoot by legislating the Combinations Act of 1799, which forbade 'association' of any group of two or more people with the intention of discussing ways to increase wages or improve their working conditions, simply inflamed the hostile relations between workers and employers. There was, in fact, very little difference between their relationship and the 'planter-slave' relationship in the Americas which the British so roundly criticized and condemned as 'uncivilized'. The Enactment of the the the Combinations Act, with its clear intent, was aggressive provocation and highly inflammatory towards workers and workers' rights. The government had openly invited hostile actions by trying to suppress the workers who were already thoroughly suppressed, and could bear little more; they had been pushed too far.

By 1812, government expenditures on 'poor relief' had risen almost 400% from thirty-two years earlier in 1780. Fewer and fewer people could make a living working at the mills and factories, and in Yorkshire, Lancashire, and Nottingham, resistance to installation of the Industrial Revolution's second generation machines was strong. In some cases, mill-owners in Yorkshire did not install any new machinery for fear of the reaction of workers already distressed by other more fundamental concerns of just 'making ends meet' and keeping their families housed, clothed, and fed. Instead of the government considering the problems from the perspective of the hard-pressed working poor, Parlia-

---

1   The riots were named after Lord George Gordon, the leader of the Protestant Association, who opposed the repeal of anti-Catholic legislation. He was acquitted of high treason, but twenty-one others were hanged.

ment, which was controlled by the landed gentry, enacted laws which favoured only themselves and members of the upper classes. To further punish workers for their acts of belligerence and growing unrest, they simply enacted more laws to remove privileges of clothworkers and clothmakers which had taken them decades to achieve. The government had set its own trap, and for the workers violence was now the only recourse, and the only viable alternative, to meet their demands.

The threat of violence was especially high in Yorkshire where cloth-workers often earned three times the 'going rate' in other districts, and they took great pride in their work and the quality of their product. Now with new legislation which took away workers' past privileges, some mill-owners took advantage of their weakened position to install new machinery which they had not introduced earlier for fear of reprisal. The two machines particularly offensive to the Yorkshire workers were cloth-dressing machines known as the 'gig-mill' which raised the nap on woollens, and the 'shearing-frame' which trimmed away excess, fly-away nap. Their pride was sufficiently injured and their jobs were now sufficiently threatened for them to take firm, aggressive action to make their feelings known and give backing to their threats; without action their threats would be hollow. The stage was now set for action, and Luddism was about to rise to a new level, from one of threats and intimidation to property destruction and violence.

To add to the misery of the workers by the introduction of these new machines, hand loom spinners and weavers were now feeling the effects; many of them were being dropped as skilled craftsmen and replaced by unskilled labour, their wages were being reduced, and rents for cottages and looms were being raised arbitrarily. And, insult was added to injury when they observed the shoddy, mass-produced goods which replaced their fine, high-quality goods which they made with craftsmanship, care, and attention to detail. By the end of 1811, tensions had reached a boiling point, and Luddism reached 'fever pitch'. Men met in secret; their faces were painted black and their names were replaced by numbers all to prevent identification, even to one another. Such tactics paids dividends in the end since few Luddite were ever captured and tried, and even fewer betrayed by their own number. They trained briefly, planned heavily, and appeared as silent, disciplined, masked gangs under the direction of a regimental leader when they made their attacks. Their commander-in- chief was none other than the mysterious, legendary, ubiquitous, and phantom-like 'General Ludd' whose very name frightened children of the middle-classes, but was revered and venerated by the lower classes.

The exact origins of 'General Ludd' are sometimes disputed, but according to the author, Christopher Hibbert (The English A Social History 1066 - 1945), Ned Ludd was, in fact, a real person who lived in Leicestershire. Unfortunately, Ned was simple-minded and was teased unmercifully by the village children. He endured their torments, taunts, and cruelty until one day they went too far; he became enraged and began to chase them. As the children fled, they scattered in every direction for fear of their lives, and Ned then focused on one child and followed him into his cottage. He searched everywhere, but the child was nowhere to be found, perhaps hiding under a bed or out the back door, but Ned would not be denied some satisfaction. In the main room of the cottage, he found two knitting frames and smashed them to pieces in his fury and frustration. Soon the story spread far and wide, and when the Luddite Riots began and machines were mysteriously smashed, it was immediately credited to Ned Ludd. And so arose the myth and the legend, and the scapegoat, Ned Ludd, was later elevated to the rank of 'general'. General Ludd then became a hero across North England within the next decade, and 'his' signature appeared at the bottom of handbills, warnings, threats, pamphlets, and posted broadsheets throughout the textile districts.

The Luddites were widely and generally feared by mill-owners, the middle-class of merchants, the clergy who generally supported the mill- owners and the government,[2] sympathizers, other Luddites, and particularly individuals who defied them and worked at reduced rates. The Luddites were known to be equally just to members of their cause, and merciless to those whom they opposed or stood in their way. No person or machine was safe unless it was 'officially sanctioned' by 'inspectors' or 'committees' who visited cottages, villages, and pubs to give their stamp of approval. Those who opposed the cause, made bold threats against them, or raised their ire, could be boycotted, censured, beaten, or even killed. Luddism and Luddites were now something to be feared as the underground workers movement took hold, expanded, flexed its muscles, and made good its threats.

In early 1812, the 'machine-breakers', as the Luddites were known, expressed their displeasure and took positive action by smashing and pulling down new machinery, intercepting and destroying them while enroute to the mills, intimidating and threatening the lives of mill- owners, and inflicting major damage and property destruction at various mills. These attacks were most common in Yorkshire and Lancashire, and in each and every attack, the modus operandi, purpose, and results were generally the same. Mill-owners and their families now feared for their lives, property was being destroyed by militant gangs, their manufacturing output was declining, and they expected their government to step in and bring the attacks to a halt.

By February of 1812, the British Parliament enacted legislation aimed generally at the Luddites which proved effective and slowed down their activities. The government moved a large number of troops into the area for protection of the mills, and secondly made it a capital offence to break or destroy certain types of new machinery. These new laws put a 'damper' on the activities of many who reconsidered their positions rather than swing at the end of a rope. A second hypothesis to explain the slowdown of Luddite attacks claims that Luddism was working and being effective; the installation of new machines was now being delayed, and workers were now getting more work and higher wages. And although the Luddite attacks had now subsided, the most memorable one was about to happen in April, and Rev. Brontë, then minister at Hartshead-cum-Clifton, was at the very centre of the action. It was his personal 'witness' to these events at his very doorstep which he passed down to his children and which Charlotte used as the 'centrepiece' and main action of her novel, *Shirley*.

Up to February and March of 1812, most of the damage and destruction by the Luddites was done at smaller mills in Lancashire and Yorkshire. Emboldened by their own suc-

---

2   Rev. Brontë fell into this category of clergy.

cesses, facing bold threats by some powerful owners and punitive actions by Parliament, some Luddites thought that it was time to attack bigger mills to impress upon owners and authorities alike that they were serious, committed, and not to be intimidated. In early April, secret meetings[3] were held and plans were made to attack Rawfolds Mill, Liversedge, to send a clear message that Luddism was not dead. Preparations were being made on both sides.

On the night of April 11, 1812, the Luddites gathered at Dumb Steeple, blackened their faces or wore masks, shouldered pikes, muskets, 'Enochs' (giant iron hammers), and an assortment of other destructive weapons and marched silently toward Rawfolds Mill, Liversedge, owned by William Cartwright. Cartwright himself had been preparing for such an attack and had hired private, armed guards, made use of some of the soldiers sent into the area, and barricaded himself and a few, loyal workers inside the mill compound. He even had vats of sulphuric acid placed at the top of the stairs to tip onto the heads of the intruders if they managed to break into the mill. When the battle began, it was a fearsome fight which lasted twenty minutes, but the mill force held firm, and the Luddites retreated. There were numerous injuries on both sides, and two severely injured Luddites were left behind. The mortally wounded men were carried to the Star Inn in Roberttown where the younger man, John Booth, had his leg amputated but died of his injuries shortly afterwards along with the other man. Neither of the dying men betrayed any of the others involved in the attack.

William Cartwright soon became a hero to mill-owners, judges, the middle class, persons who preached 'law and order', and the authorities in general. The failed attack was a turning point in Luddism and Luddite efforts, and a second, planned attack on a mill near Huddersfield was called off. The owner, William Horsfall, was thoroughly hated, despised, and detested by the common worker, and he once boasted that he would 'ride up to his saddle girths in Luddite blood', as local legend has it. Horsfall's mill was so well-guarded with soldiers and cannon that the Luddites realized that an attack on the mill would be futile. Instead, they remained in hiding and ambushed him on the moors as he rode home after a trip to Huddersfield. He died of his wounds, and it was this incident which inspired Rev. Brontë to exchange his shillelagh and walking stick for a pair of pistols. From that time onward, and for many years to come, the Reverend never went walking alone on the moors without a loaded pistol. Also, for several decades afterwards, he kept a loaded pistol beside his bed at night and discharged it at St. Michael's Church tower each morning from his upstairs, bedroom window. Such were the times of the early 1800s which left such a profound impression on Mr. Brontë, and later his children.

The Luddite Riots in Yorkshire and the assassination of William Horsfall set off a massive search for the Luddites responsible. Dozens were captured, taken to the gaol in York, and tried for their crimes. A few were set free, some were sent to penal colonies and seventeen were eventually hanged. In the meantime, the turmoil became even greater when a distraught merchant who had lost everything and blamed the government for his losses, shot Spencer Perceval, the Prime Minister, to death in the lobby of the House of

---

3   Some of their meetings were held in an upstairs room of the Shears Inn on Halifax Road, Hightown, Liversedge.

Commons. Supporters of Luddism, fanatics, and malcontents were joyful at the news of the assassination and put up reward posters calling for the 'head' of the Prince Regent.

In the months following the Luddite Riots and the murder of William Horsfall, thousands of armed troops were sent into the West Riding of Yorkshire to suppress these acts of violence, and, in effect, the capturing, gaoling, and sentencing of those responsible put a general end to Luddism. For a long time afterward, William Cartwright relentlessly pursued those Luddites who attacked his mill and managed to escape, but not one person was ever brought to justice; the people of Yorkshire were very 'tight-lipped' and remained silent throughout. In the years and decades that followed, the stories surrounding the people and events of the day were turned into songs, myths, and legends which were handed down from generation to generation as part of the local lore.

Some isolated attacks on machinery occurred into the fall of 1812, but generally speaking the riots and violent acts had stopped by mid-summer. The last incident of machine-smashing occurred five years later in 1817, at a large factory in Loughborough, Leicestershire, but, in retrospect, it appears that the entire rise of Luddism was not only doomed to failure but also seemed to be symptomatic of an even greater problem, one which had to do with the sharing of wealth and prosperity with all classes of people in Britain, and not simply spreading it among those of the upper classes who already possessed an inordinate amount of England's wealth.

During Charlotte's stay at Roe Head, she and other classmates passed by the site where Horsfall was murdered on the moors, and we can only speculate on the impact that this may have had on her, as it tied in with the tales of those told to her by her father about these same events. Another important event connected to the Luddite Riots and Rev. Brontë must also have been passed along to Charlotte. Late one night as Rev. Brontë returned unexpectedly to the church, he came across a group of Luddites burying one of their dead. Since he was a 'law and order' preacher, an anti-Luddite, and preached against their actions in his church, he was confronted with a moral dilemma. Should he alert the authorities of this late night venture, or should he respect the rights of the living to bury their dead in peace and dignity; Rev. Brontë chose the latter.

Although the Brontë children were all born after all the incidents of the Luddite Riots in Yorkshire, they were in their teens and early adulthood when another group of disaffected people arose in England and began to threaten the very fundamental establishments of the country. The Chartist Movement, which officially began in 1838, had its 'grass roots' origins almost a decade before with economic problems developing in the agrarian, labour sector. Agriculture had been on the decline for decades going back to the origins of the Industrial Revolution, was now in 'depression', and many farmers and labourers were in a ruinous state. Labourers were earning starvation wages, and farmers were selling their products at rates much lower than they had in the past.

When much of Britain's agricultural lands were partitioned with stone fences and enclosed to raise sheep for the wool industry, fewer farm- labourers were needed, and those labourers moved to towns, villages and cities where mills and factories had been established to secure employment. In the rural areas, hamlets and small villages were almost deserted, and where once there was a thriving population, only a handful remained.

The dissatisfaction with the government, the powers that be, and the wealthy upper classes, grew into anger, and by the 1830s erupted into disturbances throughout the country. For the governments, the middle-classes, the nobility, and aristocracy, it was déjà vu of Luddism and the Luddites. In actual fact, there was no connection whatsoever between the two groups, but they certainly took their cue from the Luddites and emulated their efforts in several ways. The gangs of men who destroyed property often blackened their faces or wore hoods and costumes, preceded their attacks with letters of warning and threats, and they were led not by 'General Ludd', but by their own 'Captain Swing'. In addition to destroying farm machines and cutting fences, their favourite tactic was arson and putting hayricks and barns to the torch. Arson was a capital offence, and in the end, in a twist of ironic, black humour, many did 'swing' for their 'Captain'.

The roots of discontent were, once again, very basic and fundamental to these rural, agrarian folk simply trying to eke out a living from the land. The situation went from bad to worse, and they finally began to protest against enclosures of land, their restricted use of grazing commons, low wages which barely provided a sustainable living, employment of foreigners (mainly Irish workers) at lower rates, and new threshing machines which were taking away much-needed jobs at harvest time, a season which provided their greatest income. Loud protests eventually turned to violence, and in some cases lives were lost, but for the most part there were warnings, intimidations, loud, boisterous gatherings with violent language and the display of fearsome weapons, but no damage. In the end, thousands were arrested, some were acquitted, hundreds were imprisoned, hundreds more were sent to penal colonies in Australia and elsewhere, and nineteen were hanged. Once again, the efforts of the common folk was thwarted, suppressed, and crippled by harsh, punitive actions of a government which seemed indifferent to their concerns, however well-founded they might have been. The government's chief aim appeared to be to restore law and order, and return to the status quo.

With many past, failed experiments in uprisings and revolts by the people with the usual and 'standard' outcome being imprisonment or death, the Chartist Movement took a more peaceful and democratic approach to the problem. With slow beginnings and small groups in London, the followers of William Lovett, and a radical friend from the London Working Men's Association, came 'The People's Charter' of 1838. It did not take long for its followers to be called 'Chartists' who made six very basic demands of the government in power. They wished to see: Parliament held on an annual basis; universal male suffrage; votes conducted by secret ballot; equal electoral districts; an end to property qualifications for members of Parliament; and annual salaries for members of Parliament. The purpose and intent of these demands were obvious; with these demands in effect, ordinary workers could then be elected to Parliament and endeavour to make changes on behalf of the voteless, working poor who made up the majority of the population, produced the goods of the land, paid the bulk and burden of the taxes, but had no say or representation in the Parliament of the land.

The Chartists were alive and well in Charlotte Brontë's day, and were, in fact, a popular and growing movement. Charlotte and her family could not have divorced themselves from these issues since the family did subscribe to several political and religious magazines, and generally, and regularly, discussed political matters from an early age. Rev. Brontë, as in the case of the Luddites three decades earlier, was always sympathetic to the plight of the common worker, but he was also a firm believer and backer of the government, and 'law and order' first. The demands of the Chartists were very basic, and even in the broadest sense could not be seen or interpreted as 'revolutionary', or treasonous; they simply sought change and improvement to the plight of the working poor and lower classes. The upper classes, who were firmly in control, were, however, suspicious and fearful regarding where their demands would lead, since the French Revolution and what had happened in France, was still in the minds of many.

The Chartist Movement grew rapidly, and supporters were neither shy nor reluctant to show their feelings, especially hatred, for the governing and ruling classes. It showed strong support and solidarity of the working class; the crowds at meeting places became larger and larger. First, there were hundreds, then thousands, and at an oath-taking, swear-in ceremony in Lancashire, the crowd was estimated at 10 000. Some impressive torch-light parades attracted as many as 50 000 people, and the biggest rally of all, with a crowd of approximately 200 000, met in Halifax on Whit Monday, 1839, to lend their support. Several months later, a general strike was called, but it met with only partial success. The Chartists meant for their movement to be peaceful, but if they could not obtain their demands 'peaceably', they would considered taking them 'forcibly', and this understanding struck fear in the hearts of the upper classes.

In the same year, 1839, as one might expect, it was only a matter of time before one of the protests got out of hand, or the government and its army over-reacted. Such was the case in Newport, Monmouthshire (Wales), where a crowd of 7 000 armed men marched to demand the release of one of their spokesmen from Newport Gaol. The army felt threatened, opened fire, and killed twenty-two protestors. In 1842, a petition of three million names was sent to London, and six years later, a massive protest rally was planned for London. When the government flexed its muscles, and brought in 150 000 special constables and reserve regiments to deal with any trouble, the Chartist Leaders called off the rally in the face of the government hard line, and possibly to ward off potential casualties. From that point onward, the Chartist Movement slowly declined towards disintegration, and the best and most effective opportunity the people of the day had to 'better themselves' slipped away, and was lost. Had the Chartists developed a more powerful, nation-wide organization and been more persistent, it is likely that they would have succeeded and brought their desired results to a speedy conclusion. Unfortunately, without their Movement, its backing, and the constant pressure of protests, the government acted at its leisure, and final results were slow in coming.

It is highly unlikely that Charlotte and her sisters would not have taken an interest in such newsworthy events and the social issues which these protests brought to light. Their father may even have made comparison with the Luddites and their actions years before. Although the Brontë children were never desparately poor or starving, their father was in constant touch with such people and their desparate struggles with poverty, which was never far away. The sympathies of the Brontë children, as well as their moral and religious beliefs, were generally parallel to that of their father's. Charlotte's sympathies are quite evident in *Shirley* where Robert Moore and Shirley Keeldar, the first a mill-owner and the latter with an aristocratic background, wealth, and property, are the protagonists. They are presented as the law-abiding citizens without blemish while the Luddite pro-testers are portrayed as lawless hooligans bent on destruction. The two sides are portrayed strictly in 'black' (Luddites) and 'white' (Moore and Keeldar) with no 'middle ground'.

In retrospective objectivity, excluding the property destruction, injuries and death, we can more clearly see, and freely understand, the fundamental grievances which drove the two movements, Luddism and Chartism, whose underlying symptoms went far be-yond the obvious manifestation of their anger. In this respect, Charlotte was never able to completely remove herself to a comfortable distance and objective viewpoint; she was too closely tied to the religious beliefs of her father, and aunt, and the restrictive, moral views of Victorian society. No matter how she tried to 'break free' from these restric-tions, she was always still loosely in its 'clutches' and could not come to terms with the fact that perhaps violence and revolution were the only options that desperately poor people had at their disposal.

20

OTHER VICTORIAN WRITERS

Since all of the Brontës were highly intelligent, precocious, and voracious readers from the very early stages of their lives, we do know that they were influenced by writers of their time, and before, but to what degree and by whom is a matter of conjecture. We do know that Charlotte, in particular, was highly influenced by the poems of Wordsworth, Cowper, Southey, Campbell, Milton, Shelley, Keats, Byron, Hazlitt, Hunt, and possibly the Brownings. In works of prose, the Brontës enjoyed the writings of Sir Walter Scott, and for Charlotte, her interest was also piqued by writers like Jane Austen, Mary Wollstonecraft, Mary Shelley, and contemporaries like her hero, William Makepeace Thackeray, the early works of Charles Dickens and that of Elizabeth C. Gaskell[1] and Harriet Martineau. As for Branwell, who may also have had an interest in all of the above writers, he particularly had an interest in writing for *Blackwood's Magazine* and wrote to them several times.

Branwell's letters to both Wordsworth and Blackwood's were never answered. The lack of response was attributed to his tone, thought to be arrogant, and an 'air' of supreme confidence in his own writing ability, and although Blackwood's did not issue him a response, his correspondence was kept in their archives.[2] Branwell was particularly inspired by the works of James Hogg, a contributor to Blackwood's, William Cowper and his poetry and life bordering on insanity, as well as the opium-induced visions of Thomas De Quincey, which he outlined in 'Confessions of an English Opium Eater', 1822, and those of Samuel Taylor Coleridge in 'Kubla Khan; a Vision in a Dream', 1816. These were highly intriguing to Branwell, and they may very well have encouraged him to experiment with laudanum. Branwell also wrote to Hartley Coleridge and received not

---

1 Elizabeth C. Gaskell was eventually the person asked by Mr. Brontë to write an authorized biography of Charlotte's life.
2 Daphne DuMaurier makes reference to this in her book, *The Infernal World of Branwell Brontë*.

only a reply from him but also encouragement since the young Coleridge thought that Branwell's poetry had merit.

We do know that Charlotte wrote to both Southey and Wordsworth and received replies from both. The reply from Wordsworth was polite and courteous, but the letter she received from Southey was polite but not encouraging. Southey was definitely from the 'old school' of poetry and was also firmly entrenched in Victorian thought. In his reply to Charlotte dated 12/03/1837, he first states that Charlotte does possess poetic talent and then adds a cautious note. Southey says:

> You evidently possess & in no inconsiderable degree what Wordsworth calls "the faculty of Verse.".... Whoever therefore is ambitious of distinction in this way, ought to be prepared for diappointment.

but then he advises:

> Literature cannot be the business of a woman's life: & it ought not to be. The more she is engaged in her proper duties, the less leisure will she have for it, even as an accomplishment & a recreation.

Such a reply must have shocked Charlotte who was for the emancipation of women and the breaking down of social barriers which were so prevalent in the upper classes of Victorian society, and to which Robert Southey so strongly adhered.

The Brontës were 'fierce politicians', as Mary Taylor described Charlotte, and were followers of politics, political figures and events and issues of the day. And since the Rev. Brontë had always been interested in the army, guns, and military matters, his particular hero was Wellington, who also became Charlotte's favourite. Admiral Nelson who stopped the French fleet at Trafalgar, and perhaps prevented the invasion of England, and thereby changed the course of history, was also a second favourite. Admiral Nelson was once named the Duke of Bronté, which encouraged the young, Cambridge University student to change his name from 'Brunty' to 'Bronté', but it was eventually changed to Brontë (see Chapter 1).

Branwell's rich, vivid and highly active imagination may have also been stirred by books in his father's library which included the writing of many of the contemporary poets. Other prose works which impressed him included *The Life of Napoleon* by Sir Walter Scott, *The History of Rome* by Oliver Goldsmith, and children's classics like *Aesop's Fables*, and the *Arabian Nights*. Even the painting, 'Belshazzar's Feast' by John Martin, whose intricate detail appeared to have fascinated them for hours at a time, intrigued him and inspired him into making his own intricate creations which are so prevalent in his juvenilia.

Branwell was particularly enthralled by *Blackwood's Magazine*, an Edinburgh periodical set up as a rival to the *Edinburgh Review*, which was a Whig-leaning magazine. Blackwood's became immensely popular with the reading public for its hard-hitting articles on leading Scottish political figures, its attacks on the 'Cockney School' of poets which included Hunt, Hazlitt, and Keats, and its numerous dialogues known as the "Noctes

Ambrosianae'. One of the magazine's editors, James Hogg, was a particular favourite of Branwell's, and inspired him with his poetry, and his many contributions to the magazine. When Hogg died in 1835, Branwell again wrote to Blackwood's pleading with them to read his work and hinted that he be considered a trial replacement for Hogg. His letter was never answered.

In many respects, the novels of the Brontës have been classified as 'romance' with manifestations, elements, and links to Romantic writers and poems of previous decades and the preceding era. The poems of Wordsworth were probably the most alluring, since they typified and epitomized those of the Romantic era, and he was considered one of its founders along with Samuel Taylor Coleridge. Wordsworth's works like 'Lyrical Ballads', 'Tintern Abbey', and 'The Prelude' were just some of his works with which the Brontës would have been familiar. In addition to this, Wordsworth's description of Nature, a theme which was close to their hearts and minds, and his use of 'ordinary language' about themes from 'ordinary life' were not unlike theirs.

Each of the Brontës spent a good deal of time and effort in writing poetry in their early life, along similar lines of theme, structure, and rhythm employed by Wordsworth and his contemporaries. Although the Brontës continued to write poetry throughout their lives, Charlotte indicated in a letter Henry Nussey dated 11/01/1841, that she had more or less given up on poetry. She stated:

> Once indeed I was very poetical, when I was sixteen, seventeen eighteen and ninteen years old - but I am now twenty-four approaching twenty-five - and the intermediate years are those which begin to rob life of some of its superfluous colouring. At this age, it is time that the imagination should be pruned and trimmed - that the judgement should be cultivated - and a few at least, of the countless illusions of early youth should be cleared away. I have not written poetry for a long while.

Another factor which may have encouraged Charlotte and Branwell to write to Wordsworth was the fact that the great and legendary Romantic poets lived in the Lake District which has only Lancashire between them and Yorkshire and was not that distant. In the last few years of her life, Charlotte did make several trips to The Lake District and at one time met with Harriet Martineau at the Knoll, in Ambleside, only a short distance from Wordsworth's last home at Rydal Mount. It seems unlikely that she would have missed the opportunity of visiting this great poet's home so near at hand.

The novels of the Brontës, like most other sincere, creative and original authors, stand out as unique and different, but if an effort is made, we can find traces of the past which influenced her. Anyone who has read the works of Sir Walter Scott cannot help but become totally absorbed in the character, the history, and the geography of his novels. The Brontës enjoyed the works of Scott and owed much to him in writing their famous novels incorporating, as Scott had done, rural themes, 'peasant' life, and regional speech based in West Yorkshire. All three of these elements are evident, and most fully integrated in *Wuthering Heights,* which is the most unique novel in the history of English Literature, and perhaps World Literature. Secondly, the historical nature of Charlotte's

Shirley makes use of these same elements and again, less so, in *Jane Eyre*, and is also to be found in Anne Brontë's, *The Tenant of Wildfell Hall*.

The social issues raised in these last two novels have derived their influences not only of their author's own doing but also of writers like Jane Austen, Mary Wollstonecraft, Elizabeth C. Gaskell, and Harriet Martineau, all important female, 'celebrity' authors of the day. The breakdown of the rigid, social class structure which Charlotte Brontë so eminently and successfully portrayed in *Jane Eyre*, and the emancipation of women's rights and freedoms which she so strongly brought forward in *Shirley*, may have had their impetus from works like *A Vindication of the Rights of Woman* (1792), by Mary Wollstonecraft whose ideas challenged the existing social structure, and 'woman's place' in society.

Harriet Martineau, a renowned and celebrated writer of the time, became a friend of Charlotte Brontë's after Charlotte's work gained fame among the literati. Martineau came from humble origins and 'knew' poverty well. In her youth, she was devoutly religious and her first work, *Devotional Exercises*, 1823, brought her fame and fortune. Her later works, published in a series of short stories, and entitled *Illustrations of Political Economy*, showed her concern for social reform and earned her national respect. She travelled widely and her opinion was sought in many quarters. When she finally settled in The Lake District, she became friends of the Wordsworths who lived nearby. Charlotte met Miss Martineau for the first time in December, 1849, and one year later in December, 1850, Charlotte stayed with her at the Knoll in Ambleside. Their friendship 'cooled' somewhat after Martineau wrote her highly anti-theological *Laws of Man's Social Nature*,1851, and after she sharply criticized one of Charlotte's later novels. Charlotte also confided, in her later years, to Mary Taylor that Miss Martineau's openness and frankness were qualities which bothered her, and that, too, led to the 'cooling' of their relationship.

Another person of influence who also became friends with Charlotte Brontë was none other than her eventual biographer, Elizabeth Gaskell, who in 1848, wrote her first novel, *Mary Barton*, after the death of her infant son. The novel would, no doubt, have been of considerable interest to Charlotte since it deals with the impoverished conditions of unemployed mill-hands and their families in Manchester. The story takes place during the 1840s, when many people were out of work and in dire straits. The story was also unique in that its central characters were all strictly working class, and mill-owners were secondary characters. After its release, the book was not well received by the middle-class of mill- owners and 'high Tories' who took it as an affront. By contrast, Charles Dickens was highly impressed with the novel and invited Mrs. Gaskell to provide submissions for his new, weekly periodical, 'Household Words', which began in 1850.

Charlotte Brontë met Elizabeth Gaskell for the first time in 1850, and became friends over the years. Six months later in June, 1851, Charlotte visited Mrs. Gaskell at Plymouth Grove, her home in Manchester. While there, Charlotte began her last novel, *Villette*, and perhaps even asked for her ideas and opinions, but this, of course, is highly speculative. Charlotte returned to Plymouth Grove again in April, 1853, for a week's visit, and five months later, in September, Mrs. Gaskell visited the Parsonage for four days and met Mr. Brontë for the first time. She took an immediate dislike to Mr. Brontë and formed a highly negative opinion of him which she aired in her first edition of Charlotte's biography.

Perhaps Mrs. Gaskell is best known, not for her novels, but for her biography, *The Life of Charlotte Brontë*, 1857. Three months after Charlotte's death, Rev. Brontë wrote to Mrs. Gaskell suggesting that she write an authorized biography of his daughter to counteract the many unauthorized and inaccurate stories that began to surface about her and the family. Gaskell agreed, the work began, and the biography was two years 'in the making'. When the finished work appeared in March, 1857, many of her descriptions and opinions of people still living bordered on libel. She and her publisher, Smith, Elder & Co., were forced to remove some passages from their second edition and issue apologies to those affected. Rev. Brontë, in general, was pleased with her biographical work on Charlotte, but was hurt by her negative portrayal of himself. In a letter to Mrs. Gaskell, he indirectly scolded that we are all sinners, including her, and that someday we will all have to answer for our mistakes. Rev. Brontë died in June, 1861, and Mrs. Gaskell died suddenly of heart failure only four years later in 1865, at the young age of fifty-five.

Being voracious readers, having knowledge of contemporary literature, and being interested in the social issues of the day, the Brontës must have been familiar with the works of Charles Dickens who was just coming into vogue in the 1840s. The author appears to have had a happy childhood until the age of twelve when his father was sent to a debtor's prison, and from there it descended into a life of misery. With hard work in a blacking warehouse, and diligent effort and determination, Dickens was able to work his way up, first as an office boy, and then as a reporter for the Morning Chronicle. These memories and experiences coupled with his rough and painful initiation into 'life in Victorian times' inspired him to write his first novel, *Pickwick Papers*, in 1837, and others later which were highly popular and highly successful.

Dickens was a moralist and a 'socialist' and saw the many shortcomings, inconsistencies, and inequities of Victorian society which he used as a recurrent theme in many of his novels like *Oliver Twist* (1838), *David Copperfield* (1850), *Bleak House* (1853), and *Hard Times* (1854). In the 'Introduction' to *Bleak House*, G. K. Chesterton made the following observation of Dickens and his purpose in writing:

> Dickens had a singularly just mind. He was wild in his caricatures, but very sane in his impressions. Many of his books were devoted, and this book [Bleak House] is partly devoted, to a denunciation of aristocracy - of the idle class that lives easily upon the toil of nations.

and Chesterton also quoted Dickens himself who briefly outlined his assessment of the Victorian social 'tyranny':

> This tyranny,... shall not be lifted by the light subterfuge of a fiction. This tyranny shall never be lifted till all Englishmen lift it together.

This statement, in fact, closely parallels Anne Brontë's feeling and purpose in her writing of *Agnes Grey* which she made reference to in the 'Preface to the Second Edition' of *The Tenant of Wildfell Hall*, July, 1848. Dickens was the first English writer to display a 'social conscience'.

The writings of Dickens, like those of the Brontës afterward, particularly Charlotte's, captured the popular imagination of readers in the lower classes who could identify with the lowly protagonists who were much like themselves and who suffered many of the same fates in factories and workhouses. Now, writers like Dickens and the Brontës were speaking up on issues in their fiction, and with their fiction, on behalf of the socially disadvantaged. This was definitely new and revolutionary in British society, and whereas French peasants and ordinary French folk took to the streets armed with muskets, pikes, bayonets and cannon in violent, armed revolution, British writers were finally achieving changes, ever so slowly, in a 'bloodless revolution' with pen and paper. And just as Dickens was criticized for his verbosity, sensationalism, and 'want of construction' by the aristocracy, and critics, so were the Brontës with their novels and their views of Victorian society's hypocrisy and shortcomings.

Another parallel which can be drawn between the Brontës and Dickens was the living arrangements of the two families. After Mr. Brontë's wife died, his sister-in-law, Elizabeth Branwell, or 'Aunt Branwell', came to live in the Brontë household to take charge of it, and to help raise six children. And although it is said that Mr. Brontë did propose marriage to Elizabeth and she refused, the continued living arrangement was considered 'scandalous'. Marrying one's sister-in-law after the death of one's wife was an 'impropriety' in the eyes of Victorian society. Charles Dicken's situation was not much different when in 1858, his wife, Kate, left him, and Dickens continued to keep his wife's sister, Georgina, in his employment as his housekeeper. Naturally, there were many 'whispers', wagging tongues, and scandalous stories which circulated regarding this arrangement long after his wife's departure.

The work of the Brontës and Dickens have similarities in that they both wish to place Victorian society and its mores 'under a microscope', question the unquestionable, challenge the status quo, point out the glaring inequities, the insupportable inequalities, the obvious unfairness, the tremendous poverty, and the hopeless suffering, and 'call to task' the social make-up and class structure which allows these conditions to exist. Although Dickens more closely deals with the aspects of poverty and inequalities, the Brontës challenged the class structure and its beliefs which suppressed the wishes and desires of women to make an honest contribution to society at large other than just being submissive wives and mothers, or teachers and governesses, as the society of the day dictated. Neither did they expect to cause revolutionary changes with their writings, but with diligence and constancy bring about revolutionary changes 'of thought' in the governing classes to effect changes for the betterment of the poor and defenceless members of society who had no 'voice', or 'choice', in how their lives were governed and directed by forces, powers, laws and decrees completely beyond their control.

Another author of celebrity and importance to the Brontës who preceded them by one generation was Jane Austen whose novels were very well- received and widely read in the early part of the 19th Century. Miss Austen had several things in common with the Brontës beginning with the fact that both families had well-cultivated and well-educated fathers who were both members of the clergy. Both families were large, close and affectionate with the Brontës having six children and the Austens having seven. Jane Austen, like the Brontë children was intelligent, precocious, widely read, and enjoyed many of the same authors and poets. The similarities also include the facts that Jane Austen remained unmarried throughout her life, like Emily and Anne Brontë, although she had several suitors and one serious 'brush' with marriage. In fact, she did accept one proposal of marriage one day, but quickly retracted it the next. This moment of indecision seems to be 'played out' in a minor way in the plots of many of her novels. Miss Austen also wrote a great deal of 'Juvenilia' and left behind many letters to family and friends which later proved invaluable in reconstructing her biography although much of the material was censored by her sister Cassandra after Jane Austen's death. It is also a coincidence of fact that both Jane Austen and Charlotte Brontë each had one novel published posthumously, and both left behind unfinished novels. Charlotte's unfinished novel, perhaps by no coincidence, was entitled, *Emma*, which certainly leaves us all to wonder why the same title. It might also be noted that both authors, Austen and Brontë, lived relatively short lives and died at ages forty-two and thirty-eight, respectively.

Although there was a large readership and interest in Jane Austen's novels, and praise of her work by Sir Walter Scott in the *Quarterly Review* of 1815, there were dissenting voices, criticisms and [later] detractors including Elizabeth Barrett Browning, D.H. Lawrence, and even, Charlotte Brontë who found her writing too 'limited' and restricted. She says in a letter to W.S. Williams, dated 12/04/1850 :

> ... She [Jane Austen] does her business of delineating the surface of the lives of genteel English people curiously well;.... : she ruffles her reader by nothing vehement, disturbs him by nothing profound; the Passions are perfectly unknown to her;.... Her business is not half so much with the human heart as with the human eyes, mouth, hands and feet; what sees keenly, speaks aptly, moves flexibly, it suits her to study, but what throbs fast and full,... - <u>this</u> Miss Austen ignores;...

The comment sounds more like a gentle backhand than a compliment, and two years earlier in a letter to dated 12/1848 to G. H. Lewes, the literary critic, she is even more direct in her criticism of the work of Jane Austen pointing out its lack of 'bright, vivid physiognomy', 'open country', 'fresh air', 'blue hill', and 'bonny beck'. Jane Austen was not as closely tied to Nature as the Brontës, and, therefore, this 'omission' was immediately noticed by Charlotte.

Upon first glance, one might agree with Charlotte since Austen's writing did appear to follow a 'formula' of success and many of the plots were similar. The theme, the 'dispatch' of young women in the upper classes through planned and 'strategic' marriages, was the same, and her bubbly, sparkling approach and style were repeated successfully. There is also little question that *Pride and Prejudice*, *Sense and Sensibility*, *Emma*, and others were all read with interest, and pure enjoyment, then, as they are today. The recurrent use of available young men and women in search of marriage, high society, hero and heroine, arranged marriages versus those of natural attraction, etc. as part of the plot structure cannot be denied. These repetitve elements lend credence to Charlotte's criticism that her writing is 'limited', but one must also admit that the reader learns a great deal about Georgian and Regency times in the early 1800s, particularly about court-ship and marriage rituals. We also learn about their society and leisure activities which include art, dance, music, outings, and various games. To Charlotte Brontë, it was too close to her era for her to notice, but today, we value the social insights Jane Austen's works provide much more highly.

In more recent times, beginning with D.W. Harding's stunning and ground-breaking essay in 1940, 'Regulated Hatred..', in which he claimed Jane Austen displays a 'hid-den', or perhaps unconscious hatred for many aspects for the society in which she lives and is so closely identified with, we are forced to give serious thought to his hypothesis and look at her works in a completely different light. A reader of discernment can easily elicit many passages and situations which are open to interpretation, hold a deliberate ambiguity, or were perhaps simply veiled with subconscious meaning. On the other hand, if her works are permeated with 'regulated hatred', and it was done consciously, there is a need for a complete re-evaluation and re-assessment of Jane Austen's work.

This same hypothesis is touched on by authors S.M. Gilbert and S. Gubar in their book, *The Madwoman in the Attic: The Woman Writer in the 19th C. Literary Imagina-tion*, which suggests that overt 'demeanour of meekness' and quiet subjection to patriarchal rule is, in fact, a well-camouflaged cover for her underlying distaste of the whole social make-up and class structure of which she was part. The works of Gilbert and Gubar also investigate the idea of 'concealed plots' used by authors to get their true meaning and feelings, which cannot be overtly displayed to their readers. Some might argue that her works are nothing more than satirical good humour of social, mating rituals of her times seen through the eyes of a middle-aged woman. And others might argue that her novels reflect the wider and more serious political tensions which were growing between classes in English society after the French Revolution and the Revolutionary Wars. Whatever the arguments, we cannot deny that many of the passages are simply tongue-in-cheek mockings of authority, or challenges to conventions of the day. It is highly doubtful that the alert, intelligent, and widely-read Charlotte Brontë could have possibly missed these underly-ing thoughts, currents, and themes in Jane Austen's writing.

One of the most important and admired writers of the day who impressed Charlotte Brontë was William Makepeace Thackeray who wrote *Vanity Fair* in 1847, the same year that Charlotte published *Jane Eyre*. *Vanity Fair* was also Thackeray's first, major novel, and today, it is certainly the one for which he is best remembered. Charlotte was simply enthralled by his novel, and he was her contemporary, literary hero. She described his wit as 'bright', his humour as 'attractive', and his genius as 'serious', and when the second edition of *Jane Eyre* was published, Charlotte dedicated the book, "To W. M. Thackeray, Esq This Work is Respectfully Inscribed By The Author". This dedication was perhaps somewhat inappropriate since she did not know him well, and secondly, Thackeray's wife was in an insane asylum which parallels the plot of *Jane Eyre* and Bertha Mason, the 'mad woman in the attic' of Thornfield Hall. In May and June, 1851, Charlotte visited London and attended the lectures by Thackeray on 'The English

Humourists of the 18th C', but as so often happens, she was far less impressed with him 'in the flesh' than the image she had conjured up of him in her mind.

Perhaps one other author of note in the search for influences of novel writing may be Samuel Richardson (1689 - 1761) who is often considered to be one of the chief founders of the modern novel and who wrote important novels such as *Pamela* (1740-41), and *Clarissa* (1747-48), both written in epistolary form[3] which was popular at the time. The novel *Pamela* has some very basic similarities to *Jane Eyre* in that the female protagonist, a lady-in-waiting to 'Mrs. B.' with no wealth or means, is pursued by her son, 'Mr. B.' when Lady B dies. The remainder of the story deals with her imprisonment, her gradual, growing affection for 'Mr. B.', and ultimately their marriage. In the end, Pamela Andrews reforms her profligate husband and becomes the 'perfect wife' and mother, and one who is admired by all. The crossing of social boundaries in marriage is the basic comparison with Charlotte's character, Jane Eyre. This novel and others by Samuel Richardson such as *Pamela, Part II*, written because of the great demand after his first novel, was later followed by *Clarissa*. Such novels may well have planted some 'seeds' for the Brontës production of novels with themes such as overcoming class boundaries in *Jane Eyre*, the use of letters in Anne Brontë's *The Tenant of Wildfell Hall*, and the use of multiple narrators in *Wuthering Heights*.

Such were the wide and varied literary experiences of the Brontës, and it is difficult to know precisely which authors or literary works affected them, in what way, and how deeply. But we can be certain that their keen, intelligent, inquisitive, young minds acted like sponges, drawing information from many sources whether it was local people or characters they, in fact, knew or imaginary characters, places, and incidents they conjured up in their own minds, or 'drew' from in a 'well' of their own making. However wide or deep was their own 'well', we know not, but we do know that it was vast, and it was from this source that their ingenious plots and characters were derived and devised.

The effect of writers like Shelley, Byron, but especially that of John Milton, upon Charlotte and Emily Brontë was so great upon their writings, conflicts, plots, and plot elements that it is treated separately in a final chapter entitled, 'Emerging Feminism'. These influences were sparked to ignition not only by the Victorian society in which they lived but also the misogynous writings of John Milton in his epic poem, *Paradise Lost*, and other writers of the day who believed, practised, and espoused these patriarchal principles. Shelley and Byron, on the other hand, were far more egalitarian and radical in their outlooks and provided indirect and vicarious 'encouragement' for their 'cause'. Therefore, a thorough understanding of Brontës works is not complete without an investigation into this important factor, and consideration of its impact.

---

3   One made up primarily of letters and journals.

21

MARY TAYLOR - A FORCE AND INSPIRATION

Like most people, Charlotte Brontë, inspite of her high intelligence, self-reliance, strong character, and independent thought, was influenced by the people around her, and, of course, some more than others. She was undoubtedly influenced by her father, sisters, brother, aunt, and household servants in her younger years, but during her formative years of young adulthood away from home, Charlotte was particularly influenced by two people she first met at Roe Head School in January, 1831. These two persons were Mary Taylor and Ellen Nussey, and of these two, Mary was definitely a greater influence in her thoughts, beliefs, and principles. The three of them kept up a correspondence with each other for the rest of their lives when they went their separate ways after Roe Head.

After Charlotte Brontë's death, both Mary Taylor and Ellen Nussey provided information to Elizabeth C. Gaskell who was requested by Rev. Brontë to write an authorized biography of Charlotte's life. Ellen Nussey had kept almost all of their correspondence, and Mary Taylor, in contrast, had kept almost none. Mary Taylor had 'wander lust' and was much too 'nomadic' to hoard letters and material, and as a result, these valuable letters were lost forever to posterity. Years later, Mary Taylor regretted not having kept them, yet she was able to provide a great deal of valuable information and insight into Charlotte Brontë's life, and their friendly relationship over the years. Mary Taylor provided Mrs. Gaskell with two, lengthy letters from her home in New Zealand where she was still living at the time of Charlotte Brontë's death. The information Mary sent in the first letter to Mrs. Gaskell, dated 18/01/1856, was used in the first edition of '*Life*'[1], and the new information she provided in the second letter was utilized in the third, and subsequent editions.

Neither Mary nor Charlotte made friendships easily since they were both wary, suspicious, and 'cautious' of newcomers. Mary Taylor still remembered the day, January

---

1   *The Life of Charlotte Brontë* by Mrs. Gaskell is hereby abbreviated simply as '*Life*'.

17, 1831, when Charlotte first arrived at Roe Head School in a covered cart. She recalls Charlotte in her old-fashioned clothes in her letter to Mrs. Gaskell dated 18/01/1856:

> She looked [like] a little old woman, so short-sighted that she always appeared to be seeking something, and moving her head from side to side to catch a sight of it. She was shy and nervous, and spoke with a very strong Irish accent...

Mary Taylor also recalled that they thought her very ignorant because of her lack of knowledge of grammar and geography, but she also astounded them with her knowledge of other subjects like politics, religion, poetry, poets, painters and their paintings, and other famous people. It did not take long for them to recognize her keen intellect, and perhaps genius. Mary also recognized that Charlotte could not play the games which other children played, and when they finally convinced her to do so, they soon realized that she could not see the ball, so they 'put her out'. Mary also mentions that it was about this time, early in their relationship, that she told Charlotte that she was 'very ugly'. Years later, Mary tried to make amends and told Charlotte how impertinent she had been, but Charlotte only anwered that she had done her a great service by the remark and did not hold it against her. She did not elaborate on the 'service' provided.

It may have been after this remark that Charlotte and Mary were 'cool' to one another for a long time, as Ellen Nussey described it, but it did not last, and their mutual respect for each other's intellect drew them together again. In time their friendship grew, flourished, became strong, and lasted until the end of their days. Over the years, they visited each other's homes and became friends with other members of their respective families, and it was through these early meetings and visits that Charlotte's world became exposed to a whole new set of ideas, values, influences, beliefs, and principles which were completely foreign to her.

Charlotte was a clergyman's daughter and their family had very fixed, rigid, conservative ideas and opinions which were closely tied to their politics. The Taylors, on the other hand, could not have been more diametrically opposite in their thoughts and ideas on religion and politics. To Charlotte they were Radical Dissenters, but they were also closer to what we might term today as 'free-thinkers'. For Charlotte, this turned into a great, hidden benefit, since it opened up a whole, new vista of ideas and approaches to a variety of subjects, and life in general, for which she had previously received only a one-sided, parallaxed view. The complexity of the Taylor family in the West Riding, their diverse financial, business and banking interests made them a 'peculiar, racy, vigorous' stock[2] with a cosmopolitan approach and view, as opposed to the narrow, conservative views and opinions usually put forward in West Yorkshire.

When they first met in 1831, they were both in their early teens, separated by only one year between them, Charlotte being the older. As their friendship grew, Charlotte recognized qualities in Mary, and her younger sister Martha, which she had never encountered before. Mary was bright, intelligent, spirited, stubborn, proud, fiercely independent, competitive, radical and very political; qualities which were intriguing, and

---

2   The Yorkes as described in *Shirley*, Chapter 9.

ideas which were provocative. For the first time outside of her own family circle, Charlotte had met someone with a level of intelligence she could respect, and which was on par with her own. With this interaction of new and different ideas not only with Mary but also with Joshua Taylor, her father, Charlotte took on an 'education' of a completely different kind. It did not take long for their conversation to turn to controversial topics of religion and politics; Mary recalls in her letter dated 08/01/1856, to Mrs. Gaskell:

> We used to dispute about politics and religion. She, a Tory and a clergyman's daughter was always in a minority of one in our house of violent Dissent and Radicalism.

and,

> We had a rage for practicality, and laughed all poetry to scorn. Neither she nor we had any idea but that our own opinions were the opinions of all the sensible people in the world, and we used to astonish each other at every sentence.

Charlotte was so intrigued, impressed, and influenced by the Taylors, with the exception of Mrs. Taylor, that she clearly portrayed them in *Shirley* as the 'Yorkes'. Perhaps the one who intrigued her most was Mary's father, Joshua, whom she portrayed as Hiram Yorke[3], a travelled, worldly, and learned gentleman with cosmopolitan views. Mary took her fierce independence from her father whom Charlotte described as 'difficult to lead' and 'impossible to drive'. His independence, Radical anti-Establishment views, energetic business initiatives, and unorthodox, maverick approach to topics and subjects of all kinds, fascinated Charlotte and opened her mind like a grand 'Revelation' and 'Revolution' of inspiration. The flames of thought had been ignited.

Mary Taylor was portrayed in *Shirley* as Rose Yorke, Hiram Yorke's daughter, who strongly favoured her father, who never had a harsh word for her, and regularly avoided her mother. Rose is featured as being 'childlike', highly spirited, even more so than her father, stubborn, and intelligent, with novel and original ideas. Rose is only outshone by her younger sister 'Jessy', who, in reality, is Mary's younger sister, Martha.

Jessy Yorke, like Martha in life, was lively, vivacious, loquacious, gay and chattering, highly original, and very passionate and affectionate. She was also described as engaging in conversation, exacting, generous, brave, fearless, and openly defiant. By constrast, she could also be both gentle and 'rattling' but always 'likeable' with her charm, personal magnetism, and 'winning ways'. And in real life, Martha was vigorously and rudely outspoken to the point of being 'sassy' and openly defiant to Miss Wooler, headmistress at Roe Head, for which she occasionally received a 'box on the ear' as punishment. Inspite of this, Martha was not only her father's 'pet' at home but also a favourite with other students at the school. Her lively manner, originality, forthrightness, good humour, and good nature attracted many friends.

---

3   Mr. Taylor was also portrayed as Hunsden Yorke Hunsden in *The Professor*.

The Yorke family as a whole was described by Charlotte as having a 'great mental capacity', much more so than any collection of families from the area. She describes the family in *Shirley*, Chapter 9 as follows:

> ... in the aggregate: there is as much mental power in those six young heads, as much originality as much activity and vigour of brain, as - divided amongst half a dozen commonplace broods - would give to each rather more than an average amount of sense and capacity.

In addition, Charlotte calls them of 'good blood', 'strong brain', 'turbulent', proud and, 'intractable', but "wanting polish, wanting consideration, wanting docility, but sound, spirited, and true-bred as the eagle on the cliff or the steed in the steppe". But the only Taylor for which Charlotte could not find kind words, and described negatively, was their mother 'Mrs. Yorke', who was said to be gloomy, humourless, serious and grave, cynical, suspicious, pessimistic, dreary, funereal, and a general 'kill-joy'. Upon the death of Mr. Taylor, in real life, in 1840, the family quickly split up and went their separate ways; only their eldest son, Joshua III, remained with his mother, but only until 1845, when he, too, decided to leave. Their home, 'Red House' in Gomersal, is 'Briarmains' in *Shirley*, and today it is a museum opened to visitors and students of the Brontë legend and legacy.

Mary Taylor was an inspiration to Charlotte in many ways, but primarily as an example of independent thought and means. Mary's strong character, unorthodox views and uncompromising principles and beliefs were a 'guiding light' for Charlotte's reserved nature, which until their meeting, had been one of 'quiet acceptance'. Rose Yorke's statements in *Shirley* are a reflection of Mary Taylor's search for a meaningful life. Rose Yorke responds to Caroline Helstone:[4]

> I am resolved that my life shall be a life. Not a black trance like the toad's, buried in marble; nor a long slow death like yours in Briarfield rectory.

and,

> Better to try all things and find them empty than to try nothing and leave your life a blank. To do this is to commit the sin of him who buried his talent in a napkin - despicable sluggard!

Mary's view parallels that of her father's and is opposite to that of her mother's who strongly believes the Victorian notion that a woman's 'place' is in the home giving birth to children, and looking after those children. Mary's unorthodox views also run counter to that of her friend, Ellen Nussey, whom Charlotte portrayed as 'Caroline Helstone'. On numerous occasions, Mary Taylor did her utmost to spur Ellen 'into action', a career, or to travel, but Ellen was completely intransigent in everything, and her views were very 'Victorian', and closely aligned to those of Mrs. Taylor.

---

4   Caroline Helstone is often thought to be the portrayal of Ellen Nussey or Anne Brontë, or perhaps even a composite of both.

Early in their relationship, Charlotte recognized Mary Taylor's 'strength of character', boundless energy, and personal 'power'. In a letter to Ellen Nussey, dated 03/01/1841, Charlotte stated:

> Mary alone has more energy and power in her nature than any ten men you can pick out in the united parishes of Birstal and Gomersal. It is vain to limit a character like hers within ordinary boundaries - she will overstep them. I a morally certain Mary will establish her own landmarks, so will the rest of them.

and to her sister Emily, Charlotte makes reference to Mary in a letter dated 02/04/1841:

> Mary has made up her mind she can not and will not be a governess, a teacher, a milliner, a bonnet-maker nor housemaid. She sees no means of obtaining employment she would like in England, so she is leaving it.

Mary was also the chief inspiration for Charlotte and Emily to go to Brussels and study there. It was at this time in late 1841, that Miss Wooler offered Charlotte the opportunity to take over the new Roe Head School at Dewsbury Moor since Margaret's sister was relinquishing it. Charlotte had, in fact, accepted the offer, but as late as September 29, 1841, she still had not had a reply from Miss Wooler. In the meantime, Charlotte had changed her mind, and Mary Taylor's constant encouragement to improve her 'attainments' had 'kindled a fire' and 'cast oil on the flames' for her thirst for knowledge and travel. At the last moment, she refused Miss Wooler's offer and asked her Aunt Branwell for a loan with which she and Emily could attend school in Brussels to learn French, and possibly German. When her aunt agreed to the loan, plans were set, and in February, 1842, Charlotte, Emily, Rev. Brontë, Mary Taylor, and her brother Joseph, set out for Brussels via London. By packet, they made their way to Ostend and from there to Brussels where they settled into Pensionnat Heger which was cheaper than Chateau de Koekelberg where Mary and Martha Taylor were attending. Had it not been for this travel and experience, Charlotte would not have been able to write two of her future novels, *The Professor*, and *Villette*, both based on her experiences there.

Mary, besides being energetic, was a restless and active person; she could not stand the sedentary lifestyle which she saw in Charlotte, and especially their friend, Ellen Nussey. In a letter dated 01/11/1842, Mary Taylor tells Ellen:

> I have chosen to go to Germany - activity being in my opinion the most desirable state of existence - both for my spirits, health, and advantage.

Mary remained in Germany for more than a year teaching English at a German, boys' school. This, to Charlotte and Ellen, was beyond their comprehension since it was something that was not done in Victorian England; boys had men teachers and girls had lady teachers. It was also something that neither of them would consider doing, or think appropriate.

In late 1844, when Charlotte heard of Mary Taylor's firm plans to go to New Zealand, Charlotte was devastated because someone who had always been there for her, and was as solid as granite under one's feet, was now leaving the hemisphere altogether. Mary's absence to Belgium and Germany was but a few days' journey, but from New Zealand, the trip home would take at least three to four months. In the 1840s, it was like travelling to another planet; Charlotte was devastated. However, she did not believe that Mary would remain there for any length of time which shows that she still did not fully understand, or grasp, her friend's strength of character, determination, and depth of resolution. In this regard, Charlotte completely misjudged her. In a letter to Ellen Nussey dated 16/04/1844, Charlotte states:

> Mary Taylor is going to leave our hemisphere. To me it is something as if agreat planet fell out of the sky. Yet, unless she marries in New Zealand, she will not stay there long.

But, in fact, Mary Taylor stayed in New Zealand for fifteen years, from 1845 to 1860, and did not return until five years after Charlotte's death.

From half a world apart, Mary Taylor continued to be an influence on Charlotte Brontë, their friendship and correspondence continued regularly, but even when she was relatively settled, she did not save Charlotte's letters. In Wellington, Mary established a shop with her cousin Ellen Taylor in 1850, which proved successful and profitable. And when Ellen died in late 1851, Mary was forced to take on an assistant who eventually took over her interest when she decided to return to England in 1860. In New Zealand she bought land, built buildings, rented out accommodation, and continued on a novel which she had started years before.

Mary wrote with a definite purpose in mind, and it was clearly not simply to amuse or entertain. She was a straight-forward person with a social conscience who went directly to the point and hammered it home. Her thoughts were riddled and driven by her beliefs and philosophies, and she wanted to put these ideas forth in a novel. Unfortunately it took her almost five decades to complete, and it was published as *Miss Miles* in 1891, only two years before her death. Had she finished it immediately in the late 1840s, or even 1850s, there is a good possibility that her provocative ideas would probably have made her a literary notable of the time like Harriet Martineau and Elizabeth Gaskell, but by 1891, its publication date, the ideas presented were no longer 'revolutionary' or even 'avant-garde', but simply 'old hat'. Her timing was badly off, and Mary Taylor had clearly missed her 'moment in the sun'.

When Mary first received a copy of *Jane Eyre* and *Wuthering Heights*, she was truly shocked and amazed. In her letter of 24/07/1848, she was surprised by it being, "so perfect as a work of art." For some reason, she did not believe that Charlotte had it 'in her' to achieve such a major work, but beyond the initial surprise came Mary Taylor's criticism. Mary offered this general observation, and chastisement, in the same letter:

You are very different from me in having no doctrine to preach. It is impossible to squeeze a moral out of your production. Has the world gone so well with you that you have no protest to make against its absurdities?

Perhaps Mary wasn't looking hard enough to see the major moral issues of 'love conquers all' and the neat, precise boundaries of Victorian society, which considered marriage between classes a transgression, being broken by the lowly Jane Eyre. Also, Charlotte Brontë wanted to make it clear that heroines do not always have to be tall beauties of the upper classes to capture the hearts and imagination of Victorian readers. In her own novel, Mary Taylor used the 'sledge hammer' technique to make her points, and as a result any artistic qualities of the work were masked, submerged or 'flattened' by her blunt approach. Charlotte's approach was far more subtle, and effective. Mary's only words for Emily's novel were shock and wonderment, and she referred to it as that 'strange thing'.

Mary valued 'freedom' and 'occupation' above all else, and although Ellen Nussey was her friend, she constantly tried to get her to leave home and take up work. In a letter dated 09/02/1849, Mary tells Ellen:

Wishing for something to turn up that wd [would] enable you to work for yourself instead of for other people and that no one shd [should] know that you were work- ing. Now no such thing exists. There are no means for a woman to live in England but by teaching, sewing or washing. The last is the best. The best paid the least unhealthy and the most free.

Although Mary detested people who did not work, or at least attempt it, Ellen was her friend, and therefore her remarks were 'tempered' somewhat and made less pointed and direct than was her habit. But inspite of all Mary's entreaties to Ellen, nothing worked or prompted her to seek active employment, or move away from home.

Mary's own happiness centred not only on her 'freedom' but her ability to fend for herself, earn her own living, and be completely independent. Marriage was never really an option for Mary since she had early on believed that marriage was a sure way of giving up one's freedom and independence, and becoming dependent on someone else; this she found morally reprehensible and also quite unacceptable. In a letter to Charlotte dated 13/04/1850, Mary states that:

It was from my father I learnt not to marry for money nor to tolerate any one who did and he never wd [would] advise any one to do so or fail to speak with contempt of those who did.

and, in a letter three months later, dated 29/04/1850, Mary comments about the illusions her brother harbours for his own impending marriage. Mary does not see marriage as the answer to all his problems. She tells Charlotte:

> By the eagerness with which he seeks to be married he evidently hopes more from the change than it will bring. It is certainly better to be married but to look forward to such great things is just insuring disappointment.

Her comment that, "It is certainly better to be married, but...", leaves us to wonder whether she was referring specifically to her brother in his set of circumstances, or whether she meant it to be 'all-inclusive', including herself in the process. If she included herself by this statement, she did not elaborate on her concept of 'marriage', but we can be assured that it was radical, and not a 'Victorian view'.

Before getting married, Mary Taylor thought that women's first duty, and right, should be to 'learn to earn', to ensure one's own economic security, self-assurance, and, of course, personal independence. Upon her first reading of *Shirley*, Mary scolded Charlotte severely in that same letter of April, 1850, for her comments on women's right to work which Mary did not think went far enough. She harshly scolded Charlotte with these words:

> And this first duty, this great necessity you seem to think that some women may indulge in - if they give up marriage and don't make themselves too disagreeable to the other sex. You are a coward and a traitor. A woman who works is by that alone better than one who does not and a woman who does not happen to be rich and who still earns no money and does not wish to do so, is guilty of a great fault - almost a crime - A dereliction of duty which leads rapidly and almost certainly to all manner of degradation.

Mary Taylor took great delight in being responsible for her own shop which she and her cousin Ellen set up jointly in Wellington, New Zealand. In this letter of April, 1850, she delights in telling Charlotte about their new business, and the wonders of being self-employed, self-directed, and completely independent. She describes their new, business venture:

> I have set up shop. I am delighted with it it (sic) as a whole - that is it is as pleasant or as little disagreeable as you can expect an employment to be that you earn your living by. The best of it is that your labour has some return and you are not forced to work on hopelessly without result.

Some years later in a letter to Ellen Nussey dated 08/01/1857, upon hearing of the illness of a mutual friend whom they considered 'young', Mary mentioned that her health and well-being had been excellent. She attributed most of it not only to her lifestyle but also to the fact that she is responsible for herself, and to herself. This personal freedom is the key; she asserts:

> ... but it is very great to me for it is just the difference between everything being a burden and everything being more or less a pleasure.

Mary's observation holds a timeless truth which is as valid today as it was in 1850. Her personal lifestyle, love of labour, and her dedication to personal independence seems to have agreed with her very well, and in so doing she avoided the pitfalls, and stress, to which others succumbed.

Although Mary Taylor always displayed the appearance of an impenetrable shield of armour, she was only human and had occasional bouts of insecurity, loneliness, and depression. In rare instances, 'cracks' and 'chinks' did appear in her otherwise solid exterior, and were exposed. In an undated letter to Ellen Nussey (possibly fall 1844), Mary confesses some of her misgivings about herself, and life in general:

> I am alone & melancholy. We sometimes take it into our heads - at least I do, to
> wonder what we live for, to look all around & see nothing in this world getting up for
> in the morning.

And after the death of Ellen Taylor, her cousin and business partner, on December 27, 1851, Mary further confides to Ellen Nussey in a letter dated 11/03/1851, that she fears she will become "a stern, harsh, selfish woman". Mary, always ready with harsh criticism for others, could also be self-deprecating, as she is in a letter to Charlotte dated 13/08/1850. She recognizes her own faults and states:

> I am wofully (sic) ignorant terribly wanting in tact and obstinately lazy, and almost
> too old to mend. Luckily, there is no other chance for me; so I must work.

To her friends, Mary was always supportive and optimistic although she had difficulty in expressing sympathies and condolences; she was kind but direct and blunt. After the rapid, successive deaths of Branwell, Emily and Anne, Mary tried to buoy up Charlotte's failing spirits, although somewhat clumsily, with these words, in a letter dated 05/04/1850:

> Railway shares wil (sic) rise, your books will sell and you will acquire influence and
> power and then most certainly you will find something to use it in which will interest
> you and make you exert yourself.

And to Ellen Nussey, when Rev. Francis Upjohn and his wife made a proposal for her to move in and look after them in their declining years for a 'future consideration', Mary wrote a stinging, mock response to 'Mr. Clergyman and Mrs. Clergyman' in which she castigated them for such an 'impudent proposal'. In the end, Ellen heeded Mary Taylor's advice, and the advice of Charlotte, and did not accept the proposal which was 'frought with difficulties', as Mary pointed out.

After Charlotte Brontë's death in 1855, Mary Taylor cooperated with her biographer, Mrs. Gaskell, and provided her with as much information as she could remember. Mary was not a keeper of letters, but after Charlotte's death, she deeply regretted not having kept them. In any case, she sent two, lengthy letters to Mrs. Gaskell which were very helpful, and on which the author relied heavily in certain cases. The only letter of

Charlotte's which Mary had kept, the letter of September 4th, 1848, in which Charlotte outlined the need for, and the details of the 'pop visit' (as referred to by Mary) to London in July, 1848, by Anne Brontë and herself. This proved invaluable, since the only other account of their meeting with Mr. Smith, Charlotte's publisher, and W.S. Williams, Smith's reader, was given almost fifty years later by Mr. Smith himself, in 1900. Charlotte's account, written only two months after the incident, is considered to be far more accurate than Mr. Smith's written five decades later.

Mary Taylor, at first, was determined to help put forward an accurate description of Charlotte Brontë's life and sacrifices, and was cooperative in the early years. In a letter to Ellen Nussey, dated 10/05/1856, Mary berated Rev. Brontë as that "selfish old man", and commented on Charlotte's 'selflessness'. She states:

> No one ever gave up more than she did and with full consciousness of what she sacrificed. I don't think myself that women are justified in sacrificing themselves for others, but since the world generally expects it of them they should at least acknowledge it.

And, in a letter, fifteen months later to Mrs. Gaskell, dated 30/07/1857, Mary makes an observation on a comment someone made about Charlotte's life of 'poverty and self-suppression'. Mary Taylor returns to her point of women and 'industry'; she firmly states:

> Neither of them seem to think it a strange or wrong state of things that a woman of first-rate talents, industry, and integrity should live all her life in a walking nightmare of 'poverty and self-suppression'. I doubt whether any of them will.

Following Mary Taylor's return to England in 1860, Mary soon tired of endless requests for interviews regarding the life of the Brontës. She despised the public curiosity into their lives and refused all further interviews on the subject. Once back in her native Yorkshire, and Gomersal in particular, her industrious nature continued, and she built a new home, 'High Royd', in which she lived to the end of her days. She was only forty-three years old when she returned and continued to write and travel often to Europe, but as a contributor to the Brontë legacy, she became recalcitrant and reticent. It was over this very issue that Mary Taylor and Ellen Nussey eventually became estranged from one another. In a letter to Thomas J. Wise, dated November, 1892, Ellen Nussey made this disparaging remark about her old friend, Mary Taylor:

> Mary Taylor the "Rose York" in *Shirley,* is living, but has always proved herself *dead* to any approach on the Brontë subject, and it is understood that long ago she destroyed her letters. She is so peculiar she might prove otherwise than helpful.

In her later years, after her return to Yorkshire, Mary's works carried a recurrent theme which basically stated that 'women, like men, from every social class, needed purposeful and useful employment, not only for the good of society but for their own personal mental health and well-being', and that 'staying at home and doing nothing was more of a hardship than work itself'. These themes were present in both her works, *The First Duty of Women,* published in London, 1870, which first ran as a series of articles in *Victoria Magazine*, and which was later published as a book, and her novel, *Miss Miles*. These articles were direct, forceful, harsh and even bitter about the fact that middle-class women had few options in their lives outside of 'marriage'. And for those who were 'overlooked' by marriage, or those who chose to remain single, they could only look forward to lonely, empty lives. As well, for those who lived in 'doomed marriages', or 'troubled marriages', their outlook was equally bleak.

In her second, more creative work, *Miss Miles, or a Tale of Yorkshire Life 60 Years Ago*, she was reminiscent about her early years with her friends and family at home in 'Red House'. She also tried to hold up her recurrent themes of female self-sacrifice, the hatefulness of dependence for women, and 'marriage' as women's only solution, to closer public scrutiny. Mary Taylor was one of the new generation of writers in the 19th C. who demonstrated and helped evolve a 'social conscience'. Mary's solution, for women, demonstrated in her books, was to 'learn to earn', to go out into the world to make a living on their own, to employ their mental faculties in all areas, including science, and to strongly object to the 'submissiveness' expected of them. These themes Mary incorporated into a complex plot, but her delay in producing her book in a timely fashion, and published only two years before her death, simply made her books 'passé'.

Mary's only other book was one she co-authored with four other ladies who travelled and hiked with her in Germany and Switzerland in the 1870s. The book is entitled, *Swiss Notes by Five Ladies*, published in Leeds, 1875. In the book, she is the inveterate, 'Frau Mutter', the eldest member of the group who has the 'will' but not always the 'way'. One of her stories recounts a true, life-and-death situation she experienced on a glacier in which she loses her way among ice ridges, moraines, and deadly crevasses. The brave and courageous 'Frau Mutter' faced death, but lived to tell the tale.

There is no doubt that Mary, Martha and Joshua Taylor all had an influence on Charlotte Brontë, and there is also no doubt that Charlotte's lengthy friendship and close relationship with Mary Taylor over the years had a strong influence over Charlotte's formative years during and after Roe Head, and in Brussels. Through the influence of the Taylors, Charlotte was able to re-evaluate her own personal beliefs and principles, and listen openly to the beliefs and principles of others. These new thoughts and ideas were 'explosive' and intriguing to Charlotte's young, inquisitive and keen mind yearning for new information.

In their later years, as mature adults, Charlotte was able to learn vicariously through Mary's wide range of experience and travels, and at one point even joined her in Brussels to expand her own world and her own education. In the last ten years of Charlotte's life, they knew each other only through their continued correspondence, but they never ceased to be friends or exchange thoughts and ideas. Charlotte always respected Mary Taylor and her family for their keen intellect, knowledge, strong personal qualities, some of which Charlotte herself could easily aspire to, their dedication to beliefs and principles, and their vitality. The admiration and respect Charlotte Brontë held for the Taylors was, in fact, mutual.

Mary Taylor died in 1893, at the age of seventy-six, two years after her novel, *Miss Miles*, was finally published; she had lived a 'full life', just as she had proposed for herself in her early years.

The friendship of Charlotte Brontë and Ellen Nussey was a special friendship which lasted from the time of their first meeting in January, 1831, to the time of Charlotte's death in March, 1855, a span of twenty-four years. To properly pursue the intensity, and understand the meaning, of their enduring friendship requires a chapter of its own; it simply cannot be summed up in a few paragraphs or a few pages. The definitive work on this special friendship was done by Barbara Whitehead of Thornton-Bradford in West Yorkshire. Her work is entitled *Charlotte Brontë and her 'dearest Nell' - The story of a friendship* (1993).

22

ELLEN NUSSEY - A SPECIAL FRIENDSHIP

There can be no doubt that of all the friendships that Charlotte Brontë cultivated and maintained, her friendship with Ellen Nussey was the closest, the most prolonged, and the most enduring. They first met at Roe Head School as students in January, 1831, and although Charlotte did not care for Ellen when they first met, a friendship began, and grew stronger through the years. In a letter to William S. Williams dated 03/01/1850, Charlotte sums up the slow but steady growth of that friendship:

> When I first saw Ellen I did not care for her - we were schoolfellows - in the course of time we learnt each others faults and good points - we were contrasts - still we suited - affection was a first germ, then a sapling - then a strong tree: now - no new friend however lofty or profound in intellect - not even Miss Martineau herself - could be to me what Ellen is, yet she is no more than a consciencious, observant, calm, well-bred Yorkshire girl... but she is good - she is true - she is faithful and I love her.

Ellen Nussey was a stark contrast, in almost every conceivable way, to Mary Taylor, one of Charlotte's greatest influences, and to Charlotte, Ellen contrasted in a minor way, but still their opposing natures attracted one another. Just as Mary Taylor was forceful, political, ambitious, eager, and anxious to see the world and 'test' the world, Ellen was equally content with her family, her sourroundings, her situation, and her social 'station' in life. Ellen was quiet, calm, reserved, sociable, loving, religious, loyal, selfless, and extremely devoted to family and friends. As the youngest member of a large family of twelve children, Ellen quickly learned to be an 'listener' and 'observer' of her parents and siblings which rendered her compliant nature.

Several things drew Charlotte and Ellen together. Firstly, their birthdays were only one day apart, although Charlotte was Ellen's senior by one year. Their education was similar, and both attended the same school, Roe Head, and associated with the same friends. Their backgrounds, too, were similar with their parents coming from middle-class society, with the exception of Mr. Brontë, but he was a clergyman, as were several of Ellen's brothers as well as Mary 'Mercy' Nussey who became a 'sister' in the Moravian sect. Both had similar interests and tastes in literature, and both were strong advocates and members of the Church of England. Also, the two girls lived only twenty miles away from one another which allowed frequent visits and helped nurture their early friendship. These same factors also fostered the friendship between Ellen and Mary Taylor, and Mary and Charlotte.

In addition to these similarities, there were also other parallels and 'parallels by contrast'. Charlotte had lost her mother at age four, and Ellen had lost her father at age nine. Aunt Branwell came to live with them at the Parsonage and look after the young Brontë children whereas Ellen, her mother, and several sisters moved to Rydings to live with an uncle. Charlotte was the oldest of the four children, and by contrast Ellen was the youngest of twelve children. Charlotte had lived through an outbreak of typhus at Cowan Bridge, and Ellen had survived the 'black pox' in the village of Little Gomersal while at the Moravian Ladies Academy. Charlotte's family was dependent on their father's 'living' and income, and Ellen, her mother, and sisters were financially dependent upon their uncle Richard. Both also expected to make their living by becoming teachers or governesses, and both loved Nature, the outdoors, animals, and both were pious and 'close to God'.

Ellen was also faithful, loyal, modest, steadfast, socially refined, cultured, gentle, understanding, charming, and she showed a quiet reserve and serenity. All of these qualities immediately endeared themselves to Charlotte who found in Ellen a trustworthy confidante, someone she could appeal to and rely on with all her personal confidences. Ellen's qualities were a product not only of her quiet homelife and 'breeding' but also the result of fundamentalist principles espoused, and taught, at the Moravian Ladies Academy which she attended until December, 1830.

Although the Brontë sisters were a very close-knit family, Charlotte felt the need to expand her 'social horizons' which also included a wider circle of friends. Ellen Nussey, Mary Taylor, and Charlotte's new friends and class-mates at Roe Head met those needs, and her growing friendship with Ellen was of increasing importance to her. When the three friends parted from Roe Head for the summer, Charlotte did not expect to hear from them again, and she was pleasantly surprised to receive an invitation from Ellen to visit Rydings in September, 1832. New friendships were made between Charlotte and the Nussey family including Ann, Mary 'Mercy', Mrs. Nussey, and Richard Nussey. The respect and affection between them was immediate and mutual. Charlotte was also introduced to a number of Nussey family friends, relatives, and associates, and although Charlotte was at first shy, many of them became Charlotte's own friends in later years. This first visit sealed their emerging friendship and placed it on a firm footing; from that moment on, their friendship never waned.

Charlotte's visit to Rydings was reciprocated with a trip to Haworth Parsonage in July, 1833. This was Ellen's first visit to the area of the Worth Valley, and she described it as 'wild and uncultivated' and remarked on its sparse population. Having lived in the area of Birstall, Gomersal, Batley, Dewsbury, Mirfield, Heckmondwike, Liversedge, and Cleakheaton, Haworth and its immediate surroundings would indeed seem like a desolate hinterland. Behind the Parsonage was a seemingly endless expanse of purple moor, the village was small, and its location was isolated on the Eastern side of the Pennines.

The immediate acceptance of Ellen Nussey by all members of the Brontë family, including the 'remote' and taciturn Emily, is a testament to Ellen's good character and amiability. They immediately recognized in Ellen her well-bred manners, her fine personal qualities, especially that of 'neatness' which was so important to Charlotte, her friendliness, her cheerfulness, and her 'suitability' as a friend for Charlotte. In return, and in time, Ellen became a good friend with all the Brontës, and was invited to Scarborough by Anne on her final, fatal journey in search of fresh, sea-air and good health. Also, the only letters of Emily's which briefly survived, were those of Emily to Ellen which indicates their friendship, the one and only friend Emily ever had outside of her own family.

Ellen proved endearing to Aunt Branwell, a lady 'of birth', who found her to be quite respectable and suitable in every respect. Rev. Brontë also had high praise for Ellen and held her in the highest esteem and regard. And, the final 'seal of approval' came from none other than Tabby, the servant, who did not take kindly to everyone who entered the Parsonage, especially strangers. Tabby, like many people from Yorkshire, was a shrewd judge of character, and her immediate acceptance of Ellen was a 'good sign'. Branwell, then a boy of sixteen, was also enchanted by the youthful visitor, but he had met her at least twice before, once at Roe Head, and once at Rydings when he escorted Charlotte there the previous fall. In later years, Ellen wrote down her first impressions of that first visit which are now recorded for posterity.

It was these first two visits which solidified Charlotte's and Ellen's new friendship, left lasting impressions for both, and set the foundation for an enduring relationship, broken only by Charlotte's death. When their first letters were exchanged, a pattern of six letters per year was set which continued with fair regularity for the next twenty-four years. And it was these same letters, saved scrupulously by Ellen over the years of their friendship, from 1831-1855, which have provided the 'backbone' and historical accuracy needed by scholars for their research. Without them, the flow of information and research, which continues even today, would have ceased long ago, and had Arthur B. Nicholls and Mary Taylor not destroyed all of their letters, our reconstructive, biographical histories would be even more accurate and more complete. But, for what we do have, scholars and historians are deeply indebted to Ellen Nussey for meticulously saving Charlotte's letters.

When Ellen visited her brother John Nussey in London in February, 1834, Charlotte was worried that she would lose Ellen as a friend. Charlotte could not imagine, and did not believe, that anyone could encounter London and not be changed by it dramatically and permanently. Much to Charlotte's surprise, Ellen returned much the same as when she had left, and was quite unmoved and unaffected by the 'glitter', the romance, the 'pull' of the great metropolis, her interaction with high society, and a visit to St. James' Palace. Undaunted by her visit, Ellen's unbending and unswerving nature and manner in the face of all these alluring stimuli proved to Charlotte that she was of steadfast personality, and character. These qualities of serenity and even-temperament persisted throughout Ellen's life, and fulfilled Charlotte's need for an 'anchor' of stability to which she could attach her emotions in a turbulent and 'impermanent' world.

As their friendship grew, Ellen, and particularly her circle of friends and society, had an increasing influence on Charlotte, although it may have been almost imperceptible. Charlotte, who first knew only the amiable society of her siblings, was now 'branching out' and expanding her social contacts as she matured into a young lady and became more confident. Ellen's friends and 'social circle' were now fast-becoming Charlotte's friends and 'circle', and Charlotte was universally being accepted by that 'society'. With this new confidence, along with an offer to teach at Roe Head where she had been a student, Charlotte could now enhance and build a new group of friends and associates in the parishes surrounding the school, without the direct intercession of Ellen. Charlotte was now emerging as her 'own person', but the fact that Ellen lived so near at hand, was also a factor in Charlotte's decision to accept the teaching position. Ellen's stability, steadfastness of character, and closeness, provided that 'zone of comfort' which Charlotte still required.

With Rydings and Roe Head a little more than a mile apart, Ellen was able to visit the school, and Charlotte often went there on weekends, or at least was able to associate with Ellen on Sundays at Birstall Church before or after the service. Also, contact was continued over this short distance by personal messenger through Ellen's brother, George, who passed by Roe Head frequently on his way to Huddersfield to carry on business. Ellen would often commission George to throw a packet and letter over the garden wall alongside the road. This unorthodox mail delivery continued to strengthen and cultivate their growing friendship.

During this time, the two friends were also able to provide comfort and support to one another, since life-problems began to develop for each of them. Charlotte was growing weary, bored, and exhausted from her teaching duties at Roe Head. As a student there, Charlotte was happy enough, but as a teacher, the situation was quite different. The teaching load was heavy, onerous, and Charlotte highly resented having to cater to students' whims, demands, and constant requests for services which she thought they should be capable of providing for themselves. The relentless and tiring work led to mental anxiety, depression, and physical exhaustion. To add to her heavy workload, Roe Head School was moved to Healds House in Dewsbury Moor in the summer of 1837. Charlotte's thoughts increasingly moved away from teaching to writing, partially to escape from the dreariness and monotony of her work.

Ellen's problems were brought about by the illness, and finally death, of her uncle Richard Nussey in 1835, from whom she, her mother, and sisters so heavily relied upon for financial support; now he was gone. His will left much of the estate to others, and although Ellen's brother John, the royal apothecary in London, purchased the property, he had someone else in mind to occupy it. Her uncle's death, the uncertainty of the situation, and the likelihood of a move was traumatic for Ellen, since she and her family had lived at Rydings for ten years from 1826-1836. In addition to their forced move from Rydings to Brookroyd, Ellen's mother was ill, her brother William was suffering debilitating depression, and Sarah had always been a dependent from infancy. At this time, as Ellen was approaching her twentieth birthday, there was no opportunity for her to 'spread her wings', follow her dreams, or pursue a life of her own because she was indispensable at home. With Ellen's quiet manner, her pious devotion, and sense of Christian duty, she acquiesced to their needs without a whimper.

The years of 1837-38, were times of trial and tribulation for both families. In December, 1837, Anne Brontë became severely ill at Healds House, the new school, and Charlotte, under severe stress, strain, anxiety, and pressure 'lashed out' at her friend and head mistress, Margaret Wooler, for not recognizing her failing condition sooner. In Haworth, Tabby, their faithful servant, broke her leg on an icy road near Christmas, and the Brontës looked after her over the holiday. In the New Year, 1838, Ellen's brother, Henry, fell from a horse, struck his head, and suffered some brain damage which plagued him for the rest of his life. In June, Ellen's brother, William, suffering from severe depression, drowned himself in the Thames River in London.[1] In April, Emily Brontë left Haworth to teach at Law Hill, Halifax, and her letters to Charlotte were extremely worrisome to her, and a cause of great anxiety. Socially and politically, some of the disturbances, demonstrations, and disruptions caused by the Chartist Movement were localized in their immediate area. Also, the implementation of the Poor Laws[2], although slow in coming, were finally upon them and caused a great deal of social unrest, tension, and distress which both Ellen and Charlotte felt deeply. Such were the tumultuous times of 1837-38, and their common bond of misery brought them even closer together than ever before.

On March 01, 1839, Charlotte received her first marriage proposal, and not surprisingly, it came from Henry Nussey, Ellen's brother, whom she had known for almost seven years. Although Charlotte was tempted to accept because it would make Ellen her sister-in-law, and they could then spend a great deal of time together, or perhaps even live together, she had to face the truth. Charlotte liked Henry well enough as a friend, but she was not in love with him, and she found him much too serious for her liking. In addition to the fact that Charlotte was a 'romantic' at heart, and he was not, Henry was not her intellectual 'equal'. Her high level of intellectual activity would not be stimulated by such a match. Five months later, Charlotte received her second proposal from Rev. Bryce whom she had met only once, but Charlotte rejected it without hesitation. Such relationships and proposals were at the core of many of their letters and discussions which required a close and confidential exchange of information.

There can be little doubt that the trip taken by Ellen and Charlotte to Bridlington in East Yorkshire in July, 1839, 'cemented' their already firm relationship. In addition to this memorable trip, it was here that Charlotte garnered vivid and indelible sights, sounds, and smells of the sea which she later used in her novel, *Villette*. Their holiday together

---

1   As Royal apothecary, John Nussey, Ellen's brother, is said to have altered the death certificate to cover up this ignominious act. It is believed that it was so well done that many members of the family were never aware of his true cause of death. Whitehead, B. *Charlotte Bronte,...and her dearest Nell,* p. 77.

2   Enacted in 1834, these highly unpopular laws set up the infamous 'workhouses'. It took several years to implement them.

gave these two close friends ample time to talk over a number of topics, subjects, issues, gossip, and plans for the future. Both were looking for posts as teachers, but Charlotte worried about her best friend, whom she thought could not survive the harsh, real world of 'governessing'.

With the arrival of William Weightman in August, 1839, as the new curate to Rev. Brontë, the lives of Ellen and Charlotte took a new turn. It appears that both of them were 'interested' in him at one time or another. Examination of their letters indicate that Charlotte was perhaps in love with him first, but he also showed interest in Ellen. As an amiable, affable character, as he was to all his parishioners and all women, Charlotte interpreted his actions as 'flirtatious' and warned Ellen away from him. These actions were indicative of their highly possessive natures when it came to guarding their affections for one another, and the threat of interlopers 'stealing away' their hearts. They each lived with that fear and that their precious friendship would be brought to an end. There is also evidence that a few years later, William Weightman and Anne Brontë may have had strong feelings for one another.

A year later, in 1840, Ellen had two new suitors, John Bradbury and Osmond Parke Vincent; the latter was quite serious about Ellen and a strong contender for her affections. Ellen was now twenty-three years old, of 'marrying age', and ready to fall in love. O. P. Vincent didn't propose to Ellen, but 'fished' for information regarding her feelings for him through her brother Henry. Ellen, on the other hand, asked her closest friend, Charlotte, for advice and thoughts on the situation. Charlotte, acting in her own self-interest, wanting to keep Ellen 'for herself', and afraid of losing her close and devoted friend, discouraged her from pursuing the relationship. In a letter to Ellen, Charlotte intimated that she would probably not see Ellen again if she was to marry. This veiled threat, bordering on 'emotional blackmail', was enough for Ellen to turn down the proposal when it finally did come. In later years, Ellen lived to regret her decision, but at the time when she was forced to choose between her friend or a husband, Ellen was not prepared to give up Charlotte. Neither Ellen nor Mr. Vincent ever married in their lifetime.

In March, 1841, when Charlotte accepted the job of governess to the Whites at Upperwood House, Rawdon, Ellen, still at Brookroyd, was only nine miles away, about half the distance from Haworth. Visits back and forth took place, and occasionally Charlotte spent the weekends at Brookroyd. In June, 1841, Ellen and Charlotte had their first, brief estrangement when Ellen promised to go to Haworth but did not arrive. Charlotte was deeply hurt, disappointed, and then angry; Ellen had an opportunity to go elsewhere and took it, but did not inform Charlotte. Four months later, it was Ellen's turn to be disappointed.

In the summer of 1841, both Ellen and Charlotte received letters from Mary Taylor and her brother John, who were both on the Continent. Martha Taylor had been installed in a school in Brussels, and Mary's letter was inspiring enough to stir a 'burning desire' in Charlotte to want to study there as well. If Charlotte followed through with her plans, Ellen would probably not see her again for a year or possibly two. In an ironic twist of fate, Ellen may have prevented this entire scenario had she gone to Haworth in June as she had planned, since it was Charlotte's intention to discuss their plan to open a school of their own. A vague notion of beginning a new school in Bridlington, the site of their first trip together, had even been considered. Charlotte had already been offered Miss Elizabeth Wooler's new school at Healds House, and had, in fact, accepted the offer. Had Ellen gone to Haworth as proposed, Charlotte may have followed through on the school plans for Healds House, Dewsbury, and there is little doubt that Charlotte would have made a place for Ellen there as a teacher since she was well-qualified. But this was not to be.

Charlotte's decision to go to Brussels for additional studies, marked a new phase not only in her own personal life but also in her friendship with Ellen. Ellen had been deeply hurt by the fact that Charlotte had acted so quickly on Mary Taylor's suggestion and had not asked her opinion. Charlotte left Upperwood House in mid-December, 1841, and then left for Brussels in early February, 1842. Although invited to Haworth, Ellen was unable to see Charlotte before she left for the Continent. This new phase of Charlotte's life marked an increasing self-determination on her part, and a widening rift of her dependence on Ellen. It is also indicitive of the fact that the two were now adults, fully in control of their own lives, and no longer teenagers and young adults full of idealism, but coming to grips with reality and maturity with an 'air' of confidence. At the same time, the Nussey family were even more dependent on Ellen than ever before, and she was increasingly becoming the 'root' and 'anchor' of the family.

After returning to Haworth in November, 1842, upon Aunt Branwell's death, Emily remained at Haworth but Charlotte returned to Brussels, this time as both a teacher and a student. In a brief visit to Haworth, Ellen and Charlotte talked over the idea of Ellen joining Charlotte in Brussels, but the plan was interrupted by the illness and death of Sarah Nussey, her dependent sister. By this time, loneliness, anxiety, and homesickness were having its effects on Charlotte, and not even Ellen's letters were able to sustain her and keep her out of deep depression. As a repeated pattern in her life, Charlotte was always attracted to the man, and disliked the wife, when she met married couples, particularly those for whom she worked. Charlotte, unable to help herself, fell madly in love with M Heger, and his wife ran 'interference' between them to protect her marriage. When M Heger did not return Charlotte's affections, she was quite devastated, and this eventually resulted in her quitting the school and returning home to England.

Ellen, in later life, was either unwilling or unable to admit that Charlotte had been deeply in love with M Heger and she repudiated that idea to the very end. At the same time as Charlotte's obsession with Heger, Ellen had her suitors as well: O. P. Vincent, John Taylor, and Joe Taylor all showed interest in her, but she was too busy maintaining the family to think of her own personal happiness. A scholarly examination of the letters indicate that Ellen's letters were more detailed than ever at this time whereas Charlotte's show a distinct change in tone and character after her stay in Brussels. The change from her lively, buoyant, optimistic, and effervescent writing style to one more staid, sober, and melancholy was no doubt brought on by the deaths of William Weightman, Martha Taylor, and Aunt Branwell, as well as her unrequited love for M Heger.

In June, 1845, Henry Nussey's marriage to Emily Prescott resulted in Ellen's invitation to Charlotte to come to Hathersage, the site of his new curacy. There Ellen was to mind the cottage while it was being renovated and extended while Henry and his new bride were on their honeymoon. This was the second major holiday in which Ellen and Charlotte's friendship was renewed, refreshed, and rejuvenated. Also, it turned out to be a 'gold mine' of information, characters, and sites, 'stored away' for future use, which Charlotte later relied on heavily for her novel, *Jane Eyre*. Had it not been for these events and Charlotte's visit there, *Jane Eyre*, may never have been written, or ir may have turned out quite differently.

Ellen and Charlotte were occasionally 'testy' with one another if their regular flow of correspondence failed to arrive, or was overdue. Such was the case in the fall of 1845, when Ellen sent off a 'sharp' letter to Charlotte, but what she did not know was that the Brontës were, in fact, very busy putting together their first book, *Poems*, for publication. For the Brontë sisters, it was a time-consuming activity and caused them anxiety. Charlotte could not explain the cause of her neglect because she was sworn to secrecy about their work and their authorship, particularly at Emily's behest. Charlotte was finally able to pacify Ellen by making a trip to Brookroyd in late February and early March, 1846.

At this time another irritant was developing between the two, close friends, and that was the growing relationship between Charlotte and Arthur B. Nicholls, and early rumours of their possible marriage. Ellen was not exactly enthralled by the idea. Once again, it was an ironic twist that when Ellen first met curate Nicholls, she liked him and saw 'good' in him, whereas Charlotte's first impression was that he was narrow-minded and bigoted. As time went on, their assessment and positions were reversed, and after Charlotte's death, Ellen held only animosity for Nicholls. Ellen could not help but feel that somehow he was responsible for her early demise.

Friendships, like most other relationships, 'grow' and develop as the individuals involved grow, develop, and mature. As two, mature adults, no longer young idealists with hearts and emotions to explore, and in constant need of confidences, Charlotte had learned to 'swallow' her grief, mistakes, failures, and triumphs without having to confide everything in Ellen. As a result, Ellen was now 'in the dark' about several aspects of her 'inner life'. She did not confide in Ellen completely about M Heger, her growing interest in A. B. Nicholls, and told her nothing about their writing, their book *Poems*, their manuscripts, or their writing goals. Such factors are indicative of a 'new plateau' in their friendship, and of a small, but ever-increasing, divergence and separation in the two personalities. In their youthful years they did not believe that they could live without each other's close and continuous confidence, but that was all changing.

As evidence of their growth apart, Ellen began to cultivate new friendships which was before perhaps unthinkable. Even now, Ellen was careful not to show too much interest in her new friends and tried to bring Charlotte into the friendship by having her new friends write to her to introduce and 'establish' themselves. In this respect, Mary Gorham, Ellen's new friend from Earnley, was successfully brought into the circle, but with Amelia Ringrose, Charlotte was not drawn toward her and gave her a 'cool' reception. Charlotte's high level of intelligence made it difficult for her to communicate with, cope with, and develop friendships with those of lesser intellect. The 'chemistry' of friendship with Amelia just wasn't there. Charlotte like to choose her own friends who were few and special; Ellen being more gregarious made friends easily and had many.

The rift in Charlotte and Ellen's friendship also widened when Charlotte gained some fame and fortune, unknown to Ellen, after the publication of *Jane Eyre*. Another world had now opened up to Charlotte, of which she intended to take full advantage, except that after several years of celebrity, Charlotte discovered that the 'glitter' of fame was not exactly what it was made out to be. The world of publishing, authors, literati, soon 'wore thin' with Charlotte, and she re-evaluated the meaning and importance of these new advantages in her life against those of remoteness, anonymity, tranquility, and personal happiness. In the end, Charlotte preferred the quietness and anonymity of homelife, and the society of her Yorkshire friends, to that of London's glitter and the high society now available to her.

While fame and fortune were still in its bright, early stages (1848-49), Charlotte began urging Ellen to pursue happiness through marriage if she could find it. Ellen's life was never short of suitors, but she had already 'thrown away' a chance of happiness through marriage with O. P. Vincent largely at Charlotte's behest. Now, Rev. Thomas Allbutt, Vicar of Dewsbury and recent widower, was showing interest in Ellen, and Charlotte no longer appeared to have any qualms about Ellen's marriage, if it was to happen. Since Ellen had not pursued marriage as a result of her fear of Charlotte's reaction, and the possible damage to their long friendship, that barrier now appeared to have been lifted. Also, by lifting this barrier on Ellen, Charlotte was also 'clearing a path' for her own pursuits in this 'direction', almost as something inevitable in her future.

Ellen was a dedicated reader, devoted to English literature, and like others read the highly acclaimed *Jane Eyre*. Immediately Ellen recognized the style, places, several characters, and some of the events within the plot, as those of her friend, Charlotte Brontë. Ellen had, in fact, watched Charlotte correct the proofs in the garden at Brookroyd in September, 1847, only a month before its publication. Charlotte said nothing of her activities there, and Ellen was too polite to ask. When Ellen wrote to Charlotte to confirm her authorship, Charlotte denied it simply to protect Emily and to uphold her oath of secrecy. There is no doubt that Charlotte would have enjoyed sharing the pleasures of her success with her best friend, but this was not possible as long as Emily was alive. Charlotte was not forced to keep her oath of secrecy long.

In the fall of 1848, Charlotte's world fell apart, and she needed Ellen more than ever. In successive tragedies, Branwell's condition deteriorated dramatically, and he died suddenly on September 24th, 1848. Only three months later, on December 19th, Emily passed away, and Anne was already seriously ill. Charlotte was sorrowful and grieving at Branwell's death, but she was devastated by Emily's passing. Their brother had more or less brought about his own death through dissipation, but Emily was the 'tower of strength' in Charlotte's life. Throughout Emily's final stages, Charlotte suffered extreme anguish and torment knowing that they could do nothing for her and that death was inevitable. Charlotte wrote to Ellen begging her to come to Haworth to console and comfort her after Emily's death. Ellen arrived within days and stayed two weeks, leaving on January

9th,1849. It was then that Charlotte revealed the truth of their authorship and provided Ellen with personal copies of their first four novels.

With the death of Emily and the illness of Anne, we can see from correspondence that Ellen was not only a friend of Charlotte's but also of Anne's. Many of Anne's and Emily's friends were acquired through Charlotte, and Ellen and Anne had a special fondness for one another. When Anne realized that her illness was not getting any better, and that there was a possiblity of recovery by venturing to a better climate, Anne asked Ellen to accompany her to Harrogate or Scarborough. Ellen magnanimously made the offer that Anne convalesce at Brookroyd, but the Brontës in an equally magnanimous gesture, refused the offer, since it would be burdensome to Ellen. In the end, both Charlotte and Ellen accompanied Anne to York, and finally Scarborough where she died.

After the death of her three siblings, Charlotte's friendship with Ellen again strengthened largely out of need for moral support, and courage to face the future without them. Charlotte now relied on Ellen more than ever since Emily and Anne were no longer there to talk to and consult with. After Anne's death, Charlotte's work on *Shirley* came to a halt, and it required some effort on Charlotte's part to return to it. By early September, 1849, the *Shirley* manuscript was in the hands of her printer, and by late October it was published. Had it not been for the solace and comfort of Charlotte's dear friend, the period of recovery may have taken many more months or even years. Again in late December, 1849, Ellen visited Charlotte at Haworth for two weeks. It was the first anniversary of Emily's death which only made Charlotte's holiday season bleak, depressing, and full of anxiety. Only Ellen could provide her with the level of comfort she needed; Ellen had proved herself a loyal, trusted, devoted friend once more.

For the next two years, Ellen and Charlotte continued their reciprocal visits, and in March, 1851, Charlotte visited Brookroyd and later in July, Ellen visited Haworth. The visit in July was after Charlotte's visit to London in June as a guest of her publisher's family. It was the year of the Great Exhibition, and at the insistence of the host, they visited it many times, much to the annoyance of Charlotte who intensely disliked the much-touted Crystal Palace. While she was there, Charlotte attended the lectures of Thackeray, a fellow, contemporary writer whom she held in awe. The visit was exciting but Charlotte was always happy to be home.

Ellen's very presence was often the 'elixir' that Charlotte needed to lift her from illness and depression; such was the power of Ellen's friendship and presence. In June of 1851, while visiting Elizabeth Gaskell in Manchester, Charlotte began her last novel, *Villette,* which was a complete re-make of the ill-fated *Professor.* Six months later in January, 1852, the contents of her book, based on her experiences in Brussels aroused latent and suppressed romantic memories, emotions, and anxieties, such that Charlotte immediately fell into serious depression. Ellen answered Charlotte's call, arrived in Haworth, and Charlotte was soon better, but she relapsed after Ellen left. The uplifting spirit and the comfort Ellen provided could not be doubted. Two months later, Charlotte went to Brookroyd to recuperate after her depression was treated with pills that were toxic to her, and secondary substitute pills were equally bad.[3] Once again, Ellen's companionship and tender care revitalized Charlotte. After her recovery, Charlotte continued her writing, and *Villette,* completed in October, 1852, was published in January, 1853.

With the completion of *Villette,* Charlotte again had some freedom but was beset by a new set of problems. In December of 1852, curate Nicholls proposed to Charlotte, and she refused largely because of her father's violent reaction to the whole affair. The tension between the three parties was high. In January, 1853, the first reviews of *Villette* were out, and they were mixed. One of the most highly critical reviews of her new work was by Harriet Martineau, and this ended their friendship. Ellen worried about the reviews, and Charlotte's reaction to them, for her sake, because she did not take criticism well.

In the meantime, Ellen had a conundrum of her own to deal with. An elderly couple had offered Ellen an inheritance of an unspecified amount if she would look after them in their old age, and an annuity would be paid out to her upon their deaths. Both Charlotte, and Mary Taylor in letters from New Zealand, strongly advised against its acceptance, seeing that the proposal was fraught with difficulties, vague, and subject to the vagaries of fortune, making the entire venture highly speculative and extremely risky. During Ellen's visit to Haworth in January 1853, the situations were discussed and friendly advice given on both sides. In spite of Charlotte's advice, Ellen accepted the offer on a trial basis, but it soon became evident that the situation was untenable, and the relationship incompatible. Ellen gave it up and went to visit her brother Joshua at Oundle. Charlotte was highly pleased at the outcome.

In the latter months of 1853, it appears that Charlotte had finally made up her mind to accept curate Nicholl's offer of marriage. Ellen expressed her shock and amazement at the idea of their union, and Charlotte's reply was sharp. As a result, their friendship suffered a temporary setback, but this time it was more serious and severe. Ellen then wrote of her concerns to Mary Taylor in New Zealand and received an equally sharp rebuff defending Charlotte's right to pursue happiness, and what she thought was right for herself. It is most likely that Ellen saw this as a definitive break in their long-standing relationship, and suspected that after their marriage, things would be different. Ellen was right; after Charlotte's marriage to Nicholls, things were different, and it was Nicholls who came between them. Nicholls's possessive nature would have preferred to see Ellen at a much greater distance, have less influence, and much less contact.

From that moment on, their friendship and relationship was never the same. Charlotte's thoughts and interests were now concentrated on her future husband, her role as a wife, and alterations to the Parsonage to mark his arrival there as full-time resident, and part of the family. Both Ellen and Rev. Brontë felt 'abandoned' and 'rejected' by Charlotte as she became totally pre-occupied with her forth-coming marriage. Rev. Brontë became crusty, grumpy, and more obstinate, while Ellen avoided Charlotte and Haworth altogether, primarily because of her growing dislike of Nicholls. Some of Charlotte's previous

---

3   The pills contained mercury. Secondary medication included quinine which was also toxic to her system. Whitehead, B. *Charlotte Brontë,.. and her 'dearest Nell'.* p.169.

letters had indicated that Nicholls had serious flaws in his personality, and it seemed enigmatic to Ellen that Charlotte should now be drawn to him, especially as a husband.

After Ellen's initial shock and anger, she eventually resigned herself to the fact that Charlotte was about to marry. In a noble gesture, Ellen invited Charlotte and Nicholls to Brookroyd but Nicholls declined, and Charlotte came on her own. Elizabeth Gaskell also invited both, and again Nicholls refused which indicates either his arrogance and stubbornness, or that he sensed how deeply they disliked him. Both Ellen and Margaret Wooler accepted Charlotte's offer to be bridesmaids at her wedding, and they arrived in Haworth the day before. After the wedding, the newly-weds left for Ireland for their honeymoon and to visit Nicholls's relatives there. They briefly stopped in Wales, and it is a testament to the strength and bond of their friendship that Charlotte spent part of her wedding night writing a letter to her best friend. Ellen, on the other hand, was still deeply hurt and did not respond as Charlotte had requested.

Ellen did not see Charlotte until two and one-half months later in late September, 1854. What surprised Ellen most was that Charlotte radiated with happiness and joyful exuberance; this was something entirely new for Charlotte. From her general appearance and her own statements, she was truly happy for the first time in her life; it was even better than being a literary celebrity. During a walk on the moors with the newly-weds, Charlotte told Ellen that she had an idea for her next book, but her husband was against the continuation of her writing. Nicholls wanted a 'traditional' wife, not a famous author, and he did his utmost to keep Charlotte as busy as possible. As far as Nicholls was concerned, Ellen was as much a threat to him as was Charlotte's writing; both competed with him for her attentions.

Such 'draws' on her powerful intellect and individualism may have played on Nicholls's insecurities, and he continued to be threatened by them. Before long, he began to interfere in their friendship by censoring, or at least 'over-seeing' and 'directing', the contents of Charlotte's letters. He insisted, through Charlotte, that Ellen burn her letters after reading them, since he did not approve of their contents. Such was the extent of control that Nicholls had over his new wife. It is also a point of speculative interest to see how this scenario would have 'played out' if they had been married longer.

After the September, 1854 visit, Ellen never saw her friend Charlotte alive again. Several visits were scheduled but all were postponed and eventually cancelled due to unforeseen events, circumstances, and visits by other guests. Another 'wrinkle' in the friendship appeared when Charlotte thought she was pregnant and turned her writing to Amelia Taylor[4] for advice. Ellen was hurt and felt slighted that Charlotte did not write to her whereas Amelia was delighted that Charlotte had consulted her above all others. Charlotte's reasoning was clear; Amelia had already had one child, and Ellen had never been married.

---

4   Amelia Ringrose was originally the beaux of George Nussey before his mental illness developed in 1845. She eventually married Joe Taylor, Mary's brother, and had one daughter by him.

Ellen continued to worry about her dear friend's health in spite of her marriage to Nicholls and recognized early warning signs that escaped others. Ellen, early on in their friendship, noticed that Charlotte had a delicate constitution, was somewhat fragile, suffered frequent migraines, and needed constant rest, relaxation, and attention. She also recognized that since her marriage these requirements were not being met, and that the marriage relationship and social requirements of being a clergyman's spouse, and being a wife to the demanding Nicholls were taxing her strength to the limit. Charlotte's letter to Ellen indicating that she had not completely recovered from her 'November cold' was an ominous sign. In mid-January, Charlotte indicated that she wanted to visit Ellen at Brookroyd, but it was later followed by letters from her husband saying that Charlotte was too ill to travel, or even write. These were forebodings of worse things to come. In mid-February, Charlotte wrote a short, hastily scrawled note to Ellen; it was her last communication to her friend.

On March 30th, 1855, Rev. Brontë wrote a letter to Ellen telling her that Charlotte was now on her death-bed, and to come at once if she wished to see her alive again. Ellen set out immediately upon receiving the letter, but when she arrived at Haworth, she discovered that Charlotte had died during the night. It was an extremely difficult time for Ellen, but she helped with the funeral arrangements. Charlotte was buried on Wednesday, April 4th, 1855; the close and wonderful friendship of twenty-four years had come to an end.

Although her best friend was now gone, Ellen spent the remainder of her life defending the name and honour of Charlotte Brontë. She had now become the 'chief defender' and prime source of information not only on Charlotte but also the Brontë family since other sources such Rev. Brontë, Nicholls, and household servants were not speaking. Nicholls and Rev. Brontë were both devastated, lonely, and reluctant to talk about family members, all now dead and gone, and whose memories only evoked sadness and anxiety. It also became known that Ellen had hoarded and saved all of Charlotte's letters which now proved invaluable to any biography that was to be written, and for general historical and literary value. In all, it appears that Ellen had saved over 350 letters.

Reports and articles criticizing Charlotte as 'coarse' and 'unladylike' in her writings were fiercely repudiated by Ellen. Charlotte was now 'reverent' and 'god-like' in Ellen's memory and neither aspersions nor any degree of criticism would be tolerated by her best friend who rose to defend her whenever necessary. Ellen felt incapable of writing a biography on Charlotte herself and eagerly encouraged several writers to produce biographies which paralleled her own views and opinions about her beloved Charlotte. When Elizabeth Gaskell was finally commissioned, in June 1855, to write an authorized biography on Charlotte, Ellen was pleased and gladly loaned out most of her letters for research purposes. During the production of the work, Ellen was to be the key source of information, and following its completion, she was to proof-read the final copy.

As time went by, Rev. Brontë who had always been very fond and full of compliments for Ellen, suddenly found fault with her, and she 'fell out of grace'. It is thought that perhaps Nicholls was now a strong personal influence over Rev. Brontë, and since Ellen and Nicholls were now at loggerheads over issues like the letters, the biography, and proof-reading, Nicholls was hostile towards her. The 'bad blood' between them only got worse. A second factor was Elizabeth Gaskell using Ellen as a source of information on the Brontë family which was otherwise unattainable. Both Rev. Brontë and Nicholls wanted much of the information suppressed and were unhappy that Ellen was providing it. She was no longer considered a member of their 'inner family circle' nor did she find favour in their eyes.

With the death of Charlotte, a large 'chunk' of Ellen's life was 'torn away', and nothing could replace it. The influence that Ellen had over Charlotte in their close friendship was now reversed, and the friendship was now about to influence and dominate her for the rest of her life. Ellen had had a good, youthful relationship with Mary Taylor, but when she returned to England in 1860, and built 'High Royd', it was just not the same. The element which could 'bind them' was now gone. Many things had changed, but primarily it was the death of Charlotte which had changed Ellen's life and affected her relationship with Mary. Ellen's final link with the Brontë family was severed after a visit to Haworth in December, 1860, where she met with Nicholls and Rev. Brontë. This was their last meeting, and Rev. Brontë died six months later in June, 1861.

Although Ellen was prodded and urged by friends and fans of the Brontës to write a book, Ellen was reluctant to do so. She was truly in awe of her great friend, but she also wanted to preserve the sanctity of that relationship and the confidences which Charlotte had conveyed to her. Even in death, the preservation of that relationship was uppermost in her mind and could not be betrayed by her loyal, trustworthy friend. Ellen's loyalty and dedication to her friend's memory did not waiver, and no amount of money could purchase a betrayal.

As the years progressed, Ellen was still the faithful guardian of the Brontë letters, but she did look to the future and the proper placement of the letters. Ultimately she wanted the letters to be preserved for posterity and hoped that the British Museum[5] would be interested. Unfortunately, various forces were pulling her in different directions and unscrupulous minds were already at work devising ways to separate Ellen from her valuable letters. This desire for proper placement of the letters combined with the fact that Ellen still believed that neither Gaskell nor any other writer had done Charlotte proper 'justice' made Ellen ripe for exploitation by those whose aims were simply greed.

For the remainder of her life, Ellen spent a great deal of her time dealing with both legitimate and fraudulent persons trying to gain access to the Brontë letters for the purpose of researching them and writing books while others were simply out to market them for personal gain. The train of interested parties included Wemyss Reid, Rev. A. Wilkes, Sydney Biddell, Mary Robinson, William Scruton, John Horsfall Turner, Dr. Erskine Stuart, Augustine Birrell, Dr. Wm. Wright, Clement Shorter, and the person who ultimatley defrauded Ellen of many of her letters, Thomas J. Wise. In addition to aiding and collaborating with the above, Ellen answered dozens of letters requesting information about the Brontës, or requesting bits, scraps, and pieces of Charlotte's letters. Much of her remain-

---

5   In 1884, Wemyss Reid made efforts to broker a sale of the Brontë letters to the British Museum through Lord Houghton, but they did not appear to be interested. Whitehead, B. *Charlotte Brontë,... and her 'dearest Nell'* p.230.

ing time was spent helping the poor, giving assistance to the church and various local schools and social agencies for the betterment of her fellow man.

Ellen spent the last few years of her life in torment after being defrauded of her letters by T. J. Wise. There was no one to help her, and any legal recourse would be time-consuming, taxing on her failing health, raise the level of her already-heightened mental anxiety, and very costly. Also T. J. Wise was not a man to be trifled with, and he was easily able to silence Ellen with legal threats and bullying tactics. With the ensuing, widespread retailing of Brontë letters by Wise and his undercover associates, many people assumed that Ellen was behind the sales resulting in her reputation being sullied by innuendoes. Ellen, now in her late seventies, was old, frail, and unable to launch a sustained legal fight. She had only the interest of her friend at heart and the preservation of her letters, and through it all, she suffered the most and profited the least.

The last years of her life were spent quietly at her last home at Moor Lane House, although she was bitter and upset at the treatment she had received, especially from Shorter and Wise, and the disappearance of her most highly-prized possession, the Brontë letters. She had many friends, especially among the poor, who called after her at her home to convey their 'good wishes' when she fell ill. She died peacefully and quietly at her home on November 26, 1897, an unwaivering friend to Charlotte Brontë to the very end.

23

LIVES AND TRAGEDIES

The life of the Brontës reads like a Shakespearean tragedy, and not even the great bard himself could have produced in his fictional genius the tragedies of reality which plagued the family. And the one person who watched all the tragedies unfold before his very eyes was Rev. Brontë who saw his family members die, one by one, until only he was left. Through each of these tragedies he suffered greatly, and only his steadfast religious beliefs carried him through these tribulations.

In the end, we must ask ourselves just how these deaths affected the remaining Brontës and their writing, if at all. Barring their occasional differences and approaches to life, the Brontës were a fairly 'tight-knit' family, perhaps 'brought together' or 'thrown together' by the centripetal forces of tragedy. This is only a natural, human and psychological reaction to tragedy of any type, but repeated as they were with the Brontës, it surely must have 'weighed heavily' on their minds in a deep-rooted, unconscious fashion. And as the tragedies repeated themselves, it may have seemed to be a test of their 'wills', their strength, and their belief in God, for few could have suffered, and endured, the 'taxing' nature of these tragedies and kept their sanity, hopes, and beliefs.

For the first seven years of the Brontë children's lives, things appeared to go well for them. In 1812, Rev. Brontë met Maria Branwell when she was visiting her uncle, John Fennel, the headmaster of Woodhouse Grove School, near Bradford, where the young Mr. Brontë had been appointed 'examiner' of Scriptures. The attraction was instant and mutual, and after a 'whirlwind romance' of only a few months, the passionate Irishman proposed to Maria. She accepted, and the marriage was set for December 29th at Guisely.

Immediately upon their marriage, they moved into Clough House on Halifax Road, Hightown, Liversedge. In early 1814, their first child, Maria, was born and later baptised April 23rd, at St. Peter's Church, Hartshead. The following year, on February 8th, 1815, their second daughter, Elizabeth, was born and later baptised on August 26th at Rev.

Brontë's new curacy at Thornton, a few miles away. It was here that the family spent their most blissful years from 1815 to 1820.

During this time, the family lived at 72 Market Street, Thornton, just a short walk away from Thornton Church, his new assignment. And it was during this time that four more children were born in the 'dining room'[1] where the Georgian fireplace[2] made it the warmest room in the house, and therefore, the likely birthplace of Charlotte (1816), Patrick Branwell (1817), Emily Jane (1818), and Anne (1820). These were the years when the family was young, happy, 'whole', and looking forward to a pleasant and prosperous future. The first tragedy had not yet struck.

Following Anne's birth in January 1820, Mrs. Brontë was not well and did not appear to be recovering; in fact, she appeared to be getting worse. Mrs. Brontë's health problems were probably not helped by the move to Haworth a few months later, in April, only three months after Anne's birth. By January, 1821, in a letter to a friend, Rev. Brontë was fully aware that her situation was hopeless, and that her death would be a 'blessing' compared to the pain and suffering that she was going through. It appears from information in letters that Mrs. Brontë had a form of stomach cancer which, in those days, was completely untreatable, and therefore, terminal.

In the latter stages of her illness, Mrs. Brontë refused to see her children, primarily because she did not want them to see her in such a condition, and traumatize them. Secondly, she found it difficult to look at her young children knowing that in a short time, they were all going to be motherless. Her overwhelming concern, right up to the time of her death, was for the welfare of her children, and not her own. The children carefully obeyed, as they were instructed, the new house rule to keep quiet for the sake of their sick mother.

By mid-September, Mrs. Brontë's sufferings were finally over, but those of her children were about to begin. The eldest children, Maria and Elizabeth, were now seven and six years old, respectively, and, of course, they were much more aware of the importance of the event of the passing of their mother. The other children were much younger, Anne being only one and a half years, and did not fully comprehend, or appreciate, the dreadful significance of this first, great tragedy, and loss. Their mother was buried several days later underneath the centre aisle of the old Haworth Church in the family vault. This was but the first of many tragedies to come.

Shortly after her death, Mrs. Brontë's sister, Elizabeth Branwell, came to assist Mr. Brontë with his six, small children as a 'temporary' measure until the family situation was stabilized once more. Aunt Branwell, as she came to be known to the family, had no intention of staying in the cold, northern climes of England and wished to return to the warm, friendly, southerly coast of Penzance in Cornwall. Also, no one really expected Mr. Brontë to remain unmarried for long. His position and standing in the community, along with his position, general attractiveness, and fine bearing were thought, surely, to find him a new wife. Mr. Brontë tried several proposals to several women, but none were

---

1   Designated the 'dining room' by present owner, Barbara Whitehead, who is slowly restoring the former Brontë home.
2   When the fireplace cover was removed, the original Georgian fireplace was found in tact.

accepted; he then gave up and remained a widower for the rest of his life. Also, the fact that he did not re-marry extended Aunt Branwell's stay until finally she became a permanent resident at the Haworth parsonage.

The next four years were relatively stable, and once again the family settled into a routine with a sense of 'normality' returning to the devastated family. Then again, the stage was set for a second round of tragedies when Rev. Brontë, looking for an economical way to educate his six children, was informed of the new Clergy Daughters' School, which opened in January of 1824. With the low, subsidized rate of only £14 per year, Rev. Brontë could not pass it up and began enrolling his children.

Rev. W. Carus Wilson, wishing to be a philanthropic patron to his fellow clergymen, set up the school at Cowan Bridge near the spot where the Leck Fells spill out onto the plains. It was a poorly chosen site with many problems: sanitation and potable water were lacking; food provided was inadequate for growing children; the site was subject to cold, northerly winds in winter, and the building was inadequately heated. All of these circumstances led to a dangerous and unhealthy environment. On Sundays, the students were marched, summer and winter, two and one-half miles to Tunstall Church, where Rev. Carus Wilson preached, and where they remained the better part of the day in the unheated church before marching back to the school. It did not take long before there was an outbreak of 'low fever' early in 1825. Many became ill, Maria Brontë among them; some died and were immediately buried in the Tunstall Churchyard Cemetery.

When Rev. Brontë received a letter on February 14, 1825, indicating that Maria was ill, he quickly went to the school to bring her home. She lingered in illness for several months but died at Haworth on May 6th. Just three weeks later, a second letter arrived informing him of Elizabeth's illness. He immediately left and removed her from the school on May 31st, and returned the very next day to remove Charlotte and Emily before they, too, became ill. Elizabeth was seriously ill and died two weeks later on June 15th.

Once again, their world was upset by this double tragedy and was traumatically felt by all who remained. Anne was only five years old and perhaps had the least memory of the event, but Branwell, now almost eight years old, was the most deeply affected. He was 'beside himself' with grief over the loss of his beloved Maria who had been like a 'mother' to him, as well as the rest. Branwell was haunted for months and years following her death, and some of his poetry years later[3], had her as its subject. He wandered the house searching and hoping to find her. Just six weeks after Maria's death, Elizabeth, his second oldest sister, also died adding further to his grief, and the family's grief. It is reasonable to believe that many of Branwell's problems later in his life were the direct result of his traumatosis which scarred him for life.

Added to the terrible grief the family suffered was the shock which these tragedies brought. For Aunt Branwell, whose basic Calvinist 'creed' was that 'man was put on this earth to suffer', this belief perhaps carried her through these tumultuous and grievous times, but for the Brontës who lived by a different creed, the tragedies were difficult to understand. For Branwell, it perhaps laid the basic groundwork for his later 'godless'

---

3   The poem 'On Caroline' is a prime example. The beginning of the third stanza shows that he suffered a form of 'survivor guilt'.

actions and bohemian lifestyle, in which he seemed either to show his wantoness or to 'punish' God for what He had done. The loss of his two eldest sisters, especially Maria, appeared to haunt him for the rest of his life.

For Emily and Anne, who were both younger, the effects were somewhat less, since they both had their older sister, Charlotte, from whom they could seek support and consolation. For Charlotte herself, the effect was exactly the opposite; now she was the eldest child, and felt responsible for assisting and caring for her younger siblings. Charlotte was only nine years old, and still a small child herself, but she now 'shouldered' the responsibility of an adult. Such a weighty responsibility must have taken its 'psychological toll' on such a young child, but she accepted the challenge. For the remainder of her life, she was the 'senior sibling', who, besides Aunt Branwell, was a general overseer of the Brontë children, and it was a responsibility she took very seriously.

That Charlotte was affected by these tragedies is perhaps witnessed by the fact that she could, and did, carry a grudge in spite of her strong, religious beliefs. This is evident in *Jane Eyre* and her portrayal of Rev. W. Carus Wilson, as 'Rev. Brocklehurst', and 'Miss Scatcherd'[4], and her depiction of the treatment they received at their hands. Helen Burns, portrayed as learned and stoical, is none other than Charlotte's beloved sister Maria, who received particular, cruel treatment at the hands of Miss Scatcherd. Like Maria, Helen Burns had a great and powerful faith in God and Eternity and considered life too short to dwell on animosity. The loss of Maria was something which weighed heavily upon Charlotte's mind and is clearly revealed in *Jane Eyre* as an act of vengeance, and exposure, on the perpetrators[5] of these cruel misdeeds. And although 'forgiveness' is one of the basic tenets of Christianity, Charlotte could not find it within herself to forgive what she considered 'unforgiveable'.

So accurate were Charlotte's descriptions of 'Lowood School', its administrators, teachers, and students, that shortly after *Jane Eyre* was published, many readers who were former students at Cowan Bridge School instantly recognized the people, places, and events which Charlotte described. The only mystery which remained was the identity of the writer, 'Currer Bell', but for some the 'dots' were easy to 'connect'. Considering the time, the place, the people, and the events described, the 'short list' of possibilities for the real author was quickly narrowed down still further. For some, the Brontës figured highly on that list.

These tragedies had another indirect effect on the Brontë children brought about by their father who refused to send his children to school after the deaths of Maria and Elizabeth, lest they, too, suffer the same fate. As a result, the children became withdrawn, and in the case of Emily, almost reclusive. This continued and sustained withdrawal from society at large, made them exceptionally shy, quiet, and reserved, particularly in the presence of others unknown to them. With their close friends, their demeanour was quite different; they were overt, sociable, and happy. They rarely mixed with other village children except on Sundays at the church where their father preached.

---

4   Her real name is thought to be 'Miss Andrews'.

5   The 'perpetrators' were still alive at the time of the publication of *Jane Eyre*, and would certainly have read about themselves, or at least have heard about it.

In the case of Branwell, Rev. Brontë was hesitant, and reluctant, to let the boy out of his sight. Whereas the young girls would be taught what they needed to know by their aunt, Branwell's education was carefully administered by his father who taught him classic languages, along with other subjects. It was not long before Branwell demonstrated his brilliance, and possible genius, through his learning. Unfortunately, coupled with his high level of intelligence, came what appears to be sociological behaviour disorders including temper-tantrums, severe misbehaviour, and hyperactivity which made him difficult to control. Much of this may well have been the result of the severe shock and trauma which he suffered in his early years.

These untreated disorders which affected Branwell so greatly early on, and which were briefly outlined in Chapter Five, seem to have simply had a greater negative, cumulative effect on his developing character in his young adulthood. These unresolved psychological and emotional issues were far more damaging than his father, or close family members, could possibly have imagined. The family's solution to his uncontrollable temper, and ravings, was to simply let him have 'his way', which eventually resulted in his own lack of personal responsibility, and 'weak character', as Emily pointed out. His work history and life history from youth to young adulthood is proof enough of a disastrous, mistaken, and misguided upbringing which was not helped by the pampering of his father, Aunt Branwell, and 'soft spoiling' by his sibling sisters. The end result was an unmitigated disaster.

Mid-way through their lives, from 1825 to 1842, a period of seventeen years went relatively smoothly until another set of disasters occurred which affected all of them, and once again, tested their 'mettle' and beliefs to their limits. In early September, 1842, their father's curate, William Weightman, who had been a virtual joy and 'ray of sunshine' in their otherwise bleak and dreary lives, suddenly became very ill. Branwell spent a great deal of time at his dear friend's bed-side, but three days later, on September 6th, he died. Once again, Branwell was devastated at his loss. This was a complete shock and trauma to the entire family; the joy and happiness which had entered their lives in August, 1839, as the new curate to Mr. Brontë, was now gone.

This time, three people felt his passing more than any of the others; they were Rev. Brontë, Branwell, and Anne. For Rev. Brontë, William Weightman was a delightful and diligent co-worker who was well-liked by his parishioners, and especially Mr. Brontë who looked upon him as a 'son'. Branwell had quickly become friends with Weightman because of their similar ages, talents, intelligence, and interests, coupled with his charming ways. For once, Branwell had a close friend whose company he could enjoy but was now suddenly taken away from him. In a letter to his friend, Francis Grundy, dated 25/10/1842, Branwell explains his sorrow, and his delay in writing. He says:

> I have had a long attendance at the deathbed of the Rev. Mr. Weightman, one of my dearest friends, and now I am attending at the deathbed of my aunt, who has been for twenty years as my mother. I expect her to die in a few hours.

For Anne, his death may have been even more grievous, since there was the possibility that she and William Weightman might have had a serious interest in one another as future 'partners' in life. Charlotte remarked in one of her letters to Ellen Nussey of how the two of them reacted in church as they sneaked glances at one another during the service.

Following his death, some of Anne's poems appear to be directed to a 'lost love' which is most often assumed to be none other than William Weightman. The first stanza of the poem, 'A Reminiscence', is undoubtedly about her happy remembrances of him. It reads:

> Yes, though art gone! and never more/Thy sunny smile shall gladden me; But I may
> pass the old church door,/And pace the floor that covers thee.

Also, in *Agnes Grey*, the new curate at Horton, Mr. Weston, although quite different in personal qualities from William Weightman, is thought to be at least inspired by him. In her novel, there is a great deal of interaction between them, and 'coincidentally' when they both leave 'O-', they both are re-united in 'A-', where their relationship is renewed, and 'raised a notch', to the point where Mr. Weston proposes marriage to Agnes and she accepts. In the end, they have three children, live modestly, and live 'happily ever after'. One can only surmise that this is perhaps the idyllic life she would have chosen for herself had things turned out differently.

For the remainder of her life, Anne never married or had a serious relationship with anyone, and like her sisters, she was shy, quiet, and reserved. After Anne wrote *The Tenant of Wildfell Hall*, Charlotte was her most severe critic, and not only condemned the subject of the novel but also that it was inconsistent with her nature. Charlotte also made the observation in her 'Biographical Notice of Ellis and Acton Bell' that:

> ... hers was naturally a sensitive, reserved, and dejected nature; what she saw sank
> very deeply into her mind; it did her harm.

The above statement was made in reference to her choice of subject, thought to be about their brother Branwell's dissolute ways as disguised in the character of Arthur Huntingdon. But we must also assume that if Anne was sensitive enough to be affected by her brother's gradual demise, and it 'sank... into her mind' and 'did her harm', so likewise did the other tragedies which affected them, namely the three tragedies of September and October, 1842. Charlotte goes on to add in the same paragraph about Anne that:

> She was a very sincere and practical Christian, but the tinge of religious melancholy
> communicated a sad shape to her brief, blameless life.

What Charlotte identified as 'a tinge of religious melancholy' may have, in fact, been symptoms of 'depression' in a mild to moderate form. Anne's earlier religious crisis during her stay at Roe Head School in 1837, may also have been 'depression' of a deeper, 'clinical' variety, as we identify it today. In any case, we can only surmise this from our readings today, since it was not diagnosed as such then; 'depression' was not readily identified as a debilitating emotional or pyschological illness in Victorian times. The source of her 'depression', if it was that, can perhaps be attributed to a number of origins, their continued life-tragedies being one of them.

It was not long after William Weightman's death that another tragedy was in store for them in mid-October, 1842. Martha Taylor, Mary's younger sister, the lively, vivacious, gay, and 'chattering', 'Jessy Yorke' of *Shirley* suddenly became ill at the Chateau de Koekelberg in Brussels and died several days later on October 12th. The tragedy again affected Charlotte and Emily, who were present in Brussels at the time, just as it did Mary Taylor. The length, the symptoms, and the progression of the illness were identical to those of William Weightman. Martha had also brought 'rays of sunshine' into their lives during Charlotte's visits to 'Red House' in Gomersal, and to the rest of the Brontës during her visits to the parsonage at Haworth. Even Branwell was 'taken' by her prattling, jovial, manner in a house which was usually 'directed' by a sober and serious-minded approach to life, first by Rev. Brontë, and secondly by Aunt Branwell.

The two, successive deaths, both of relatively young people, surely would have reinforced the 'fickleness' and impermanence of life on this Earth, especially in Victorian times, when neither a great deal was known about certain illnesses and diseases nor how to treat or combat them. The death of young Martha would also certainly have stirred up memories of the deaths of Maria and Elizabeth, their two, older sisters. To add to the trauma was the fact that Martha died in a distant land, away from home and family, and had to be buried there on the outskirts of Brussels in the Protestant Cemetery. Charlotte vividly recalled the visit to Martha's grave she had taken there with Emily, and Mary Taylor in the fall of 1842. The visit is described in *Shirley* [6] (Chap. 23) where Charlotte relives the scene of their deep sorrow and their great loss. She says:

> ... but they each knew that a gap, never to be filled, had been made in their circle. They knew they had lost something whose absence could never be quite atoned for so long as they lived;...

The deaths of William Weightman and Martha Taylor were difficult enough to contend with, but they were yet to suffer more grief in quick succession. Shortly after Martha Taylor's death in Brussels, Aunt Branwell, now sixty-six, fell ill at Haworth. Her illness was quite unlike that of either Martha's or William's, but her suffering was no less. In fact, her suffering was perhaps greater since she suffered much longer. Aunt Branwell fell ill with stomach pains in mid-October, and they only increased in intensity with the passage of time. Her illness continued, and after two weeks of intense suffering, on October 29, 1842, she died.

The official cause of death was listed as "exhaustion caused from constipation", but this only 'begs the question' as to what caused the constipation. Charlotte later described it as an ' internal obstruction', but it may also have been complications as the result of

---

6   The scene is also described, less accurately, in Chapter 19 of *The Professor*.

appendicitis or a 'strangulated' bowel each of which could have caused similar symptoms. In any case, hers was not an 'easy death', and when it came, it was almost a 'blessing'. In a letter to Francis Grundy, dated 29/10/1842, Branwell explains:

> I am incoherent, I fear, but I have been waking two nights witnessing such agonizing suffering as I would not wish my worst enemy to endure; and I have now lost the [guide] and director of all the happy days connected with my childhood.

Charlotte and Emily were both in Brussels at the Pensionnat Heger when they first received a letter on Wednesday, November 2nd, informing them of their Aunt Branwell's serious illness. The very next day, a second letter arrived informing them of her death on October 29th, and although they continued their packing to return home immediately, they missed the boat on Friday and were unable to leave Belgium until Sunday, November 6th. After travelling day and night for two days, they arrived home on the morning of Tuesday, November 8th, but Aunt Branwell had been buried five days before on November 3rd. And in a letter to Ellen Nussey, dated 10/11/1842, Charlotte laments over the recent, sad occurrences[7] and the emptiness that they now endure. She says:

> I have seen Martha's grave - the place where her ashes lie in a foreign country Aunt - Martha Taylor - Mr Weightman 'are now' all gone - how dreary & void everything seems - Mr Weightman's illness was exactly what Martha's was - he was ill the same length of time & died in the same manner - Aunts disease was internal obstruction. she was ill a fortnight

Once again the world of the Brontës had been badly shaken, but as before, it soon settled into a relatively peaceful routine for the next six years until Charlotte's life was rocked again by another series of three tragedies. In the intervening years, all remained stable with the exception of the gradual decline of their brother Branwell whose series of personal setbacks led to moral decline with disastrous results. In the end, he appeared to be a 'beaten man' and a man without hope; all that he had tried had come to nothing. And his hopes, plans, and scheme for marrying into wealth, through the hand of Mrs. Robinson when her husband passed on, were dashed when, in fact, Mr. Robinson did pass away, but Mrs. Robinson declined to see him again, or have anything further to do with him.

Following this, Branwell was a 'shattered being' and soon sank deeper into the use of alcohol and laudanum, his old 'stand-bys' to find comfort for his mental anguish. With its constant use, and lack of proper food and sustenance, he soon sank further into oblivion. In the end, he was hardly recognizable, even to his close friend Francis Grundy, and only two days before his death, he made his last venture out of doors to the Black Bull Inn. On

---

7   In addition to the three successive deaths of W. Weightman, Martha Taylor and Aunt Branwell, there was a fourth death of which Charlotte was to hear later. While in Brussels, they became friends of the Wheelwright girls from Yorkshire, four of whom were attending Pensionnat Heger at the same time as Charlotte and Emily. The family's youngest daughter, Julia, only seven years old, died of typhus fever in November, 1842, when Charlotte and Emily had returned home after Aunt Branwell's death.

Sunday morning, September 24th, 1848, he passed away[8] suddenly, much to the horrible grief of his father who could not be comforted. For Charlotte, Emily, and Anne, their only brother and youthful pride and joy of the family, was now gone. This was the first time since the loss of Maria and Elizabeth that they had lost a member of the 'firm four' who had been constant companions to one another since their births.

In a letter to W. S. Williams of Smith, Elder & Co., dated 29/10/1848, five days after Branwell's death and two days before his funeral, Anne Brontë wrote to him on behalf of her sister, Charlotte, who was ill herself. She said:

> My sister wishes me to thank you for your two letters, the receipt of which gave her much pleasure, though coming in a season of severe domestic affliction, which has so wrought upon her too delicate constitution as to induce a rather serious indisposition, that renders her unfit for the slightest exertion.

And although Charlotte was devastated by their loss, she explains in a letter to W.S. Williams, dated 02/10/1848, a day after Branwell's funeral, that his loss has affected her differently from the others. She clearly states:

> I do not weep from a sense of bereavement - there is no prop withdrawn, no consolation torn away, no dear companion lost - but for the wreck of talent, the ruin of promise, the untimely dreary extinction of what might have been a burning and a shining light.

During Branwell's final illness and death, Charlotte also came down with an illness, later diagnosed as 'bilious fever' which lingered on. This illness, and the anguish she suffered over Branwell's death, resulted in her being unable to continue on her second novel, *Shirley*, for the time being. In a letter, dated (?)18/10/1848, to W.S. Williams, she explains her delay:

> My book, alas! is laid aside for the present; both head and hand seem to have lost their cunning; imagination is pale, stagnant, mute. This incapacity chagrins me; sometimes I have a feeling of cankering care on the subject, but I combat it as well as I can; it does no good.

The funeral, held a week later on Sunday, October 1st, was a cold, wet, dreary day with Emily taking charge of arrangements. Following the funeral, Emily came down with a severe cold which only seemed to get worse. She never left the house again, and her rapid decline, outlined in Chapter Three, stunned everyone. She died on December 19th, 1848, and of all the family tragedies, it appears that Emily's death took the greatest toll on Charlotte, and she was never really the same person again. The first mention of Emily's cold and 'obstinate' cough are given in a letter to Ellen Nussey, dated 29/10/1848, and in

8   After Anne's death in 1849, in a letter to W.S. Williams, Charlotte claimed that 'consumption' had taken all five of her siblings, but Branwell's symptoms, and sudden death, are inconsistent with TB, and were more likely the result of complications from several, on-going illnesses.

another letter to W.S. Williams, dated 02/11/1848, Charlotte makes mention of a more serious 'slow inflammation of the lungs' but does not seem seriously alarmed at that point. This same letter shows how Emily's qualities, although 'peculiar' are the ones which make her the more endearing. Charlotte reveals her close attachment to her sister and says:

> When she is ill there seems to be no sunshine in the world for me; the tie of sister is near and dear indeed, and I think a certain harshness in her powerful, 'and' peculiar character only makes one cling to her more.

In a letter to Ellen Nussey, dated 29/10/1848, Charlotte, in a rare instance of candour, begins to show her occasional elements of doubt in her faith when the death of Branwell weighed heavily on her mind. She admits to Ellen:

> The late sad event has I feel made me more apprehensive than common - I cannot help feeling much depressed sometimes - I try to leave all in God's hands, and to trust in his goodness - but faith and resignation are difficult to practise under some circumstances.

The same letter also shows Charlotte's reluctance to form any close bond, implying that life on this Earth is tenuous at best. She says to Ellen, in reference to Harriet Heald's serious illness:

> ... she has been some years out of health now - these things make one <u>feel</u> as well as <u>know</u> that this world is not our abiding-place. We should not knit human ties too < fast > 'close' - or clasp human affections too fondly - they must leave us or we must leave them one day

In the letter of 07/11/1848, to George Smith, Charlotte mentions that "my dear sister Emily who is at present too ill to occupy herself with writing, or indeed with anything but reading" is, in fact, getting worse. And only five days later, on 12/11/1848, in a follow-up letter to George Smith, Charlotte alludes to Emily's declining health again saying, "I wish I could speak of my dear Sister as convalescent, but as yet her state inspires only anxiety" suggesting that her health is not improving, and simply deteriorating.

By November 23, 1848, in a letter to Ellen Nussey, Charlotte expresses, for the first time,' alarm' and a lack of hope. She describes Emily's illness to Ellen in these words:

> - she has not rallied yet - she is very ill: I believe if you were to see her your impression would be that there is no hope: a more hollow, wasted pallid aspect I have not beheld. The deep tight cough continues; the breathing after the least exertion is a rapid pant - and these symptoms are accompanied by pain in the chest and side.

And Charlotte now even considers, in this same letter, the possibility of Emily's demise which previously she did not believe. She confides to Ellen:

More than once have I been forced boldly to regard the terrible event of her loss as possible and even probable. But Nature shrinks from such thoughts - I think Emily seems the nearest thing to my heart in this world.

In subsequent letters to Ellen, and others, Charlotte simply indicates that Emily's health is in a downward spiral and that she refuses help of any kind whatsoever. Although Charlotte still clings to 'hope', Rev. Brontë is 'despondent', cannot be hopeful, and prepares for the worst. He is well aware of the symptoms of consumption, and has seen it all before, particularly in the cases of Maria and Elizabeth, his two, eldest daughters, who both died of it. Charlotte, however, still clings desperately to hope and is unable to 'renounce' it completely. As well, Emily refused all medicines and medical attention, and simply exacerbated the family's worries. In a desperate attempt to obtain some medical information to aid Emily, Charlotte wrote surreptitiously to a homeopathic physician, Dr. John Epps in London, via W. S. Williams of Smith, Elder & Co.

Charlotte's efforts were in vain, and Emily's rapid deterioration ended in death at approximately 2:00 P.M. on December 19th, 1848, and three days later, on December 22, she was laid to rest in the family vault of the church. And, on December 24th, Charlotte wrote an elegy for her beloved, deceased sister. The first stanza began with:

> My darling, thou wilt never know/The grinding agony of woe
>   That we have borne for thee.
> Thus may we consolation tear/E'en from the depth of our despair
>   And wasting misery.

On Christmas Day, 1848, in a letter to W.S. Williams, Charlotte once again indirectly questions God's purpose in taking such a talent as Emily in her 'prime'. Charlotte asks:

> ... I will not now ask why Emily was torn from us in the fullness of our attachment, rooted up in the prime of her own days in the promise of her powers - why her existence now lies like a field of green corn trodden down - like a tree in full bearing - struck at the root;...

Throughout the family's ordeal with Emily's illness, death and funeral, Charlotte was expected to be the stalwart person who would 'bear up' and keep up everyone's spirits. Rev. Brontë felt that if Charlotte 'failed', he, too, would 'sink', for he was now seventy-one years old, not in good health, and now Anne showed signs of illness, too. When the best doctor in the area, Dr. Teale from Leeds, arrived and made a diagnosis, the situation and prognosis was not good. Mr. Brontë and Charlotte now had a new crisis to face following two, recent and successive tragedies. Charlotte, needing support herself, wrote to Ellen Nussey on December 23rd, 1848, asking her to come for a short visit; Ellen arrived five days later on December 28th, and stayed for almost two weeks before returning home. She was there when Dr. Teale examined Anne and made his diagnosis.

Anne's decline in health was gradual at first, and letters to Ellen, W.S. Williams, and George Smith in early January and February of 1849, simply indicate the changes in her delicate health according to the changes in weather, which seemed to have an effect on her. In addition to the treatment advised by Dr. Teale, Charlotte contacted a consumptive specialist, Dr. John Forbes of London, for a second opinion. He concurred on every point of Dr. Teale, and agreed with the treatment he had prescribed; there was nothing now for Charlotte to do but 'watch' and 'wait'. In early February, in a letter to W.S. Williams dated 01/02/1849, Anne appears to be improving slightly. Charlotte reports:

> Consumption - I am aware - is a flattering malady - but certainly Anne's illness has of late assumed a less alarming character than it had in the beginning; the hectic is allayed - the cough gives a more frequent <respite> reprieve, Could I but believe she would live two years -

In a letter to Ellen Nussey, dated 16/02/1849, Charlotte again shows concern for Anne's failing health. She states:

> She continues very much in the same state - I trust not greatly worse - though she is becoming very thin - I fear it would be only self delusion to fancy her better -

And in a letter to W.S. Williams in a letter, dated 01/03/1849, Charlotte explains that she is too pre-occupied to continue on her manuscript for *Shirley*. She frets about the disease's threat to Anne's health, and its subsequent effect on herself and her writing. She laments:

> - Oh if Anne were well - if the void Death has left were a little closed up - if the dreary word - "<u>nevermore</u>"[9] - would cease sounding in my ears - I think I could yet do something! -

The worries of Anne's failing health were exacerbated by the depression which followed, and remained, after Emily's death. In a letter to Ellen Nussey, dated (?16)/03/1849, Charlotte admits to the 'depression' which Ellen observed in her past letters. She states:

> The feeling of Emily's loss does not diminish as time wears on - it often makes itself most acutely recognized - It brings too an inexpressible sorrow with [it] and then the future is dark

Throughout these tragedies, it has been oddly overlooked that Anne, the youngest, and the one her siblings thought the most delicate, was, in fact, the most stalwart of the Brontë children and did 'bear up' extremely well. She was truly resigned to her fate and

---

9   This is a direct reference to Edgar Allan Poe's poem, 'The Raven', and its recurring refrain which was as popular in Britain as it was in the U.S.A.

faced Death with a firm, courageous spirit. In a letter to Margaret Wooler, dated 24/03/ 1849, Charlotte outlines Anne's serious condition and declining health, and says:

> In Spirit she is resigned: at heart she is - I believe - a true Christian: She looks beyond this life - and regards her Home and Rest as elsewhere than on Earth.

And continuing on in the same letter, Charlotte relates her deep bereavement over Emily's loss, and her own deep depression and shock which have not abated, but, in fact, gotten worse. She admits:

> Yet I must confess that in the time which has elapsed since Emily's death there have been moments of solitary - deep - inert affliction far harder to bear - than those which immediately followed our loss -... - the desolate after feeling sometimes paralyzes.

In the early part of April, Anne wrote to Ellen Nussey asking if she would be willing to accompany her, and possibly Charlotte, to some 'sea-side' or 'inland watering place' where she could convalesce during the month of May. In the same letter, Anne declines an invitation to Brookroyd, Ellen's home, as being too intrusive on Ellen and her family in her present state. Anne hoped to improve her consumptive condition through the medicinal benefits of the fresh, clean, sea-air which had been prescribed by some doctors of the time. Anne is brave and states, "I have no horror of death", and pleads to be spared not just for Charlotte's and her father's sake but also because she has many things left to do in her life.

Charlotte wrote a follow-up letter to Ellen Nussey on 12/04/1849, in which it appears that she has resigned herself to Anne's ultimate fate and reveals her continued reliance on her religion and Faith. Without it, it appears that she would be unable to cope with the situation; she is also still haunted by Emily's death. She explains:

> If there 'were no' hope beyond this world - no eternity - no life to come - Emily's fate and that which threatens Anne would be heart-breaking. I cannot forget Emily's death-day; it becomes a more fixed - a darker, a more frequently occurring idea in my mind than ever; it was very terrible; she was torn conscious, panting, reluctant though resolute out of a happy life.

In a letter to W.S. Williams, dated four days later on 16/04/1849, Charlotte has not returned to her former self even though she says, "I should like to please my kind friends at Cornhill. To that end I wish my powers would come back - ". And in regards to her returning 'to the pen', she laments:

> I try to write now and then. The effort was a hard one at first. It renewed the terrible loss of last December strangely - Worse than useless did it seem to attempt to write what there no longer lived an "Ellis Bell" to read: the whole book with every hope founded on it, faded to vanity and vexation of spirit.

The last line suggests that they still wrote 'for one another', and without Emily there to read it, and partake in it, all seemed hopeless, useless, and without purpose, except vanity.

In late April and early May, final plans were being laid for Anne's journey to Scarborough, but Charlotte had severe reservations about the trip although she did not voice them openly, but in 'couched language'. The underlying tenet of her concerns revealed in various letters were her fears that Anne may die away from home during the trip. In a letter to W.S. Williams, dated 08/05/1849, she states that the trip to Scarborough is imminent, and also pleads for 'patience' from all at Smith, Elder & Co. for her next novel, *Shirley*, which was still in the works but not complete and badly 'stalled' due to the mental anguish and depression she was suffering after Branwell's and Emily's death, and Anne's acute illness which she was presently dealing with.

Although their trip was delayed one day to Thursday, May 24th, because Anne was too ill to travel on the scheduled departure date of Wednesday, May 23rd, they finally got under way after Ellen arrived from Leeds concerned about their welfare and wondering what had happened. Charlotte, Ellen, and Anne then proceeded to York where they stayed overnight at the George Hotel, visited York Minster one last time, and then continued on to Scarborough arriving there on the 25th. On Saturday, May 26th, they went out for a donkey cart ride on the beach, and Anne took the reins herself fearing that its driver would push the beast too hard. The next day after morning prayers and breakfast, they walked a little, and Anne sat near the beach while Charlotte and Ellen enjoyed the scenes nearby. The day ended with a spectacular, and unforgettable, sunset.

On Monday, after arising early and having a light breakfast, Anne sat in an easy chair. She was quiet and calm, and at about 11:00 A.M., she felt a 'change' come over her. A doctor was sent for but it was too late; death was imminent. She died several hours later at about 2:00 P.M. Ellen later added an account of Anne's death in her diary; she stated:

> So still, and hallowed, were her last hours and moments it was more like a translation[10] than death. There was no thought of assistance, none was needed.

After Anne's death, Charlotte wrote W.S. Williams two letters, six days apart, one on May 30th, and another on June 4th, in which she appeared to still be in a mild state of shock. Anne had just died and been buried, and Charlotte compares her death and its bereavement with that of Emily's five months earlier. They were perceived differently however, and Charlotte still is haunted by Emily's passing, the images of which keep coming back. She states:

> I could hardly let Emily go - I wanted to hold her back then - and I want her back hourly now - Anne, from her childhood seemed preparing for an early death - Emily's spirit seemed strong enough to bear her to fulness of years -

---

10 Ellen may have meant to use the word 'transition'.

In yet another letter to W. S. Williams, dated 13/06/1849, Charlotte expresses her dread at returning home from Bridlington to Haworth after Anne's death; she can only look forward to it with apprehension and solitude. She writes:

> - it will be solitary - I cannot help dreading the first experience of it - the first aspect of the empty rooms which once were tenanted by those dearest to my heart - and where the shadow of their last days must now - I think - linger for ever.

Upon her return to Haworth on June 21st, three weeks after Anne's death, one of the first things that Charlotte did in her mournful state was to write a poem commemorating Anne's life. The first stanza reads:

> There's little joy in life for me,/ And little terror in the grave; I've lived the parting hour to see/ Of one I would have died to save.

The remaining stanzas simply show her sense of loss and despair. She was now all alone, and this was the first time that she returned home without it being a pleasant experience. In a letter to Ellen Nussey, dated 23/06/1849, she wrote about her feelings on returning home. She said:

> ... this time joy was not to be the sensation. I felt that the house was all silent - the rooms were all empty -... the sense of desolation and bitterness took possession of me - the agony that was to be undergone - and was not to be avoided came on -

and she went on to mention that evenings, the time when they used to gather in the sitting room,[11] were the worst time of the day. Charlotte remembered the times they spent there together discussing their writings; she reflected:

> Now I sit by myself - necessarily I am silent. - I cannot help thinking of their last days - remembering their sufferings and what they said and did and how they looked in mortal affliction -

For the remainder of her short life, Charlotte appeared to be haunted and affected by her siblings' deaths. The parsonage was empty and lonely, and no longer did she have the friendship and kinship of her siblings. They were all gone now except for herself and her father. Being from such a close-knit family, the trauma and anxiety of their separation was extremely painful. It was not something which she could put aside easily; they had been there for almost all her life, and now they were gone forever.

In the years that followed, in addition to completing her last two novels, *Shirley* (1849), and *Villette* (1853), Charlotte visited her friends often and travelled to London more frequently to partake of its culture and meet other writers. These frequent trips away from home may simply have been a conscious, or unconscious, effort to escape the solitude and gloom of the parsonage, her home, which was once filled with the joyful

---

11 Also called the 'dining room'.

laughter of a large, cohesive family. Now it was a house of loneliness, despair, silence, and memories of better and happier days.

Five years later, Charlotte was married to Rev. A.B. Nicholls, and experienced some months of extreme happiness and joy, but shortly, that too was gone. In her 38th year, after only nine months of 'wedded bliss', Charlotte died and was buried in Haworth Old Church along with other members of her family. And so ended the Brontë legacy of writers; the literary giants of Yorkshire were all finally laid to rest.

24

EMERGING FEMINISM

No analysis of the Brontë novels would be complete without at least a superficial look at their underlying purpose and their emerging feminist views which clashed directly with the strongly upheld patriarchal system of the day. Probably the most interesting and effective critique ever written on the works of the Brontës, which reveals not only an inner driving force to write but also 'concealed forces', was put forth by authors Sandra M. Gilbert and Susan Gubar in their detailed analysis entitled, *The Madwoman in the Attic: The Woman Writer and the Nineteenth Century Literary Imagination*. Their work exposes an influence which began to 'stir' in the Brontës, and other intelligent female writers of the 19th C., who recognized and understood societal and cultural forces at work and responsible for their plight in a tightly-controlled patriarchal society.

They contend, with almost undeniable support, that all four of Charlotte Brontë's novels and Emily Brontë's *Wuthering Heights* have 'concealed plots', all of which are driven by an up-welling of rebellion brought about by the 'place' assigned to them in Victorian society. Their literary efforts indicate not only a 'surface story' which can be enjoyed by a superficial reader but also a deeper, hidden, and underlying message and story questioning the principles of their society which 'traps' and 'enslaves' their gender. These Victorian strictures limited their contributions to society and made them submissive, subservient, second-class citizens whose sole contributions were to be nothing more than housewives, tea-servers, and mothers, in marriage. As well, these limited options for women gave them no outlet for their creative ambitions and talents other than sewing, painting, drawing, or as teachers and governesses.

Victorian society in the 19th C. was strictly patriarchal in all its facets. The church, government, politics, law, and literature were all derivatives of a patriarchal past which held firmly in the times of the Brontës. Creative, inquisitive, and intelligent female minds which had the inclination to rebel were either held firmly in check by the 'powers that be', were intimidated into acceptance, simply capitulated after futile attempts to escape, or took the 'path of least resistance'. But for some like Mary Wollstonecraft, her daughter Mary Shelley, Jane Austen, and Charlotte and Emily Brontë, 'submission' was out of the question. They were among the emerging feminists of the 19th C. who meant to challenge the archaic and untenable beliefs in, and adherence to, male supremacy.

As voracious, precocious, and intelligent readers, it was soon evident to the young Brontës that society did not favour their gender, and their questioning minds soon rebelled against these inequities. Born into a clerical family, and their father a clergyman, the Brontë children were first exposed to male domination in the Church of England. From the Archbishop down to the lowly curates, the church was directed and controlled solely by men, and being constantly exposed to many of the vicars and curates who visited the Parsonage on a regular basis, it was evident that some of them were of very average intelligence, and quite unimpressive. In the Catholic church, the situation was known to be even more oppressive, and it was viewed almost as a 'papist mafia'.

In addition to the make-up of the church was the make-up of the Bible which they studied at home and in the church. Man was made in the image of God, a male; Christ was God's son; the twelve apostles were male; man was created first and woman second as a companion and adjunct to man. All of this placed women in a secondary and submissive role to man, a place of inferiority to their 'superiors'. As a result, women's minds were thought not to be equal to that of man's, and not of sufficiently sound judgment which would allow them to hold office in the church, government or public administration, the professions, or to contribute to literature. Knowing that these widely-held beliefs were completely untenable, it soon became a driving force for a small but determined group of 19th C women writers including the Brontës.

In law, women were held in equal contempt since the laws of primogeniture automatically disinherited them by giving property and assets to the eldest male of the family, and forced females to be dependent on their male siblings and near relatives for assistance, and an 'existence', usually through an annuity. Should the male inheritor become dissipated, or lose his inheritance through bad or careless investments, as sometimes was the case, female members of the family would lose their annuities, become destitute, and be forced to face the vagaries of an unforgiving and hostile world which they were not prepared to face either literally or figuratively.

As a form of creative expression, and a medium through which they could challenge patriarchal society, the Brontës looked to writing. In their early years, they did so as a form of self-entertainment and an outlet for their creative talents. Their mother and father had done so before them, they were voracious readers, and besides walks onto the lonely moors, they channeled their creative energies and imagination into miniature books of poetry and prose featuring Angrian and Gondalian tales for themselves, and each other.

As they grew older and tried to make their way in life by writing, certain realities of the times faced them. When Charlotte wrote to Southey and Wordsworth, she received a kind reply with muted praise for her talents and efforts but was 'warned off' writing as a career for females. She was advised to stick to the traditional roles of women, and, of course, as these responsibilites grew, she would have no time for writing. Later, to cover their role as female writers, Charlotte, Emily, and Anne adopted androgynous names to confuse publishers and readers alike. In their first attempt at writing (*Poems*,1846), this was not enough to help them get started. Their future lay in prose, not poetry, and when their first novels were successful, their enigmatic names kept readers and critics guessing as to whether they were male or female.

The discouragement by Southey and Wordsworth to become writers perhaps, and probably, had the opposite effect and simply stirred their desire even more and raised their angst and ire against the patriarchal society which governed and circumscribed their lives. All of the forces and controls in law, government, administration, society, and literature which allowed a patriarchal society to exist and perpetuate itself appeared to be based on a universal misogyny. As Charlotte and her sisters matured into young ladies, Victorian patriarchal writing and poetry, and the misogyny upon which it was based, became underlying 'anti-forces' in the writing careers of Charlotte and Emily, and a source of deep-seated discontent which they sought to amend.

Nowhere in English literature could they find a more shining example of patriarchal 'superiority' than in the Bible and the origins of Christianity, upon which their very beliefs were founded from early childhood. A rebellion against their own religious be-liefs would be a 'rebellion' against their own father who taught and espoused these very beliefs. And nowhere in literature could they find a more stinging example of their culture's misogyny than in John Milton's epic poem, *Paradise Lost*, which describes the downfall of mankind precipitated by Eve's disobedience, giving rise to both Sin and Death for mankind. Therefore, nowhere in their lives could they find female role models who were sources of 'good' nor could they foresee any hope whatsoever for their gender. This misogyny and woman's plight in Victorian times became a recurrent theme in Charlotte's novels.

Although the Brontë children adored their father, he was both a product and a prime example of the patriarchal society in which they lived, and he was not a proponent of women's rights. Also, John Milton was one of his favourite poet's, but Emily in her quiet, rebellious, but brilliant, fashion sought to oppose, and even rectify, the misogy-nous 'underpinnings' of the patriarchal society upon which Milton expounded, and which her father espoused. Throughout their book, *Madwoman...*, authors Gilbert and Gubar point out the "Miltonic overtones" which can be found in the various Brontë works but most evident, to a discriminate reader, in *Wuthering Heights*.

According to the two authors, *Wuthering Heights* is about man's central 'fall', much like Milton's *Paradise Lost*, except that the situation is reversed with Catherine Earnshaw falling from an apparent hell, the 'hell' of Wuthering Heights, to the 'paradise' of Thrushcross Grange. But, in fact, this fall into paradise proves to be her undoing and her true 'hell' on earth. While at Wuthering Heights, Catherine was in an euphoric, 'natural' state of bliss, her 'heaven', with her alter-ego, Heathcliff. Her ascent into the cultural 'heaven' of Thrushcross Grange and the physical love of Edgar Linton is not the 'heaven' she expects it to be. The end result is a descent into the hell of madness, and the only 'heaven' she can now hope to achieve is death and a re-uniting in the 'hereafter' with her true love, Heathcliff.

In effect, Emily Brontë seeks not the origins of man but the origins of 'woman', and not in Heaven but in woman's ascent into heaven from hell. From what little we do know about Emily, she appears to have been more of a Pantheist, with Mother Nature as her 'god', than a strict believer of a theistic, Christian 'God', as she was taught to believe in from early childhood. Such a belief may have been spawned and nurtured by patriarchal society and culture in which she lived, patriarchal poetry and prose of her time, and the apparent universal misogyny which they encountered in English literature and particularly in Milton's work. In his own life, Milton, perhaps bitter over his own circumstances and blindness, was a domestic tyrant who ruled with a 'heavy hand' over his daughters, and hated women in general.

Emily Brontë was also influenced in her writing by another of her favourite writers, Byron. As an outcast in exile for his non-conformist views, ways, and lifestyle, he perhaps gave rise to Wuthering Heights' demon and devil, anti-hero Heathcliff who is Byronic in looks, words, actions, and deeds. At other times, the conflicts and conversations, particularly the most dramatic scene in the kitchen of Thrushcross Grange is typical of Shakespearian high-drama. And, the opening of Catherine Linton's coffin after Edgar Linton's death is Mary Shelley's story style at its gothic best. Emily was not hesitant in occasionally borrowing from different styles, genres, and generations, if it served her purpose.

The authors Gilbert and Gubar interpret *Wuthering Heights* roughly in the following manner as a story of "origins and renewals" carefully worked out by Emily Brontë. The story bears anti-Miltonic themes which counter and re-interpret his mythological understandings of the origins of man. In it, Catherine Earnshaw was a daughter of Nature, the original 'Mother' who 'fell' into decline by being enticed by earthly, 'heavenly' culture through her meeting with the Lintons. Once absorbed into 'culture', she and Heathcliff became 'fragmented' with their "fierce, primordial selves disappear(ing) into nature," (*Madwoman...*, Ch.8, p.303) and Catherine adopted the 'cultural world' of the Lintons. (For both Catherine Earnshaw and Emily Brontë, this was the real, 'living hell'.) The teachers and facilitators of this culture simply perpetuate the patriarchal society in which they live. Also, this society can only be successful if it manages to aggressively remove the "rebelliously Satanic, irrational, and 'female' representatives of nature" (*Madwoman...*, Ch.8, p.303)

After Edgar Linton's proposal, Catherine's decline and 'fall' are swift. Heathcliff's return, after a three-year absence, re-ignites her rebellious nature and she rebels against her 'imprisonment' of marriage and the suppression of 'self'. When Catherine cannot recognize herself in the mirror, the reader realizes that she has also lost her identity. Her feeling of powerlessness and rage at her inability to alter her future and her situation leads Catherine to realize that her only escape is death. And shortly after the birth of her daughter, she dies. This concludes the first half of the novel.

Without 'his' Catherine, Heathcliff swiftly unravels and becomes 'monstrous' and diabolical and exacts revenge on those who stand in his way. He attempts to subvert the legitimate order of succession and through his manipulation removes both Hindley, and later his own son Linton, to obtain ownership of Wuthering Heights and Thrushcross

Grange. With the growth and solidification of the relationship between Hareton and the young Catherine Linton, Heathcliff sees that his end is near. Their relationship reminds him of the fleeting heavenly paradise he once had, but which escaped him, and when Edgar Linton dies and Heathcliff opens her coffin, he is further driven to join her. Only then will he enjoy his 'paradise'. Heathcliff now sees young Catherine's relationship with Hareton as "a re-telling of the story the 'right' way" (*Madwoman...*, Ch.8, p.301), that is, the way it might have been for himself and Catherine Earnshaw had she not married Edgar Linton.

In *The Professor*, according to the authors Gilbert and Gubar (*Madwoman...*) they see Charlotte Brontë assuming the role of an 'impersonator', William Crimsworth, in order to investigate the state of women in 19th C. England and patriarchal society. William Crimsworth, the narrator of the story, attempts to reveal the 'trapped' and 'buried' nature of women's lives from a sympathetic, male point of view.[1] This story, as do her other novels, contains women 'seeking escape' from the dreary life set out for them in Victorian society. In Charlotte's early childhood writing of Angrian tales, this was easily overcome by the use of male identities and narratives complying with conformities of the day, and which Charlotte employs in her first, full-fledged novel. This was also adopted in order to evade the gender identity of the author since female authors were not yet universally accepted.

In a nutshell, the novel delves into the lives of females as disinherited members of a patriarchal society. William Crimsworth, as the second son of the family, is also familiar with the feeling of disinheritance. As a disaffected, disinherited member of society, William Crimsworth provides a 'platform' from which Charlotte can launch her anger, and explore the anguish of the dispossessed. William Crimsworth can do this with sympathy since his situation differs so little from that of a woman's. As one who has lost his rights to inheritance, he, too, is highly limited in the careers available to him.

From his 'platform', Crimsworth's sympathetic stance attacks the Victorian idea of the 'perfect lady', accepted images of women, and their accepted, and expected, roles in society. He also expounds on the tyrannies and hostilities of his own patriarchal household, especially that of his brother, and the suffering of those within. This may reflect Charlotte's feelings about her own family and household where her father was in 'firm control', and her younger brother Branwell who became more tyrannical and despotic as he grew older. In William's case, he finally rebelled against the tyranny of his older brother Edward and took a whip to him; such is his symbolic retaliation against feelings of restraint and restriction, enclosure, and 'burial'.

William's flight and escape symbolizes his new-found freedom away from the imprisonment of his tyrannical and despotic brother and family. From his position as a teacher at a Belgian boys' school, Crimsworth is able to 'objectively' describe the female students in the neighbouring girls' school. His description and sketches of the Belgian girls are not exactly flattering, and he points out their negative qualities. The school's curriculum in his view is simply a means by which females are indoctrinated and held in check for their subservient roles, and not for creative contributions to 19th C. society.

---

1   For many critics, this feature was the book's major, inherent flaw which doomed it.

Such studies and curriculum simply perpetuate the status quo and will not advance the cause of women.

Coupled with the subservient nature of women is also the 'monster side' with 'monstrous traits' such as vanity, duplicity, scheming, flirtation, and lying, all instilled and used to advance their way in the patriarchal society in which they live and must exist. All of these characteristics, traits, and qualities are adopted because they conform to what patriarchal society expects of them. These qualities are best portrayed in Zoraide Reuter who exhibits all of these characteristics simply to advance her own cause and position. In *Villette,* the character is re-named Mme Beck who displays the same characteristics, and both are meant to portray Mme Heger in real life whom Charlotte disliked and distrusted.

Throughout the novel William Crimsworth throws out pieces of wisdom showing how he despises many of the qualities typically admired in a woman by men in Victorian society. This, of course, is Charlotte's rebellious 'voice' against such stereotyped views which she wishes to challenge and change. Charlotte also makes her views known through the character of Frances Henri who is thin, pale, and small, much like the author herself, and like the characters 'Jane Eyre' and 'Lucy Snowe' in successive novels. Frances Henri makes her 'way' through the novel in a slow, plodding, unassuming, and inobtrusive way, and in the end is successful. Her quiet, yet deliberate, manner may almost be categorized as passive-aggressive.

Both William Crimsworth and Frances Henri have suffered suppression, injustice, poverty, isolation, and 'orphanhood' as well as hostility. They are both intelligent, intellectual, and idealistic with 'designs' and desires to change their world of oppression, despotism, and slavishness in a patriarchal society. Frances Henri in particular must learn to cope with a world which frowns on female desire to improve or better oneself and to be competitive with their male counterparts. It is a vicious world which suppresses female endeavour and richly rewards tyranny and hypocrisy against reason itself.

Coming from a Swiss-English family, Frances represents her bifurcated background and fragmented self who does not become whole again until she unites with William Crimsworth and returns to England with him. In marriage, William appears to have found himself a wife who does not exactly fit the Victorian mould and ideal but fits with *his* ideal of a woman suitable to him. Frances, on the other hand, appears to 'back-slide' into the traditional feminine roles expected of her as a wife during the evening, but during the day she is a modern, expressive, dynamic, and self-directing woman with a 'wilfulness' which William would like to curb, contain, and curtail.

There is no doubt that the novel *Jane Eyre* caught readers off-guard when it was first published in 1847. Critics were quick to condemn it for its perceived courseness and sexuality, but there was also an underlying rebellious attitude which was seen as highly anti-Christian. For a woman to refuse to submit to her 'social destiny' in Victorian times was both sacrilegious and 'heretical', and to seek equality of rights for women was the sign of an "unregenerate and undisciplined spirit" (Elizabeth Rigby, *Quarterly Review*, 1848).

In *Jane Eyre*, the authors Gilbert and Gubar (*Madwoman...*) once again reveal Charlotte Brontë's feminist 'messages' of starvation, repression, rage, and rebellion in a plot which is far more open and obvious than the complex and hidden ones of *The Professor*. From the outset, the story is eminently clear with a progression of Jane Eyre's life from its unhappy beginnings to a happy ending. *Jane Eyre* once again portrays a story of injustice and 'boundaries' which makes the protagonist feel 'trapped' and 'enclosed' and fill her with a desire to escape. In her journey through life in a patriarchal society, she successively feels oppression, starvation, madness, isolation, and 'coldness' to varying degrees. Hers is a lonely, solitary struggle through a maze of physical, emotional, and psychological obstacles which she eventually overcomes through her own perseverance.

From the opening, we see Jane Eyre as a small, weak, plain, orphaned child who is excluded from her adopted family, and one who is oppressed, sad, and dejected. Her situation only becomes worse as she is tyrannized by an older step-brother. Jane Eyre was angry, frustrated, and felt the pangs of injustice at the hands of a patriarchal society at an early age. She was alone, isolated, vulnerable, without 'clear standing' anywhere, but she had pride and was defiant. Gilbert and Gubar liken her tale to that of John Bunyan's *Pilgrim's Progress* with a succession of flight, escape, starvation, and near madness repeated throughout the novel. Her initiation into the injustice is through John Reed, but she has yet to meet the Rev. Brocklehurst and St. John Rivers.

John Reed is successful in his tyranny over Jane Eyre. This results in her 'expulsion' from Gateshead and her second encounter with patriarchal tyranny and injustice at the hands of Rev. Brocklehurst, the 'black pillar' of Lowood School. Here tyranny, deprivation, and oppression run rampant over the poor, orphaned girls who are at the mercy of the school and its 'benevolent' founder. At Lowood, Jane Eyre meets two persons, Miss Temple and Helen Burns, who influence her life through their kindness, but she could not adopt their ladylike, passive approach, Helen Burn's religious resignation, or Miss Temple's continued suppression of her feelings. If anything, Rev. Brocklehurst fires up even more rebellion within her and she redoubles her determination to succeed. Following eight years of repression, Jane moves on to the next phase of her life.

After leaving Lowood, Jane Eyre accepts the position of governess to a small child at Thornfield Hall. Gilbert and Gubar point out the deep-seated and symbolic meanings of Thornfield as her 'crown of thorns', like Christ, and Bertha Rochester as representative of Jane Eyre's hidden, buried rage. In this case, the rage is confined to rooms in the third floor attic, and Rochester's secret wife is representative of Jane's 'secret self'. Grace Poole represents not only a 'pool of mystery' but the "dark 'pool' of the woman's behavior" (*Madwoman...*, Ch.10, p.351), representing the mystery of Jane Eyre's own life, and perhaps also the key to unlocking it. And, the attic itself becomes the 'focus' and 'ignition point' for all of Jane's pent-up emotions, problems, rebellion, and rage.

After the entry of Edward Rochester into the story, Jane Eyre, a poor, plain governess, begins to interject her own personal qualities and elements into the 'mix', and this is where the real story begins. At once we see the clash of character and social classes and the barriers which by convention keep them apart. Slowly those barriers dissipate but not before a series of events depict the social 'distance' between them, or at least expected of them. It is here that the author, Charlotte Brontë, shows her anger and rage at the dictates of a society which keeps them apart.

Although Rochester and Jane Eyre are master and servant, they are 'equals' in other ways from their first meeting. Rochester's intimate confidences to Miss Eyre and his casual association with a lowly governess aroused the ire of Victorian critics. He was middle-aged and rich, although brooding, while she was young, small, plain, poor, and rebellious; neither was handsome. Rochester immediately recognized in her something completely different from all the females he had known before. She had 'power', soul, and an innate strength of character, which he himself lacked and needed, even though men were expected to be strong 'masters'.

Jane sees through his facade and his character weaknesses. Rochester's charades and trickery are perhaps nothing more than a 'covering up' of inadequacies, or a means of obtaining 'power' and advantage over females, or even a sign of his own insecurities. His only 'power' and 'advantage' over Jane Eyre is his own experience and carnal knowledge, whereas Jane is a young virgin and completely inexperienced. As their relationship grows and they are engaged to be married, he begins to treat her like a new 'toy' and 'plaything'. Jane is unaware that through his age and his experience, he is exploiting her youth and inexperience, and being her 'patriarch'.

Jane does not see marriage in the traditional sense but Rochester does. This simply invokes her ire and rebellion at his and society's expectations. Her lonely pilgrimage through life has not prepared her to be a submissive, Victorian wife and mother; she expects to meet Rochester 'head on', and on equal terms. This cannot be as long as Bertha exists and is married to Rochester, and Jane's disturbing dreams are a prelude to the unraveling of their relationship. The unresolved problems between them will not allow a union on those equal terms which Jane so dearly cherishes.

Ultimately, Jane's goal of independence and equality with Rochester are elusive and difficult to obtain. For her small size, Jane is brave, indomitable, and irrepressible although fighting the battle alone occasionally takes its toll. According to authors Gilbert and Gubar, Bertha Mason Rochester is Jane's "dark double" who acts out Jane's own hidden anxieties and suppressed, unconscious desire to destroy Thornfield, a symbol of Rochester's masculinity and power, and of patriarchy itself. And, in the end, Bertha not only carries out Jane's secret desires but also destroys herself in the process removing the final barrier to their union. Rochester's injuries, the loss of a hand and near total blindness, and his state of helplessness brings them to a point of equality where, in fact, Rochester is now dependent on Jane rather than vice versa.

Before her final re-union with Rochester, Jane suffers more loneliness, isolation, separation, hunger, and near starvation after her 'escape' and flight from Rochester and Thornfield and wanderings on the moor. Once again, as many women in a patriarchal society, she found herself homeless, without assets, with no place to go, and assuming a false name; she was saved at the 'last minute' by discovery by the Rivers family. Once fully recovered, she finds herself again the subject of petty tyrannies at the hands of St. John Rivers, as well as pressures and coercions to marry him for the sake of Christian charity and the fulfilment of missionary work abroad. If her severance from Rochester and Thornfield served a purpose, it was to finally bring Jane to maturity and find her true self, and rightful place, in the world. And finally, St. John Rivers discovery of her true identity, and the inheritance which it entails, made her a truly independent person on a financial and economic par with Rochester. This now guarantees her with 'social equality' as well.

Jane is then forced to face a dilemma and the discrepancy of two ways of life. St. John Rivers offers her a life of toil and hardship and promises little, but accepting his offer would mean compromising the very principles and beliefs which her pilgrimage was meant to achieve. By becoming Mrs. St. John Rivers, Jane would have to betray her own nature and constantly give in to restraint, patriarchal domestic dominance, and the slavish demands of the stiff, cold St. John Rivers, all of which she staunchly opposes. It would also mean foregoing the equality she so eagerly sought in marriage; St. John Rivers' stern and dictatorial ways would never entertain such a thought. The fact that she rejects his offer is a testament to the strength of her character, her determination, and the near achievement of all her 'pilgrimage goals'.

The retracing of her steps to Thornfield, and then Ferndean, conclude Jane's pilgrimage and union with Rochester. Finding Thornfield destroyed, she finally makes her way to Ferndean where she finds Rochester blind and crippled. Now, in a new and remote setting, and under new circumstances for both, Rochester and Jane are able to unite in equality and equanimity. Away from the trappings of a restrictive, patriarchal system, and with the final barrier (Bertha) to their marriage gone, their love and union can flourish and blossom without the restrictions of an oppressive society.

Charlotte's novel *Shirley* has essentially the same plot elements as those in *The Professor* and *Jane Eyre* but this time hunger of the oppressed worker and the down-trodden is inextricably tied to the 'hunger' of women for a relevant and purposeful life and place in English society in the 19th C. The element of 'hunger' of the workers and that of women striving for recognition is interwoven throughout the novel. If any reader wondered at the sex of the author, Currer Bell, that question is clearly answered and 'identified' here, particularly in Chapter 20, where Caroline Helstone makes her famous speech to the "Men of England!" and "Men of Yorkshire!" It clearly draws attention to the plight of women in Victorian society and leaves no doubt about the intent of the originator.

An earlier reference to 'Milton's Eve' in *Shirley* (Ch.18) also leads the reader to believe that the author is a woman. Shirley cautions Caroline that "... we are alone; we may speak what we think" which implies that her question about Milton's *Paradise Lost* (*Shirley*, Ch. 8, p. 240) would sound heretical to male ears. She says:

> Milton was great; but was he good? His brain was right; how was his heart? He saw heaven; he looked down on hell. He saw Satan, and Sin his daughter, and Death their horrible offspring.

And later in the same paragraph she adds, "Milton tried to see the first woman; but, Cary, he saw her not". Such an attack on Milton, and his patriarchal view of society where women occupied a spot near the bottom rung of the ladder, leaves no doubt as to where Charlotte stood on the subject, and reveals her misgivings about the great 17th C. author.

Shirley is a 'woman's woman' who has the strength of character and integrity which defines a person of outstanding quality. By her very position of power and independence, she is not about to be 'manhandled' by the men about her who would, in fact, like to control her. Her free-thinking and independent-mindedness is completely beyond their control, much to their dissatisfaction. On the other hand, Robert Moore is shown to be weak, ineffectual, and a somewhat unscrupulous, unprincipled male who foregoes his promising relationship with Caroline Helstone to pursue Shirley for the purpose of an 'economic union' to shore-up his failing business. The sterling qualities of Shirley, both moral and ethical, are demonstrated by her refusal of his offer, and, therefore, the negative qualities of Robert Moore are brought sharply into contrast.

Other males in the novel come out equally badly as poor examples of the species in19th C. Victorian society. Besides the three curates who reveal less than admirable qualities about themselves as 'gentlemen' and 'men of the cloth', Hiram Yorke and Rev. Helstone stand out for particular criticism. The former is a proponent and 'hell-raiser' for various injustices, as perceived by himself, whereas the latter is a 'hell-raiser' and defender of the status quo. Neither one comes across as an admirable character as compared to either Shirley or Caroline, and both were pursuers of the same young lady, Mary Cave. Although Rev. Helstone 'won' her affections, Mary was the ultimate 'loser', dying soon after their marriage where she found even more loneliness, isolation, and desolation than ever before.

Caroline, in her soft, quiet way, goes about her business, achieves what she ultimately desires and is not afraid to criticize the man she loves, Robert Moore, for his harshness to mill workers. His treatment of her and the workers eventually comes back to haunt him and almost costs him his life. Caroline is looking for her 'place' in the world, and she despises the treatment of women in her time where they are treated as 'chattels', like other acquired property, or as mere adjuncts to their husbands lives. She eventually comes to the conclusion that all men are "selfish", and to combat her feelings of loneliness and helplessness, and 'deflect' her ineffectiveness, she duplicates Miss Ainley's example and devotes all her energies to hard work and religion.

Caroline idolizes Shirley for her freedom and independence and wishes the same for herself. Through her she recognizes that the 'root cause' of women's tribulation is their dependence on men and the system of patriarchy which contributes to their 'slavery' and 'confinement'. Caroline would like to show some semblance of independence by becoming a governess, but her family and friends think it a degradation, and 'unworthy' of a lady. Without marriage into a family of equal bearing and status, her prospects are bleak. Only Shirley seems to have broken her chains of bondage; she is an Eve - a Titan - not Milton's Eve, but "Jehovah's daughter, as Adam was His son" (*Shirley*, Ch. 18, p. 241). Eve and Adam are on equal terms without subservience one to the other, but Shirley's vision of Eve as Mother of mankind differs from the traditional, 'Miltonic view'. She refuses to enter the church and responds to Caroline, "... I will stay out here with my mother Eve, in these days called Nature. I love her - undying, mighty being!" (*Shirley*, Ch. 18, p. 241). Shirley sees Eve not as the Biblical Eve but as an Omnipotent, powerful force, quite equal to any male counterpart, and whose future generations will "bring forth a Messiah" (*Shirley*, Ch. 18, p. 240).

Shirley defies all the stereotypical images men of the 19th C. had of Victorian women. Besides being independent and powerful, she did not conform to the false heroines created by male authors of the period. Shirley was not a monstrous, aggressive seductress with deviant, crafty guile hoping to tempt an unsuspecting male into her web of sin, but she was an astute business woman, and full participant of capitalism, bettering her male counterparts with her intelligence, skill, and knowledge. And, although Shirley was generally treated with respect, male counterparts bore her a hidden grudge, perhaps spurred by an injured male pride, and male workers resented her because of the perceived anomalous power and authority she wielded over them. But when the pitched battle of owners and workers broke out at Hollow's Mill, both Shirley and Caroline were forced to sit on the sidelines and were relegated to simple 'observers', as women of the Victorian period often were. As 'observers', they were able to provide the reader with a 'running commentary' on this historic fight which symbolizes not only the exploited worker of the newly-emerged Industrial Revolution but also the hungry desire of women to battle their oppression which binds them down, holds them back, and keeps them in their 'place'.

With her rejection by Robert Moore, Caroline Helstone becomes lovesick and then highly discontented. As her real mother, Mrs. Pryor (unknown to Caroline), with 'prior knowledge' of life and love advises her daughter that neither marriage nor a job as a governess will relieve the symptoms of boredom and loneliness that she is experiencing. In Caroline's dramatic monologue to the "Men of England!" and the "Men of Yorkshire!", she places the blame squarely on their shoulders also adding that only they hold the key to unlocking their chains and granting them freedom. On the other hand, Rose Yorke[2] responds that women are their own jailors, allow these conditions to exist and continue, and live within the constrictions set out for them by their male patriarchs. Caroline is living proof of Rose Yorke's contention since she had chosen to bury her 'talents'[3], suppress her feelings, and accept patriarchal supremacy and domination.

Although Charlotte Brontë began this novel with radical intentions, it 'fizzled out' in the end and became a traditional, literary romance with a happy ending. Shirley, who defied literary, sexual images as a wealthy, independent business woman, and who appears to be headed for complete female independence and freedom from male subjugation and domination, succumbs to Louis Moore, brother of Robert, her tutor, master, lover, hero, and 'keeper' by the end of the novel. Caroline does exactly the same when Robert Moore 'realizes' his mistake, returns to his senses, and once again successfully pursues her. The ending, therefore, takes an unexpected twist and 'turn' and is somewhat of a betrayal, a 'let down', and a 'sell out' to the feminist principles Charlotte appears to

---

2   Rose Yorke was Mary Taylor in real life who lived her life by her own rules, was 'beholden to no one', and lived free of any restrictions/constrictions imposed by society. She, in fact, epitomized the 'free woman' that Charlotte Brontë only talked and wrote about and that Caroline Helstone wanted to be.

3   In this case 'talents' has a double meaning. It refers not only to her mental and physical skills but also 'money' as in the Biblical parable.

promote throughout the length of the novel. Both Shirley and Caroline submit and 'sink' into the traditional roles of housewives and dependents in the hands of their husbands in a patriarchal, Victorian society, and Charlotte appears to submit to the literary conventions and dictates of writers of the day. The ending and message would have been far more powerful if Charlotte had pursued a different ending, one which corresponded more closely to the ones she set out to tackle at the opening of the novel.

To mitigate the change of heart and the intent of Shirley, and that of the author, Shirley qualifies his 'conquest' by indicating that it was more of a submission on her part than a victory on his. Also, any student of the life of Charlotte Brontë must also take into account that Charlotte herself was now in the earliest stages of her own relationship with Arthur Bell Nicholls when she wrote this novel and the statements, "Louis would never have learned to rule if she had not ceased to govern", and "The incapacity of the sovereign had developed the powers of the premier" (*Shirley*, Ch. 37, p. 476), may have been either a subliminal message, or even an open one, to both Rev. Nicholls, and her father, about her own inner feelings. Her views on love, marriage, and equality within that partnership differed widely from the prevailing Victorian view.

In Charlotte's last novel, *Villette*, her concerns and personal pessimism regarding the fate of 'woman' in a patriarchal society appears to hit its lowest depths and anxiety. This is probably consistent with her own personal, loveless situation and the deep loneliness and sadness she experienced at the loss of her beloved siblings. It is also Charlotte's final attempt, through fiction, to deal with her unrequited love for M Heger in Brussels, an event in her life which haunted her for many years, and possibly to the very end. Life for her appeared to hold out no glimmers of happiness, and little hope. Lucy Snowe, the protagonist of *Villette*, is an 'extension' and an 'expression' of that hopelessness. She is, like Charlotte Brontë herself, truly alone in the world, and her name itself suggests a cold, lonely, terrifying existence filled with anxiety and despair.

Authors Gilbert and Gubar see in Lucy Snowe a female with a "buried life", not the literary one which Romantic poets and prose writers celebrated and romanticized, but a real one of loneliness, homelessness, poverty, unattractiveness, sexual discrimination, and the stereotype-casting (of women) which make them feel victimized. For them, their 'buried life' is a suppressed life from oppressive forces of a patriarchal, Victorian society. The celebrated authors and writers of the day, almost all male, simply did not understand the 'internalization' that women suffered as a result of their 'lot' in life. It was impossible for them to understand because they were part of the oppressive forces and part of the problem.

Romantic writers like Wordsworth revelled in their Freudian 'buried life' and sought escapism through poetic searches for a 'Lucy' of their dreams, whereas for Lucy Snowe, her life was 'buried' in a reality she dealt with every day as a matter of course, and could not escape. Through the 'parodic' eyes of Lucy, the reader obtains a new and direct view of solitary women in a Victorian society dealing with almost insurmountable obstacles. And, for Lucy Snowe, almost every imaginable obstacle of culture, society, and physical make-up are against her. Nature has not been kind to Lucy Snowe, and for those who seek to oppose literary and social conventions of the 19th C., life is even more difficult and brutal.

Lucy Snowe's journey begins, once again as an orphaned child living with her god-mother, her son John Graham Bretton, and little Paulina Home. Her anomalous position in the family allows her to be an 'observer', and she is withdrawn, taciturn, and submissive with rebellion 'burning' deep within her. As a person without a home it sets the stage for her 'troubled journey' as she 'shuffles' along from one home to another. In the home of a lady where Lucy has accepted a position as her 'companion in-waiting', we find that Miss Marchmont is one who has suffered life-long, mental anguish as the result of the death of her lover on Christmas Eve. The fact that she has suffered such debilitating anxiety and lasting 'damage' demonstrates the utter sacrifices that females endure when they give their lives to 'love'. Such devotion and dedication is bound to result in that 'buried life' of suppression and anxiety, as was the case with Miss Marchmont. After Miss Marchmont's sudden passing, Lucy moves on to Labassecour.

Once in Villette, Lucy's life quickly becomes involved in an entanglement of psychic facets with 'mirrored', double images which perhaps reflect and manifest her confused, psychic state. Victorian women, particularly those without means or position, struggled desperately with their physical and emotional needs for love, and the dreadful consequences of perhaps not finding it. Without love or support, they looked forward to a life of bleakness and despair with increasing anxiety, growing desperation, and festering internalization and 'paralysis' as their prospects diminished.

Mme Beck is a duplicitous character who employs covert activities of spying and surveillance on those she considers a threat to herself and her own 'sphere'. Her methods and her stealth symbolize 'repression' as well as the length to which desperate individuals will resort to in obtaining their goals. Those of Mme Beck were primarily ones of self-interest, and to maintain an 'edge', she needed to apply subterfuge. Her daughter, Desirée, a 'daughter of repression' was also a symbol of inner revolt, and she, too, reacted in an unruly fashion.

Lucy's internalization of oppression and repression from the external world are simply added to the mental anxiety she already suffers from emotional turmoil and her search for self, freedom, and even self-indulgence. Ginerva Fanshawe is the embodiment of the unconscious desires that Lucy Snowe wishes for herself. These unresolved, personal issues and the general imbalance of 'reason' and 'imagination', restraint and indulgence, are tortuous, making her life a 'living hell' and eventually lead to her complete, mental breakdown. The garden at Mme Beck's school is also symbolic in that it is an 'island' away from interference, an area of self-expression and indulgence free from prying eyes, and beyond the control of those who wish to manipulate the lives of others.

Charlotte's use of characters assuming the opposite sex demonstrates her search for the power of, or knowledge of, the male species, or perhaps a hidden desire to escape her own sex. In *The Professor*, she assumes the sex of a male through her protagonist, William Crimsworth, although rather unsuccessfully, to see things from a different, sexual perspective, and perhaps to inspire male readers to adopt a different, more modern and moderate view of women in their Victorian society. In *Jane Eyre*, Edward Rochester assumes the character of a female gypsy with the power of prophetic insight into human lives. In *Shirley*, the protagonist, Shirley Keeldar, adopts the power and position generally reserved for males, whereas her suitor is her former tutor, the equivalent of a lowly governess. And, in *Villette*, Lucy Snowe takes on the role of a man in a play, but only partly dresses up in men's clothing. Such cross-dressing and cross-sexual roles allow Charlotte to explore the world from the 'other side'. With a simple change of clothes, the participant can shed their sexuality and briefly be 'liberated' from society's 'bondage' and boundaries.

Perhaps one of the highlights and climaxes of *Villette* is Lucy's brief flirtation with the Roman Catholic church and her visit to the confessional. The novel is highly anti-Catholic and reflects the views of the author. To her, and Lucy Snowe, the church is as restrictive as Victorian society, patriarchal in its mythical origins and present-day operations and conventions, and nuns are simply seen as 'slaves' of the church. This visit brings her into the alluring grasp of Père Silas who is as persuasive and seductive as the snake, Sin, in the Garden of Eden. Lucy manages to 'escape' but even at a distance knows that a return visit will likely result in her 'fall', and conversion. Once converted, she would become a 'prisoner' within its restrictive, patriarchal walls forever.

Lucy's visit to the confessional and her flirtation with the Roman Catholic church is also symbolic of a repeated theme and topic in Charlotte Brontë's novels. As in real life, and as with Emily's *Wuthering Heights*, Charlotte has difficulty coming to grips with the male mythology of Christianity, especially in Catholicism, and the exclusion of women from that mythology except as sinners. Emily's approach and message is direct and inescapable, but Charlotte's appears to be more ambivalent, indirect, and 'waffling', as in the conclusion of *Shirley*. That exclusion from the foundations of Western religions, and the secondary status of women in Victorian society, was hurtful and degrading to Emily and Charlotte, as evidenced by the hidden messages in all of their novels.

Also, in an unconventional literary style, Charlotte employs 'trickery', and 'deceit' in a mild form, in her *Villette* plot since we do not learn, until late in the novel, that 'Dr. John' is in fact, Dr. John Graham Bretton, the son of Lucy's godmother with whom she stayed as a youngster. He was also the young gentleman who helped her locate her missing trunk after their arrival in Villette. Although some critics found this misleading, literary analysts Gilbert and Gubar examine why a "voyeur", Lucy Snowe, "narrates a fictional biography". They explain in (*Madwoman...*, Ch. 12, pp. 418-19):

> .... Lucy's life, her sense of herself, does not conform to the literary or social stereotypes provided by her culture to define and circumscribe female life.... So she finds her using and abusing - presenting and undercutting - images and stories of male devising,...

Thus, for Lucy Snowe and all females of 'confinement', she must use non-conformist and unconventional literary techniques to give 'voice' to their plight and overcome the "silent submission" of women.

Charlotte Brontë's chapter 'The Cleopatra' also provides Lucy with a platform from which to expound on the false roles, bordering on the ridiculous, which men assign women in real life and in culture. This is accomplished through the visit to the museum to see the over-sized, reclining, naked Cleopatra who is adored for her great beauty. The woman in the painting appears to bear no resemblance to reality for Lucy, or other women; she is simply a sexual object for "worshipping connoisseurs". Lucy ridicules the person in the painting as "extremely well-fed" with that "affluence of the flesh" (*Villettte*, Ch. 19) as well as lounging about in midday without any clothes. After surveying the painting for a while, she comes to the conclusion that "it was on the whole an enormous piece of clap-trap;... " (*Villette*, Ch. 19) and then moves on to a 'still life'.

Dr. John Bretton's change of heart and mind regarding Ginerva Fanshawe indicates his 'growth' and 'maturity' in the realization of the true and valued qualities of women as opposed to the superficial ones, like beauty, which first endeared him to Ginerva. Lucy tries to quieten his anger and assures him, "She is not actuated by malevolence, but sheer, heedless folly. To a feather-brained schoolgirl nothing is sacred" (*Villette*, Ch. 20). Dr. John takes exception to this but realizes that Lucy is, in fact, right.

On one of her trips to London, Charlotte was taken to see a live performance by Rachel, the renowned French tragic actress, who excelled in fierce, passionate roles. This greatly impressed and intrigued Charlotte, and she used this experience in *Villette* and portrayed her as 'Vashti', an actress who gave intense, dramatic performances packed with energy and artistic, self-expression. But instead of Vashti's passionate performances resulting in her 'freedom', as one might expect, it leads to her self-destruction as she internalizes the conflicts of the characters she portrays. Also, it does not result in her acceptance into high society, but rather her exclusion from it. With each performance, Vashti 'rises like the phoenix', is 'consumed', and 'falls' again. Thus, she never attains a permanent place in 'heaven'; her revolt against the tyranny of heaven is never heard, and is futile. In the end, Vashti is herself 'consumed' by the heat of her own 'burning' perfor-mance. In the reference to Vashti, we also find a parallel to Charlotte as a writer whose self-expression and challenges to a patriarchal system rooted in the past bring her public criticism, not accolades. Her critics evaded the cultural issues which she raised and fo-cused mainly on the fact that the author was female.

Another feature in *Villette* is the recurring appearance of the nun's apparition which is perhaps a manifestation of Lucy's fears and anxieties. The nun, and her vows, symbol-ize purity, self-denial, and a life devoted to Christ and their fellow man. The nun's apparition is a constant reminder of the conflicts which tear at Lucy and the choice she must make, neither of which is appealing. The nun's way is total devotion and dedication to God, the Father, and the patriarchal priesthood, as opposed to obedience in marriage in the patriarchal, Victorian society on the other hand, which is not much different. The apparition is a protest to a male-dominated world and the injustices that it entails to the female population. The nun's reappearance may also symbolize women's rebellion for the guilt of sin which they are made to bear during their sojourn on earth - told over and over again that Eve was the mother of Sin, females are burdened through life with the 'weight' and guilt of sin.

Lucy's attraction to Dr. John is a submission to her physical and emotional needs, and his letters are 'foods' of sustenance which she devours in private and in her leisure behind locked doors. When the letters to Lucy stop, it is tantamount to starvation, but it also triggers a skepticism, cynicism, and rejection of romantic love. For Lucy, romantic love can only end in rejection, heartache, and further demoralization and loss of self-esteem. For Polly and Dr. John, their relationship intensifies and Lucy Snowe has an increased admiration for Paulina to the same extent that Dr. John falls in her estimation. As a person of fine and true character, her growth has outstripped his, and just as Dr. John fades from her 'romantic picture', Lucy is increasingly attracted to M Paul.

In both *Jane Eyre* and *Villette*, the heroine's romantic involvement defies literary convention as someone tall, dark, and handsome. Both Edward Rochester and M Paul do not measure up to the glamourous images created by the Romantic writers of the past and her other contemporary novelists. M Paul is small in stature, dark in complexion, not young but middle-aged, indulgent, and despotic with a tendency to cruelty and tyranny. Although they both share the same, worthy goals and ideals, their nature and styles are 'testy' and 'combative' which stresses their intellectual equality. Their inequality is evident in the clash between Lucy's desire for her own freedom and equality with her male counterparts, and his patriarchal views, stuck in the antiquated past, which expected her subservience. M Paul did not believe that the feminine mind was on an equal par with that of males. He was soon to collide with her strength of character, individuality, independence, intelligence, and unswerving determination.

Mme Walravens is easily identified as 'witch material' primarily from her odd appearance, older age, and malevolence toward others who are happier than herself. Authors Gilbert and Gubar claim that "Madame Walravens is yet another vindictive madwoman in the attic, and like Bertha Mason Rochester, she is malevolently enraged,... " (*Madwoman*, Ch.12, p. 431). From Père Silas, Lucy learns the real story of Mme Walravens, Justine Marie, and M Paul, who despite his outward appearance and petty tyrannies, epitomizes self-sacrifice and denial for the benefit of others. Mme Walravens had actually opposed his marriage to Justine Marie who then entered a convent and died. M Paul is still devoted to his dead angel, Justine Marie, after twenty years, has encumbered himself with the support of Mme Walravens, Père Silas, Dame Agnes, and other charities, and lives in penury as a result.

Neither Mme Walravens nor Mme Beck typify or exemplify Victorian 'ladies' by any means. Mme Walravens appears to be possessed with special 'powers' which we usually associate with the 'black arts' or mystic, Eastern cultures. Mme Beck on the other hand is controlling, manipulative and secretive, filled with mystery and intrigue, and more like the two-faced Roman goddess Janus, a god of doorways and passageways. But both are agents and sycophants for patriarchal society and culture without any desire to better the lot of women. To avoid the scrutiny of critics and a critical society, they simply renounced their femininity by becoming androgynous; both have become 'defeminized', and almost 'de-humanized'. As the novel nears its end, we find that Lucy has, in fact, made noticeable progress in her life's journey, her search for self, independence, and self-expression. The journey has not only been physical with aesthetic observations along the way but also one of psychological struggle with growth in confidence and maturity, and a better sense of self. Lucy is now able to focus on her own concerns for the present, and the future, 'weighed' against her own past. The repression which Lucy has suffered and the restraint which she has practised now receded and diminished, and she is gradually freed from her 'fictional world' of confinements and concealments. She then emerges as a more whole and unified person with the ability of articulating herself well against more formidable 'opponents' like Père Silas and M Paul.

With this new-found freedom, Lucy is now able to perceive things differently from her own perspective and that of others. The 'looking glass' is a repeated feature in Charlotte's novels whereby she occasionally perceives herself, which is often not the perception of others. The looking glass proves unreliable in separating truth and reality from perception and imagination; the perception and 'image' of oneself is not always the truth and reality of others. The images one 'sees' in the mirror may be as fleeting and unreal as the images of the nun - they either 'skirt' and confound reality or they are figments of the imagination.

The author has made the ending of *Villette* intentionally ambiguous. It also evokes the irony that although it was M Paul who has made her 'whole', she can only feel that 'wholeness', independence, and power in his absence. With his absence goes the tyranny of his patriarchal mastery which generally typifies the ending of a traditional,19th C. novel. It also cleverly and quietly removes the symbol of that patriarchy through 'accidental' design; Lucy will now carry on without M Paul (and probably quite well), and he will be but a memory and a projection of her imagination. If this novel is, in fact, a depiction of her own life and a fictionalized, autobiographical account of her relationship with M Heger, Charlotte indicates that she is a 'survivor' and has managed to live very well without him although he occasionally enters her thoughts and evokes 'mixed memories'.

In all of her novels, Charlotte attacks patriarchal society and culture and the customs and traditions that it spawns and engrains in their constricted lives. In *Jane Eyre*, this is done openly and brazenly; in *Shirley*, it is done bravely and directly, and in *The Professor* and *Villette*, it is done more obscurely and intricately and is delicately interwoven with characters and plot elements which require thought and analysis. In each case, it attempts to subvert the status quo of 19th C. literature with its images of masculine power and supremacy, and those of female submission and servitude. Also, each heroine is shown to be unique, intelligent, independent, thoughtful, understanding, and sympathetic with a sense of pride and determination, and a set of personal goals. In her novels, Charlotte has shown herself to be brave enough, and even courageous enough, to tackle the untenable and indefensible, but firmly held, patriarchal principles and beliefs of the day through the art of writing. In her short life, although longer than any of her other sisters, Charlotte has shown herself to be among the giants of 19th C. writers of English literature, and at the forefront of women's issues which were not broached directly until more than a century later.

        *   *   *   *

APPENDICES

APPENDIX A

THE BRONTË CHRONOLOGY

1776, (date unknown)	Elizabeth Branwell (Aunt Branwell) born Penzance Cornwall
1777, March 17	Patrick Brontë (Rev.) born St. Patrick's Day, Emdale, County Down, Ireland
1783, April 15	Maria Branwell (Mrs. Brontë) born Penzance, Cornwall
1802	Patrick Brontë enters St. John's College at Cambridge University as 'sizar'
1806	Patrick Brontë ordained by Bishop of London as clergy-man for Church of England
1806 - 1809	Mr. Brontë is curate at Wethersfield, Essex
1809 (Jan. - Dec.)	Mr. Brontë is curate at Wellington, Shropshire
1809 (Dec.) - 1811	Mr. Brontë is curate at Dewsbury, Yorkshire
1811 - 1815	Minister at Hartshead-cum-Clifton, Yorkshire

1812	Rev. Brontë appointed Examiner of Scriptures at Woodhouse Grove School under Headmaster, John Fennell
1812	Rev. meets Maria Branwell who is niece to John Fennell. Strike up immediate relationship.
1812, Dec. 29	Maria Branwell becomes Mrs. Brontë. Ceremony held at Guisely Church, Guisely, near Leeds
1814 (date unknown)	First daughter Maria born. Baptised at St. Peter's Church, Hartshead, April 23rd
1815, Feb. 8	Elizabeth, second daughter, born. Baptised Aug. 26, at Thornton Church, Thornton, near Bradford
1815	Mr. Brontë appointed perpetual curate, Thornton Church, Thornton
1816, April 21	Charlotte born. Baptised June 29, at Thornton
1817, June 26	Patrick Branwell, first and only son, born at Thornton. Baptised July 23rd
1818, July 30	Emily Jane born at Thornton. Baptised Aug. 20th
1820, Jan. 17	Anne born at Thornton. Baptised March 25th
1820, Feb.	Rev. Brontë appointed Perpetual Curate at Haworth
1820, April	Brontë family makes trek with seven ox-carts from Thornton. Move into Haworth Parsonage
1821, Jan.	Early signs of severe illness for Mrs. Brontë
1821, Sept. 15	Mrs. Brontë buried in family vault beneath old Haworth Church. Aunt Elizabeth Branwell arrives to look after young family for 'interim' period
1824, July 1	Maria and Elizabeth enrolled at Cowan Bridge School, near Kirkby Lonsdale. Charlotte enrolled in August and Emily in November

1825, Feb.	Low fever breaks out at Cowan Bridge School. Many children become ill and some die. Maria removed Feb. 14, and taken home to Haworth
1825, May 6	Maria dies at Haworth. Buried in family vault
1825, May 31	Mr. Brontë removes Elizabeth, who is now very ill, from Cowan Bridge School
1825, June 1	Mr. Brontë returns and removes both Charlotte and Emily from school
1825, June 15	Elizabeth dies at Haworth. Buried in family vault
1825, (Nov. ?)	Tabatha Akroyd replaces Nancy and Sarah Garrs as help at Parsonage. Both sisters are betrothed and marry. Tabby serves Brontës for thirty years
1826, June 5 (?)	Rev. Brontë returns from Leeds with toy soldiers ("Twelves") for Branwell. Actively stirs their imaginations for their early writings
1831, Jan. 17	Charlotte enrolled at Roe Head School, Mirfield. There she meets Ellen Nussey, Mary Taylor and Miss Margaret Wooler, Headmistress, who all become life-long friends
1832, June	Charlotte leaves Roe Head. Now assists her aunt and father in teaching younger siblings
1835, July	Charlotte takes offer of teaching position at Roe Head. Emily enters as free pupil, but stays only a few months. Anne takes her place at school
1835 (autumn)	Branwell goes to London to enroll at Royal Academy but returns home several days later with no money
1837, Dec.	Anne suffers stress and religious crisis. Returns to Haworth to be with family
1838, June	Branwell becomes portrait painter in Bradford. Stays with Kirbys but returns to Haworth, May, 1839, in debt and pursued by creditors

1838, Sept.	Emily takes position as teacher at Miss Patchet's School at Law Hill, Halifax. Stays till March, 1839, and then leaves abruptly
1838, Dec.	Charlotte leaves post at Roe Head. Finds duties overwhelming; needs more time to herself
1839, April	Anne takes job as governess to Inghams at Blake Hall, Mirfield. Stays there until December
1839, May-July	Charlotte becomes governess to Sidgwicks at Stonegappe, Lothersdale. Left three months later
1839, Aug.	Wm. Weightman appointed curate to Rev. Brontë. Brings much-needed life and joy to Brontë family
1839, Sept.	Charlotte holidays with Ellen Nussey at Bridlington
1840, Jan.	Branwell takes job as tutor to Mr. Postlethwaite at Broughton-in-Furness. Dismissed in June.
1840, May	Anne takes second job as governess to Robinsons at Thorp Green Hall, Little Ouseburn, near York. Remains there almost five years
1840, Sept.	Branwell hired as clerk on new Leeds-Manchester railway at Sowerby Bridge near Halifax
1840 (date unknown)	Martha Brown, sexton's daughter, age twelve, enters service of Brontës; remains with family until Rev. Brontë's death in June, 1861
1841, March	Charlotte becomes governess at Upperwood House, Rawdon to a Mrs. White. Leaves in December
1841, April	Branwell promoted to clerk-in-charge at Luddenden Foot, also near Halifax
1842, Feb.	Rev. Brontë escorts Charlotte and Emily to London and then Brussels where they enroll at Pensionnat Heger as students

1842, April	Branwell dismissed from railway due to irregularities in accounts
1842, Sept. 6	Wm. Weightman, age 26, dies suddenly. Buried in Haworth Old Church
1842, Oct. 12	Martha Taylor, Mary's sister, dies of cholera in Brussels while at Koekelburg Pensionnat
1842, Oct. 29	Aunt Branwell dies, age 66, after 21 years of dedicated service to Mr. Brontë and his children. Buried in family vault at Haworth Church. Emily and Charlotte return home from Brussels
1843, Jan.	Charlotte returns to studies in Brussels. Emily remains at Parsonage as housekeeper, and Anne takes Branwell to Thorp Green as tutor to young Edmund Robinson
1844, Jan. 4	Charlotte returns home from Brussels after completion of studies
1845, May	A.B. Nicholls appointed new curate to Haworth to assist aging Rev. Brontë
1845, June	Anne resigns position at Thorp Green over Branwell's illicit affair with Mrs. Robinson
1845, July	Branwell dismissed by Mr. Robinson. Charlotte visits Ellen Nussey at Hathersage
1845, (autumn)	Charlotte 'discovers' poetry written by Emily on her desk. She urges sisters to publish their work.
1846, May	*Poems* , their first book of poetry published by Aylott & Jones at own expense. Only 2 copies sold. Use pseudonyms Currer, Ellis, and Acton Bell
1846, June	Charlotte finishes, *The Professor*, but it was rejected by many publishers
1846, July	Emily's, *Wuthering Heights*, and Anne's, *Agnes Grey*, manuscripts complete. Sent to publishers and finally accepted by Thomas Cautley Newby

1846, Aug. - Sept.	Charlotte accompanies father to Manchester for eye operation. There she begins *Jane Eyre*
1847, Oct.	*Jane Eyre* published by Smith, Elder & Co. of 65 Cornhill, London, to instant success and acclaim
1847, Dec.	Thomas Cautley Newby rush *Wuthering Heights* and *Agnes Grey* into print after success of *Jane Eyre*
1848, June	Anne's second novel, *The Tenant of Wildfell Hall*, published by Thomas Cautley Newby. Second edition put into print in July after its immediate success
1848, July 7	Charlotte and Anne rush to London to prove their identities to Smith, Elder & Co. after Newby claimed that the three 'Bells' were only one person
1848, Sept. 24	Branwell, age 31, dies from consumption and complications from alcohol and laudanum use. Rev. Brontë devastated
1848, Oct. 1	Branwell buried in family vault of Haworth Old Church on wet, cold Sunday. Emily catches cold at funeral and never leaves the house again
1848, Dec. 19	Emily, age 30, dies from consumption, and is buried in family vault of Haworth Old Church a few days later. Anne is already ill with consumption
1849, (Jan. ?)	Dr. Teale, specialist, diagnoses Anne in advanced stages of consumption. Prescribes strict regimen of food and medicine for her comfort
1849, May 28	Anne, age 29, dies at Scarborough where Charlotte and Ellen Nussey had taken her in hopes of sea-air cure. She was buried in St. Mary's Churchyard Cemetery overlooking the sea
1849, June	Charlotte and Ellen Nussey remain at Filey and Bridlington after Anne's death, upon Rev. Brontë's suggestion. There Charlotte and Ellen recover from their ordeal

1849, Oct.	*Shirley*, Charlotte's second successful novel, published and released by Smith, Elder & Co.
1849, Dec.	Charlotte invited to London to stay with family of George Smith, one of her publishers. There she met Wm. M. Thackeray and the well-known writer, and new friend, Harriet Martineau
1850, March	Charlotte visits with Sir James Kay and Lady Kay-Shuttleworth at Gawthorpe Hall, near Burnley
1850, June	Charlotte visits London again. Dines with Thackeray and has portrait done by George Richmond, a well-known portrait painter of the day
1850, July	Charlotte visits Edinburgh with George Smith and friends
1850, Aug.	Charlotte meets Elizabeth Gaskell for first time at Briery Close, Windermere, while staying with the Kay-Shuttleworths
1850, Dec.	Charlotte visits Harriet Martineau at The Knoll, Ambleside, in The Lake District
1851, May - June	Charlotte visits London. Sees Great Exhibition, Crystal Palace, and attends lectures by Thackeray
1851, June	Charlotte stays with Mrs. Gaskell at Plymouth Grove, near Manchester. Begins her last novel, *Villette*
1852, June	Charlotte stays alone at Filey, East Yorkshire, and visits Anne's grave in Scarborough
1852, Dec.	A.B. Nicholls proposes to Charlotte, but she turns him down after her father's vehement objections
1853, Jan.	Charlotte visits London for last time. Smith, Elder & Co. release *Villette* , her last novel
1853, April	Charlotte again visits Mrs. Gaskell at Plymouth Grove, Manchester. Stays there one week

1853, May	A.B. Nicholls resigns his curacy at Haworth, and later transfers to Kirk Smeaton, Pontefract
1853, Sept.	Mrs. Gaskell spends few days at Haworth Parsonage. Charlotte visits Marg Wooler at Hornsea, East Yorkshire
1854, Jan.	A.B. Nicholls visits Mr. Grant at Oxenhope, and Charlotte meets with him several times
1854, April	Charlotte's engagement to Rev. Nicholls announced after Rev. Brontë withdraws his objections
1854, June	Rev. Nicholls resumes duties as curate at Haworth
1854, June 29	Charlotte married to A.B. Nicholls by Rev. Sutcliffe Sowden at Haworth. Marg Wooler 'gave her away', and Ellen Nussey was her only bridesmaid
1854, July	Charlotte and new husband take honeymoon in Ireland where she meets his relatives
1855, Jan.	Charlotte catches cold while walking on wet grass during visit to Kay-Shuttleworths at Gawthorpe Hall. Charlotte never recovers from this illness
1855, Feb. 17	'Tabby' Akroyd, their beloved servant of thirty years, dies at age 84. She is buried in churchyard in front of the Parsonage
1855, Mar. 31	Charlotte dies of consumption, and complications arising from early stages of pregnancy. Buried in family vault of Haworth Old Church, April 4th.
1855, June	Rev. Brontë writes to Mrs. Gaskell and asks if she would like to write the biography of Charlotte
1857, March	*The Life of Charlotte Brontë* published by Smith, Elder & Co. after two years of research done by Elizabeth C. Gaskell

1857, June	Charlotte's failed first novel, *The Professor*, is published by Smith, Elder & Co. for first time, with an preface by Rev. A.B. Nicholls
1861, June 7	Mr. Brontë dies at age 84, and is buried alongside Charlotte in family vault of Haworth Old Church. Rev. Nicholls resigns his post, leaves the Parsonage and returns to Ireland
1861, Oct.	Household effects of Parsonage and Rev. Brontë put to auction. Records from this sale later important in recovery of many of the historic artifacts
1872 - 1878	Rev. John Wade, the new curate, begins changes and renovations to Parsonage. Gable wing is added
1879	Haworth Old Church demolished and new one built. Only original tower is saved; vault left in tact
1880, Jan. 19	Martha Brown, trusted servant of the Brontës, dies at age 52. Buried in cemetery beside the Parsonage
1893, Dec. 16	Lord Houghton named first president of The Brontë Society formed at meeting in Bradford Town Hall
1895, May 18	The first Brontë Museum opens to public above Yorkshire Penny Bank in Haworth
1897, Nov. 26	Ellen Nussey, Charlotte's life-long friend, dies at Gomersal, age 80 years
1906, Dec. 2	A.B. Nicholls, Charlotte's husband, dies at Banagher in Ireland at age 88.
1928, Aug. 4	Brontë Parsonage Museum opens to the public after being purchased for £3000 by Sir James Roberts and presented to The Brontë Society
1928 - 1929	Bonnell Collection, named after American collector of Brontë books, manuscripts, and drawings, donated to The Brontë Society

1944	Brontë Memorial tablet placed in Poet's Corner of Westminster Abbey, London
1960	Extensions to rear of Parsonage and new Bonnell Room opens to the public
1964, July 4	Dedication of new Brontë Memorial Chapel in Haworth Church
1975	Manuscript collection of Seton Gordon presented to Brontë Parsonage Museum
1980	Brontë Society purchases 44 Brontë manuscripts from Grolier Collection
1984, Oct.	Brontë portraits put on temporary loan to Brontë Museum by National Portrait Gallery
1988	Brontë Parsonage Museum celebrates Diamond Jubilee
1993	Brontë Society celebrates its centenary year.

APPENDIX B

THE BRONTË FAMILY TREE

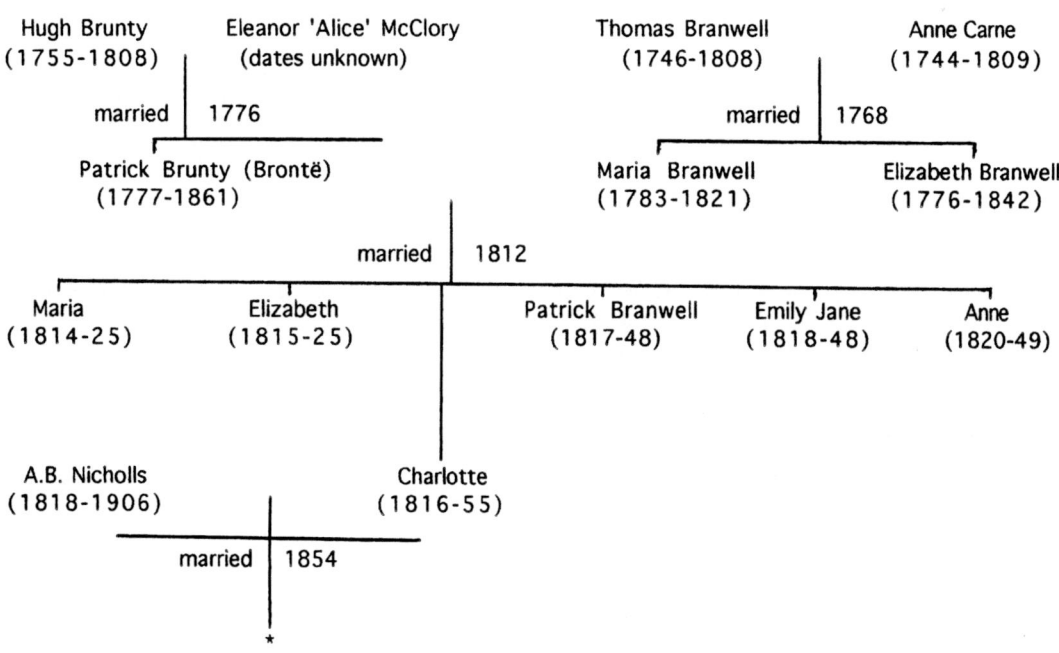

* Family dies without any heirs or successors.
** For precise birth and death dates, see Appendix A: The Brontë Chronology.

APPENDIX C

REVEREND ARTHUR BELL NICHOLLS
(1818 - 1906)

Rev. Arthur Bell Nicholls was born in Ireland in 1818, but surprisingly little is known about his early upbringing except that he was raised by an uncle of moderate means. He came into the service of Haworth Parish as a curate in May, 1845. Even during his stay there, and the time of his marriage to Charlotte Brontë, little information was either collected or survives today. Seen simply as a late adjunct, and not as a direct influence on any of Charlotte's writings, he has perhaps been shunted aside. Also, he was a quiet, reserved, and private person who preferred to remain out of the 'limelight'. His importance appears to be in the legacy which followed, and his contributions toward the legacy with the correspondence, manuscripts, letters, and material effects left to his charge. Others might argue that his real significance lays in the early death of Charlotte, only nine months after they were married, but this is purely speculative and academic.

In the years after Charlotte's death, he faithfully looked after his parish duties in Haworth, carried on correspondence with a host of Brontë fans, and lived up to his promise to care for Rev. Brontë in his old age. This he did faithfully until Rev. Brontë's passing on June 7, 1861. After his duties and promises were discharged, and the household effects of the Brontës were sold at public auction in October of that year, he resigned as curate, and returned to his native Ireland.

With his marriage to Charlotte, the acting successor to Rev. Brontë, and his direct connections with the family, Arthur Bell Nicholls became the sole heir and guardian of legal rights to her materials. Published materials, and future publications, were now legally under his control, and often deferred to him. This later caused friction between Nicholls and Ellen Nussey, who held hundreds of Charlotte's letters which were now invaluable to her biography and any future academic studies of her life. Some of these letters contained information on Rev. Nicholls himself of which Charlotte had written to Ellen prior to their marriage. Ellen astutely kept these away from Nicholls although he suspected their existence and wanted them back.

Immediately following Charlotte's death, beginning in June, 1855, Nicholls was an important source and consultant, on a wide range of material, to Elizabeth Cleghorn Gaskell, Charlotte's biographer. Although not in complete agreement with everything that was written in the first edition, both he and Rev.Brontë were generally pleased with the positive light shed on Charlotte's life and work.

Some of Charlotte's correspondence, still in her possession when she died, which Nicholls deemed sensitive, private, and inappropriate, but which may have provided important biographical information on him and her relationship with him, was destroyed. Much of the remaining material which he took back to Ireland with him was kept out of circulation until the very last years of his life when he agreed to part with them through Thomas J. Wise and his operatives. He, too, was under the misguided belief that this man would see that these materials, so valuable to the literary history of Victorian England, would be placed in the safe care and public domain of the National Museum and in British libraries. Unfortunately his trust, like that of Ellen Nussey's, was badly misplaced in profiteers operating under the guise of honest-brokers for valuable public treasures.

Much of the Brontë material ended up in the hands of Thomas J. Wise through clever promises, never fulfilled, and sold on the open market for profit. As a result, much of the material was spread far and wide around the world through sellers and collectors. Over the years, much Brontëana has been returned through generous donations, like the Bonnell Collection, and individual contributors. Arthur Bell Nicholls is also to be credited for having kept much of this important material in his safe-keeping for many years. Although a few items were lost or destroyed by him, we can be now appreciate the valuable contribution which he made toward its preservation.

With the purchase of Haworth Parsonage in 1928, by Sir James Roberts, its subsequent presentation to the Brontë Society as a museum and its subsequent development, so little is known about Arthur Bell Nicholls that his former den and study is now used as a display room for relics from Haworth Old Church, which was torn down, except for the original tower and rebuilt in 1879, by Rev. John Wade, the successor to Rev. Brontë and Rev. Arthur Bell Nicholls.

Upon Nicholls return to Ireland, he is purported to have married his cousin Mary Bell, resigned from the clergy, and taken up farming. His quiet, reserved manner, his newly-acquired country life, and his resignation from the Church allowed him to live in relative peace and obscurity for the remainder of his life, away from the legend which was growing rapidly in England. His is said to have continued a correspondence with Martha Brown, a Brontë servant, and she is said to have visited him in Ireland. Nicholls reticence and aloofness simply added to the many unknown factors surrounding his life.

SOURCES AND REFERENCES

Altick, Richard D. *Victorian People and Ideas*. New York: Norton & Co., 1973.

Bainbridge, Cecil. *The Brontës and Their Country*. Burley-in-Wharfedale: Dales PR, 1993.

Banks, Lynne Reid. *Dark Quartet - The Story of the Brontës*. New York: Delacorte Press, 1976.

Barker, Juliet R.V. *The Brontës* . London: Weidenfeld and Nicholson, 1994.

Brontë Society. *Brontë Parsonage Museum*. Haworth, Yorkshire: Author, 1989.

Brontë Society. *Brontë Parsonage Museum, Haworth: A Souvenir Guide*. Haworth, Yorkshire: Author, 1998.

Brontë, Anne. *Agnes Grey and Poems*. London: Orion House, 1997.

Brontë, Anne. *The Tenant of Wildfell Hall* . London: Penguin Classics, 1994.

Brontë, Charlotte. *The Professor* . London: Penguin Classics, 1995.

Brontë, Charlotte. *Jane Eyre* . Ware, Hertfordshire: Wordsworth Editions Limited., 1992.

Brontë, Charlotte. *Shirley*. Ware, Hertfordshire: Wordsworth Editions Limited., 1993.

Brontë, Charlotte. *Villette*. London: Penguin Classics, 1994.

Brontë, Emily. *Wuthering Heights*. Ware, Hertfordshire: Wordsworth Editions Limited., 1992.

Drabble, Margaret (Ed.) *Oxford Companion to English Literature (Rev. Ed.)*. Oxford: Oxford University Press, 1995.

Du Maurier, Daphne. *The Infernal World of Branwell Brontë*. London: Gollancz, 1960.

Gardiner, Juliet. *The World Within - The Brontës at Haworth: A Life in Letters, Diaries and Writings*. London: Collins & Brown, 1992.

Gaskell, Elizabeth Cleghorn. *The Life of Charlotte Brontë*. London: Dent, 1908.

Gerin, Winifred. *Charlotte Brontë: the evolution of genius*. Oxford: Clarendon Press, 1986.

Gilbert, Sandra M. and Susan Gubar. *The Madwoman in the Attic: The Woman Writer in the Nineteenth-Century Literary Imagination* (2nd ed.). New Haven, Conn., Yale Univ. Press, 1984.

Hibbert, Christopher. *The English: A Social History 1066 - 1945*. London: Harper Collins, 1998.

Law, Alice. *Patrick Branwell Brontë*. London: Philpot, 1924.

Leapman, Michael. *Great Britain: DK Travel Guides*. London: Dorling Kindersley Limited, 1999.

Norris, Pamela (Ed.) *The Brontës* . London: Everyman, 1997.

Pinion, F. B. *A Brontë Companion : Literary Assessment, Background And Reference* . London: MacMillan, 1975.

Ratchford, Fanny E. *The Brontë's Web of Childhood*. New York: Columbia University Press, 1941.

Smith, Margaret (Ed.). *The Letters of Charlotte Brontë: Volume One* (1829-1847). Oxford: Clarendon Press, 1995.

Stevens, Joan (Ed.). *Mary Taylor, Friend of Charlotte Brontë: Letters From New Zealand and Elsewhere*. Auckland, NZ: Auckland University Press, 1972.

Whitehead, Barbara. *Charlotte Brontë and her 'dearest Nell': The story of a friendship* . Otley, West Yorkshire: Smith Settle, 1993.

Willis, Irene Cooper. *The Authorship of Wuthering Heights*. London: Hogarth Press, 1936.

SUGGESTED READINGS

Alexander, Christine. *The Early Writings of Charlotte Brontë*. Oxford: Blackwell, 1983.

Allott, Miriam F. *The Brontës, The Critical Heritage*. London: Routledge & K. Paul, 1974.

Bentley, Phyllis E. *The Brontës*. London: Home & Van Thal, 1947.

Bentley, Phyllis E. *The Young Brontës*. New York: Roy Publishers, 1961.

Bentley, Phyllis E. *The Brontë Sisters (Rev. ed.)*. New York: Longmans, 1967.

Blom, Margaret H. *Charlotte Brontë*. Boston: Twayne Publishers, 1977.

Brontë, Anne. *The Poems of Anne Brontë A New Text And Commentary*. London: MacMillan, 1979.

Brontë, Charlotte. *The Belgian Essays: A Critical Edition*. New Haven, Connecticut: Yale University Press, 1996.

Brontë, Emily. *Gondal's Queen : A Novel in Verse*. New York: AMS Press, 1973.

Brontë, Emily. *The Poems of Emily Brontë*. London: B.T. Batsford, 1992.

Brontë, Patrick B. *The Poems of Patrick Branwell Brontë: A New Text And Commentary*. New York: Garland, 1990.

Chitham, Edward. *A Life of Anne Brontë*. Oxford: B. Blackwell, 1991.

Craik, W.A. *The Brontë Novels*. London: Metheun, 1968.

Crandall, Norma. *Emily Brontë, A Psychological Portrait*. Rindge, New Hampshire: R.R. Smith Publisher, 1957.

Davies, Stevie. *Four Dreamers and Emily*. New York: St. Martin's Press, 1997.

Davies, Stevie. *Emily Brontë*. Bloomington: Indiana University Press, 1988.

Everitt, Alastair G. *Wuthering Heights : An Anthology of Criticism*. New York: Barnes & Noble, 1967.

Frank, Katherine. *A Chainless Soul : A Life of Emily Brontë*. Boston: Houghton Mifflin, 1990.

Fraser, Rebecca. *Charlotte Brontë*. London: Methuen, 1988.

Fry, Christopher. *The Brontës of Haworth*. London: Davis-Poynter, 1975.

Guzzetti, Paula. *A Family Called Brontë*. New York: Dillon Press, 1994.

Harland, Marion. *Charlotte Brontë at Home*. New York: G.P. Putnam's Sons, The Knickerbocker Press, 1899.

Harrison, Ada M. *Anne Brontë, Her Life and Work*. Hamden, Connecticut: Archon Books, 1970.

Hewish, John. *Emily Brontë : A Critical And Biographical Study*. New York: St. Martin's Press, 1969.

Hopkins, Annette B. *The Father of the Brontës*. Baltimore, MD: John Hopkins Press, 1958.

Keefe, Robert. *Charlotte Brontës World of Death*. Austin, TX: University of Texas Press, 1979.

Knies, Earl A. *The Art of Charlotte Brontë*. Athens, OH: Ohio University Press, 1969.

Langland, Elizabeth. *Anne Brontë, the Other One*. Totowa, NJ: Barnes & Noble, 1989.

Lock, John. *A Man of Sorrow : The Life, Letters and Times of the Rev. Patrick Brontë, 1777 - 1861*. London: Nelson, 1965.

Lloyd Evans, Barbara. *Everyman's Companion to the Brontës*. London: Dent, 1982.

MacKay, Angus M. *The Brontës ; Fact and Fiction*. New York: AMS Press, 1973.

Maurat, Charlotte. *The Brontës' Secret*. London: Constable, 1969.

Mill, John Stuart. *On Liberty and The Subjection of Women*. Ware, Hertfordshire: Wordsworth Editions Limited., 1996.

Moore, Virginia. *The Life and Eager Death of Emily Brontë, a Biography*. London: Rich & Cown, Ltd., 1936.

Morrison, Nancy B. *Haworth Harvest : The Lives of the Brontës*. London: Dent, 1969.

Passel, Anne. *Charlotte and Emily Brontë, and Annotated Bibliography*. New York: Garland, 1979.

Peters, Maureen. *An Enigma of Brontës*. New York: St. Martin's Press, 1974.

Peters, Margot. *Unquiet Soul : A Biography of Charlotte Brontë*. Garden City, NY: Doubleday, 1975.

Peters, Margot. *Charlotte Brontë : Style in the Novel*. Madison, WI: University of Wisconsin Press, 1973.

Pollard, Arthur. *Charlotte Brontë*. London: Routledge & K. Paul, 1968.

Sherry, Norman. *Charlotte and Emily Brontë*. London: Evans Bros., 1969.

Shorter, Clement King. *The Brontës and Their Circle*. New York: Kraus Reprint, 1970.

Shorter, Clement King. *Charlotte Brontë and Her Sisters*. New York: C. Scribner's Sons, 1905.

Sinclair, May. *The Three Brontës*. Port Washington, NY: Kennikat Press, 1967.

Smith, Margaret (Ed.). *The Letters of Charlotte Brontë with a selection of letters by family and friends, Volume One 1829-1847*. Oxford: Clarendon Press, 1995.

Smith, Margaret (Ed.). *The Letters of Charlotte Brontë with a selection of letters by family and friends, Volume Two 1848-1851*. Oxford: Clarendon Press, 2000.

Spark, Muriel and Derek Stanford. *Emily Brontë, Her Life and Work*. London: Owen, 1953.

Spark, Muriel. *The Brontë Letters*. London: Nevill, 1954.

Stevenson, W. H. *Emily and Anne Brontë*. New York: Humanities Press, 1968.

Stoneman, Patsy. *Emily Brontë: Wuthering Heights*. Columbia Critical Guides. United States: Columbia University Press, 2000.

White, W. Bertram. *The Miracle of Haworth: A Brontë Study*. London: University of London Press, Ltd., 1937.

Willis, Irene Cooper. *The Brontës*. New York: MacMillan, 1933.

Wilks, Brian. *The Brontës*. New York: Viking Press, 1975.

Winnifrith, Tom. *A New Life of Charlotte Brontë*. New York: St. Martin's Press, 1988.

Winnifrith, Tom. *The Brontës*. New York: Collier Books, 1977.

Winnifrith, Tom. *The Brontës and Their Background: Romance and Reality*. New York: Barnes & Noble, 1973.

Wise, Thomas J. *The Brontës, Their lives, friendships, and correspondence*. Philadelphia: Porcupine Press, 1980.

Vine, Steven. *Emily Brontë*. New York: Twayne, 1998.

INDEX

Lightning Source UK Ltd.
Milton Keynes UK

177945UK00002B/55/A